EAST COAST/WEST COAST

EAST COAST
WEST COAST

Patrick Douglas

DONALD I. FINE, INC.

NEW YORK

"Open the Door, Richard"
Words by "Dusty" Fletcher and John Mason
Music by Jack McVea and Dan Howell
© Copyright 1947 by Duchess Music Corporation,
1755 Broadway, New York, New York, 10019
Rights administered by MCA Music Publishing, A Division of
MCA INC. Used by permission. All rights reserved

"The End of the World" and "Epistle To Be Left in the Earth"
are from *New and Collected Poems* by Archibald MacLeish
Copyright © 1985 by the Estate of Archibald MacLeish.
Reprinted by permission of Houghton Mifflin Company.

Library of Congress Cataloging-in-Publication Data

Douglas, Patrick.
East Coast/West Coast.

1. Regionalism—United States.   2. Untied States—
Civilization—1970   .   I. Title.
E169.D68   1988   973   88-45379
ISBN 1-55611-098-7

Manufactured in the United States of America

10   9   8   7   6   5   4   3   2   1

DESIGNED BY IRVING PERKINS ASSOCIATES

What then is the American, this new man?

—*Hector St. John de Crèvecoeur*

INTRODUCTION

THIS IS NOT A BOOK about hot tubs or surfboards, or about whatever it is that may be replacing whatever it was that may or may not have replaced the so-called Me Decade. Rather (at the risk of sounding overly portentous), it is a book about certain larger forces moving inexorably within the ocean of recent events even as the fads and trends toss to and fro upon the surface. Specifically, it is a book about the *effects* of those forces and what they portend (that word again) for the American mind.

For most of the nation's history, the American character has been partly if not largely determined by a special relationship—that between the East Coast and Europe. Today, that relationship has begun to lose its traditional sway. The reasons: the center of the world economy is shifting from the Atlantic Basin to the Pacific; and within the United States, population (along with economic and political power) is shifting from the East Coast toward the West.

These two movements, of course (especially the latter), are by now well known. What is less well known is that both of these movements, like the rumblings of large techtonic plates along a major fault line, signal basic changes in American society. All told, these changes are reshaping not only the country's economy and its politics but its general culture, and indeed its perception of reality itself. Our starting point in describing these effects is the system of thought that gave birth to the American republic—namely, eighteenth-century rationalism (imported of course, from Europe). This rationalism had at least two aspects, one scientific, the other political and social. Today, in the United States, both these aspects are in decline or open to serious challenge. The challenge to rationalism in a scientific sense is brought about mainly by the shift of power from the Atlantic Basin to the Pacific. The decline of rationalism in a political and social sense is caused mainly by the shift of power within the United States itself.

The latter trend first. Political rationalism, in theory at least, made each man the architect of his form of government and indeed of society itself. As long as the theory was not taken too literally, the system seemed to work well enough (and sometimes, as at the Constitutional Convention, it worked to near perfection). But for much of its history, the United States has been undergoing a process of "democratization," caused partly by its population's westerly migration, and partly by the transfer of the entertainment capital from New York to Los Angeles. Over the past few decades, this process has resulted in a noticeable change in some of the country's major institutions.

One of those institutions is politics, which has recently produced a series of "failed" administrations and a corresponding depreciation of American leadership in the world at large. Today, the country is faced with the threat of imminent national decline, but it is not at all certain it can elect a president with the intelligence and vision even to acknowledge the problem, let alone deal with it.

Yet the failure of the presidency (Reagan's popularity notwithstanding) is merely symptomatic of a general cultural deterioration. And we'll take a look at three institutions that reflect it— namely, the theater, publishing (both books and magazines) and television news. Taken together, these three changing institutions embody the democratization of the American mind.

Of the two general trends we'll be considering—the decline of political rationalism and the challenge to scientific rationalism—it is the former that in the short run is likely to be the more pronounced (and the more disturbing). But in the long run, it is the latter trend—caused mainly by the shift of power from the Atlantic Basin to the Pacific—that will produce the more profound results. In effect, these results will ensue from the meeting of East and West, Orient and Occident—that is, from a melding of the scientific rationalism of the latter hemisphere and the mysticism of the former.

Already, this union is producing some different ways of seeing things—in physics, in medicine, even in sports. But the most dramatic messages from this gradually unfolding *terra incognita* are being returned by the little-known discipline of parapsychology. Considered together, these various findings suggest nothing less than a new way of regarding (new at least in the rational West) what we are wont to call reality.

PART I

The Decline of Political and Social Rationalism

1

Open the Door, Richard:
The Decline of Class
and the Entrance
and Apotheosis
of the Average Man

(A small group of revelers, gathered on a sidewalk, is pounding
on the door of the house of a friend. Eventually, a woman
down the way throws open a window and calls into the night.
One of the revelers turns to another.)
"Hey, man, did you hear what the lady said?"
"No, man. What'd she say?"
"She said we sure look common out here in the street."
"Common! Why, man, I got class I ain't even use yet."

—From, "Open the Door, Richard,"
a popular song of the forties

THE MIDNIGHT BANTER of Richard's friends was meant to be
taken ironically, of course: if ever there was a no-class bunch, it was
the gaggle of night owls flapping about in front of Richard's door.

Still—if the notion that "I got class I ain't even use yet" could be
expounded, willy-nilly, by any group of n'er-do-wells, and repeated
gleefully by middle-class bobby-soxers . . . Perhaps the institution
of social class was not what it had been.

Nor was it. By the 1940s, when "Open the Door, Richard" was
amusing teenagers and annoying parents across the land, the
American class system was more or less a shambles—much like, in
fact, the famed Vanderbilt mansion on Fifth Avenue, the razing of
which, in 1942, was regarded by many as the beginning of the end.

And since then? Well, what's the name of the last song you
remember that mentioned the word "class"? Or for that matter, the
word "common"?

3

Nor is that all. The place formerly occupied in our national esteem by what used to be referred to as the upper classes is now given over to a different type of hero: the average man (or person, if you prefer).

To many Americans, the suggestion that there has recently occurred anything resembling a decline of class may seem rather odd in an age which, for materialism and greed, is unsurpassed since the 1920s. But as we shall see—or as any member of the country's dwindling aristocracy could tell us at the outset—the prominence of such traits is not a refutation of the argument in favor of the decline of class, but rather its confirmation.

For a still larger group of Americans, the argument in question will seem somewhat odd for a quite different reason: the widely held assumption that ours is, and always has been, a more or less classless society. This assumption is also favored by foreign observers. As Paul Fussell explains in his nasty little book called *Class:* "Class distinctions in America are so complicated and subtle that foreign visitors often miss the nuances and sometimes even the existence of a class structure."[1] Especially susceptible to such oversights are visitors of the Tory persuasion, such as Henry Fairlie:

> One spring day, shortly after my arrival [in the United States], I was walking down the long, broad street of a suburb, with its sweeping front lawns (all that space), its tall trees (all that sky), and its clumps of azaleas (all that color). The only other person on the street was a small boy on a tricycle. As I passed him, he said "Hi!"—just like that. No four-year-old boy had ever addressed me without an introduction before. Yet here was this one, with his cheerful "Hi!" Recovering from the culture shock, I tried to look down stonily at his flaxen head, but instead, involuntarily, I found myself saying in return: "Well—hi!" He pedalled off, apparently satisfied. He had begun my Americanization.
>
> "Hi!" As I often say—for Americans do not realize it—the word is a democracy. (I come from a country where one can tell someone's class by how they say "Hallo!" or "Hello!" or "Hullo," or whether they say it at all.) But anyone can say "Hi!" Anyone does.[2]

Anyone doesn't. One recalls, for example, the amusing experience of Will Barrett, Walker Percy's Last Gentleman, when he transferred from Princeton to the university of his native Alabama. Particularly disconcerting to Barrett was the students' habit of greeting total strangers they encountered on campus by calling out "Hi!" Nonetheless, Barrett resolved to master the greeting, and after practicing alone in the room where he lived, he decided to risk an actual encounter. Approaching a fellow student on a campus walkway, he waited until just the right moment: " 'Hi!' I bellowed. Oh Lord—a good twenty feet too soon." (Anyone who attended a Southern college as I did, will recognize that Percy has got it exactly right.)

The actual status of social class in the United States is quite different from that suggested by either of these preconceptions. To state the matter briefly (and maybe a little stuffily), America at one time possessed a recognizable upper class, what might even be termed an aristocracy.* This class was based in part on wealth, of course, but more important, it was based on a sense of *noblesse oblige* toward the public good and the life of the mind. More important still, its ideals and standards were generally accepted as those to which society as a whole should aspire.

In more recent times, this has all changed considerably. As Paul Fussell puts it, "the whole society could be said to be engaged in a process of class sinking. Prole Drift, we can call it . . ."[3] But in a broader sense, what we are discussing here is not the blurring of class distinctions per se. Rather, it is the process that Tocqueville observed so astutely in *Democracy in America*—to wit, the gradual transformation of Western society from an aristocracy into a thoroughgoing democracy, with all that suggests in the way of values and tastes.

In the United States, where the transformation is mainly taking place, the chief engines of the process are the two major shifts we'll examine in Chapters Two and Three: the continuing western migration (continuing, that is, since the founding of the colonies but especially prevalent since the California Gold Rush and even more so during the past twenty years) and the transplantation of the entertainment capital from New York to Los Angeles.

The results of this process of democratization are not—as is

* The word is used here less in the modern European sense than in the original Greek sense of *aristos* ('best') and *kratia* ('rule').

5

popularly believed—simply a matter of who gets into the country club (a rather democratic institution, in any case). Instead, they permeate our whole society, affecting not only our politics, but (as we shall see in subsequent chapters) several of our major socio-cultural institutions as well—among them, television news, the theater, and books and magazines, not to mention the movies and television shows that did so much to help the process along.

The reasons this influence is so strong and pervasive are not hard to find, at least if one reads Tocqueville (as few of the people who quote him seem to). The following observations are taken from Volume II. (Incidentally, it's a shame to quote Tocqueville at any-thing less than paragraph length. As John Stuart Mill observed in his review of the work, "M. de Tocqueville's ideas do not float upon a sea of words; none of his propositions are unmeaning, none of his meanings superfluous." Nonetheless, in the interest of space, we'll condense his prose considerably, while at the same time providing more than the meaningless squiglets our distinguished visitor is usually accorded.)

> Where the ranks of society are unequal . . . men living at these aristocratic periods are . . . naturally induced to shape their opinions by the standard of . . . a superior class of persons, while they are averse to recognizing the infallibility of the mass of the people.
>
> The contrary takes place in ages of equality. The nearer the people are drawn to the common level of an equal and similar condition, the less prone does each man become to place implicit faith in . . . a certain class of men. But his readiness to believe the multitude increases . . . for it would seem probable that, as men are all endowed with equal means of judging, the greater truth should go with the greater number . . . and opinion is more than ever mistress of the world. . . .
>
> The public, therefore, among a democratic people, has a singular power, which aristocratic nations cannot conceive; for it does not persuade others to its beliefs, but it imposes them and makes them permeate the thinking of everyone by a sort of enormous pressure of the mind of all upon the individual intelligence. . . .
>
> By whatever political laws men are governed in the ages of equal-ity, it may be foreseen that faith in public opinion will become for them a species of religion, and the majority its ministering prophet.[4]

According to Tocqueville, these ages of equality would appear to be more or less inevitable in Western society, for as he pointed out elsewhere in Volume II, democratic communities "will endure poverty, servitude, barbarism, but they will not endure aristocracy."[5] Events have certainly borne out this claim—even in terms of the quasi-aristocracy that came to exist in the United States.

One of the ways we've erased aristocracy is retroactively, through the formulation of our national myths. Thus, New England (and, by extrapolation, much of the rest of the country as well) was supposedly founded by the Pilgrims—simple, homespun folk who, as every schoolchild knows, landed at Plymouth Rock in 1620. No sooner had they done so than they set about inventing Thanksgiving dinner . . . .

It's true enough the Pilgrims were an egalitarian lot. It's also true they were not the chief founders of New England. That role, of course, belonged to a far larger and far different group called the Puritans, who arrived about ten years later.

Among the first Puritan settlers (whose lead ship, the *Arbella*, is referred to by old-line Bostonians as "the second boat," to distinguish it from the more plebeian *Mayflower*) were the following: Sir Richard Saltonstall, wealthy nephew of the lord mayor of London and progenitor of the only American family to boast ten consecutive generations of Harvard men; John Winthrop, a justice of the peace at age eighteen and later the first colonial governor of Massachusetts; John Whitney, founder of the famous Whitney clan; John Phillips, whose descendants established the well-known academies at Andover and Exeter; Edmund Quincy, father of a family that produced three mayors of Boston and a president of Harvard; and Thomas Leverett, whose son served seven times as colonial governor and whose grandson became one of the great Harvard presidents. (These same names appear throughout the history of Massachusetts in various permutations: in this century, Leverett Saltonstall served as governor.)

Fifteen years after the *Arbella's* arrival in 1630, the colony's settlers included not only the graduates of Harvard (founded in 1636), but 130 alumni of Oxford and Cambridge—giving Massachusetts, as Tocqueville pointed out, the highest proportion of educated citizens the world had ever seen.

To be sure, New England was not the only part of the New World to spawn an embryonic aristocracy. Twenty years after the autocratic acts of Charles I sent a wave of Puritans washing into Boston Harbor, his untimely decapitation sent legions of Cavaliers hieing to Virginia. Many of these newcomers were people of considerable means, and aided by the state's topography and climate, they eventually developed an impressive network of large plantations. By the time of the American Revolution (which of course was mainly a colonial revolt, rather than an actual social upheaval), the upper classes of Virginia and New England constituted a national aristocracy—one which was as formidable for its erudition as it was for its wealth. As historian Richard Hofstadter observed in his classic study of *Anti-Intellectualism in American Life:*

> When the United States began its national existence, the relationship between intellect and power was not a problem. The leaders *were* the intellectuals. Advanced though the nation was in the development of democracy, the control of its affairs still rested largely in a patrician elite: and within this elite men of intellect moved freely and spoke with enviable authority . . . . The intellectual as ruling-class gentleman was a leader in every segment of society—at the bar, in the professions, in business, and in political affairs. The Founding Fathers were sages, scientists, men of broad cultivation, many of them apt in classical learning, who used their wide reading in history, politics, and law to solve the exigent problems of their time. No subsequent era in our history has produced so many men of knowledge among its political leaders. . .[6]

Writing specifically of Virginia, Charles S. Syndor remarked:

> . . . the high quality of Virginia's political leadership in the years when the United States was being established was due in large measure to those very things which are now detested. Washington and Jefferson, Madison and Monroe, Mason, Marshall, and Peyton Randolph, were products of the system which sought out and raised to high office men of superior family and social status, of good education, of personal force, of experience in management: they were placed in power by a semi-aristocratic political system.[7]

Yet in a larger sense, Virginia's aristocratic system left some things to be desired. Because it was based on a plantation economy, the population was widely dispersed, and there were no cities of any size. (At the time of the revolution, the largest was Norfolk: population 7,000.) While this arrangement no doubt suited Thomas Jefferson just fine, it also meant that Virginia for many decades was without those amenities of civilization that some of the other colonies took for granted. There were very few newspapers, no theater companies, and (despite Mr. Jefferson's architectural accomplishment at Charlottesville) no Harvard. Virginia lacked a focal point for the life of the mind, and with the notable exceptions of the writers of the Constitution and the Declaration of Independence, the state produced few men of letters.

Another reason for Virginia's decline was the state's total eclipse in the realm of politics. After occupying the White House for thirty-two of the nation's first thirty-six years, the Virginia dynasty ended with John Quincy Adam's election in 1824. A few years later came the tidal wave of Jacksonian democracy (about which a bit more later), then the rise of sectional strife and finally, of course, the Civil War. Not only did the war destroy the region's plantations, but a scion of one of the state's best families (whom Lincoln had offered the command of the Union armies) had the misfortune to serve as leading general on the losing side. Five short years after surrendering at Appomattox, he died.

For all these reasons, then, one must look northward for a full-blown example of American aristocracy. And the place where the eye comes to rest, of course, is Boston.

Rather than compare Boston to Tidewater Virginia, we might do better to compare it to another venerable northern city: Philadelphia. At the time of the nation's founding, Massachusetts and Pennsylvania were two of the three most populous states (the third being Virginia). But by the end of the century, there was a considerable difference in the size of their principal cities. Philadelphia, with a population of 70,000, was the leading city in the country. (In terms of size, New York was second, with 60,000.) Boston, meanwhile, lagged far behind, with a population of only 25,000. This gap was never really closed, of course, yet Philadelphia—despite its role as host to the Constitutional Convention and as national capital from 1790 to 1800—made only a minor contribution to the country's public and intellectual affairs. Boston, on the other hand—and especially its upper classes—made

9

a contribution that was far out of proportion to its size. "The plain fact of the matter," writes Cleveland Amory in *Who Killed Society?*, "is that a very small number of Boston Families were able to produce an Aristocracy which, for accomplishment, was one unmatched by any British or for that matter any titled Aristocracy anywhere."[8]

Why the great disparity? An interesting answer is provided by sociologist E. Digby Baltzell in a lengthy book entitled *Puritan Boston and Quaker Philadelphia: Two Protestant Ethics and the Spirit of Class Authority and Leadership.* Baltzell begins by describing the two groups of settlers in terms of their English origins. The Puritans, he points out, came from "the most sophisticated and prosperous parts of England"[9]—mainly London and the southeastern counties—and many, like John Winthrop and John Harvard, were educated at Cambridge, "the nursery of New England Puritanism." Thereafter, the Puritans spent their lives as "ministers and magistrates," the latter often serving in the House of Commons.

Equally important (more so, actually, in Baltzell's view) was the Puritan Ethic, under which life was regarded as a "calling" that imposed upon each citizen—especially the wealthy—a long list of duties. (*Noblesse oblige*, as it were.)

The Quakers, according to Baltzell, were quite different. Drawn from England's poor, backward, northern counties, they were swept up in a religious revival which was not unlike the Great Awakenings that have periodically stirred the American heartland—but which contrasted sharply with the staid Puritan reform movement within the Church of England. Rejecting the notion of an educated clergy, the Quakers espoused instead the "individualistic and subjective doctrine of the Inner Light," along with a "radical egalitarianism."[10]

These attitudes, in turn, were reflected in the cities that the Quakers and the Puritans founded in the New World. Philadelphia was basically egalitarian and anti-authoritarian. In time, of course, Philadelphia developed a rather well-known upper class (whose members quietly shifted over to the fashionable Episcopal church from the much less fashionable Quaker meeting house). But lacking any aristocratic ethic, the Philadelphia well-to-do tended to value material comfort and the privileges of caste over any sense of obligation to the intellectual and political life of city, state or nation. As a result, they made relatively little impression on any of these fronts. The city's most famous citizen (by far) is still Benjamin Franklin, who was actually born in Boston and whose autobiography, in Baltzell's words, remains "the greatest manual of careerist Babbittry ever written." [11] The city's chief contribution to American publishing was Franklin's magazine, the *Saturday Evening Post*. And its only notable man of letters was Owen Wister, the chronicler of the cowboy.

Boston, on the other hand, was basically hierarchical and authoritarian, and it produced an upper class with a strong sense of duty both to the life of the mind and the body politic. As a result, Baltzell argues, it also produced "the most influential upper class in American history."[12]

Admittedly, the Boston aristocracy could seem rather austere. As T. S. Eliot remarked during his undergraduate days at Harvard, "Those of us who can claim any New England ancestors may congratulate ourselves that we are their descendants, and at the same time rejoice that we are not their contemporaries."[13]

Boston's austerity was particularly apparent in the matter of manners, and particularly when the city had occasion to allude to its soon-to-be *bête noire*, New York. In 1838, for example, a Boston matron named Mrs. John Farrar published a popular volume entitled *The Young Lady's Friend,* in which she felt it necessary to warn her readers against what she referred to, delicately, as "jiggling":

> Some girls have a trick of *jiggling* their bodies (I am obliged to coin a word to describe it) . . . than which nothing can be more ungraceful. . . . It must have originated in embarrassment, and a desire to do something, without knowing exactly what; and being adopted by some popular belle, it became, at one time, a fashion in New York, and spread thence to other cities.[14]

By the same token, the Boston austerity is evident in what Cleveland Amory describes in *The Proper Bostonians* as "that most curious of all Proper Bostonian customs—the love of funerals and funeral going":

> First Family social history starts with funerals and ends with funerals. . . . Long before there is, from a life insurance point of view, actuarially any risk at all, hymns are chosen, Bible verses selected,

11

pallbearers nominated, and occupants of front-row pews designated. . . .

One latter-day Boston merchant, asked point blank why he attended funerals with such obvious enjoyment, managed an equally point-blank reply: "Melancholy, Sir, is the one great passion of my life."[15]

Along with melancholy, Boston early on acquired a reputation for parochialism. As Edith Wharton remarked in her autobiography: "It was not until I went to Boston on my marriage that I found myself in a community of wealthy and sedentary people seemingly too lacking in intellectual curiosity to have any desire to see the world."[16] To which a Boston matron allegedly responded: "Why should I travel, when I'm already there?"

In similar fashion, a Boston woman was asked whether she didn't think that Robert Cutler, a Bostonian then serving as special assistant to President Eisenhower, had made quite a name for himself in Washington. "Yes," she replied, "I suppose he has—but after all, it's not Boston: it's just national."

Be that as it may, Boston's influence was felt not only on a national and local level, but regionally as well. For example, the early Puritan culture of Massachusetts Bay spawned the culture of Connecticut, including its oldest university, Yale (founded in 1701). In turn, Connecticut Puritans spread into northern New Jersey, where in 1746 they founded the College of New Jersey, the name of which they later changed to the classier-sounding Princeton.

Back in Boston, the original Puritans had founded the Boston Latin School in 1635 (a year before Harvard), and four years later they set up America's first printing press. The city's library opened in 1656, and by the eve of the revolution, Boston boasted five newspapers (as compared to three in the much larger city of Philadelphia). Institutions such as these—together of course with Harvard—soon formed the basis of a major Boston influence upon the country's intellectual life.

"I must study politics and war," wrote John Adams in a letter to his wife, "that my sons may have liberty to study mathematics and philosophy. My sons ought to study mathematics and philosophy . . . in order to give their children a right to study painting, poetry, music, architecture, statuary, tapestry and porcelain."[17]

12

Over the next few generations, the Adams family tree came more or less to assume the shape of these arboreal aspirations.

John Adams himself ("that finest of American conservatives," in the words of Richard Hofstadter)[18] is described by Baltzell as "the most judicious and penetrating conservative political philosopher in our history."[19] His son John Quincy studied in Paris, Amsterdam, Leyden, and The Hague, as well as at Harvard, where he later occupied the chair of rhetoric and oratory. In addition, he served for many years as head of the American Academy of Arts and Sciences, and as secretary of state under James Monroe. As president, he sought to make Washington the leader of a program of education and scientific advancement, in part by establishing a national university.

John Quincy's son, Charles Francis Adams I, served (like his grandfather) as ambassador to England (where he convinced his hosts to resist forming an alliance with the Confederacy). Charles's son Henry wrote the splendid *Mont Saint-Michel and Chartres* and *The Education of Henry Adams*. (A "worldly sophisticate," Henry nonetheless maintained an ironic sense of his own sophistication. "Everyone," he once said, "carries his own inch-rule of taste, and amuses himself by applying it, triumphantly, wherever he travels.")[20]

Also significant in the field of letters were several members of the Lowell family, notably Amy, James Russell, and Robert. In addition to writing poetry and criticism, James Russell served as first editor of the *Atlantic Monthly*— which became, like Harvard, a major institution through which the Boston aristocracy influenced the growth of American thought.

Among the early contributors to the *Atlantic* were Emerson and Hawthorne, which points up the fact that Boston played a pivotal role in the first great flowering of American literature. Alluding to the 1840s and 1850s as "the height of Boston's hegemony over the American mind," Baltzell goes on to argue that "no other city in America and very few in Western history as a whole have equaled Boston . . . in dominating the ideas and values of a developing nation."[21]

Aside from the realm of intellect, another area in which Boston dominated American values was politics. This dominance did not result solely from sending officials and advisors to Washington (although there have certainly been plenty of those). For many years, Boston also imparted a certain *tone* to American political life—one which consisted, in Baltzell's words, of "class authority and deference democracy."[22] As John Adams explained it: "Go into every village in New England, and you will find that the office of justice of the peace, and even the place of representative, which has ever depended only on the freest election of the people, have generally descended from generation to generation, in three or four families at most."[23] Or in Baltzell's words, "the best people, in wealth and family reputation, were elected to office time after time in town after town for over 200 years."[24]

This system was also reflected in the Massachusetts delegations that signed the Declaration of Independence and the Constitution. In the former group, all four delegates were members of the upper class of Massachusetts Bay and graduates of Harvard. In the latter group, which met at a time when most of Boston's prominent citizens were occupied at other public duties, the number of Harvard graduates dropped to three out of four.

Nor did the system end there. "In Boston," Baltzell points out, "Brahmin leadership in the mayor's office was typical down to the Civil War."[25] The governor's office has been occupied by sixteen Boston Brahmins (the most recent being Endicott Peabody, 1963–65), all but two of whom were graduates of Harvard. As for Congress, Baltzell asserts that, "From the nation's founding to the present, no other state, including aristocratic Virginia, has sent a more cohesive class of distinguished gentlemen to the Senate than has Massachusetts."[26]

Even more noteworthy, perhaps, is the fact that in Massachusetts, the worlds of politics and intellect were not at all segregated (as in most places, especially today), but were closely intertwined. For example, representatives of both groups formed an organization called the Saturday Club, which met for dinner once a month at Boston's venerable Parker House. In addition to various politicians, businessmen, and presidents of Harvard, the club included Oliver Wendell Holmes, James Russell Lowell, Emerson, Hawthorne and Henry James.

Although the Saturday Club still exists, a number of the attitudes that characterized the Boston aristocracy have virtually disappeared. Among them:

14

• An aversion to the world of "business," even among many of those who were in business themselves. As Charles Francis Adams II observed in his autobiography, published in 1916:

> Business success—money-getting . . . comes from a rather low instinct. Certainly, so far as my observation goes, it is rarely met in combination with the finer or more interesting traits of character. I have known, and known tolerably well, a good many "successful" men—"big" financially . . . famous during the last half-century; and a less interesting crowd I do not care to encounter. Not one that I have ever known would I care to meet again, either in this world or the next.[27]

• Adherence to a strict code of ethics (even in business). "My father never talked much about 'Family'," recalled Charles Francis Adams IV, president of Raytheon. "But the day I went to work he told me, 'I believe you have a reputation for honesty. God help you if you lose it.' That was all he said."[28]

• A distaste for ostentation. This entailed an avoidance of "publicity" of any kind, and an insouciance toward material possessions ("shabby genteel," as the style is often called). According to a recent survey, the latter trait is still evident in Boston today. Its residents buy the fewest fur coats per capita of any large city (despite the frigid winters), and the fewest Cadillacs. Luxury cars in general account for only 7.5 percent of the cars sold in Boston, compared to 13.3 percent in Los Angeles and 14.6 percent in New York.

• Finally, under the heading of Puritan duty, one might mention the fact that when John Quincy Adams had completed his term as president, he was virtually penniless. Nonetheless, he then served for seventeen years in the House of Representatives.

On a national level, the decline of Boston aristocracy ostensibly dates from John Quincy Adams's landslide loss to Andrew Jackson in 1828—an event that historian Henry Steele Commager likens to an earthquake. But like most earthquakes, this one had been building for quite some time.

*   *   *

15

Mainly because of topography—a low coastal plain, bordered on the west by a long range of mountains—the original American settlements had developed for more than a hundred years as Atlantic communities closely tied to Europe. Their residents regarded themselves as English citizens (as of course they were), and most of their institutions were also distinctly English: the colonial governments (modeled, more or less, on Parliament), the New England schools (modeled on Eton and Oxbridge). Finally, and most important, was the colonial assumption that (to a degree we would find surprising today) the tastes and standards of the indigenous aristocracy should serve as a model for society.

Much of this system, of course, is still intact on the East Coast today. All the old New England schools are still going strong, as is (to a lesser extent) a class system modeled on that of the British. (If you doubt this, consider the fact that the East Coast is the only section of the country where a person's class—as in England—is immediately revealed by the way he speaks.) Finally, there is the endemic Anglophilia. As Henry Adams once remarked, "the true Bostonian always knelt in self-abasement before the majesty of English standards."[29] Or as Van Wyck Brooks observed: "The more the center of gravity of the nation shifted toward the West, the more the Boston mind, thrown aback on itself, resumed its old colonial allegiance."[30]

More recently, Cleveland Amory pointed out in *The Proper Bostonians* (1947), that "the whole tone of Boston Society, from oatmeal and Dundee marmalade at dawn through a day which may well be topped off with a bedtime snack of the London *Illustrated News*, is still English."[31] Today, one might mention the automatic absorption of anything emanating from the BBC, but the "old colonial allegiance" is best revealed, perhaps, in a small vignette from the ceremonies commemorating the 350th anniversary of Harvard.

When the university had celebrated its 300th anniversary a half-century earlier, the president of the United States was Harvard alumnus Franklin Roosevelt, who naturally had accepted an invitation to speak at the school's commencement. But this time around the White House was occupied by Ronald Reagan (like Andrew Jackson—with whom John Quincy Adams refused to ride down Pennsylvania Avenue on Inauguration Day—an unlettered rustic from the western frontier). What to do? Eventually, Harvard resolved its dilemma by declining to proffer an invitation to the president of the United States, and inviting instead—Prince Charles.

But a century after the original Bostonians had honored an earlier Charles of England (for whom the city's principal river was named), a different sort of society was emerging along the East Coast's western edge. Rather than being an appendage of Europe, it was distinctly American; and far from being aristocratic, it was decidedly egalitarian.

"The frontier was one of the forces that did most to shape American life," writes Henry Steele Commager. "Moving across the continent as population advanced from the Atlantic ... it profoundly affected the American character. It was more than a line—it was a social process. It encouraged individual initiative; it made for political and economic democracy; it roughened manners ... it bred a spirit of local self-determination coupled with respect for national authority."[32] Most important of all, perhaps, the frontier (and its later glorification in myths and movies) spawned a sense that the tastes and values of the average man were quintessentially American, while those of the East were decadently European.

As Commager points out, there have been several of these frontiers in American history: the Appalachian Mountains, the Mississippi and Ohio valleys, and finally, the vast trans-Missouri West, comprising half the area of the United States and constituting, in Commager's words, "the most democratic and American frontier of all."[33]

Much of this egalitarianism is still apparent, of course, today—most notably in places such as Texas and Southern California, but even in an older and relatively class-conscious place such as San Francisco. For example, Stanford University is often described (at least in California) as the Harvard of the West. (Actually, it's more like Princeton, but never mind.) Nonetheless, the school is expected to compete on the football field with the likes of USC and Oklahoma. (Even more surprising, it often does.)

Throughout the history of the United States, Western egalitarianism has repeatedly rolled eastward. In the 1890s, for instance, came the rise of Populism, during the course of which a thirty-two-year-old Wisconsin historian named Frederick Jackson Turner published a celebrated essay on the "The Significance of the Frontier in American History."

Up until then, U.S. history had been generally regarded (especially on the East Coast) as an offshoot of that of Europe. But Turner argued a very different case. "American democracy," he declared, "was born of no theorist's dream; it was not carried in the *Sarah Constant* to Virginia, nor in the *Mayflower* to Plymouth. It came out of the American forest, and it gained new strength each time it touched a new frontier."[34]

Turner pointed out that, "The East has always feared the result of an unregulated advance of the frontier, and has tried to check and guide it."[35] Such a policy, for example, was followed by Presidents Washington, Jefferson, and John Quincy Adams, but when Andrew Jackson reached the White House, he adopted a rather different approach. In the words of John Quincy Adams, Jackson "formally recommended that all public lands should be gratuitously given away to individual adventurers and to the States in which the lands are situated."[36] The result was a land rush unique in the history of the world.

Out of all this emerged a series of frontier societies with several salient characteristics. In Turner's words: ". . . the most important effect of the frontier has been in the promotion of democracy. . . . The frontier is productive of individualism. . . . It produces antipathy to control, and particularly to any direct control. The tax-gatherer is viewed as a representative of oppression."[37] (At the same time, the frontier was anxious for internal improvements such as railroads, as well as for the protection of the U.S. cavalry. Thus, the frontier was noticeably nationalistic.)

Having approached the frontier as "Europeans" (either literally or figuratively), the settlers eventually added some of the trappings of civilization—"but the outcome," in Turner's words, "is not the old Europe. . . . The fact is, that here is a new product that is American. . . . Thus the advance of the frontier has meant a steady movement away from the influence of Europe, a steady growth of independence on American lines."[38]

Indeed, "as society on her eastern border grew to resemble the Old World in its social forms,"[39] the frontier spawned "a new type of democracy and new popular ideals."[40] These entailed "a passionate hatred of aristocracy,"[41] and "the exaltation of the common man."[42]

Nor did such ideals remain confined to the frontier. Instead, they gradually spread eastward, partly through expansion of the suffrage laws, partly through the results of national elections and partly through simple osmosis. As a result, Turner declared, "the true point of view in the history of this nation is not the Atlantic Coast; it is the Great West."[43]

During the two decades after Turner's Frontier Thesis appeared, it quietly revolutionized the study of American history. Then, outside the confines of history departments (where it continued to be the subject of periodic revisions and re-revisions over the next half-century), it was just as quietly forgotten.

But the truth is that Turner's thesis does much to account for the place in American history of more recent phenomena: the rise of Hollywood movies in the twenties; the explosion of Hollywood television in the fifties; and in a more general sense, what might be called the California effect, whereby a social movement arises on the West Coast and gradually spreads eastward. By the same token, the thesis might profitably be applied to the elections of Richard Nixon and Ronald Reagan (not to mention the subsequent Eastern counterattacks: Watergate and the Iran-*contra* scandal). For the moment, though, we'll return to the election in which it all began: Andrew Jackson's landslide victory over John Quincy Adams in 1828.

We'll have more to say on this particular subject in a subsequent chapter ("The Democratization of Politics"). For now, we'll simply take note of some "election analysis" by selected historians, chief among them Richard Hofstadter:

> The contests in 1824 and 1828 between Jackson and John Quincy Adams provided a perfect study in contrasting political ideals. . . . The last President to stand in the old line of government by gentlemen, Adams became the symbol of the old order and the chief victim of the reaction against the learned man. . . . He represented a kind of leadership which had outlived its time. . . .
>
> As Adams embodied the old style, Andrew Jackson embodied the new; and the opposition between these two in the politics of the 1820s symbolized what America had been and what it would become. In headlong rebellion against the European past, Americans . . . feared

19

that their own advancing civilization was "artificial.". . . . Jackson's advocates praised him as the representative of the natural wisdom of the natural man. . . . Among his other gifts as as national leader . . . he was able to offer reassurances as to the persistence of native vigor and the native style.[44]

Hofstadter observes that the spirit of the age was vividly reflected by George Bancroft as he "rhapsodized over Jackson's unschooled mind":

> Behold, then, the unlettered man of the West . . . the farmer of the Hermitage, little versed in books, unconnected by science with the tradition of the past, raised by the will of the people to the highest pinnacle of honour, the central post in the civilization of republican freedom. . . . What policy will he pursue? What wisdom will he bring with him from the forest? What rules of duty will he evolve from the oracles of his own mind?[45]

Or in the words of Henry Steele Commager, "Jackson had the Western faith that the common man is capable of uncommon achievement. Westerners . . . did not believe for a minute that the great prizes of public life were reserved for the rich, the well born, and the educated. The coon hunter had as good a right to them as the Harvard graduate."[46]

In the election of 1828, writes Hofstadter, "the issue was posed to the voters mainly as a choice between aristocracy and democracy." And when the final returns were in, "Adams was outdone in every section of the country but New England. . . . Jackson's triumph . . . was overwhelming."[47]

Nor was that the end of it. "By 1840," Hofstadter continues, "the conquest of the Whig Party [Adams's old party] by the rhetoric of populism was complete."[48] That year, the Whigs nominated William Henry Harrison, whose mansion on the banks of the Ohio River was portrayed in campaign literature as a simple log cabin.

Observing the silly spectacle from Washington, John Quincy Adams discerned "a revolution in the habits and manners of the people."[49] Morgan Dix reported: "This appears to be the first time in our history in which a direct appeal was made to the lower classes by exciting their curiosity, feeding the desire for amusement. . . . Since that day the thing has been carried farther, until it is actually a disadvantage to be of good stock and to have inherited 'the grand old name of gentleman.' "[50]

"The rise of democracy as an effective force in the nation," wrote Frederick Jackson Turner in his original essay, "came in with Western preponderance under Jackson and William Henry Harrison, and it meant the triumph of the frontier—with all of its good and with all of its evil elements."[51]

"By mid-century," concludes Hofstadter, "the gentleman had been reduced to a marginal role in both elective and appointive offices in the United States, and had been substantially alienated from American politics. . . . It was not merely Jacksonianism that was egalitarian—it was the nation itself."[52]

* * *

With all the opulence and splendor of this city, there is very little good breeding to be found. We have been treated with assiduous respect; but I have not seen one real gentleman, one well-bred man, since I came to town. At their entertainments there is no conversation that is agreeable; there is no modesty; no attention to one another. They talk very loud, very fast, and altogether.[53]

The speaker is Proper Bostonian John Adams, and as you may have guessed, this city that Mr. Adams found not to his liking was New York. His misgivings, moreover, proved prescient. For during the latter part of the nineteenth century, New York became the setting for a transformation of America's upper classes.

Today, of course, we think of New York as the East Coast's capital (to say the least), but in Adams's day (and well beyond), the situation was quite different. To the south, leadership rested with rural and aristocratic Virginia; to the north, with Puritan and aristocratic Boston. In between was the so-called Middle Region, which was unlike either. As Frederick Jackson Turner pointed out in his Frontier Thesis:

The men of the frontier had closer resemblances to the Middle Region than to either of the other sections. Pennsylvania had been the seed-plot of frontier emigration. . . . New York . . . was an open door to all Europe. . . . The Middle Region was less English than the other sections. It had a wide mixture of nationalities, a varied society

21

. . . a varied economic life, many religious sects. In short, it was a region mediating between New England and the South, and the East and the West. It represented that composite nationality which the contemporary United States exhibits.[54]

It also represented, in the case of New York, the wave of the future.

New York's ascendancy began, as it happened, in the same decade that saw the end of the Virginia dynasty, the banishment of Boston from the White House, and the rise of the frontier. In 1825, the state of New York completed the Erie Canal, giving its principal city direct access to the farm products and raw materials of the interior. Not long afterward, New York became the fastest growing metropolis in the country.

Following the cataclysm of the Civil War, the growth of New York—and the nation in general—entered an entirely new phase. Over the next forty years, the country's population rose from 31 million to 76 million, and the number of states increased by twelve. Steel production (protected by a stiff tariff) surpassed that of Britain by 1890, and by the turn of the century, surpassed that of Britain and Germany combined. The number of miles of railroad track grew from 30,000 to 200,000.

The number of millionaires grew even faster. During the 1840s, there were fewer than 20 in the entire country; in 1892, the *New York Tribune* published a list of 4,047. The following year, the Census Bureau estimated nine percent of the nation's families owned 71 percent of the wealth. Much of this ownership existed, of course, in the form of trusts, which rose in number from 82 in 1898 to 318 only six years later.

Meanwhile (Lord Acton's dictum having come into play), corruption increased on an enormous scale. In the words of Henry Commager, the period "brought into prominence a class of men who were eager for money and power, coarse in their tastes, and unscrupulous in their acts. . . . A vulgar, brassy, greedy element was more conspicuous than ever before."[55]

And what of our old friend the gentleman; how did he fare in the Gilded Age? Not at all well. Richard Hofstadter described the scene:

> The newly rich, the grandiosely or corruptly rich, the masters of great corporations, were bypassing the men of the Mugwump type—

the old gentry, the merchants of long standing, the small manufac-
turers, the established professional men, the civic leaders of an
earlier era. In a score of cities and hundreds of towns, particularly in
the East but also in the nation at large, the old-family, college-
educated class that had deep ancestral roots in local communities and
often owned family businesses, that had traditions of political leadership, belonged to the patriotic societies and the best clubs, staffed
the governing boards of philanthropic and cultural institutions, and
led the movements for civic betterment, were being overshadowed
and edged aside in the making of basic political and economic decisions. In their personal careers, as in their community activities,
they found themselves checked, hampered, and overridden by the
agents of the new corporations, the corrupters of legislatures, the
buyers of franchises, the allies of the political bosses. In this uneven
struggle they found themselves limited by their own scruples, their
regard for reputation, their social standing itself. To be sure, the
America they knew did not lack opportunities, but it did seem to lack
opportunities of the highest sort for men of the highest standards.
In a strictly economic sense these men were not growing poorer as
a class, but their wealth and power were being dwarfed by comparison with the new eminences of wealth and power. They were less
important, and they knew it.[56]

Hofstadter points out that many of these people could trace their
ancestry (in spirit, at least) to New England:

While men of the Mugwump type flourished during those decades
most conspicuously about Boston, a center of seasoned wealth and
seasoned conscience, where some of the most noteworthy names in
Massachusetts were among them, they were also prominent in a
metropolis like New York and could be found in some strength in
such Midwestern cities as Indianapolis and Chicago. None the less,
one senses among them the prominence of the cultural ideals and
traditions of New England, and beyond these of old England. Protestant and Anglo-Saxon for the most part, they were very frequently
of New England ancestry; and even when they were not, they tended
to look to New England's history for literary, cultural, and political
models and for examples of moral idealism.[57]

Even so, this great American pageant of the changing of the
guard was played out mainly in New York, where most of the new
money was concentrated. In a sense, New York became a stage for

a confrontation between the ideals of aristocracy and those of plutocracy—the former holding, for example, that the worth of any enterprise should be determined partly by its likely effect on the life of the mind and the public good, the latter holding that its worth should be determined solely by the life of the marketplace. In the end, plutocracy largely prevailed, though the contest is still being waged today (most dramatically, at the moment, in the field of network television news).

To be sure, New York had always claimed a fair number of aristocrats. (In a purely economic sense, the colony of New York was probably the most upper-class of all.) In the old days of patroonships along the Hudson River Valley, there were the Dutch Van Rensselaers, Van Burens and Stuyvesants, as well as the English Livingstons, Morrises and Jays. Later came the well-known "telephone exchange" families—Rhinelanders, Beekmans, and Schuylers (originally from Albany)—and finally such prominent clans as the Whitneys (originally from New England). In addition to their several cultural contributions, most of the members of the Whitney family displayed their aristocracy in the manner prescribed, that is, by displaying rather little of it at all. "As children," recalls Jock Whitney, "we were the reverse of snobs, and we liked people in almost inverse proportion to their so-called 'social' position."[58] As he grew older, Whitney became widely known for such "social" pursuits as polo, but he nonetheless refused to be listed in the *Social Register,* calling it a "travesty of democracy" with "absurd notions of who is and who isn't socially acceptable."[59]

Another member (and astute observer) of the New York aristocracy was Edith Wharton, who was born in that city in 1862. In her autobiography, *A Backward Glance,* many of her observations concerned the differences between New York and her husband's hometown of Boston. For example, she found that Boston families, as compared to hers, were "far more assiduously cultivated,"[60] whereas those of her set in New York were more worldly: "I remember once saying that I was a failure in Boston (where we used to go to stay with my husband's family) because they thought I was too fashionable to be intelligent, and a failure in New York because they were afraid I was too intelligent to be fashionable."[61]

Be that as it may, the "fashion" in New York was soon to change—and not, for the most part, in the direction of Boston. A new class of "the uneducated rich" was on the rise, and though Wharton herself spent much of this period in Europe, a novel of hers called *The House of Mirth* described the heady atmosphere of turn-of-the-century New York:

> Rosedale, in particular, was said to have doubled his fortune, and there was talk of his buying the newly-finished house of one of the victims of the crash, who, in the space of twelve short months, had made the same number of millions, built a house on Fifth Avenue, filled a picture-gallery with old masters, entertained all New York in it, and been smuggled out of the country between a trained nurse and a doctor, while his creditors mounted guard over the old masters, and his guests explained to each other that they had dined with him only because they wanted to see the pictures.[62]

In such an atmosphere, the innocent, prosaic world of Wharton's childhood was subjected to "sudden extinction"—though not without leaving a few tiny traces. In *A Backward Glance,* Wharton recalled that her uncle, Thomas Newbold, had assembled a collection of Madeira that was regarded as among the best in town. Following her uncle's death, the collection was sold, an occurrence that led to the following notation: "After my marriage, dining in a nouveau riche house of which the master was unfamiliar with old New York cousinships, I had pressed on me, as a treat not likely to have come the way of one of my modest condition, a glass of 'the famous Newbold Madeira.' "[63]

Yet another witness to the changing of the guard was Wharton's good friend Henry James, who, shortly after the turn of the century, returned for his first visit to the United States in twenty-five years (an experience he recorded in a fascinating book, *The American Scene*). Among his early stops was of course New York, a place that from the harbor he found to hold a certain allure:

> . . . the multitudinous sky-scrapers standing up to the view. . . . Like extravagant pins in a cushion already overplanted, and stuck in as in the dark, anywhere and anyhow . . . are impudently new and still more impudently "novel" . . . all of which uncontested and unabashed pride, with flash of innumerable windows and flicker of subordinate gilt attributions, is like the flare, up and down their long,

narrow faces, of the lamps of some general permanent "celebration."[64]

On landing, however, Mr. James was, let us say, taken aback. The "assault of vulgarity,"[65] the "crudity of wealth,"[66] "the huge American rattle of gold"[67]—all resolved themselves, in James's mind, into a "concert of the expensively provisional,"[68] or simply, "the loud New York story."[69] Reeling from the effects of his observations, James was moved to envision the future of New York as that of "a huge, continuous, fifty-floored conspiracy against the very idea of the ancient graces."[70]

As the writings of Wharton and James suggest, the tone of New York social life around the turn of the century was considerably different from what it had been, say, a quarter-century before. Whereas during the earlier period a certain decorum and restraint prevailed (at least by the standards of New York), social fashion was now determined by richer and less retiring families such as the Astors and the Vanderbilts—"the Astorbilts," as they were popularly known.* To employ Cleveland Amory's useful distinction, they were not Aristocracy but Society.

This Society soon attracted a lot of attention, not only in the East but across the country. As Mrs. J. Van Rensselaer King, an aristocratic New Yorker, recalled in her memoirs:

> The West was yielding tremendous riches. . . . Steel barons, coal lords, dukes of wheat and beef, of mines and railways, had sprung up from obscurity. Absolute in their territory, they looked for new worlds to conquer. The newspaper accounts of New York society thrilled the newly rich. In a great glittering caravan the multimillionaires of the midlands moved up against the city and by sheer weight of numbers broke through the archaic barriers.[71]

Along with the Astorbilts, the *arrivistes* formed a New Regime that was characterized by what today we would call conspicuous consumption—consumption on a scale that the inhabitants of Beverly Hills, in their wildest fantasies, have never even contemplated, let alone practiced. There were the Fifth Avenue mansions

---

* Although both these families—especially the Astors—first rose to prominence during the earlier period, their style of living was considerably more typical of the new regime than of the old (a fact attested to by their very notoriety).

("pompous," sneered Henry James); the "cottages" at Newport ("mistakes," said James); the houses at Palm Beach and elsewhere; the dreadnaught yachts; platoons of servants; herds of polo ponies; fleets of cars; sky's-the-limit debutante parties; elaborate dinners; dress balls to end all dress balls. Of the last, the more noteworthy were held at a place called Sherry's (which Wharton readers will recall from *The House of Mirth*).

For one such soiree, costing $200,000, the establishment's ballroom was transformed into a replica of the Hall of Mirrors at Versailles. On another evening, the 1,200 guests were suddenly transfixed by the sight of a swan (presumably artificial) circling overhead. On cue, the obedient swan exploded, showering the guests with 10,000 tiny pink roses.

Sherry's was also the site of a much-discussed dinner (given by a recent arrival from Chicago) at which guests were seated on horses (real ones). As the horses contentedly munched hay, their occupants gazed about at the cavernous ballroom, which for this occasion had become a woodland garden, with trees, shrubs and flowering plants. Live birds sang in the undergrowth, and attendants in white breeches and scarlet riding coats scurried about.

As the evening wore on, the guests were served dinner, which each consumed, as best he could, from a short wooden table slung across the shoulders of his by now reluctant mount and anchored, precariously, against the animal's quivering flanks. From time to time, the guest could quench his thirst from a bottle of champagne secured in a saddlebag and accessible by means of a long rubber tube.

As I say, the Horseback Dinner was much discussed in social circles, but perhaps the most talked about event of this genre was the dinner given by Mrs. Stuyvesant Fish for the Prince del Drago. Seated at the head table, resplendent in his regalia, the prince, on closer inspection, turned out to be a chimpanzee.

Today, of course, New York has grown much more respectable. Brooke Astor, for example, widow of the great-great grandson of old John Jacob, has become one of the city's major benefactors, in the best aristocratic tradition.

In seemingly similar fashion, New York has grown fond of raising an eyebrow at the rest of the country (its attitude being roughly comparable to that of nineteenth-century London toward the British empire—New York, of course, being the Empire State). "I have heard urbane New Yorkers describe someone as 'very American,' " writes Calvin Trillin.[72] The average American would be surprised to learn that the description is not meant as a compliment.

Yet like most such remarks, this one suggests a certain insecurity (an attitude characteristic of an upper middle class, rather than of an aristocracy). Trillin calls this attitude "rubophobia," which Donal Henahan explains in the *New York Times* as follows: "The person who contracts rubophobia does not fear rubes or hicks, as you might suppose, but being mistaken for one. In Manhattan this is a special problem, inasmuch as almost all its residents are from somewhere else, and that somewhere is likely to be a provincial backwater. That is why New York is always full of would-be gentlemen and ladies dedicated to upholding lofty standards that they only recently adopted."[73]

The *New York Times* displays similar tendencies. As the paper opined in an editorial opposing a plan to spruce up the state's new license plates with an image of the Statue of Liberty: "Let South Dakota flaunt Mount Rushmore on its plates. Let North Carolina, home of the Wright Brothers [Weren't they from Ohio?] boast about being 'First in Flight.' New Yorkers, secure about their state, should not need to hustle its virtues on their bumpers.... To appropriate Miss Liberty would wrong New Yorkers by making them look like provincial hicks."[74] (The *Times*'s advice was ignored. Miss Liberty was appropriated anyway.)

One reason such rubophobia is rampant in New York these days could be that—just as in the days of Mrs. J. Van Rensselaer King— New York has become Mecca for the rich and *nouveaux riches* from around the country and elsewhere. In the words of Tom Wolfe:

> The San Francisco matron who decides it's time to graduate from Merla Zellerbach's column in the *Chronicle* to the party-picture pages of *W* . . . the Hong Kong currency arbitrager who wants his daughter to become princess of a world bigger than Kowloon . . . the Australian who inherits a business from his daddy and wants to prove he's not merely a rich booby of the outback . . . the Argentinean who wants to get out of the pampas before his capital is shrunk to nothing by inflation . . . the Baltimore real estate developer who makes his first $10 million (the boundary line, replacing the old "millionaire")

only to discover that no one in *tout le monde* knows who he is . . . plus
the usual crowd of French rag-trade counts, Italian liquid-asset
refugees, British publishers, Cincinnati lavatory-puck manufactur-
ers yearning to be known as industrialists, and young Dallas and
Houston second wives (of the old boys) who want to meet some
people they've read about for a change at parties—in short, the
international tribe of those who want to be *where things are
happening*—today, in the last quarter of the twentieth century, head
not to Paris or London but to New York.[75]

Nor is New York unreceptive. As Charlotte Curtis puts it, "The
city is wide open, full of instantly accepted outsiders."[76] Thus: Two
of the city's newest and most popular party-goers are known collectively as "the two Anns." Their last names are not (as one might
otherwise suppose) Vanderbilt and Whitney, but rather Getty and
Bass; and they hail not from New York, but rather from, respectively, San Francisco and Ft. Worth. Mrs. Getty, in fact, was recently
elected to the board of the Metropolitan Museum, ahead of a long
line of local aspirants who doubtless considered themselves more
deserving. Why did this occur? One clue may lie in the fact that Mrs.
Getty's husband, Gordon, was until recently ranked as the richest
man in the world, and the couple dispenses about $5 million a year.
(Brooke Astor, by way of comparison, gives away anywhere from
$2 to $12 million.)

As it happens, the Gettys, in the style of San Francisco, are
relatively unflamboyant (Gordon, in fact, is a serious composer of
some success). But one could not necessarily make the same observation of all the other recent arrivals, and partly for this reason,
New York remains as always fast-talking and turbulent. And despite the city's best intentions, little gaucheries persist: Susan Gut-
freund achieving overnight success as a hostess, having obtained
much of her training at 30,000 feet; William F. Buckley, Jr., who
usually seems to be under the impression that he is Eustace Tilley,
going on and on about his Cadillac; Donald Trump going on and
on about everything . . .

But New York's shortcomings, say some observers, are considerably more serious. In the words of Louis Auchincloss, "We've
fabricated a society of wolves and coyotes. Why does anybody think
we're better than we were in the Robber Baron days?"[77]

Auchincloss's assessment would seem to have been amply borne
out by the recent scandals on Wall Street, which also serve to

demonstrate the accuracy of a statement by E. Digby Baltzell. In *Puritan Boston and Quaker Philadelphia,* Baltzell observes that an "elite" society—i.e., one made up merely of all persons who have reached the upper levels of their chosen fields—"is all too prone . . . to be composed of individuals motivated by the standards of success and individual self-interest, rather than by any class standards of honor or duty."[78] (Incidentally, the most sought after dinner guests in New York not long ago were people such as Ivan Boesky and Claus von Bulow. Criminal chic?)

Another writer makes much the same charge. In his novel *Hard Money* (a thoroughly dislikable book, by the way), Michael M. Thomas describes "the new Manhattan establishment" as "a miserable collection of shameless opportunists and gratification seekers: the men were principally paper merchants gorged on inside info and big lines of credit; the women were marked by a social ambition so obvious as to be unconscionable; the whole lot were vulgar, loud, unlettered, parasitic, and marked, above all, by an insecure, humorless self-esteem based on and derived from possessions."[79]

There's more:

> As ever, an entire army of people existed whose sole function was to help the newly rich spend their money in the right way. There were people who knew about toile de jouy and velvet, who knew about which orchids and souffles were currently "in" and which little country wines and legumes were "out," and which were the "right" periods of Jasper Johns and Billy Baldwin, and what "this year's" flower beds should look like, and what columnists to cultivate, and who could help get people into what clubs, and what it would take, and which charities to support and committees to strive for. It was now possible, in no longer than it took to write the check, to acquire for oneself what it had taken other people years to learn about and assemble and cultivate, from wine cellars to friends to gardens. There was no such thing as right by precedence, no point to connoisseurship. No man's island of taste and sensibility was his own, to savor and take pride and pleasure in; someone was now always on the fringes, ready to trump your ace with his checkbook if he liked the look of what you'd put together.
>
> Arrayed behind the purveyors of instant glorious living, and plugged into them, stood a vast machinery of gush, positively humming with a thirst for material. Glossy life-style journals, gossip

columns, special Sunday supplements in the *Times,* now the life-style journal of record. The ink on the check would barely be dry; the last clever gewgaw from the Pimlico Road would have barely been un-crated and arranged ever so artfully; the last painting of Jack Russell terriers would have been straightened to plumb over the Adam mantel ripped from some great country house; the white-gloved Ganymedes from Glorious Food would have been stationed, Pouilly Fumé in hand, behind each chair, when *Architectural Digest* or *House & Garden* or some breathless androgyne from some Living section somewhere would appear, trailing florists and photographers, to declare the assemblage one for the ages, of a piece with Sissinghurst and Ferrieres and Dunecrag. I thought it a game played by whores and tipsters.[80]

Gracious. Mr. Thomas may be right (if rather overwrought) about the present state of New York society. But he seems unaware that the press coverage such people receive today is a flyspeck compared to the coverage they received in the early part of the century—when, in the words of one grande dame, "the entertain-ments and ceremonies of Society were given more space than the proceedings of the Congress."[81]

One such entertainment the press particularly liked was Reggie Vanderbilt out for a spin, accompanied by his pet bull terrier—the latter attired in leather leggings, a tiny leather jacket and a pair of miniature goggles. Also prominent in the press was Grace Vanderbilt—*the* Mrs. Vanderbilt. Asked about denials that Mrs. Vanderbilt ever sought such publicity, her sister-in-law ex-claimed—"Publicity? Grace invented it!"[82] Invented, perhaps, but scarcely deserved. By all accounts, she was a dreadful woman—egocentric, demanding and virtually devoid of conversation.

A man who accepted an invitation to one of Mrs. Vanderbilt's regal dinners recalls that no sooner had the guests been seated than the dining room fell absolutely silent, save for the sepulchral clink of solid silver upon delicate china. Mrs. Vanderbilt, lost in her Vanderbiltness, spoke not a word. Eventually, to stave off sleep, the man began idly inspecting the placecards of his fellow guests (none of whom he had ever seen or heard of) and made a curious discovery. The last names of all those around him began with the same initial. The realization quickly dawned. Mrs. Vanderbilt had instructed her secretary to go through her address book and invite everyone from the section next in line. This was the *R* list.[83]

"For such a woman to be taken so seriously for so many years, not only by the columns and the tabloid press but also by visiting royalty," writes Cleveland Amory, "is certainly something of a comment on the downhill slide of Society in general."[84]

Other evidence of downhill slide abounds. Reggie Vanderbilt, for example—he of the goggled terrier—died of drink in 1925, two years after his second marriage. (Among his survivors was a year-old daughter named Gloria.) Of the Vanderbilt clan in general, Amory writes that "the workings of too much money and publicity and too little character and stability were, with certain notable exceptions, inexorable."[85] His diagnosis of the Astors' troubles, of which there were many, is more or less the same: "too much money and too many marriages."[86] Amory adds that beginning with the 1930s, "one is faced with a kind of all-embracing breakdown."[87]

Toward the end of that decade, Reggie Vanderbilt's sister Gladys was left a widow, and for many years thereafter, she lived alone in a suite of rooms on the top floor of the family's now-deserted Newport mansion, The Breakers, where Reggie had died. At one point, oddly enough, she enrolled, under an assumed name, in a Dale Carnegie course in How to Win Friends and Influence People; but for the most part, she sat at her window and watched the tourists troop by the mansion to (as she put it) "view the remains." Thus ensconced, she also had occasion to reflect on how things went awry. "I guess when all is said and done," she concluded, "the people who should have set the standard, didn't."[88]

Meanwhile, Aristocracy had begun an intermittent comeback of sorts, at least on a national political level. The first instance occurred in 1901 when President William McKinley was assassinated, and a young vice-president named Theodore Roosevelt was suddenly elevated to the White House. A graduate of Harvard (the first Harvard president since John Quincy Adams), he was also a member of that school's Porcellian Club ("the *ne plus ultra* of college clubs,"[89] in the words of Cleveland Amory). In addition, he was a scion of one of the most aristocratic families in New York.

Admittedly, not every member of the Roosevelt clan has subscribed to the adjective *aristocratic*. "Hells bells," exclaimed Theodore's daughter Alice to an interviewer in 1960, "the Roosevelts aren't aristocrats at all in the sense of the word as I use it. As a matter of fact, I like the world 'patrician' better, but the Roosevelts aren't that either. It's nonsense. The Roosevelts were Dutch peasants who achieved burgherhood by making respectable marriages—which few of them, I might add, have done since."[90] (Despite her disclaimer, Alice Roosevelt Longworth was undeniably an aristocrat, and as the foregoing remarks suggest, she abhorred the middle-class propensity for circumspection. Visitors to her Washington apartment report that a settee in the living room held a pillow that bore the inscription: "If you can't think of anything nice to say about someone, come sit next to me.")

Like his daughter Alice, Theodore Roosevelt was also an aristocrat, and as such he held a haughty disdain for the "decorous" and "ignoble" lives of many of his upper class acquaintances. As E. Digby Baltzell points out in *The Protestant Establishment: Aristocracy and Caste in America*, a large part of the American upper class, by the turn of the century, had become essentially a caste, interested mainly in guarding its privileges. But Roosevelt, he adds, "spent his life trying to justify, rather than protect, his inherited advantages. . . . He mistrusted and often despised the bourgeois mind, which has, after all, always reveled in luxury, snobbery and the pecuniary values."[91]

Or as Roosevelt recalled in a letter to a friend:

> I used to hunt at Hempstead. The members of the Four Hundred who were out there rode hard and well, and I enjoyed riding to the hounds with them. But their companionship before and afterwards grew so intolerable that toward the end I would take a polo pony and ride him fourteen miles over before the hunt and fourteen miles back after the hunt, rather than stay overnight at the club. . . . The life of the Four Hundred, in its typical form, strikes me as being as flat as stale champagne.[92]

Rather than spend his life sipping stale champagne, Roosevelt opted, early on, for livelier pursuits—as a cowboy and big game hunter out West (where, according to Baltzell, he adopted Federick Jackson Turner's view of the power of the frontier to mold character) and later as a Rough Rider on San Juan Hill. All of which, of course, made him enormously popular with his fellow citizens; and all of which raises an obvious question.

Was the general public able to draw the distinction between the

33

caste member that Roosevelt never was and the aristocrat that he nonetheless remained? Or did it see him mainly in a simpler sense: as the rich Harvard kid who had renounced his Eastern ways and become a real American. Did it regard him as a patrician assuming his rightful place in the White House? Or more on the order of that valued guest at a revival meeting: the former sinner who has seen the light.

Another difficulty with a strictly "aristocratic" interpretation of the Roosevelt administration stems from a paradox peculiar to all such presidencies: in the end, to some degree, they all have the effect of enhancing the image of the average man.

In the United States, the aristocratic ideal (such as it is, or was, at least) has never entailed a closed upper class, a social caste. Anyone with sufficient intelligence and taste could hope to ascend to the aristocracy (at least, in the persons of his progeny, two or three generations hence). Beyond that, patrician presidencies have all been imbued with a sense of *noblesse oblige:* of concern for the poor, the illiterate—the masses. (Thus, when certain of Theodore's cousin Franklin's contemporaries branded him "a traitor to his class," they had the wrong class. He was merely observing *noblesse oblige* on a very large scale.)

The problem arises when these patrician ideals are eventually expressed in popular form. Concern for the poor and their wasted potential becomes (to some degree) praise for the average man as he exists in fact. Hence, in the Progressive movement that was launched by Teddy Roosevelt and his fellow Mugwumps, "the dominant popular philosophy of politics"—wrote Richard Hofstadter—was contained in William Allen White's book *The Old Order Changeth* (1910). "America, White believed, was in the midst of an inexorable 'drift' toward democracy," and his book "was full of references to the intelligence, the self-restraint, the morality, the breadth of view of the average man, the emergent New Citizen."[93]

At any rate, with the advent of World War I, Progressivism ceased to progress; and with the return to "normalcy" that followed, the Mugwumps were once more consigned to oblivion. Society, so to speak, was back in the saddle.

*　　*　　*

34

Society soon discovered that a return to public favor had its rewards. In 1923, for example, a pair of advertising agencies, William Esty and J. Walter Thompson, began seeking out Society figures to endorse their clients' products. They found them. For a testimonial to the wonders of Pond's cold creme, Thompson enlisted Mrs. August Belmont and (surprisingly) Alice Roosevelt Longworth. For an endorsement of Camels, Esty eventually corralled a whole herd of socialites, including Mrs. Hamilton Fish, Jr., Mrs. Adrian Iselin, Mrs. Thomas M. Carnegie, Jr., Miss Anne Douglass Gould, Mrs. Anthony Drexel Biddle, Mrs. J. Borden Harriman, Mrs. Rodman Wanamaker and (surprisingly again) Mrs. Powell M. Cabot and Mrs. James Russell Lowell.

But in staking its reputation on its commercial drawing power, Society was treading on dangerous ground; and eventually the ground gave way. Thirty years after it all began, the use of Society endorsements had virtually disappeared. To understand how this came about, we return to the early twenties, to the age of the flapper and bathtub gin.

Even before Society began kicking the social traces to push cold creme and Camels, it was tripping the light fantastic in a new subculture called Café Society. Up until then, entertaining had been mainly a private affair, and the guests had been one's own kind. (A pair of dancers, say, might be brought in to perform after dinner, but they were never permitted at table. In the words of one such dancer, a woman named Irene Castle, "Celebrities of today have no idea how socially unimportant you were in the old days.")[94] Now, all of a sudden, everyone was dining out, and with the oddest sort of companions: actors, singers, songwriters . . . and people from—*Hollywood*.

In the words of writer Leo Rosten:

> It was Café Society that bridged the gap between Hollywood and Park Avenue. In the night clubs and restaurants of New York, the scions of the East met the gay, bright people of Broadway and Hollywood—persons whose names would make a dowager shudder. Café Society gave new money the social contact for which it yearned, and old money the escape from stagnation which it desperately needed. . . . In the Stork Club, 21, the Colony, El Morocco—Society and Show Business gazed upon each other, and each found a new affinity. Debutantes and playwrights, *bon vivants* and radio singers,

millionaires and movie queens formed a new and fluid social set, a set which embraced the continental and the *nouveaux riches,* a social circle centered in New York but with a circumference which included London, Long Island, Biarritz and Beverly Hills.[95]

In a sense, the Hollywood crowd was merely repeating an earlier migration: just as Eastern social climbers who failed to make it in New York often found success in (of all places) London, so the Hollywood set, snubbed by the ladies of Pasadena, moved on to New York. Even so, their visits were soon reciprocated. Within a few years, Whitneys and Vanderbilts were showing up at parties in Beverly Hills, as well as for the races at Santa Anita. Tangible displays of affection followed. Jock Whitney invested heavily in Hollywood movies, as did a son of FDR and a Lodge of Boston.

Still, the status of the Hollywood *arrivistes,* like that of the American emigrés to England, remained very much in doubt—a fact of which the Hollywoodians were well aware. Accordingly, wrote Leo Rosten, they had "no real sense of their own importance" and were "singularly deferential to the prestige of others." Their "hunger for social recognition" was "pathetic," causing them to "revere, and surely overvalue, the old, the traditional, the accepted," and to engage in an "unconscious aping of the higher elites in American life."[96] Coincidentally or not, many of Hollywood's movies during this period were paeans to those same higher elites.

The adulation actually began in the 1920s, soon after the emergence of Café Society. Later on, with the arrival of sound—and of Eastern playwrights to churn out the scripts—it rapidly became more or less unrestrained. For one thing, the new scriptwriters were contemptuous of their adopted home ("Millions are to be grabbed out here," cabled Herman Mankiewicz to Ben Hecht in a now-famous telegram, "and your only competition is idiots."); for another, they were homesick for the East.

As Pauline Kael has pointed out, there was a certain cultural lag at work here: what the playwrights brought to Hollywood in the thirties was really the Broadway spirit of the twenties. But no matter. The films they wrote had an irresistible appeal. Movie critic Richard Schickel, who grew up on those films as a child in the thirties, recalls the world they portrayed as the Great Other Place:

> It was a place where people tended to be beautiful (or at least well-dressed), witty, thoughtful, sexy and able to handle wine lists,

menus printed in French, and registering together at a hotel even if they weren't married. The men were often to be found in dinner jackets or even tails. At play, yachting costumes and jodhpurs were favored by both sexes. In the evening the women wore dresses that were, to our untutored eyes, barely distinguishable from their negligees, in that they were cut of shimmery white satin that clung sensuously to their bodies. These people lived in penthouses also very white and high-key, glittery with mirrors and appointments we can only in retrospect identify as art deco. They often had white pianos.

For the weekends, there was always Connecticut.[97]

Many of the movies that Schickel recalls have since become known as "screwball comedies"—movies such as *Nothing Sacred, Easy Living, Bringing Up Baby, His Girl Friday, My Favorite Wife* and *Too Many Husbands.* In a book called *Movie-Made America,* cultural historian Robert Sklar describes the genre as follows:

More often than not, the characters in screwball comedies were wealthy, and their wacky behavior showed audiences how funny and lovable and harmless the rich could be. Who could hold anything against Irene Dunne or Cary Grant after the hilarious last half-hour of *The Awful Truth,* which included Dunne playing a drunk at a posh social gathering, throwing away the knob on a blaring car radio, releasing the handbrake so the car crashes, and the two of them riding on the handlebars of police motorcycles? Or dislike Katharine Hepburn and Grant after the somersaults and games in the playroom in *Holiday?* Or find anything but charming Dunne's romance with Douglas Fairbanks, Jr., in *Joy of Living* after they go roller-skating together?[98]

In retrospect, however, the high jinks of the screwball comedies—the later ones, at least, around 1940—were deceptive, for they concealed a subtle change already taking place in the relationship between the Hollywood crowd and the sort of people they so engagingly portrayed on the screen. One of the first to notice the change was Dudley Field Malone, when he dryly observed that "Hollywood is the town where inferior people have a way of making superior people feel inferior."[99] The change was also apparent back in New York, where a great-grandson of *the* Mrs. Astor experienced what he later described as the greatest thrill of his youth on the day he had cocktails at "21" with Humphrey Bogart.

Writing of Maury Paul ("Cholly Knickerbocker"), the Gotham columnist who coined the term "Café Society," Cleveland Amory observed: "The irony was of course that, before his death in 1942, Paul lived to see the world of celebrities overwhelm his Café Society the way he and it had overwhelmed the Old Guard."[100]

For Paul, a rather fussy, high-strung man, the final straw came in the form of a party he attended where the other guests included a slew of Hollywood notables such as Marlene Dietrich and Clifton Webb. As the evening progressed, Paul became so irritated that nobody was talking about *him,* that he finally stamped his foot and announced: "You're all such crashing bores and Goddamned exhibitionists! Goodbye, please!" And with that he walked out.[101]

During the course of researching his book *Who Killed Society?* Cleveland Amory conducted an informal poll as to who, in fact, did. The first two answers were (predictably) the Servant Problem and the Bureau of Internal Revenue. The third was Hollywood.[102]

A possible explanation was offered by Dixon Wecter in *The Saga of American Society,* published in 1937:

> Hollywood can supply more glitter than a Society which has grown a trifle weary of its past magnificence and also a little timorous of its future. Hollywood's strings of pearls are longer, its Cattleyas rarer, its Hispano-Suizas newer, and its divorces bigger and better. And to some extent it has stolen the show.[103]

Indeed it had. In fashion, for example, Hollywood had "usurped the role of Society in establishing styles," as Leo Rosten put it.

> The hat which Greta Garbo wore in *Susan Lennox* put thousands of milliners to work on a style which was hailed as revolutionary. . . . Norma Shearer's bob, for *Romeo and Juliet,* altered women's hair-do for over a year and brought bitter conflict into a million boudoirs. . . . It is a familiar but ever impressive fact that when Clark Gable disrobed in *It Happened One Night* and was revealed to be *sans* undershirt, he sent the men's underwear business into a decline which, glassy-eyed manufacturers estimated, cut their business from 40 to 50 percent within a year.[104]

Hollywood was also stealing the show in the realm of marriage. Initially, such couplings involved merely a well-known actor and a prominent member of society—Randolph Scott and Mariana du

Pont, Gary Cooper and Veronica Balfe—but the former invariably received top billing. Later, Hollywood followed the example of High Society itself and opted for unions with European royalty: Douglas Fairbanks espoused England's Lady Ashley; Constance Bennett married the Marquis de la Falaise de la Coudrage, to whom Gloria Swanson had been previously wed; and so on. (Later still came the splashiest marriage of all when Grace Kelly took the hand of Prince Rainier of Monaco in a ceremony that was covered by 1,600 reporters from around the world.)

Another Hollywood marriage provided an amusing example of social succession—involving, in this case, Mrs. Hamilton McKown Twombly, a granddaughter of Commodore Vanderbilt. "For three-quarters of a century," writes Cleveland Amory, "in New York and Newport, and even, remarkably enough, in New Jersey—at 'Florham,' her incredible estate near the town of Convent—Mrs. Twombly had held what amounted to America's last court." An indication of her style of living can be gleaned from her response to a guest at Florham who inquired whether the military draft for World War II had depleted her staff of servants. "For some time," writes Amory, "Mrs. Twombly said nothing, then finally she sighed. 'This week lost four,' she said, 'from the pantry alone.' "

Amory continues as follows:

Even before this death sentence, Mrs. Twombly had observed changing times. In 1935, then in her early eighties, she had gone west—to, of all places Hollywood, California. The event was the wedding of her grandson and Flobelle Fairbanks, niece of Douglas Fairbanks, Sr. Although the reception contained, in deference to her, a sizable proportion of Eastern refugees and a well-turned-out delegation from Pasadena, Santa Barbara and even San Francisco, there was also, unavoidably, a large group of Hollywoodians. For some time Mrs. Twombly surveyed them, and then turned to a relative from New York. "In my day," she said quietly, "we had the celebrities. Now, if you please, the celebrities have us."[105]

Not quite. Two years after Mrs. Twombly's visit to California came the first nationally recognized "Glamour Girl No. 1" (a term also coined by Maury Paul). Her name was Gloria ("Mimi") Baker; her mother was the former wife of a Vanderbilt; and she herself was known, of course, as a "debutante." The following year there were half a dozen Glamour Girls—"debutantes" all—of whom the best known was Brenda Diana Duff Frazier.

By the end of the thirties, however, the time of the glamour debutante was more or less over. In part, this may have had to do with the advent of World War II; in part, it may have had to do with *Life* magazine's choice as Glamour Girl No. 1 for 1939. Her name was Lana Turner.

Two years later, in 1941, Leo Rosten observed that "Hollywood's star is rising in the larger social heavens of America. Hollywood is, indeed, supplanting Society in the public mind as a symbolic royalty."[106]

No doubt Rosten was right in his assessment, but the process he described was not simply a matter of exchanging one set of royalty for another. Horatio Alger notwithstanding, few of the people who gazed at pictures of Reggie Vanderbilt in the Sunday rotogravures imagined themselves as the next Reggie Vanderbilt. But with movie stars, the reaction was quite different. As Rosten himself observed:

> One reason for Hollywood's stars becoming national idols is that they represent a new type of hero in American experience. Hollywood's children of fortune are not the thrifty newsboys of the Horatio Alger stereotype—honest, diligent, pure of heart; here, instead, are mortals known to be spendthrift and Bohemian, people believed to lack impressive brains and given to profligate ways. Yet they have been rewarded with great lucre and honored throughout the land. . . . Furthermore, the public *sees* the actors at their trade; it *sees* how they earn their living. The public never sees Morgan making money or Ford making cars; but it does see Robert Taylor making faces. The visual evidence of the films offers the waitress a chance to compare herself to the movie queen; it gives the shoe clerk a chance to match himself against the matinee idols. It produces the thought, "Say, *I* could do that. . . ." No other industry presents so simple an invitation to the ego. . . . There is unconscious point to the dream of Hollywood which millions keep alive in their minds.[107]

Beyond that, the public regarded movie stars as, in some sense, "ours," whereas a Whitney or an Astor surely was not. Because of all this, the gap between the average person and the highest level of society (now Hollywood celebrity, in the public's mind) was narrowed considerably. Or as Robert Sklar succinctly summed it up toward the end of his book, "Movie stars were a new phenomenon in world culture, symbols who had erased all boundaries of class . . . "[108]

This effect was not simply a function of celebrity having displaced Society in the public's esteem. It resulted as well from a change in the content of the movies themselves—which, beginning in the late thirties, began to extol the virtues not of the upper classes but of the average man.

One of the reasons for this remarkable turn-around, certainly, was the temper of the times. In the midst of a severe depression, Americans had (once again) elected an aristocratic Roosevelt to the White House. And even more so than in the first Roosevelt administration, the accompanying sense of *noblesse oblige* encouraged a compassion for the troubles of the common man. Moreover, this general atmosphere seemed to build upon and enhance what Richard Hofstadter has described as "the pervasive and aggressive egalitarianism of American life"[109]—which had first exploded on the national scene in the Jacksonian democracy of the 1830s and had later found expression in the Populism of the 1890s. As for the 1930s, Hofstadter observed in *The Age of Reform:*

> In some quarters there was a revival of populist sentiment. . . . Along with this came another New Deal phenomenon, a kind of pervasive tenderness for the underdog, for the Okies, the share-croppers, the characters in John Steinbeck's novels. . . . With this there came, too, a kind of folkish nationalism . . . inspired at bottom by a real rediscovery of hope in America and its people and institutions. For after the concentration camps, the Nuremberg Laws, Guernica, and (though not everyone saw this so readily) the Moscow trials, everything in America seemed fresh and hopeful, Main Street seemed innocent beyond all expectation, and in time Babbitt became almost lovable.[110]

In addition to all that, one suspects that the democratic sentiments of late-thirties movies had a more immediate cause: Now that Hollywood Celebrity no longer felt deferential toward Eastern Society, it was just as happy to return, in spirit at least, to the popular base that had given it birth.

Whatever the exact explanation, the effects were clear. In the words of Richard Schickel:

. . . a massive effort—of just how much consciousness on the part of those engaged in it is impossible to say—was made to reeducate the public. The old exotic fancies were, in large measure, canceled out, a new fiction of ordinariness created. It was a fiction in which extraordinary people—if not always in talent, then assuredly in looks and income level—were supposed to be seen as entirely like their audience in basic values and desires. . . .

[I]t was simple enough—and pleasant enough—to believe that movie stars and suchlike wanted pretty much what we wanted—to move the family into that nice big house out in the new section of town, to buy a new car, to bring home the new console model Magnavox as a surprise for the household. I mean, what more was there to life? . . .

The nonsensical apotheosis of all this occurred during World War II. . . . Stills and newsreel sequences gave us glimpses of people like James Stewart being sworn into the service, or Tyrone Power good-naturedly peeling spuds in boot camp. . . .

Hollywood Canteen offered the most risible and exemplary such tale. In it, a young soldier played by Robert Hutton falls for Joan Leslie, playing herself, a demi-star. When she shyly encourages him, he is permitted two boons—a tour of the Warner Bros. lot and a home-cooked meal at her house, which turns out to be, wonder of wonders, a little bit of the Middle West plunked down in the middle of Hollywood. There is warmhearted Mom. There is wise and patient Pop. There is Kid Brother, only a little bratty. There is a white picket fence. There is a porch, with an old-fashioned swing where a fella and his gal can sweetly spoon. What was not there were white pianos, mirrored walls, shimmery gowns, servants or, for that matter, even a hint of a liquor cabinet. One seems to recall someone saying grace before dinner.[111]

The process of what Schickel calls "democratizing stardom" was also apparent—strikingly so—in the films of Frank Capra. In the mid-thirties, Capra directed the charming *It Happened One Night,* which bore a superficial resemblance to screwball comedies, but which actually, in the words of Robert Sklar, was "a fantasy of upward social mobility and romantic love, a comedy of submission and reward. The rich girl gives up her freedom for the hero; the poor boy weds his vitality and vision to the dominant social class."[112]

A few years later, however, Capra was turning out movies such as *Mr. Smith Goes to Washington* and *Meet John Doe.* As Sklar observes:

The major changes concerned the wealthy. . . . In the heart of the hero the rich girl's place is taken by a working woman; instead of wealth and power giving aid to the hero's dreams, it is "the people" who rally behind him. Capra's social myth requires the recognition and participation of common people to make it come true, it's a myth in which audiences are assured they, too, have a part to play.[113]

Sklar goes on to observe:

These later films have often been attacked for . . . sentimentality, demagoguery, anti-intellectualism, a belief in tyranny of the majority; for idealizing small-town and "middle" Americans who think they can do no wrong because their motives are pure and who hate lawyers, bankers, artists, intellectuals and urbanites.[114]

Finally, one should point out that such populist prejudices are also encouraged by the best-known Hollywood genre of all: the Western. We'll have more to say about Westerns in subsequent chapters. For now we'll make just a few general observations.

Those of us who grew up with Westerns (which means a large majority of Americans) are so familiar with the form that we take it almost for granted. But the Western is probably our most potent and pervasive national myth ("as much a myth," says Berkeley sociologist Will Wright, "as the tribal myths of the anthropologists").[115] Certainly it has had a greater influence on American culture than the influential Frontier Thesis of Frederick Jackson Turner; and indeed it may have had as great an impact as the frontier itself. (Incidentally, would the Western have been made such a popular form if the movie business had remained in New York, rather than moving to California?)

Just as we're familiar with the Western form, we also recall the classic Western hero as portrayed by, say, John Wayne (whom Congress, upon his death, awarded the Congressional Medal of Honor). What we tend sometimes to forget is the manner in which the Western portrayed the East. As Will Wright reminds us, in the classic Western, "The East is always associated with weakness, cowardice, selfishness, or arrogance. . . . Large scale, interesting Westerns, such as *The Big Country* [starring Gregory Peck], have been financial disasters perhaps because they made the error . . . of making the hero an Eastern dude."[116] (George Bush, please note.)

These days, of course, relatively few Westerns are still being made, but the form, and its hero, live on in countless ways. As several critics have pointed out, *Star Wars* was in a sense a Western transferred to outer space. Harrison Ford's *Witness* was a Western set in Western Pennsylvania. The Western hero as icon has survived as Dirty Harry. Recently, the Western movie *Young Guns* achieved a certain popularity with the younger set, and the mini-series "Lonesome Dove" surprised everyone by becoming a big hit on television.

With television, we come to another major step in the democratization of stardom. Movie stars, familiar as they might be, were still Stars with a capital *S*. In order to see them, one made a pilgrimage to a movie theater, stood in line and then gazed reverently upward as the larger-than-life images appeared on the screen.

But TV stars are different. The medium fosters what is known as "the illusion of intimacy." Every week, your favorite stars come right into your living room, big as life (but no bigger). They become like members of the family, trusted friends—which is exactly the way viewers greet them when encountering them on the street. The viewers feel they've known them for years, as in a sense they have, and they can't quite understand why their friends don't seem to know them.

Another difference between TV and movie stars is that the latter are regarded as more real than the characters they play, whereas with the former, who generally appear in a continuing series, the reverse is true—witness the times that "Trapper John" is stopped on the street and asked for medical advice. As a result, the illusion of intimacy is increased. Viewers feel that they know their favorites completely, every detail of their professional and private lives—the money worries (last Tuesday's episode), the problem son (the week before), the affair with the cousin's wife. . . . And it is perhaps for this reason that movie stars often do not do well on television. In the words of Hollywood agent Jerry Katzman, the networks "would much rather have Larry Hagman in a TV movie than, say, Dustin Hoffman. I'm not saying they wouldn't want Dustin Hoffman in the right piece, but Larry Hagman can get anything off the ground. . . "[117] The difference, if you will, is one of class. Dustin Hoffman, being of a somewhat higher order, is regarded as a bit too aloof, as perhaps holding a little something back. But Larry Hagman—why hell, everybody knows J.R.

Thus the process is complete: Aristocracy was superceded by Society, which has been displaced by Celebrity, which has become—a bunch of your favorite friends. American class distinctions, in the popular imagination, have disappeared.

Perhaps the best illustration of this outcome is a television series that ostensibly demonstrated the reverse—the enormously popular evening soap called "Dynasty." Like all the evening soaps (and unlike the upper-class movies of the thirties), "Dynasty" was set in the West.* (A similar series called "The Hamptons" quickly folded, as did one called "Berringer's"—read Bloomingdale's—as did one called "Tattinger's," as did another called "Beacon Hill.") Thus, despite its name, the program had virtually nothing to do with family tradition. There was rarely any mention of forebears; the protagonist, Blake Carrington, was largely a self-made man; and any "dynasty" would have to have been composed of his descendants. By the same token, the program contained nothing of aristocratic values and tastes. No one on "Dynasty" ever read a book or a magazine (except for the occasional "home design" glossy); they did not collect paintings; they did not attend the symphony, the ballet, the theater or the opera.

The only "high-class" regular on "Dynasty"—whose station we recognized because she spoke with a British accent and dawdled over champagne and caviar—was Blake's former wife, Alexis, who was also, of course, a scheming bitch. (Incidentally, Alexis did mention on one occasion that she planned to attend the ballet— "The Royal Ballet," she said pointedly, "with Anthony Dowell." The message couldn't have been clearer. Things such as the ballet are almost certainly un-American, and only a person as dreadful as Alexis would ever dream of going.)

Krystle, on the other hand (Blake's second wife), was a former

* After a run of nine years, "Dynasty" came to an end following the 1988–89 season.

secretary and the soul of niceness. Naturally, snooty old Alexis was always putting Krystle down for being just a secretary, but *we* knew that a secretary was better than a champagne fancier any day. (The name "Krystle," of course, was also revealing. It's the sort of bloodless, made-up name favored by couples who've moved to California from, say, Indiana. No more Elizabeth and Margaret. Now it's Krystle and Kirsten and Tiffany.)

The role of schools on "Dynasty" (schools in this case meaning colleges) was also instructive, being analogous to the consumption of champagne and caviar. Adam, for example, son of Alexis, was portrayed as being even worse than his mother. At one point, he tried to dispose of his brother-in-law Jeff by hiring someone to slather the walls of the latter's office with (so help me) poison paint. From time to time during the course of the series, the viewer was reminded that Adam went to Yale. Jeff, on the other hand, was so straightforward and likable that Blake Carrington tried to adopt him. Where Jeff went to school was never mentioned.

And so it went. While "Dynasty" may not have been entirely classless, its tone was quite different from the way it was described in the popular press. In general, the purpose of the series seems to have been to demonstrate the truth of Hemmingway's famous answer to Fitzgerald's assertion that the rich are different from you and me.

Television programs as a whole (about which we'll have more to say in a later chapter) also offer dramatic evidence of how the medium tends to ratify the world view of the average man. Crime, for example, occurs on television ten times more often than in real life, and televised crime grows increasingly violent. All this creates what Dr. George Gerbner of the University of Pennsylvania calls a "mean world syndrome"; and although Gerbner doesn't say so, one might speculate that such a world, in the mind of the viewer, calls for someone, some authority figure, to straighten it out.

An analogous but somewhat different perspective is provided by Ben Stein in his book, *The View from Sunset Boulevard*. Stein points out, for example, that television is "a world that largely inverts traditional standards of what is good or worthwhile. Education on television is absolutely valueless. Generally a highly educated man is a fool or a knave. Study or introspection is worthless."[118] And he observes, "No show challenges the assumption that the unexamined life is the only life worth living."[119]

In place of the stuffy world of education (i.e., the East), television offers viewers the hedonistic, egalitarian society of Southern California. (As Stein puts it, "L.A. is the original in the giant Xerox machine of television.")[120] Here, the average man does not live in a cramped row house and ride a crummy subway (literally under the feet of the well-to-do). Instead, he lives in a "spacious" split-level and cruises the endless freeways in the California sun.

One of Stein's more surprising findings (confirmed by other researchers) is that businessmen on television—especially big businessmen—are usually portrayed as evil. According to Stein, this aspect of television, like so many others, reflects the outlook of the people who write and produce the shows. As one producer confided to Stein, "You have to remember that the people here are anti-establishment, and they see businessmen as part of the establishment."[121] Stein goes on to tell of conversations with producers who were convinced the world was run by a "conspiracy of bankers and financiers and certain other people,"[122] including, by implication, Henry Kissinger. Nobody came right out and said so, but it's not hard to guess the identity of this conspiracy. It's the Eastern Establishment—or sometimes, in an even more sinister manifestation, the dreaded Trilateral Commission. In the words of Dr. George Gerbner, "television knows how to deliver a mass audience, and generally that means shows with a populist bent— anti-big business, big government."[123] Recently, Hollywood has added another villain—namely, the news media. To be sure, few if any television producers would subscribe to the views of Richard Viguerie or Howard Phillips or other such "neo-populists." But they all arrive at much the same place. Television makes strange bedfellows.

In the end, however, the impact of television comes not so much from particular programs, but rather from the nature of the television culture itself. For example, before a program is ever put on the air, it is given a screening before a sample audience whose members can signal their slightest displeasure merely by pressing a button. Later, the completed program is delivered to people right in their living rooms, where every flick of their television dials is carefully monitored. Never before has a mass of people been so assiduously courted and catered to. One can understand if members of that mass (like Molière's *bourgeois gentilhomme* when he discovered that all along he'd been speaking prose) have begun to form the impression that their whims and predilections are somehow significant.

Beyond that, television culture (and especially the commercials, which are really little thirty-second dramas) holds up a mirror to middle-class society and says that yours is the best of all possible worlds; your life is good and worthwhile and meaningful; your tastes are just fine. Because yours, you see, is the real American society, and you are the real Americans.

Westward the Course of Empire: The Shift of Power within the United States

Westward the course of empire takes its way;
The four first Acts already past,
A fifth shall close the Drama with the Day;
Time's noblest offspring is the last.

—Bishop George Berkeley[1]

WHEN IRISHMAN BERKELEY, Archbishop of Cloyne, composed those lines in 1752, he had in mind the process by which the locus of empire in the Western world had steadily followed the course of the sun, from Troy, to Greece, to Rome, to England—then on to the New World, the noblest offspring, the fifth and final act. As it happened, however, Bishop Berkeley's words received their most lasting commemoration not in the New World as it then existed. Instead, a hundred years later, in 1866, his name was given to the site of a nascent university in the newest world of all: California.

This turn of events, if perhaps ironic, was nonetheless appropriate. Virtually from the time of its inception, right up to the present day, the United States has been a nation continually on the move from East to West. It is this fact, as much as any other, that sets the country apart from the older nations of the Western world. For just as the Europeans of Berkeley's day cast off for the new worlds of Massachusetts and Virginia, so Americans ever since have set out for still newer worlds farther west. The results of this movement (as we shall see in subsequent chapters) have had a profound effect upon the American character, a character which indeed is still in the process of formation today.

*　　*　　*

That the United States was settled in the manner that it was—that is, by means of a longitudinal frontier advancing in stages from east to west—was mainly a matter of topography and international politics. Along the eastern seaboard, the numerous natural harbors led to the establishment of several small colonies, rather than a few large ones, while the presence of the Appalachian Mountains ensured that the colonies would expand along the coast, instead of extending very far inland. At the same time, a series of navigable rivers—the Connecticut, Hudson, Delaware, Susquehanna, Potomac, James, Pee Dee, Savannah—provided ready avenues for exploring the interior.

By 1700, the frontier had advanced to the highest navigation points of the coastal rivers, and fifty years later it had pushed on into the mountains. Beyond that line, another barrier presented itself in the form of the French, until the so-called French and Indian War (or the Seven Years War, as it was known in Europe) spelled the end of France as a North American power. Even so, England attempted to circumscribe western expansion by drawing what it called a Proclamation Line at the crest of the Appalachian Mountains.

With the end of the American Revolution, the United States gained control of all the land to the Mississippi River, and here again, a network of east-west waterways—the Great Lakes, Ohio, Wisconsin, Illinois, Cumberland and Tennessee—provided easy access for people and commerce. By 1800, the great fertile plain of the Ohio and Mississippi valleys was the new frontier. Three years later came Jefferson's astonishing Louisiana Purchase, which, for a price of $15 million, doubled the country's size and extended its western boundary all the way to the Rocky Mountains.

By the late 1840s, however, the steady advance of the western frontier had more or less ground to a halt. The obstacle this time was the Great Plains, a vast, arid, treeless expanse that held little appeal to European emigrants accustomed to rivers and woods. So instead, they set out westward in Conestoga wagons along the Oregon Trail, a route that eventually led them (those that survived) to the Willamette Valley, or southward to California's Sacramento Valley. In 1846, with "manifest destiny" floating in the wind, the United States went to war with Mexico, the ostensible cause being a border dispute in Texas (annexed the previous year), but the real prize was California. In 1848, soon after the peace treaty was signed, the wisdom of this aim was demonstrated when gold was discovered at Sutter's Mill.

The remainder of the century was devoted to "filling in" the lands that the wagon trains had passed by. First came the miners, as California gold fever spread eastward like an epidemic into the territories that later became Nevada (where it yielded mainly silver), Colorado, Montana, Wyoming and the Dakotas. Next came the cattlemen, with their roundups and long drives to the roaring, railhead towns of Cheyenne, Dodge City and Abilene. And finally came the farmers, aided now by deep wells and windmills for obtaining water, as well as by a much simpler device called barbed wire, essential for fencing off the open range. By 1890, the American frontier had largely disappeared.

The closing episode in this protracted process—and perhaps the most revealing—occurred in April 1889, when 6,000 homestead lots in the Oklahoma Territory (a land supposedly set aside as a permanent home for Indians) were thrown open to settlement. As D-day dawned, 20,000 aspiring Oklahomans lined up along the borders of Texas and Kansas, and at the sound of a pistol, raced to grab whatever they could. In the ensuing stampede, wagons locked wheels and overturned, children were trampled, horses collapsed from broken legs or sheer fatigue, and men were gunned down over competing claims. Sorting out the tangle of overlapping titles would take several years.

It would be a mistake, however, to describe the settlement of the west in terms of greed alone. The westward expansion is one of the great dramas of American civilization, and it was motivated as much by dreams and myths as by anything else (a concept to which we'll return in later chapters). Because of this, the West became, as Archibald Macleish described it, "a country in the mind."

Such western dreams go back a long way. Throughout the course of western civilization, in fact, there has existed what historians refer to as the Myth of the West. This myth has two strands. The more recent, which was mentioned at the start of the chapter, stemmed from imperial Rome and held that worldly power moved from east to west. Later, this belief was embraced by imperial England and was reflected in the no-nonsense names given to the western outposts of the empire: New England, New York, New Jersey, New Hampshire and so on.

The earlier strand of the myth, which stemmed from ancient

Greece, was rather more romantic. It held that somewhere to the west lay the lovely, carefree land of Elysium. As Homer described it, "No snow is there, not yet great storm, nor any rain; but always ocean sendeth forth the breeze of the West to blow cool on men."[2] This belief in a fabulous land was later espoused by the Mediterranean explorers of the New World: Coronado searching for the Seven Cities of Cibola, Ponce de Leon pursuing the Fountain of Youth, Cortez and company searching for El Dorado. As Cortez remarked to an inhabitant of Mexico: "The Spaniards are troubled by a disease of the heart, for which gold is the specific remedy."[3]

The longing for Elysium was reflected also in the name given to the westernmost setting for this visionary quest: California. Where did the name come from? The answer is that it came from a romantic narrative written by one Garcia Ordoñez de Montalvo in 1510. The narrative described an island called California, located "very close to the Terrestrial Paradise" and peopled by a race of Amazons. "Their island," wrote Montalvo, "was the strongest in all the world, with its steep cliffs and rocky shores. Their arms were all of gold, and so was the harness of the wild beasts which they tamed and rode. For in all the island, there was no metal but gold."[4]

The irony of these descriptions, of course, is that in a sense they eventually came true. First there was the place itself, a place very like the one that Homer and Montalvo had described. Then came the fateful discovery at Sutter's Mill in 1848. "Overnight," wrote historian Carey McWilliams, "California became a world-famous name, and as a name, California meant gold."[5] Within two years, the territory was a state: the Golden State, beyond the Golden Gate. Following the turn of the century came the rise of Hollywood, a place that not only manufactured myths, but itself became a mythical symbol as potent and pervasive as Elysium or El Dorado. (The ironies multiply. When the first filmmakers arrived in Los Angeles in 1908, they set up shop not in Hollywood itself, but near a place called Elysian Park, in the community of Edendale—Eden, of course, being the Judeo-Christian version of Elysium.)

Meanwhile, during the century following the Gold Rush, the state's population continued to grow by 85,000 a year, or roughly the number that had arrived in the Gold Rush boom year of 1849. "In California," wrote Carey McWilliams, "the lights went on all at once, in a blaze, and they have never been dimmed."[6] A bit boosterish, perhaps (McWilliams spent most of his life in Los Angeles), but nonetheless true. Between 1945 and 1975, California increased its population by another 200 percent, displacing New York, in the early sixties, as the nation's most populous state. In 1980, the center of population crossed the Mississippi River, meaning that for the first time, there were more people in the West than in the East. Six years later, the population center had moved another twenty miles west and ten miles south, coming to rest (temporarily) near the town of Potosi, Missouri.

By the middle of 1987, California had grown by another 4 million people since the start of the decade—far more than any other state—to reach a total population of nearly 28 million, or about 10 million more than second-place New York. During 1986, the state enjoyed its greatest spurt of growth since the boom years of World War II (when local defense industries lured thousands of new residents), with the result that better than one in nine Americans was now a Californian. That same year, San Francisco displaced Philadelphia as the nation's fourth largest metropolis. Thus, California was now home to two of the four. (The rankings: New York, 18 million; Los Angeles, 13 million; Chicago, 8 million; San Francisco, 6 million.)

But it's not just a matter of quantity; the country's various regions have been diverging in quality as well. As Neal Pierce and Jerry Hagstrom point out in *The Book of America: Inside the 50 States Today*, "The 1980 census showed the West enjoying vast advantages in the average level of residents' education, in proportion of young people, and in the numbers of families with high incomes."[7] (Today, the West still leads in all three categories.)

Meanwhile, back in the East, things were not going nearly so well. Between 1965 and 1970, for example, the Northeast* suffered a net migration loss of 715,000. (The West, during the same period, had a gain of about the same size.) During 1970–75, the loss increased to 1,342,000, and during 1975–80, to 1,486,000. From 1980 to 1985, the loss declined to 1,022,000—less serious, but still substantial.

These overall figures, however, conceal a change that has re-

---

* The Northeast is defined by the Census Bureau as consisting of New England, plus the Middle Atlantic states of New York, New Jersey and Pennsylvania.

cently taken a place in portions of the Northeast Corridor. Since 1980, for example, the New York metropolitan area has regained much of the population it lost in the 1970s, and at its current rate of growth, it will gain it all back by 1990. The Boston and Philadelphia areas are also on the rebound, while the states of New Jersey, New Hampshire, Vermont and Maine have all enjoyed net migration gains over the past several years. Between 1980 and 1986, the Northeast as a whole grew by 1.8 percent. (During the same period, the United States grew by 6.2 percent, and the West—the fastest growing region—by 12.9 percent.) Today, the Northeast and the West are roughly equal in population, with about 50 million people apiece.

This equality, though, will not last for long. The Census Bureau predicts that by the year 2000, the Northeast will have a population of 52 million, while the West will weigh in with 59 million. By 2010, the Northeast will still have only 52 million, but the West will grow to 66 million.

Within those regions, New York will remain at roughly 18 million through 2010. California will increase to 34 million by the year 2000 and 37 million by 2010, or more than twice as many people as the state of New York—which, by 1995, will have been surpassed in population by the state of Texas.

The Northeast is falling behind in other ways as well. Between 1968 and 1978, for example, the region lost a total of 800,000 manufacturing jobs. In 1970, the Northeast and Midwest together accounted for 56 percent of the nation's investment in manufacturing plants and equipment. By 1977, the two regions' combined share had dropped to 47 percent.

Meanwhile, way out west, things were taking a different turn. Between 1973 and 1986 while manufacturing employment in the rest of the country was falling by nine percent, manufacturing jobs in the Twelfth Federal Reserve District* increased by 600,000. Employment in general was just as healthy, if not more so. From 1973 to 1985, the number of jobholders in the Pacific states rose by 4,317,000, while in the Middle Atlantic states (New York, New

---

* Composed of Alaska, Arizona, California, Hawaii, Idaho, Nevada, Oregon, Utah and Washington.

Jersey and Pennsylvania), they grew by only 1,512,000—little more than a third as many. In each of these years, California led all other states by a wide margin. In 1985, for example, California added 333,000 jobs; New York was a distant second with 167,600.

One reason for California's remarkable expansion is that the state has a widely diversified economy that just keeps growing through national boom and national bust. Although few people realize it, California has long been the country's leading agricultural state; today it is the leading industrial state as well. "Of all the United States," write Neal Pierce and Jerry Hagstrom in *The Book of America: Inside 50 States Today,* "California is the one that could most easily exist alone."[8] Were it to do so, its Gross National Product (about $500 billion), would be the sixth largest in the world— greater than those of Great Britain, Italy and China.

In practice, however, California does not exist at all alone, for much of its economy is tied to national defense. In 1985, for example, the state hauled in nearly $73 billion in Pentagon spending—more than twice as much as its closest competitor, Texas, which pocketed a little over $32 billion.

Even more basic to California's success is sheer innovation. When *Science Digest* conducted a poll in 1985 as to "the year's top 100 innovations," it found that 20 of those innovations were dreamed up in California. New York was second with 13, followed by Pennsylvania with 10. A similar poll the year before found that of the "100 brightest scientists under 40," California was home to 31, more than resided in any other state.[9] Such findings are perhaps not surprising when one considers the fact that California contains the country's greatest concentration of technical and scientific personnel, and its largest number of Nobel laureates.

Another explanation for the state's propensity for innovation is historical. As Carey McWilliams pointed out in *California: The Great Exception,* when settlers arrived in the Golden State, they found that methods of operation that worked back east were counterproductive in California's peculiar physical environment. "In surveying the culture of California," wrote McWilliams, "one will find in every field—in mining, agriculture, industry, technology—that the novelty of the environment and its compulsive quality have *forced* an abandonment of the imported cultural pattern in many important respects."[10] As a result, the state became a sort of giant experimental laboratory.

Today, this tradition of the untraditional accounts in part for the fact that California leads the country in "venture capital activity." Much of that activity, of course, is concentrated in Silicon Valley, the twenty-mile stretch of former fruit orchards bounded on the north by Stanford University, which served as seedbed for many of the valley's 2,700 high-tech firms. Led by such well-known companies as Hewlett-Packard, Intel, and Apple Computer, those firms now constitute what the *New York Times* describes as "the envy of the industrial world."

If truth be known, however, the greatest concentration of high-tech firms is not to be found in Silicon Valley. Instead, it's found near a place called Los Angeles.

Over the years, the City of the Angels has steadily eclipsed the City of San Francisco in one field after another (much as, in the previous century, New York eclipsed Boston).* Population shifted south in the 1920s. Banking (if not the bank headquarters themselves) followed suit about fifty years later. Today, of course, Los Angeles not only overshadows San Francisco in everything but bridges and opera (and it's gaining in the latter); it has begun, in some ways, to challenge New York for the role of leading city.

Already, for example, greater Los Angeles is the country's largest manufacturing center in terms of the value of goods produced (as well as being the largest aerospace center in the world). In 1986, Los Angeles surpassed Chicago in banking deposits; and though it still trails New York ($130 billion to $175 billion), L.A.'s deposits have been growing rapidly, while New York's have suffered a slight decline.

Swollen by rising Pacific trade, the value of ocean-borne cargo shipped through the ports of Los Angeles and Long Beach in 1986 reached $62 billion, far ahead of the $49 billion handled by the Port Authority of New York and New Jersey. What's more, the two California ports expect their cargoes to increase 170 percent by the year 2020. This last statistic is perhaps the most revealing, for Los Angeles increasingly serves as the gateway to Asia, the fastest growing area in the world.

All of this is not to say that California's economy is without its problems. A study conducted for the state legislature in 1986 by

* The chief exception, in both cases, has been that the northern city remained the home of the more prestigious universities. Some things, fortunately, still take time.

SRI International pointed out that California is certain to suffer a decline in defense contracts as the recent military buildup comes to an end. More important, the report stated that, "While California is the world leader in advanced technology, other nations and states are challenging our position of preeminence." Japan is taking over the manufacturing and marketing of products developed in California, while states such as Massachusetts, North Carolina, Michigan and Texas are cultivating their own little Silicon Valleys.

One of California's basic shortcomings seems to be that because it has enjoyed continuous growth for so long—especially during the years since World War II—the state has come to regard prosperity as a sort of divine right, like perpetual sunshine. As a result, large-scale national projects that send other states into a frenzy of boosterism and competitive bidding are greeted by California with a barely concealed yawn. Thus, following a half-hearted wooing by California, the semiconductor industry's new research consortium, called Sematech, decided to set up shop in Austin, Texas (which had earlier been chosen as the site for another high-tech consortium). Incredible though it may seem, California lost out to Buffalo, New York, as the site of a center for research on earthquakes. And despite the fact that California invented the cyclotron, it lost the competition for the newest accelerator, the "superconducting supercollider," when (like a none-too-studious college senior sliding his term paper under the professor's door at midnight), it submitted its bid exactly two minutes ahead of the deadline.

Aside from complacency, another reason California has become blasé about such projects is that the state has developed mixed feelings about growth itself. For the past ten years or so, the San Francisco area has been skeptical if not hostile toward additional expansion (which is another reason growth has shifted to the south). Today, that hostility is showing up in Southern California as well. To be sure, the arguments advanced in the two halves of the state are usually quite different. In the liberal, middle-class north, the cry goes up over trees and open space; in the conservative, six-pack south, the complaint is heard over freeway jams. But in the end, the effects could be much the same.

Partly because Proposition 13, the famous tax-cutting measure of a decade ago, has made it difficult for local governments to raise the money for roads and sewers, rapidly growing Southern California is now a hotbed of voter initiatives to put a damper on further expansion. Eventually the movement could even produce, in the manner of Hollywood sequels, a sort of Proposition 14: The Story Continues.

Should such an anti-growth movement take hold, however, there is little reason to believe it would remain confined to California. Similar feelings are already well advanced in places such as Long Island and the Princeton Corridor, and just as Proposition 13 cloned its way across the country (arriving, finally, in Massachusetts), the sequel could be expected to do the same.

Much the same holds true for measures against air pollution. During the first few months of 1989, the Los Angeles region was forced by the federal government to devise a sweeping plan which over the next twenty years would impose severe restrictions on everything from backyard barbecues to automobiles. It could also conceivably restrict the region's growth. At the same time, however, the feds have ordered New York and New Jersey to come up with a similar plan by September 1991. Although the problems in the two regions are not entirely the same—Los Angeles leads the nation in smog, New York in carbon monoxide—officials anticipate that New York will soon be considering some of the same countermeasures that are raising questions about continued growth in Los Angeles today.

In the meantime, the Northeast in general is not at all encumbered by opposition to growth. Instead, over the past few years, the region has staged what appears to be a rather remarkable recovery from economic stagnation. During the 1980–82 recession, the Northeast suffered a net loss of employment—136,700 jobs. But during the following two years, the region *added* 745,200 jobs; and from 1984 to 1986, it added another 1,116,700; for a growth rate of 5.3 percent. This was nearly as good a record as compiled by the West, which during the last of these periods added 1,257,500 jobs, for a growth rate of 6.8 percent.

Perhaps the most impressive recovery is the one engineered by the city of New York, which in the process of pulling out of near-bankruptcy managed also to displace the city of London as the capital of world finance. To be sure, New York (like London) suffered a setback with the 1987 stock market crash (though predictions of massive layoffs proved overly pessimistic). In the future, moreover, the city will face its greatest challenge not from London but from the much more aggressive Tokyo. Meanwhile, the city's heated expansion has already begun to cool. In the words of Samuel H. Ehrenhalt, New York regional commissioner of the Federal Bureau of Labor Statistics, "The heady boom that began ten years ago is over. We've entered a period of uncertainty, of shifting economic tides."[11]

Another part of the Northeast which has staged a strong recovery is New England. In 1975, for example, Massachusetts had the highest unemployment rate in the country—11.2 percent. In 1985, it had the lowest—3.9 percent. Be that as it may, there are several reasons for raising an eyebrow at the "Massachusetts Miracle" (as Michael Dukakis was fond of calling it).

One thing to bear in mind is that (to a greater extent than Cambridge liberals like to admit) the growth along Boston's Route 128 has been dependent on the Pentagon. Thus, cutbacks in smart bombs will be felt as surely in New England as they will in California. By the same token, all those tiny Nipponese computer chips will rain alike on the just and the unjust, Route 128 and Silicon Valley.

But the reasons for taking the Massachusetts Miracle with a grain of salt are rather more basic. In the words of David L. Birch, director of the program on neighborhood and regional change at MIT, "The economic miracle per se wasn't exactly a miracle. Relative to our situation in 1974–1975, it was quite nice, but our employment growth rate for any period you want to pick has been right about the national average. . . . The only reason we look to be booming is because the unemployment rate is low, and the only reason the unemployment rate is so low is that no one moves to Massachusetts."[12] Instead, they're still moving away—some 45,000 between 1980 and 1986. Partly for this reason, employment growth in New England by 1989 was significantly slower than in the country as a whole.

"For the first time in American history," writes Lester Thurow, dean of the Sloan School of Management at MIT, "there is a region with lots of jobs where Americans are refusing to move. . . . And the Massachusetts boom has essentially ended in this unwillingness. There are simply no workers to be hired. . . . The most interesting thing about Massachusetts's now-fading boom is the extent to which it strangely reaffirms the existence of the Sun Belt as an economic force. The dampening of the economic upturn in this cold, snowy, cloudy state is further evidence of the hypothesis that the center of American economic activity will gradually move to sunny, warm states simply because that is where people prefer to live."[13]

Apparently so. According to a report by the Center for the Continuing Study of the California Economy, in Palo Alto, the economy in question, between now and 1995, will grow at a rate almost double that of the nation as a whole, generating an additional 2,200,000 jobs.

The shift of population to warm, sunny states is reflected also, of course, in the realm of politics. Following the censuses of 1950 and 1960, the Frostbelt states of the Northeast and Midwest lost a total of seven seats in the House of Representatives (while the Sunbelt states of the South and West gained an equal number). Following the census of 1970, the Frostbelt states lost eleven seats; in 1980, seventeen seats.

The biggest gainers in 1980 were Florida (four seats), Texas (three) and California (two). "The biggest loser by far," wrote Theodore White in *America in Search of Itself,* "was the State of New York, which lost five seats (four in New York City, one in Buffalo). Pennsylvania, Ohio and Illinois lost two seats each. At one time, New York had dominated the Union as much by its political weight as by its financial and cultural leadership. Starting in 1810, it had sent the largest of any state's delegation to the House. For years, its 45 congressmen had held more than one-tenth of all House seats. In 1970, California for the first time outstripped it. By the 1980 Census, New York would have only 34 congressmen, and California would have 45. . . . *Sic transit gloria.*"[14]

After the 1990 census, the Frostbelt will lose another sixteen or seventeen seats in the House. Once again, the biggest loser will be the state of New York, whose delegation will decline by three or four members. Pennsylvania, Ohio and Illinois (once again) will lose two, as will Michigan. On the winning side, Florida will pick up three seats and Texas four, the latter's delegation thereby growing to thirty-one members, equal to that of New York (or one delegate more, should New York lose four seats instead of three).

The biggest winner, however, will be the state of California, whose delegation will mushroom from forty-five to fifty or fifty-one. To be sure, such runaway growth has its drawbacks. "There's basically a hostility to California in the House," says former California representative Tony Coelho. "People keep moving west, and the delegation keeps getting bigger and bigger. Other delegations are used to having influence and suddenly they're losing it."[15]

A similar transition is apparent, of course, in the votes of the electoral college. (Since each state's electors are equal in number to its senators and representatives, a loss of seats in the House is directly reflected in a loss of electoral votes.)

According to a tally by Ben Wattenberg, when Kennedy was elected president in 1960, the Frostbelt had 286 electoral votes, the Sunbelt, 245. When Johnson was elected in 1964, the Frostbelt lead had shrunk to 12. When Nixon won in 1972, the Sunbelt, for the first time, had taken the lead, but by only four votes. With Reagan's re-election in 1984, however, the Sunbelt lead had grown to 21. Thus, there was a shift of 62 electoral votes in 24 years. In Wattenberg's words, "the magnitudes are massive."[16]

They will be even more so by the year 2000, when, according to Kevin Phillips, "domination by the Sunbelt will be far more advanced and complete than today."[17]

No Business Like Show Business: The Transfer of the Entertainment Capital from New York to Hollywood

> You can take Hollywood for granted like I did, or you can dismiss it with the contempt we reserve for what we don't understand. It can be understood too, but only dimly and in flashes.
>
> —F. Scott Fitzgerald, *The Last Tycoon*[1]

ONE OF THE MOST SALIENT FACTS about Hollywood is so obvious it is usually overlooked. In no other nation in the world has the moviemaking center been set up at the opposite end of the country from the cultural center. Yet this is what has happened in the United States, and the effects have been profound.

Such a turn of events did not, at the outset, appear very likely, if indeed the possibility occurred to anyone at all. Thomas Edison, for his part, predicted in 1890 that the new technology of moving pictures (which he was at the moment endeavoring to develop at his laboratory in New Jersey) would serve primarily to bring cultural presentations into the homes of the wealthy. Pecunious owners of his phonographs, it seems, would rush to purchase visual reproductions of operas and plays to accompany their recordings. (In later years, Edison also emphasized the opportunities for working people to encounter the rarefied higher arts.)

But things, as they say, didn't work out that way. American cities at the turn of the century were teeming with a new class of immigrants—Eastern and Southern European, usually poor, often illiterate in any language, especially English—and it was for their amusement (not edification) that the new invention was mainly employed. Along the principal streets of working-class districts, storefront theaters lined up four and five abreast, using bright lights and barkers to snare the factory hand on his way back home. Once snared, the factory hand found himself in a crowded, dark and smelly room; but at the far end, what wonders unfolded: firemen leaping from burning buildings, locomotives running backwards . . . boxing cats!

Later on, as movies grew longer, the scenes were often from everyday life: a family enjoying a day at the beach; a little morality tale called *The Kleptomaniac,* which illustrated how the legal system favored the rich over the poor. In 1903 came the first American classic, *The Great Train Robbery,* which used twenty separate shots and a dozen different locations. The audience loved it. While *The Great Train Robbery* toured the country, the number of movie theaters in greater New York grew to more than six hundred by 1908, with a daily attendance of three to four hundred thousand.[2]

All of this took place beyond the notice (beneath the notice, actually) of respectable society. In the words of writer Leo Rosten, "the movies were vulgar knickknacks, as all sensible people knew; they could never be more than a passing fad; they were cheap amusement, patronized only by the poor and the immigrant, the illiterate and the unwashed."[3] When *Harper's Weekly,* in 1907, deigned to describe this passing fad, it did so in an article entitled, "Nickel Madness."[4]

Eventually the madness proved too much. Although most of the movies were innocent beyond words—*What Demoralized the Barbershop* in 1901 was a slightly raised skirt—a few offered glimpses of female nudity; and many offered more than glimpses of various forms of mayhem. But "what was most galling to many in well-to-do city districts, suburbs and small towns," wrote Robert Sklar in *Movie-Made America: A Cultural History of American Movies,* "was the idea that workingmen and immigrants had found their own source of entertainment and information—a source unsupervised and unapproved by the churches and schools, the critics and professors who served as caretakers and disseminators of the official American culture."[5] Accordingly, in 1909, civic groups in the city of New York established a censorship board that would thenceforth pass judgment on all new movies.

As it happened, the civic groups had chosen an opportune time. Just a few months earlier, the nine principal moviemaking firms had organized the Motion Picture Patents Company, the goal of which was to create a monopoly over all phases of movie production, distribution and exhibition. Leading the company was Thomas Edison, who according to Sklar was regarded by many of his fellow citizens as "the greatest living American."[6] Most of the other producers were of similar backgrounds. Or as Sklar put it, the movies during this period were "as completely in the hands of respectable, established Anglo-Saxon Protestant Americans as they were ever to be."[7] Soon after the censorship board was formed, the Patents Company agreed that the board's volunteers could do their censoring at the company's screening room in New York.

The whole affair, however, entailed much more than the matter of censorship per se. Robert Sklar described the situation as follows:

> In New York the cultural establishment was impressed by the producers' willingness to abide by the wisdom of the charitable, educational and religious leaders who made up the board, even when it meant additional expense or lost revenue. Such cooperation seemed unmistakenly to indicate a disposition to be guided by respectable opinion. National magazines published in New York began to give movies more attentive and usually more favorable notice.
>
> It was not what movies were but what they might become that attracted the spokesmen for middle-class culture. They were fascinated by the audience the movies had won over and could command. Initially they had been disturbed by the discovery of working-class people taking part in a culture of which they had no knowledge and over which they exercised too little authority. Now the possibility of gaining control over movies suddenly opened vast new horizons, kindled impossible cultural dreams. The industrial revolution had erected barriers of experience, environment and culture between the middle and the working classes. Not since the Elizabethan Age in England had the high culture of the middle and upper classes been a truly popular culture, accessible to all social groups. But the nickelodeons could restore the past: movies would bring high culture back to the people. . . .
>
> There was one basic flaw in this middle-class dream: it rested on the continued dominance of the medium by the Patents Company producers, who, despite their apparent monopolistic power, proved unable over the succeeding decade even to survive. And as power changed hands in the motion-picture industry it passed not to middle-class reformers and cultural custodians, but to members of

the very immigrant ethnic groups they sought to influence and control.[8]

The result, concluded Sklar, was "a complete debacle for the Wizard [i.e. Edison], his leadership and his social class."[9]

Right at the outset, the Patents Company producers made a tactical blunder. As a first step to raise the general tone of movies, they decided to go after a tonier clientele (just as their counterparts in Europe, in fact, had always done). They therefore offered preferential bookings to exhibitors who agreed to set up shop in better neighborhoods, hold films for longer runs and charge a dime's admission. The only problem was that this policy left two or three thousand storefront nickelodeons temporarily high and dry, thereby providing a prize for anyone who was willing to run the company's blockade.

The first person to do so was Carl Laemmle, a German-born Jew and former clothing store manager who owned a large movie distributorship based in Chicago. After breaking with the Patents Company in 1909, Laemmle launched a production firm called the Independent Moving Picture Company, otherwise known as Imp. Within a year, about a dozen other independents had joined the fray, and the Patents Company's putative monopoly was under wholesale assault.

Eventually (and inevitably), the battle was taken up by platoons of attorneys; and in 1915, a federal court declared that the Motion Picture Patents Company was an illegal conspiracy in restraint of trade. But by then, the outcome was a foregone conclusion. Three years earlier, the Patents Company's share of total film production had dropped from nearly one hundred percent (in 1908) to slightly better than half. More important, the independent producers, in order to escape the restraints of the Patents Company, had fled to a faraway place called Hollywood.

There were, of course, other reasons for moving to California: cheap land, cheap labor (cheap, that is, in non-union Los Angeles, as opposed to unionizing San Francisco), a topography that included everything from ocean beaches to city streets to mountains to deserts, all within a hundred miles or so. . . . And the climate. A

Mediterranean climate, only better: constant sunshine, no humidity, and a temperature that varied about a dozen degrees between winter and summer.

Although the producers presumably weren't aware of it, there was still another reason why their westward migration was appropriate. The place where they would create "the greatest dream factory in the history of the world" (in Vincent Canby's words) was already awash in dreams and myths.

These extended (as mentioned earlier) from the ancient Myth of the West, to the search for El Dorado, to the modern myth of the cowboy. "More than other American regions, the West eludes definition because it is as much a dream as a fact," write Frank Bergon and Zeese Papanikolas in their introduction to *Looking Far West: The Search for the American West in History, Myth and Literature.* "Before it was a place, it was a conception. Its characteristics were invented as well as discovered. . . . Because the West has become so overlaid with legend, it is popularly assumed that a stripping of its mythic veneer would reveal the "real" West. Nothing could be less true. . . . The West and the Westerner were creations of the total American imagination."[10]

In submerging themselves in this American imagination (however inadvertently), the independent producers were aided by their isolation from the "European" cities of the East. Today, we tend to forget how real this isolation was. The only means of transportation between the two coasts was the train. The Western papers carried relatively little international news compared to those of the East, which took four to five days to reach California. There was of course no television, and several national radio programs were not broadcast in the West at all, or were offered at inconvenient hours.

To be sure, this isolation had its limits. The studios, as a rule, still maintained their business offices in New York; and this division of authority between the creative people on the West Coast and the money men on the East was a source of considerable friction as the years went by—witness the (relatively) recent Begelman affair. In his account of that affair, called *Indecent Exposure* (an account that generally adopts the New York point of view), David McClintick observes, "The heads of the film studios have—and always have had—less power to function independently of their corporate parents than has been commonly portrayed."[11] On the other hand,

John Gregory Dunne points out in *The Studio* that Darryl F. Zanuck "was a tycoon in Hollywood when the title carried with it feudal power and virtual *droit du seigneur*."[12] At any rate, it seems fairly clear that the day to day decisions as to what would actually appear on the screen were made primarily in California. And inevitably, such decisions were influenced much more by the egalitarian society of the Southland (as the *Los Angeles Times* refers to it today) than by the stratified society of the East.

Initially, the Angelenos did not much cotton to the "movie colony," whose studios they referred to as "camps," as though the workers therein were little more than roving bands of gypsies. But by 1920, the movies were the principal source of income for greater Los Angeles, which itself was rapidly changing. "Come to California!" urged a massive local publicity campaign; and the people came. Mostly they came from the heartland, to the extent that an English architectural critic named Reyner Banham would later write that, "Los Angeles is the Middle West raised to flashpoint."[13]

Gradually, the gulf between the movies and the townies started to narrow, as each, in a sense, began to borrow from the other. The townies, for their part, became preoccupied with glamor, youth and showmanship. Klieg lights announced the opening of produce markets, and attendants at drive-in restaurants dressed up like usherettes. House and shop designs were lifted from a hundred different movie sets, producing English peasant cottages next to French chateaux next to Mission adobes and Arabian minarets.

In the movie colony, the borrowing was less conspicuous but nonetheless real. "What the industry required, in the way of mores," wrote Carey McWilliams, "was a frontier town forever booming;"[14] in other words, Los Angeles. "Here," wrote McWilliams, "was the great domestic melting pot, a place which, as Morris Markey has said, 'manifests in many ways a remarkable exaggeration of all those things which we are wont to call typically American.' Here, in fact, was all America, America in flight from itself. . . . And here, of course, was the logical place to raise the tent of the institutionalized circus which is the motion-picture industry."[15] "Such a community," notes Richard Schickel, "could not have been created elsewhere. There would have been no room for it back East—no room geographically, certainly no room psychically."[16]

Among the reasons for this were the personalities of the independent producers themselves. As Leo Rosten explained in *Hollywood*:

> The men who built the motion picture industry (Fox, Laemmle, Zukor, Selig, Loew, Goldwyn, Lasky, Warner, Mayer) were not drawn from the supposedly farsighted ranks of American business. They came, instead, from the marginal and shabby zones of enterprise, from vaudeville, nickelodeon parlors, theatrical agencies, flea circuses, petty trade. They were tough-minded, hardworking, aggressive men—rude in manner, quick in their hunches, with an instinct for ballyhoo and a genius for showmanship. . . . They did not cater to small, cultivated circles. They were sensitive to mass desires, for they were of the masses themselves. They had the virtues and the failings of pioneers. They were accused of being vulgar, and with justice; yet it was their very unrefinement which fitted them so perfectly for their function. . . . It was the promoters and the showmen, not the graduates of proud preparatory schools, who sensed and satisfied the entertainment demands of a nation into which Europe's millions were pouring. . . . They stamped a vaudeville spirit onto the motion picture industry, and it still bears evidence of their crudity and strength.[17]

Thus, American movies took a different path from those of the countries that the European immigrants had left behind, which catered to a classier clientele, both then and now. Not for Americans the broodings of a Bergman or the ennui of an Antonionni. Here, the movies thrived on action, violence, the thrill of the chase.

The American movie genre that most clearly displayed these characteristics, of course, was the Western, which according to Leo Rosten comprised the major part of Hollywood's early output. Because the Western is so familiar, we tend to forget that its ubiquity is hard to explain by the bare historical facts. As Berkeley sociologist Will Wright observed in a book on Western movies: "The enormous popularity of the wild West could perhaps be attributed to cultural interest in a unique and colorful era of our history, but this explanation becomes unconvincing when the actual history is examined. The crucial period of settlement in which most Westerns take place lasted only about 30 years. . . . In contrast, the settling of the eastern frontier—from the Atlantic to the Great Plains—required at least 130 years; yet . . . this era is not rich in mythical figures."[18]

There are various explanations for the huge outpouring of Western movies (and we'll talk about some of them in the following chapter). But one which has usually been overlooked is the similarity between the Western hero and the independent producer. Like the cowboy (at least the mythical kind), the producer who fled to the American West was often something of a maverick, a loner, a driven man who bucked the system and won. Neither had much education or felt the need for much.

Another (and simpler) explanation is that the producer situated in Hollywood was right next door to all the Western settings he could possibly ever use. And even if the same nearby outcropping of rock appeared in a hundred different Grade B chase scenes, it didn't seem to matter. The audience never noticed.

Whatever the reason for the Western stampede, its imprint on the American mind was indelible. No other myth so clearly conveyed the message that the usual trappings of civilization—art, learning—are little more than pretense, putting on airs; that a man is worth only what he can do; that whatever our respective backgrounds, I'm as good as you.

Because of the Western's egalitarianism—along with that of more "glamorous" films—Hollywood eventually became the ultimate extension of the American Dream. Whereas the rest of the country, for the average person, could offer merely freedom (which was likely to result in a dead-end job in Peoria), Hollywood promised transformation. It was the place where gangling Norma Jean was magically made over into Marilyn Monroe. It bestowed, like some divine bonanza, fabulous riches and a form of immortality. If Boston was the capital of American aristocracy, and New York, of plutocracy; Hollywood (more so than Washington) was the holy city of democracy.

To be sure, such egalitarianism did not devolve in an unbroken line. By the early thirties, Hollywood was grappling with the talkies, as well as an invasion of Eastern playwrights. About the same time, a second generation of Hollywood producers, feeling rather socially insecure, was in search of respectability, which it found, for a while, by aping the ways of Eastern Society, both in its life and its art. (As Fitzgerald remarked of the Last Tycoon, he possessed "the parvenu's passionate loyalty to an imaginary past.")[19] Eventually, however (for reasons described in Chapter 1), Hollywood returned to the democratic sympathies that attended its birth.

69

Perhaps the whole matter is best revealed by what happened in Philadelphia. In 1940, Hollywood turned out *The Philadelphia Story,* a "screwball comedy" with a bit of an edge. The screenplay was written by Donald Ogden Stewart, an Eastern playwright who ten years earlier had caused something of a stir in New York Society when along with a Broadway tap-dancer named Fred Astaire, he served as an usher at a Whitney wedding. Anyway, in *The Philadelphia Story,* Katharine Hepburn, straight off the Main Line, is about to marry a middle-class social climber who doesn't understand, poor fellow, that riding clothes (like the rest of one's possessions) should appear well-worn, rather than fresh from the store window; that newspaper articles about one's personal life are to be avoided whenever possible (and certainly never encouraged). Worst of all, he doesn't understand the meaning of sailing terms such as *yare.* (It means quick-to-the-helm, nifty.) But Cary Grant understands all these things, of course; and in the end it is he whom she decides to marry. *The Philadelphia Story* is the only Hollywood movie that I can recall which takes the side of the upper class against the middle class (and not so subtly, either).

In 1959, however, came *The Young Philadelphians,* which tells the story of a woman of modest background who marries a member of the upper class. On their wedding night, the bridegroom panics, flees the hotel and soon after kills himself in an automobile crash. (You know how flighty these upper-class men are.) Not to be prevented from producing a scion, the bride searches out an old boyfriend—an Irishman, naturally, named Michael Flanagan—and takes him to bed. Nine months afterward, when her dead husband's mother confronts her with knowledge of what has occurred, she agrees to give up the family money (it wouldn't do, after all, in this later version of the Philadelphia story, to have the child reared in posh surroundings), but insists on keeping the family name. When the boy grows up (and becomes Paul Newman), he goes to Princeton and then to law school, but during the summer he works as a foreman at Michael Flanagan's construction company, where of course he wins a fight with a beefy worker who gives him trouble. In the final, obligatory courtroom scene, he outsmarts the principal prosecution witness (a supercilious butler) and wins the heart of an upperclass girl.

The not-so-subtle message of *The Young Philadelphians* is that breeding doesn't matter—or rather, that it works in inverse ratio to class. Throughout the movie, the upper class is portrayed as duplicitous and effete. Paul Newman, on the other hand, is able to triumph precisely because his parents are members of the middle class rather than the upper. By implication, all that separates the former from the latter is the mere formality of a family name.

This established, the case was closed. So far as I know, *The Young Philadelphians* was the last American movie to deal with the subject of social class.

Among the reasons for this newfound reticence was the advent of another nascent technology that profoundly altered the balance of power between East Coast and West, between elitism and egalitarianism. And interestingly enough, the new technology underwent the same cycle of class and coastal struggle that the movies had undergone forty years before. The technology, of course, was television.

When television first flickered across the national consciousness in the late forties, it was primarily a New York institution closely tied to the theater (just as it was and remained, for example, in London). This was the medium's so-called Golden Age; and each week, all year long, companies such as Philco, Westinghouse, Kraft, Ford and U.S. Steel presented hour-long dramas. "Kraft Theater," for example, served up a total of 650 plays, from its debut in 1947 until its demise in 1958. On the "Philco Television Playhouse," many of the early offerings were adaptations of theatrical classics, but "Philco," like the other programs, eventually opted for contemporary plays (most of them fresh from the typewriter). Plays such as *The Trip to Bountiful* (recently made into a movie starring Geraldine Page); *Bang the Drum Slowly; The Caine Mutiny Court Martial; Marty,* by Paddy Chayefsky; and *Patterns,* which made an overnight sensation of writer Rod Serling. (Try to imagine a writer becoming a sensation by working in television today.) In addition to Serling and Chayefsky, the list of writers included Reginald Rose, Horton Foote and Gore Vidal. The list of actors (who were likewise previously unknown) was equally impressive, including Paul Newman, Jack Lemmon, James Dean, Rod Steiger, Grace Kelly, Eva Marie Saint, Kim Stanley and John Cassavetes. The directors included Arthur Penn, John Frankenheimer, Sidney Lumet and George Roy Hill. But most impressive was the sheer volume of theater—all of it live, all from New York, the equivalent of several Broadway seasons in a single year.

True, many film critics disparage the Golden Age. Calling it the "Age of Golden Syrup," Stanley Kauffmann claims that, "The main impulse of that age was anti-Hollywood: the small screen was used to celebrate the Unbeautiful People, in contrast to the perfection-worship of Hollywood."[20] Which is another way of saying, I suppose, that the age was interested in something approaching serious drama, rather than merely entertainment. And there's no doubt the spirit was anti-Hollywood, or conversely, pro-New York. It was yet another attempt at bringing "culture to the people"; and one can only speculate on the salutary effects for American theater, not to mention the people, if television production had remained in New York, rather than moving to Hollywood.

But of course it did move. For one thing, some of the New York productions were becoming quite complex. A 1956 "Kraft Theater" presentation concerning the sinking of the *Titanic,* for example, employed 107 actors and 31 sets. The obvious solution was to shift to film or videotape; and the place to do that was Hollywood, which also offered larger studios (thereby allowing for even more elaborate sets), as well as movie stars, who could help to boost the ratings. Thus, New York drama—some of it, at least—migrated west, with mixed results. "Studio One" moved in 1958, and soon succumbed. "Playhouse 90" (which was actually created in Hollywood in 1956) enjoyed several successful seasons—best remembered for *The Miracle Worker, Requiem for a Heavyweight, Days of Wine and Roses,* and *Judgment at Nuremberg*—but it finally gave up the ghost in 1961. Weekly drama was no more.

The reasons for its demise are not hard to find. When "Kraft Theater" went on the air in 1947, the number of television sets in the United States was in the tens of thousands. In 1951 it was 12 million; in 1955, 32 million. By 1964, the television set was a fixture in 92 percent of American homes. Meanwhile, soon after television's arrival, the movie studios began taking a bath. Average weekly movie attendance dropped from 90 million in 1946 to 47 million ten years later. The answer, eventually, was obvious: Hollywood could shift its B-movie production from the large screen to the small screen. Instead of grinding out "Rustlers' Roundup" and "The Creaking Coffin," it could grind out "Gunsmoke," "Wagon Train" and "Perry Mason." New York drama never stood a chance.

There were other changes in television as well. Increasingly, it began to carry the populist message that anything that smacked of high culture or high society was suspect at best, and usually worse. Thus, each episode of "Columbo" pitted a rumpled but canny Everyman against a Southern Californian version of the Eastern aristocrat (who we always knew from the very first scene was guilty as hell).* On an episode of the "Mary Tyler Moore Show" (which as a rule was one of the few sit-coms that was actually com), Lou Grant made the terrible blunder of hiring an Easterner—a Harvard man and a professor, to boot—as on-air critic and "cultural watchdog." Naturally, this snit from Harvard proceeded to lambast all-American Minneapolis as an "intellectually famished, arid, sterile city," and eventually, even sweet little Mary lost her cool. "On the local news we're supposed to appeal to the public, not just the intellectual elite!" she shouted at the professor in the presence of a studio audience. "What news show did you ever produce, or anything else for that matter? . . . Your 'critiques' are nothing but sadistic bullying by an arrogant snob." At this point, the studio audience burst into applause (of course); and the professor (for reasons that elude me), received the classic Hollywood punishment for pomposity: a cream pie full in the face. (More applause.)

You think this sort of televised populism is a thing of the past? Well, the cream pies, maybe; but on a recent episode of "Murder, She Wrote" (which supposedly commands a relatively urbane audience, since it airs directly after "60 Minutes"), a pretentious New York police detective fails to solve the weekly homicide because he's spending all his time at the theater and such. As usual, it's left to unpretentious Jessica Fletcher (the *she* of "She Wrote") to show the police department how it's done.

The most popular new program on television these days is "Roseanne" (which may soon displace "The Cosby Show" as number one). It is also perhaps the first sit-com to express realistically the attitudes of the lower-middle class.

---

* "Columbo" was recently revived by ABC for periodic appearances on the network's weekly "Mystery Movie."

Game shows offer another case in point of how television changed as it shifted west. In New York, the shows often consisted of various sorts of experts—Bennet Cerf on "What's My Line?," Charles Van Doren on "Twenty-One," sundry fetishists on "The $64,000 Question"—demonstrating to the common folk their expertise. But in Hollywood, the participants were the common folk themselves. And with this substitution, Hollywood's promise of transformation became quite real. It was extended not just to Norma Jean Baker and Frances Gumm (later Judy Garland), but to the average couple on vacation from Kansas. And the promise was kept. With an appearance on television, there occurred a curious form of transubstantiation. A person became something other than what he was before. (The essence of this process was best described by one Lenny Skutnik, who, you may recall, achieved overnight celebrity when he rescued a passenger from a plane that went down in the Potomac River. Asked how he felt about his newfound fame, Skutnik replied, "You could put a rock on TV; and later on, people would say, 'Hey look; there's the rock that was on TV.' ")

Finally, the talk shows. When Johnny Carson moved to Hollywood in 1972, the psychological center of the country moved with him. No longer was the national imagination focused on quasi-aristocratic New York; it was now honed in on egalitarian Southern California, which was good-naturedly conjured up each night in the monologue. The rest of the show changed as well. Whereas the guests had formerly included prominent politicians—Nelson Rockefeller, Hubert Humphrey, John and Robert Kennedy—they now consisted almost entirely of Hollywood celebrities, a fact that suggested to the viewer, perhaps, that the latter were more real than the former. At any rate, the Carson studio became a mecca for all those Americans who had just blown in from the heartland.

> All their lives they had slaved at some kind of dull, heavy labor, behind desks and counters, in the fields and at tedious machines of all sorts, saving their pennies and dreaming of the leisure that would be theirs when they had enough. Finally that day came. They could draw a weekly income of ten or fifteen dollars. Where else should they go but California, the land of sunshine and oranges?
>
> Once there, they discover that sunshine isn't enough. They get

tired of oranges, even of avocado pears and passion fruit. Nothing happens. They don't know what to do with their time. They haven't the mental equipment for leisure, the money nor the physical equipment for pleasure. Did they slave so long just to go to an occasional Iowa picnic? What else is there? They watch the waves come in at Venice. There wasn't any ocean where most of them came from, but after you've seen one wave, you've seen them all. The same is true of the airplanes at Glendale. If only a plane would crash once in a while so that they could watch the passengers being consumed in a "holocaust of flame," as the newspapers put it. But the planes never crash.

Their boredom becomes more and more terrible. They realize that they've been tricked and burn with resentment. Every day of their lives they read the newspapers and went to the movies. Both fed them on lynchings, murder, sex crimes, explosions, wrecks, love nests, fires, miracles, revolutions, wars. This daily diet made sophisticates of them. The sun is a joke. Oranges can't titillate their jaded palates. Nothing can ever be violent enough to make taut their slack minds and bodies. They have been cheated and betrayed. They have slaved and saved for nothing.[21]

As suggested by this famous passage from *The Day of the Locust*, Hollywood was not alone in its ability to send a message. Beginning in the late thirties, there appeared a spate of novels (Nathanael West's *The Day of the Locust*, Budd Schulberg's *What Makes Sammy Run?* and *The Disenchanted*, among others) that portrayed Hollywood as something less than what the populace had been led to believe. As Richard Schickel points out, one of the unstated aims of these books "was to chastise the upstart film industry—after all, a powerful competitor to novels and the stage—by imbuing it with an evil, destructive power out of all proportion to the facts."[22] Schickel also notes, however, that, "This fictive tradition was late blooming, the first Hollywood novels having tended toward a sort of innocent bedazzlement."[23]

Such a cycle was to continue ever after in the portrayal of Hollywood and the rest of California by what might be described as the Eastern media—the more popular books and publications pushing the California-as-Eden myth, the more sophisticated then responding with reports of trouble in paradise.

The most recent outbreak of Edenic fever began in the 1960s, when California displaced New York as the most populous state in the union. "Soon to Be Number 1: Booming, Beautiful California," blared a cover billing on *Newsweek* in 1962.[24] But for pure purple prose, no other magazine could equal *Life:* "There is an overwhelming radiance to this land. . . . The beholder feels the spell and, suddenly, understands what makes California more than a fertile frontier, a sunny playground, a booming economic giant. . . . California—rich, vibrant, by now almost mythical—is in the 20th Century more than ever before the promised land."[25]

Another magazine in the thick of the California coverage was *Look*. The magazine's first cover story, in 1962, was fairly standard, but in 1966 the magazine published an entire issue devoted to California, in which it pulled out all the stops. California, it contended, was "a new game with new rules. . . . Hardly a major move in our national life has not been foreshadowed in the Far West."[26]

Back East, however, many people who read the magazine were not amused—least of all at *Look*. "When that '66 issue appeared," recalls George Leonard, the editor in charge of the magazine's California coverage, "all hell broke loose at our offices in New York. People at *Look* were *outraged!* One editor scrawled obscenities in red ink all over the issue. Another claimed I was schizoid and that I'd be hospitalized within a couple of weeks."*

At the city's tonier publications, the response was more restrained but equally adamant. California came under assault.

The point publication in this charge was *Esquire,* which published a special section entitled "California: Too Much Too Soon." In the lead article, called "Depressed in California," the writer complained of many things, including the fabled California climate: "It is something in the air—the air itself—that temporary residents complain acts on them like a lobotomy."[27]

Next in line was *Harper's,* which in 1967 published an article called "Turned-on and Super-sincere in California." In it, the writer sniffed at all the drug-induced chumminess in the Haight-Ashbury, and raised an eyebrow at the *Look* special issue of the year before.[28] (In so doing, he missed the emergence of the entire sixties counterculture, but never mind.)

---

* Leonard never did enter a hospital. Instead, he became a leading spokesman for the Human Potential Movement. (In nineteenth-century British colonial parlance, he "went native.") Today he lives in the town of Mill Valley, in Marin County, just a few streets away from his close friend Michael Murphy, the founder of Esalen. We'll return to Leonard and Murphy in Part II.

About this same time, Joan Didion also paid a visit to San Francisco, after which she wrote an article called "Slouching Towards Bethlehem." The title was adapted from a line in the famous Yeats poem that announced: "Things fall apart; the centre cannot hold." And suddenly, the realization dawned: California was out of control.[29]

From there it was only a short step to an *Esquire* special section called "California Evil." Written in the aftermath of the Manson murders—admittedly a ghastly event though not exactly a crime wave—the section began with an introduction that declared: "the celebration of evil has begun in California with a flair for accoutrement and ceremony that will be merchandised to all of us in time, as everything Californian eventually is. . . . We must even face the possibility that California has allowed itself to become a principality of the Devil, and that the rest of the country is not far behind."[30]

The remainder of the section—a perfunctory excursion to Charlie Manson's former ranch, a visit with a woman who claimed to be a witch, and so forth—hardly justified this startling suggestion. But never mind. If California was leading the country to ruin, something had damn well better be done. Something soon was.

"Whatever Happened to California?" read the cover billing on an issue of *MORE* in 1975.[31]

"Whatever Happened to California?" read a headline in *Time* in 1977.[32]

The message of the two pieces was of course the same: California was now passé.

The main problem with that judgment was that about the time it was rendered, the 1970s were being christened the "Me Decade." That movement also began in California.

We'll return to the matter of the Me Decade (a.k.a. the Human Potential Movement, a.k.a. the New Age) in Part II. For now, suffice it to note that there was (and is) considerably more to the movement than met the eye—except, that is, in the national press (which suddenly rediscovered California). With certain notable exceptions, the whole thing was treated as a sort of national joke. First came Tom Wolfe's seminal satire of "The Me Decade and the Third Great Awakening,"[33] then a *Harper's* cover story on "The New Narcissism,"[34] and finally, in 1978, an NBC documentary entitled "I Want It All Now."

As it happened, when the program aired, I had just arrived in

California, having just spent five years making television documentaries. I must confess that when I saw the show, my first thought was: "God, I wish I'd made that program." After doing some checking, however, I changed my mind.

Ostensibly a report on life in Marin, "I Want It All Now" was a comedy of egregious factual errors. To take just two examples, the program implied that 75 percent of the children in Marin come from single-parent homes, and that Marin has the highest level of drunken-driving arrests in the state. Both statements are wildly inaccurate.

How to explain such distortions? A possible clue is a review that A.J. Liebling wrote of Graham Greene's *The Quiet American.* Liebling noted that the American of the title ate tasteless food and was naive, sexually inexperienced and a poor speaker of French. In short, he actually resembled the stock Englishman of French novels. The narrator of the book—an Englishman like Greene—was just the opposite. He was terrific in bed, consumed haute cuisine and spoke French like a native.

Liebling went on to observe: "When England, a French cultural colony, outstripped the homeland after Waterloo and the Industrial Revolution, all that remained for the French to say was, 'Nevertheless, you remain nasty, overgrown children.' The Italians of the Renaissance said it to the French, and I suppose the Greeks said it to the Romans. It is part of the ritual of handing over."[35]

In the same year as NBC's report on the alleged misbehavior of Marin, there occurred in California an event of far more importance—the passage of Proposition 13, which paved the way for Reagan's ascension to the White House.

But today, of course, Reagan has departed; and pretty soon some smart-ass magazine will probably pose the question, "What ever Happened to California?", the contention being that this time the place is *really* passé.

Uh-huh.

4

Tippecanoe and Tyler Too:
The Democratization of Politics

Many people in Europe are apt to believe without saying it, or
to say without believing it, that one of the great advantages of
universal suffrage is that it entrusts the direction of affairs to
men who are worthy of the public confidence. They admit that
the people are unable to govern of themselves, but they aver
that the people always wish the welfare of the state and
instinctively designate those who are animated by the same
good will and who are the most fit to wield the supreme
authority.

I confess that the observations I made in America by no
means coincide with these opinions. On my arrival in the
United States I was surprised to find so much distinguished
talent among the citizens and so little among the heads of
government. It is a constant fact that at the present day the
ablest men in the United States are rarely placed at the head of
affairs; and it must be acknowledged that such has been the
result in proportion as democracy has exceeded all its former
limits.

—Alexis de Tocqueville,
Democracy in America[1]

GIVEN THE FACT that Tocqueville's visit to the United States was
made in 1831, during the administration of Andrew Jackson, his
reportage was understandable (not to mention accurate). But as
Tocqueville was well aware, the situation had not been ever thus.
In fact, from the founding of the colonies until the election of
Jackson in 1828, the country had been largely in the hands of a
patrician elite.

Today, of course, we celebrate the United States as a country
born of revolution, but in truth, the revolution was no such thing.
It was, in the main, a colonial revolt that was led by much the same
sort of people who a dozen years later in Paris would be trundled
off to the guillotine. When the revolt was over, the same sort of
people were still in charge.

79

As a result, the new state constitutions (most of which were placed in effect without consulting the voters) were rather conservative. In seven states, suffrage was extended to every male taxpayer, but elsewhere there were moderate property requirements. For office-holders, the property requirements were considerably higher; and in only four states were the governors chosen by popular vote.

Despite such checks on democracy—a form of government the ruling patricians generally abhorred—many of that class professed to see in the new constitutions the seeds of just such a movement. Along with radical stirrings in some of the western counties (notably in Massachusetts) and the general weakness of the federal government (such as it was), fears of this sort prompted the calling of a Constitutional Convention in 1787.

The "founding fathers" who gathered in Philadelphia in May of that year were in the eyes of Thomas Jefferson (who at the time was serving as ambassador to France) "an assembly of demigods."[2] Be that as it may, they were also the conservative remnant of the revolution; radicals such as Tom Paine, Sam Adams and Patrick Henry were conspicuously absent. Generally speaking, the Philadelphia assembly represented the Thermidorean reaction that any revolution—even a quasi-revolution such as that in America—is heir to.* During the four months the delegates remained in Philadelphia, their deliberations were conducted entirely in secret.

The document that emerged from these deliberations was in general less democratic than many if not most of the state constitutions. Although no property requirements were set for any federal office, suffrage requirements would continue to be set by the states (which is to say that existing requirements would be allowed to stand). Although voters would choose the members of the House of Representatives, senators would be chosen by the state legislatures; and the president would be chosen by members of an electoral college. The judiciary, of course, would be appointed by the president. Thus, of the three branches of government, only one-half of one would be selected by the public.

The first administration to take office under the new constitution generally reflected this aristocratic bent. In addition to President Washington, there was Vice-President John Adams, Secretary of

* The term *Thermidorean reaction* was not actually in use at this time, of course. It arose from the overthrow of the radical regime of Robespierre in July of 1794, a month that was known on the Revolutionary calendar as Thermidor.

State Thomas Jefferson, and Secretary of the Treasury Alexander Hamilton. An impressive line-up, to be sure, but hardly the democratic administration we think it to have been. Although Washington probably remains the most popular figure in American history, most Americans would be in for a shock were they able somehow to have met him. An aloof and rather imperious man, he was not much given to idle conversation and disliked being touched (no pressing the flesh for *this* politician). John Adams reassured his conservative friends that "democracy never lasts long. It soon wastes, exhausts and murders itself. There never was a democracy that did not commit suicide."[3] (Of course, he did not conceive of the new American government as democratic.) While Thomas Jefferson was certainly the most "liberal" member of the administration, historian Samuel Eliot Morison reminds us that "Jefferson was no social democrat but a slave-holding country gentleman of exquisite taste."[4] As for Alexander Hamilton, when someone in his presence once alluded to "the people," he announced: "The people, sir, is a great beast."[5]

The beast, meanwhile, was stirring (slouching towards Washington, as it were). Ever since the early colonial days, backwoods western settlers had resented the domination of the coastal aristocracy, and periodically this resentment broke out in armed rebellion—Bacon's Rebellion, Virginia, 1676; War of the Regulation, North Carolina, 1771; Shays's Rebellion, Massachusetts, 1786; the Whiskey Rebellion, Pennsylvania, 1794; Fries's Rebellion, Pennsylvania, 1798. Following the turn of the century, such western discontent found expression in politics, mainly through successful attempts to abolish state restrictions on voting and office holding. Then, in 1828, *le deluge:* the election of Andrew Jackson as president.

On the day of inauguration, Washington (population about 18,000) was crowded to suffocation with an estimated 10,000 visitors, some of whom had come from very distant parts to see their idol. . . . After taking the oath of office, administered by Chief Justice Marshall, and delivering his inaugural address, Jackson mounted his saddle horse and rode to the White House. An informal and unplanned inaugural parade, people in carriages, wagons, and carts, mounted and on foot, followed the President up Pennsylvania Avenue, parked their horses in Lafayette Square, and surged into the White House almost on his coattails. No police arrangement had been made, and the press of well wishers forced the President to escape by a rear window. . . . Glasses were broken and trodden under foot, punch was spilled, and damask chairs soiled by muddy boots.[6]

"I never saw such a mixture," wrote Justice Story. "The reign of King Mob seemed triumphant."[7]

Andrew Jackson (whom Thomas Jefferson regarded as a menace) soon made it plain that the old ways of doing things were in for a change. Warning of the evils of an entrenched bureaucracy, he proposed to bring in a fresh crop of workers. Of course, such a policy can be regarded as merely a justification for patronage, but it also reflected Jackson's belief that the duties of government are—or ought to be—so simple that more or less anyone could perform them. The results were soon apparent. "Jackson's first cabinet," wrote Samuel Eliot Morison, "was a collection of mediocrities, with the exception of Martin Van Buren, secretary of state. Noteworthy was the lack of anyone from Virginia or New England, the first time that had occurred. Jackson's choices registered, rather neatly, the rise of the Western and Middle states' democracy to federal power, and a brush-off to the Virginia dynasty and the Yankees."[8]

Of Jacksonian democracy in general, Morison wrote, it "catered to mediocrity, diluted politics with the incompetent and the corrupt, and made conditions increasingly unpleasant for gentlemen in public life."[9] Or in the words of historian Richard Hofstadter, "Jacksonian Democracy completed the disestablishment of . . . patrician leadership.[10] . . . it amounted to a repudiation not only of the system of government by gentlemen which the nation had inherited from the eighteenth century, but also of the special value of the educated classes in civic life."[11] (Incidentally, it also gave birth to the jackass as the symbol of the Democratic Party. Originally, the symbol was supplied by the Whigs as a means of poking fun at Jackson's ignorance; but "it is significant," wrote Morison, "that the party not only joyfully accepted this emblem but has retained it to this day.")[12]

At the end of his second term, Andrew Jackson, despite his limitations, was still wildly popular. The reasons are revealing.

"Jackson was no champion of the poor, or even of the 'common man,' " Morison observed, "but they loved him because he proved that a man born in a log cabin could become rich . . . and be elected President of the United States."[13] Remind you of any recent president you know? The parallels don't end there. As his successor, Jackson anointed the man who had loyally served him as vice-president during his second term, an easterner named Martin Van Buren. In turn, Van Buren became the only sitting vice-president to be elected president until the ascension of George Bush.

By the close of Van Buren's first term, however, the Whigs had caught on to the new way of winning. Accordingly, they chose as their presidential nominee one William Henry Harrison, hero of the Indian battle of Tippecanoe (which in fact was rather a fiasco). With the addition of one John Tyler to the ticket, the campaign slogan (a party had to have a slogan these days) practically wrote itself: "Tippecanoe and Tyler Too."

There was only one hitch. Old "Tippecanoe," the common man's candidate, actually lived on a 2,000-acre estate on the banks of the Ohio. No problem. In the campaign literature, the estate became a simple log cabin. Hence, the election's sobriquet: the Log Cabin Campaign.

> There were log-cabin badges and log-cabin songs, a *Log Cabin* newspaper and log-cabin clubs, big log cabins where the thirsty were regaled with hard cider that jealous Democrats alleged to be stiffened with whiskey; little log cabins borne on floats in procession, with latchstring out, cider barrel by the door, coonskin nailed up beside, and real smoke coming out of the chimney.[14]

Van Buren's *milieu* was portrayed in less flattering terms:

> Maine lumberjacks, Buckeye farmers, and Cajuns in the bayou country were shocked to learn that under Little Van the White House had become a palace "as splendid as that of the Caesars"; that the President doused his whiskers with French *eau de cologne*, slept in a Louis XV bedstead, sipped *soupe à la reine* with a gold spoon, ate *pâté de foie gras* from a silver plate, and rode about in a gilded British-made coach, wearing a haughty sneer on his aristocratic countenance.[15]

It was, concluded Morison, "the jolliest and most idiotic presidential contest in our history."[16] Harrison won, 234 electoral votes to 60.

The new egalitarianism was not confined to presidential campaigns. Restrictions on suffrage—common in the East, rare in the West—were gradually eliminated. (Largely as a result of this fact, and the attendant increase in political interest, the number of voters in presidential elections rose from a mere 356,000 in 1824 to a whopping 2,400,000 in 1840—a seven-fold growth in only sixteen years.) Presidential candidates, beginning in 1836, were routinely chosen by nominating conventions rather than by congressional caucus. Presidential electors were now generally chosen by popular vote rather than by the various legislatures. Elsewhere on the state level, voters elected governors and other officials, including, in many cases, members of the judiciary.

"Thus," wrote Morison, "Andrew Jackson and the brand of democracy associated with him dominated the political scene from 1828 to the Civil War. And they set a pattern of American politics which, with surprisingly few changes, has persisted into the second half of the twentieth century."[17]

Following the Civil War, the nation began that extraordinary period of private greed and public connivance known as the Gilded Age. In the words of historian Richard Hofstadter: "For a generation after the Civil War, a time of great economic exploitation and waste, grave social corruption and ugliness, the dominant note in American political life was complacency."[18] "The most significant thing about the politics of the postwar years," adds Henry Steele Commager, "was their insignificance."[19]

Way out west, however, democratization continued, in a sense, with the adoption of new state constitutions, most of which were even more liberal than those of the "western" states farther east. Most, for example, provided for some form of woman suffrage; and several instituted the initiative and referendum. Most public officials—even judges—were chosen by popular vote.

Finally, during the last decade of the century, western egalitarianism bubbled to the surface once again; this time it even had a name: Populism. Although the movement, as such, was sparked by a fall in commodity prices—both in the West and South—it also developed a lengthy political shopping list: direct election of senators, initiative and referendum, railroad regulation, an income tax and so on. And while few of those measures were immediately enacted, nearly all enjoyed a measure of success over the next twenty years. Meanwhile, Populism to some degree petered out, as it pinned its platform to the issue of "free silver" and its presidential hopes to the person of William Jennings Bryan.

Despite the Populists' failure to elevate Bryan to the White House, the quality of American presidents remained much the same as it had for the past seventy years—that is to say, not very high (the notable exception, of course, being Lincoln). Perhaps the best witness to this fact was the "second Tocqueville," who arrived on these shores toward the end of the century in the person of Lord Bryce. Soon thereafter, he produced a classic work called *The American Commonwealth,* the best-known chapter of which is titled "Why Great Men Are Not Chosen Presidents." (The final *s* is apparently an odd little Anglicism.) The most striking reason?

> The ordinary American voter does not object to mediocrity. He has a lower conception of the qualities requisite to make a statesman than those who direct public opinion in Europe have. He likes his candidate to be sensible, vigorous, and, above all, what he calls "magnetic," and does not value, because he sees no need for, originality or profundity, a fine culture or a wide knowledge.[20]

Shortly after the turn of the century, President William McKinley was assassinated, and a young vice-president named Theodore Roosevelt was thrust into the White House. With that event, the tables were suddenly turned; and for the next sixty years, the country saw a succession of presidents from the other end of the social and intellectual spectrum. The line was hardly unbroken, of course. During the twenties, the plutocrats were returned to power; and during the fifties, in Stevenson's memorable phrase, "the New Dealers were replaced by the car dealers."[21]

Nonetheless, the parade of patrician presidents is noteworthy, even if none of them quite measured up. (As President Kennedy wryly remarked at a dinner for Nobel laureates, there were now more brains at the White House table than at any time since the days when Thomas Jefferson dined alone.) At the head of the line, of course, were Theodore Roosevelt and his cousin Franklin. Next came Woodrow Wilson (who arose from modest circumstances but went on to serve as president of Princeton) and finally, John F. Kennedy (who was Boston Irish rather than Boston Brahmin, but who went to Harvard).

The more patrician of these figures displayed the patrician's contempt for the "money power," or for what Teddy Roosevelt called the "malefactors of great wealth." But they also revealed (as in the case of Franklin Roosevelt) the patrician's sense of *noblesse oblige* toward the downtrodden and the dispossessed.* Following the turn of the century, both these traits (especially the former) became evident in the Progressive movement, which took up the reformist banner that had earlier been raised by Populism. What was perhaps most interesting about Progressivism, however, was its rather optimistic view of the emerging new citizen, the Average Man. In the words of Richard Hofstadter:

> He would act and think as a public-spirited individual. . . . His approach to politics was, in a sense, intellectualistic: he would study the issues and think them through, rather than learn about them through pursuing his needs. Furthermore, it was assumed that somehow he would really be capable of informing himself in ample detail about the many issues that he would have to pass on, and that he could master their intricacies sufficiently to pass intelligent judgment.
>
> Without such assumptions the entire movement for such reforms as the initiative, the referendum, and recall is unintelligible. The movement for direct popular democracy was, in effect, an attempt to realize the Yankee-Protestant ideals of personal responsibility; and the Progressive notion of good citizenship was the culmination of the Yankee-Mugwump ethos of political participation without self-interest. But . . . this ethos . . . was less adapted to the realities of the highly organized society of the late nineteenth and the twentieth century.[22]

True indeed, as we'll see later on in this chapter. Meanwhile, we should note that for all the Progressives' professions of faith in the average man, their administrations (and those of Franklin Roosevelt to follow) were not so much government *by* the people as government *for* the people. This was particularly true in the area of foreign affairs, where, from the time of Theodore Roosevelt to that of John F. Kennedy (and beyond), much of what transpired was overseen by what came to be known as the Eastern Establishment.

* See Chapter One for an expanded discussion of this theme.

*　　*　　*

Immediately after John F. Kennedy's inauguration, the leading members of said Establishment began a three-day meeting at Washington's Sheraton-Park Hotel.* The purpose of the meeting, simply put, was to review the state of the world, and what to do about it. Among other things, the members resolved to press for United States membership in the European Common Market. "Practically everyone is agreed," remarked journalist Richard Rovere, "that in time the victory, even in this difficult matter, will go to the Establishment."[23]

Mr. Rovere's miscalculation, while amusing, is understandable. For at this point, the Eastern Establishment (Europhilia flying) was firmly in the saddle, and few could have predicted that it was about to take a very bad fall.

In its modern form, the Eastern Establishment came into being with the election of Teddy Roosevelt and the selection of Elihu Root, a corporate lawyer, as secretary of state. From Root, the line of succession runs through Henry Stimson, Robert Lovett, John McCloy, Dean Acheson, both Dulleses, nearly all of Kennedy's cabinet, Henry Kissinger (a protegé of Nelson Rockefeller's, remember) to Cyrus Vance.

In a sense, most of these men were Wall Street's emissaries to Washington, either as attorneys or financiers, and they constituted, in effect, a very exclusive fraternity. They had come, most of them, from the same sort of families, gone to the same schools, joined the same firms, the same clubs, married the same sort of women, bought summer houses at the same locations. They even had (and still have) a fraternity house—a handsome building at Sixty-eighth and Park, formerly the home of Harold Pratt of Standard Oil, now known simply as the Council on Foreign Relations.

Their power was considerable. Describing America in the fifties, Theodore White observed: "An aristocracy of old-stock Protestant

* This information was supplied by Richard Rovere in a 1962 *Esquire* article called "The American Establishment." Unfortunately, Rovere did not say just who attended the meeting, although he and John Kenneth Galbraith—another establishment-watcher—agreed that the chairman of the establishment in the late fifties was John J. McCloy, chairman of the board of Chase Manhattan.

heritage conducted national affairs. . . . At this high level they and they alone debated war and peace, the management of the national economy, industrial and scientific policy, and, if the Democrats were in power, the welfare of the lower classes."[24] In his *Esquire* article, Richard Rovere wrote that "it can, I think, be said that the Establishment maintains effective control over the Executive and the Judicial branches of government; that it dominates most of American education and intellectual life; that it has very nearly unchallenged power in deciding what is and what is not respectable opinion in this country."[25]

This power reached its peak in the period immediately following World War II, when members of the group engineered passage of the Marshall Plan, the formation of NATO, and the organization of the EEC. Thereafter, as the Lovett-McCloy generation retired from public office, the Establishment's power was wielded more discreetly, but no less effectively. Soon after his election as president, for example, John Kennedy held a long private meeting with Robert Lovett, at which Lovett put forth the Establishment's choices for cabinet posts: Dean Rusk for State, McNamara for Defense, Doug Dillon or Jack McCloy for Treasury, Mac Bundy for anything—the best and the brightest. A few years later, after Kennedy's assassination, Lyndon Johnson asked members of the Establishment to serve in a Senior Advisory Group—"the wise old men," as they came to be called*—which he hoped would lend legitimacy to the war in Vietnam.

The first little chinks in the Establishment's armor had appeared in the fifties. Senator Joseph McCarthy of Wisconsin (who had defeated the liberal Populist Robert La Follette in the 1946 Republican primary) launched a new wave of Populism. But this time Populism was not reformist, and its target was not corruption—or even Communism, its ostensible enemy—but rather the American upper class. In other words, wrote Richard Hofstadter in *Anti-Intellectualism in American Life*, it arose from "a desire to discredit the type of leadership the New Deal had made prominent."[26] "What was new about McCarthyism," wrote E. Digby Baltzell in *The Prot-*

---

* Members included John McCloy, Dean Acheson, Arthur Dean, McGeorge Bundy, Douglas Dillon and Robert Murphy.

estant Establishment, "was that it was a calculated attack on the loyalty of members of the Anglo-Saxon establishment."[27]

Thus, in his famous Wheeling, West Virginia, speech, McCarthy declared:

> The reason why we find ourselves in a position of impotency . . . is the traitorous actions of those who have been treated so well by this nation. It is not the less fortunate . . . who have been selling this nation out but rather those who have had all the benefits the wealthiest nation on earth has had to offer—the finest homes, the finest college educations, and the finest jobs in the government that we can give. This is glaringly true of the State Department. There the bright young men who are born with silver spoons in their mouths are the ones who have been worst.[28]

In a way, the idiocy of the fifties could all have been predicted. As Hofstadter pointed out in *The Paranoid Style in American Politics,* the Populist party platform for 1892—referring to an alleged European-American gold cabal—announced: "A vast conspiracy against mankind has been organized on two continents, and it is rapidly taking possession of the world. If not met and overthrown at once, it forbodes terrible social convulsions, the destruction of civilization, or the establishment of an absolute despotism."[29]

During the 1920's, wrote Hofstadter in *The Age of Reform,* "it was precisely in the West and the South, in the old Bryan country, that the public mood swung most sharply away from the devotion to necessary reforms that had characterized Progressivism at its best."[30] Bryan himself attacked freedom of thought in the Scopes "monkey" trial, while his followers joined the Ku Klux Klan and celebrated Bryan (no doubt unfairly) as "the greatest Klansman of our time."[31]

But few people, least of all the intellectuals, perceived the tack that Populism was taking. As Hofstadter explained in *The Age of Reform:*

> Liberal intellectuals, who have rather well-rationalized systems of political beliefs, tend to expect that the masses of people, whose actions at certain moments in history coincide with some of these beliefs, will share their other convictions as a matter of logic and principle. Intellectuals, moreover, suffer from a sense of isolation which they usually seek to surmount by finding ways of getting into

rapport with the people, and they readily succumb to a tendency to sentimentalize the folk. Hence they periodically exaggerate the measure of agreement that exists between movements of popular reform and the considered principles of political liberalism. They remake the image of popular rebellion closer to their heart's desire.[32]

Thus, during the 1930s, wrote Baltzell in *The Protestant Establishment,* "the common man . . . came into his own among intellectuals of the Left, who saw him as one of a chosen class."[33]

Yet as Hofstadter reminded us: "The impulses behind yesterday's reform may be put in the service of reform today, but they may also be enlisted in the service of reaction."[34]

More recently, we have seen much evidence of such popular shifts from reform to reaction. Supporters of Henry Wallace in Southern California later supported candidates of the John Birch Society. Many supporters of Bobby Kennedy's presidential bid would later support that of George Wallace. And many supporters of Franklin Roosevelt would later cheer Joseph McCarthy. Considering McCarthy's objects of scorn, the cheers were not altogether surprising. As Hofstadter wrote in *Anti–Intellectualism in American Life:*

> The right-wing crusade of the 1950's was full of heated rhetoric about "Harvard professors, twisted-thinking intellectuals . . . in the State Department"; those who are "burdened with Phi Beta Kappa keys and academic honors" but not "equally loaded with honesty and common sense"; "the American respectables, the socially pedigreed, the culturally acceptable, the certified gentlemen and scholars of the day, dripping with college degrees" . . . "the pompous diplomat in striped pants with phony British accent" [i.e. Acheson]; those who try to fight Communism "with kid gloves in perfumed drawing rooms"; Easterners who "insult the people of the great Midwest and West, the *heart* of America."[35]

Ironically, McCarthy's campaign would succeed in wounding the Eastern Establishment in a way that he could not have foreseen. During the frantic witch-hunt for Who Lost China, and for pinkos in general in the State Department, two of the department's leading Asia experts—John Paton Davies and John Steward Service—were thrown to the wolves. As a result, when the government faced another crisis in that part of the world a decade later, its two most perceptive pairs of Asian eyes were missing. Thus blinded, the Eastern Establishment—which by now was quite leery of seeming "soft on Communism"—led the country into the quagmire of Vietnam.

For the Establishment, even more than for the country at large, Vietnam spelled disaster. The best and the brightest, its hand-picked team, produced the nation's greatest calamity since the Civil War. Perhaps the brightest of all was McGeorge Bundy, of whom David Halberstam observed toward the end of his book: "above all he was a man of the Establishment, the right people deciding on the right policies in the right way, he believed in the capacity and the right of an elite to govern on its terms. The war changed all that; it not only tarnished his personal reputation . . . it saw a major challenge to the right of the elite to rule."[36]

In addition to its effect on the Establishment in general, the war was particularly unsettling for the Establishment's unoffical club, the Council on Foreign Relations. As Leonard and Mark Silk observe in their book, *The American Establishment*, "That war shook the Council as it had never been shaken before, and it is still recovering from the effects."[37]

As one might expect, the council initially supported the war, since the effort was being directed by several of its members and was sanctioned by the committee of wise old men. Then, following the Tet offensive, the council hired a new president, recruited some new members and veered to the left. Later still, after David Rockefeller had abandoned his attempt to have Henry Kissinger succeed him as council chairman, the latter was nonetheless able to install a former aide named Winston Lord (since appointed ambassador to China) in the now-vacant post of council president. Meanwhile, the pages of the council's publication, *Foreign Affairs,* were filled with recriminations by Kissinger and Bundy, each blaming the other for the catastrophe in Asia.

Today, the council is once again seeking an influential role. "But if it wants influence," observe Leonard and Mark Silk, "the council may no longer be able to rely on the closeted habits of the past."

The growth of foreign policy study—in think tanks, universities, and government planning bodies—has created a cacophony of learned analysis and advice vying for the ear of policy makers. Moreover, the country as a whole has a far greater economic stake in foreign policy than it used to, from midwestern grain farmers to southwestern oilmen to farwestern high technologists. All this . . . has made foreign policy making as confused and congested a political activity as domestic policy making has always been.[38]

As the foregoing suggests, a second reason for the council's loss of influence (in addition to Vietnam) is that the country's political center has shifted west and right. The Silks point out, for example:

A small shiver went up the council's spine when [following his withdrawal from the 1980 presidential race] George Bush, the Yankee patrician who had made his fortune and political career in Texas, resigned his membership and seat on the Board, claiming that the organization was too liberal. . . . This was an ominous sign. Had a rising tide of right-wing populism placed the Council, with its internationalist traditions, its dedication to reasoned discussion, and its hospitality to a wide range of views, beyond the Republican party's pale of acceptability?[39]

It was in presidential elections, of course, that the decline of the Eastern Establishment—and the democratization of politics—finally became visible for all to see. Between 1896 and 1945, only two presidents were born outside the Northeast, due in part to the crucial role played by the state of New York. Overall, it provided five presidents; and between 1900 and 1948, it supplied eleven of the twenty-six major-party nominations. "For a full century," wrote Theodore White in *America in Search of Itself,* "New York was the most important political state in the union, sharing with Washington, D.C., the management of the nation's affairs. . . . New York did more than that—it moneyed the politics of the nation. . . . New York's bankers and publishers imposed first Wendell Willkie, then Thomas Dewey, then Dwight Eisenhower on the Republican Party. It's rich Democrats, as well as its rich Republicans, played host to mendicant politicians from Montana to Maine."[40]

White went on to observe that "The first sense of the tilt in national leadership from Northeast to Southwest can probably be dated sometime between 1952 and 1954, when imperial New York sensed a serious financial trespass on its domain. The trespass came from Texas. There, a handful of uncouth oilmen had begun to invest in congressional candidacies across the nation. . . . In those days . . . the Texas intrusion, at least in New York, seemed outrageous.[41]

More was soon to follow. The 1956 presidential election "would be the last time," wrote White,

> that the old patrician elite of American life would be in control. . . . The Democratic convention of that year was to see the last spirited contest between gentlemen of heritage for the nomination of either party. . . . Adlai Stevenson of Princeton and Averell Harriman of Yale, thoroughbreds both, were playing politics as their class and fathers had taught them, much as Franklin Roosevelt had played politics in New York and Washington. . . .
>
> The balloting on Thursday night was concluded quickly— Stevenson over Harriman by 905½ to 210—and the party that followed it on the third floor of the Blackstone Hotel, which enlisted the social friends of both candidates, might have been drawn from the membership of the Council on Foreign Relations and their spouses, with a touch of Cook County roughnecks thrown in for fiber. Nominations in the future would be fought for by coarser men.[42]

As for the Republicans, White wrote that in the fifties, "the Republican party was the party of comfortable Northern Protestants."[43]

Thus the stage was set. In the words of Kevin Phillips:

> At some risk of generalizing too much, it is still fair to say that our parties and ideologies, once successful, have tended to entrench themselves in the Northeast—in the stronghold of the business-financial establishment and of the political power structure. Conversely, the periodic upheavals that challenge or change the structure tend to be launched in the South and West, be it the trans-Appalachian West of 1828, the Great Plains of 1896, or the dust bowl of 1932. All such insurgencies were in some measure Populist and antiestablishmentarian, which helps to give American politics its special character.[44]

In our own time, as Phillips points out, a Populist insurgency (from the right instead of the left) has taken over the Republican party. And since the Republicans have won nearly all of the recent Presidential elections,* their ascendancy is comparable to the rise of Jacksonian democracy in the 1820s, the other notable period when the Eastern elite was thrown out of office.

The first signs of the insurgency in presidential politics were seen in 1960, when the Republican nomination went to Vice-President Nixon. But Nixon was hardly in control of his party. For one thing, he was obliged to accept as his running mate one Henry Cabot Lodge, a proper Bostonian. Then too, on the eve of his party's convention in Chicago, Nixon felt obliged to fly to New York for an urgent meeting with the real godfather of Eastern Republicans— Nelson Rockefeller (who reappears, throughout this protracted political drama, like Banquo's ghost). In what came to be known as the Compact of Fifth Avenue (named after the site of the Rockefeller apartment overlooking Central Park), Nixon accepted his host's party platform. According to Teddy White, the arrangement confirmed rank-and-file Republicans in their long-held belief "that some mysterious Eastern conspiracy was always and permanently at work to frustrate both them and the Party from an expression of true faith."[45]

Four years later, the true believers took their revenge. At a place in San Francisco called, appropriately enough, the Cow Palace, western insurgents awarded the nomination to Barry Goldwater of Arizona, who had suggested that "this country would be better off it we could just saw off the Eastern Seaboard and let it float out to sea."[46] When Rockefeller took the podium to warn against "extremism," he was lustily booed. Just to add insult to injury, Goldwater chose as his running mate a New York politician named William E. Miller, whom no one ever heard of before or since. (As of this moment, Miller is the last New Yorker except for Geraldine Ferraro to have appeared on a national ticket.) Following the convention, Rockefeller sulked. As a result, California became the principal source of Republican funds for the first time in a presidential campaign, surpassing New York by 40 percent. According

* The only exceptions since Kennedy, of course, have been Lyndon Johnson, who fancied himself a Texas rancher, and Jimmy Carter, a peanut farmer and born-again Christian from southwest Georgia.

to Kevin Phillips, "the Barry Goldwater-Lyndon Johnson presidential race carved the new political geography in stone: Texas Democrat Johnson scored his best regional percentage in once bedrock Republican New England, while Goldwater ran best in the South and next-best in the West (especially the long-populist Rocky Mountains)."[47]

In 1968, the contest for the Republican nomination took place between two Californians. Nixon beat Reagan by twenty-five votes. By the time of his landslide re-election in 1972, writes Kevin Phillips, a former Nixon advisor, "Nixon was already contemplating a reshaped Republican Party—or even a new party—institutionalizing the new nonestablishment ascendancy."[48]

But Nixon, of course, had a fatal flaw, a combination of hatred and paranoia. There were many things that aroused his ire and fear—Harvard, liberals, Boston, New York, the Kennedys, Jews, artists, the media. . . . But in the end, his principal demon was the Establishment.

In the eyes of Nixon and his band of loyalists (as well as those of some left-leaning writers), Watergate was nothing more than a counter-coup by the Eastern Establishment. The charge is a fiction, of course (unless one accepts the convoluted theories that the Watergate break-in was actually an operation by the CIA that was deliberately bungled in order to ensnare the White House).

Nonetheless, future historians will no doubt note that the prosecutorial forces had a distinctly Establishment cast. There was, for example, the executive editor of the *Washington Post,* Benjamin Bradlee, who, despite his tough-guy manner, is the scion of a well-connected Boston family (among their frequent dinner guests was Walter Lippmann), as well as a graduate of Harvard and a former close friend of Jack Kennedy. There was Special Prosecutor Archibald Cox, a Harvard law professor. Attorney General Elliot Richardson, descendant of a long line of Boston Brahmins, graduate of Harvard and Harvard Law. Deputy Attorney General William Ruckelshaus, Princeton and Harvard Law. Senator Sam ("Jist a country law-yuh") Ervin, also a graduate of Harvard Law.

There were, as well, the media in New York. CBS, the network of Edward R. Murrow, who had gone after Joseph McCarthy, the network that thought of itself as the journalistic standard-bearer, and was the first to take up the Watergate cause. There was *Newsweek,* which is owned by the *Washington Post.* And the *New York Times,* the very voice of the Establishment . . .

After Richard Nixon was sent packing to California, President Gerald Ford chose as his new vice-president one Nelson Rockefeller. But with the approach of the 1976 Republican convention, where he faced a challenge from Ronald Reagan, Ford was forced to drop Rockefeller from the presidential ticket. "Despite this," wrote Kevin Phillips, "a large number of insurgent conservatives sat on their hands, preferring to see Ford replaced by a Democrat as they looked toward 1980."[49]

Let us suppose that during the 1980 presidential primaries, some neutral organization (say the League of Women Voters) distributed a questionnaire designed to weed out candidates who were clearly incompetent. Let us further suppose that the questionnaire contained, among others, the following statements, to which the candidates were to respond True or False:
   • China is the United States' third-largest trading partner.
   • The land that now comprises the United States has as much forest area as it had at the time of the American Revolution.
   • The amount of radioactive waste produced thus far by the nuclear power industry would fit inside a telephone booth.
   • During the process of abortion, fetuses often feel periods of severe and prolonged pain.
   • The SALT II treaty, although never ratified by the United States, would be illegal in any case, since it violates laws already passed by Congress.
   • Eighty percent of air pollution is produced by plants and trees.[50]
   Now, most of us would presumably agree that any candidate who answered True to even one of these statements would be highly suspect, while anyone who answered True to *all* of them would be certifiably crackers. Yet (as the reader has no doubt guessed) each

of these statements was delivered in public by Ronald Reagan.* What's more, none of them had the slightest effect on his election to the office of president of the United States, the second time by a landslide.

Years and years from now, when historians look back on the second half of the twentieth century, they will be intrigued primarily by two American presidencies, those of Richard Nixon and Ronald Reagan. They will study the first, of course, because of all of its schemes and machinations, and for what it revealed about the working of the Constitution in a state of crisis. But when they really want to learn about democracy in America, they will study the presidency of Ronald Reagan.

Both Nixon and Reagan came from California. "Indeed," writes Lou Cannon of the *Washington Post,* who has covered Reagan for many years, "it is impossible to conceive of a Reagan presidency apart from the California culture that nourished him."[51]

The political aspect of that culture was (and is) characterized in general by a rootless, restless population; a proclivity for independent voting; a virtual absence of political parties in the classic, Eastern sense; and a tendency of candidates to develop personal followings. Today, these characteristics have come to apply to the country at large, as well as to its politics. In the words of Theodore White: "American politics in the last 30 years I have been reporting them reflect far more of the California experience than the older political practices of the East. . . . California invented a new kind of politics, far more adaptable to the restless reshuffling of American people. . . . By 1980, California was preeminently the nation's political leader, providing both its President and its political style."[52]

Most of the elements of that political style were supplied by a creature called the campaign consultant, whose chief function, in White's words, was "to connect the strangers to candidates by arousing their emotions."[53] Nowadays, of course, such consultants have become quite commonplace; but all of them (according to White) can trace their lineage to the California firm of Whitaker and Baxter, which hung out its shingle as early as 1933. Unlike Eastern liberals (who, as we have seen, espoused a rather idealized

* My favorite rejoinder was delivered by the Berkeley student who appeared at a Reagan rally carrying a small sapling from whose branches hung a sign that read: "Chop me down before I kill again."

view of the average man), Whitaker and Baxter had no illusions about what they were up to. "The average American," Clem Whitaker explained, "doesn't want to be educated; he doesn't want to improve his mind; he doesn't even want to work, consciously, at becoming a good citizen."[54] Clem's thinking proved irresistible.

The firm's reputation was made in the gubernatorial campaign of 1934, in which Upton Sinclair had the audacity to run for the state's highest office. During the campaign, a group of Hollywood film moguls (acting on their own, perhaps) produced what Leo Rosten described in his book, *Hollywood,* as "a series of fabricated newsreels of appalling crudity and immense effectiveness":

> Motion pictures were taken of a horde of disreputable vagrants in the act of crossing the "California border" and prepared to expropriate the God-fearing the moment Upton Sinclair was elected. The pictures were taken on the streets of Los Angeles with cameras from a major studio; the anarchists were actors on studio payrolls, dressed in false whiskers and dirty clothes, and wearing sinister expressions. These "newsreels" were distributed *gratis* to theater owners, and were spread across the screens of leading theaters in every city in the state.[55]

Needless to say, Sinclair was soundly defeated; and "media politics" became the rule in California. As Mickey Kantor, a longtime strategist for Jerry Brown, observed a few years ago: "The question here is not whether the labor leader is backing you but who is doing your media. This is the way things have gone in California, and now it's how politics will be done in the East as well."[56]

Kantor was right, of course. "Image politics, sweeping out from California," wrote Teddy White, "would grow to dominate presidential elections, then presidential administrations, then international politics."[57]

The medium by which this image was transmitted was television, which came into political use much sooner in California than elsewhere, partly because of the dearth of party connections, partly because of the physical size of the place (800 miles from corner to corner). But recently, the rest of the country has clearly caught up. During the most recent New Hampshire primary, for example, reporters noted that what had once been a relatively personal and "human" affair was now dominated by television.

It is of course a truism to say that television has altered political reality, but in fact the effects are more profound than that. In many ways, television has *become* that reality, and not just in a tactical sense but in an almost philosophical sense as well. Each evening, for instance, politicians all over Washington—and especially out on the hustings—turn on their television sets to see which of the events in which they participated that day will be reported on the evening news. They do this not simply out of curiosity to "see how it played in the media," but rather to see which events will be certified as actually having happened. Those not certified will be more or less consigned to oblivion, while the chosen few will be accorded a status that often far exceeds their real importance. "It really doesn't make any difference what kind of law you create," remarked California Representative (and Democratic Whip) Tony Coelho, before resigning his seat in Congress as a result of a questionable financial deal. "Today, it's only the perception you create that's important. And the perception is created on TV."[58]

Such thinking also dominates political campaigns, partly because of the influence of Hollywood. For example, Gerald Rafshoon, the advertising wizard who launched Jimmy Carter on the road to the White House, had previously served as advertising chief of Twentieth Century–Fox. In the words of former NBC executive Richard Wald: "The entertainment people in television, Hollywood, are not just looking for a large audience; they're looking for all the audience. That kind of thinking, mass thinking, changes the way you operate. Old politicians were looking for part of the audience, for a coalition. They were looking at problems and saying, 'Look, this is a common problem for many of you. I'll represent you in dealing with it.' The new politicians are looking for chords. They float above the problems. They strike responsive chords. What they really want to do is cloud men's minds."[59] (Today, of course, the "chords" have become "themes," but the effect is just the same.)

Hollywood entertainment clouds the political mind in other ways as well—mainly by blurring the distinction between illusion and reality. "The TV set is a stage," says Don Hewitt, executive producer of '60 Minutes', "and on that stage, the audience watches 'Dallas' and 'Dynasty' and newscasts and paid political ads, and after a while they can't tell which is which."

*　　*　　*

A Friday evening in the fall of 1986. On television, an episode of "Falcon Crest," starring Jane Wyman (former wife of Ronald Reagan), Robert Foxworth, etc., etc. Following a commercial break, the program resumes. Foxworth is walking through his vineyard. But wait a minute. He's not talking about grapes or wine. What's he saying? Some judge is up for election. Rebozo? Renozo? What is this?

What it was, of course, was a paid political ad that just happened to look an awful lot like a scene from "Falcon Crest." Other examples of such "blurring," though less egregious, are all about:

• Sissy Spacek, Jane Fonda and Jessica Lange, after each making a movie about small-time farmers, jointly appear before Congress to testify about the plight of the family farm.

• Alan Alda delivers the commencement address at Columbia med school.

• An aging actor and a campaign consultant sit up late at night discussing the notion that if charisma is all it takes, why not go for it? One year later, in 1964, song-and-dance man George Murphy becomes a United States senator from California.*

• William Daniels (Dr. Craig on "St. Elsewhere") is invited to deliver the commencement address at *two* medical schools.

• Tip O'Neill makes a guest appearance on "Cheers." So does Gary Hart.

• Linda Ellerbee shows up on "Murphy Brown," playing herself.

• Clint Eastwood is elected mayor of Carmel, California. City government meetings, at which Eastwood presides, are overrun by tourists.

• Nancy Reagan makes a guest appearance on "Different Strokes" (and elsewhere).

• Kirk Douglas, after making a movie on the plight of the elderly, testifies before Congress.

• In a television movie called "Hollywood Wives," reporter Mary

---

* A similar development has taken place in India, where movie stars—mainly from the country's southern states—have enjoyed a considerable amount of success in politics. As in the U.S., the development in India has assumed, for the most part, a populist, anti-establishment tone.

Hart shows up with a microphone to interview guests arriving for a party, just as she does on "Entertainment Tonight" (or did, before she became an anchor).

• An organization called the California Poll conducts a public survey concerning potential Republican candidates for the U.S. Senate in 1986. The leading name—by far—is Charlton Heston. After giving the matter careful thought, Heston decides to make a television series instead, at least for now.[60]

• Jesse Jackson, in the spring of 1989, makes a guest appearance on "A Different World" (a program created by Bill Cosby, who is a supporter of Jesse Jackson).

• Pernell Roberts (Trapper John) makes a television commercial, pushing Ecotrin.

• Following his death, John Wayne is awarded the Congressional Medal of Honor.

• Fred Grandy, late of "Love Boat," is elected to Congress from Iowa.

• President Reagan and Barbara Streisand hold California fund-raisers (one Democratic), each of which nets about $1.5 million. But since Streisand's do was recorded on video, her potential take is much bigger. In Tom Wicker's column describing the events, the subhead reads: "Reagan Upstaged by Streisand."[61]

• During the Republican convention in Dallas, the platform committee throws a big bash at Southfork.

• Jeanne Wolf of "Entertainment Tonight" shows up with a microphone on "Santa Barbara," playing herself.

• As he strolls through the airport terminal in Atlanta, John Forsythe is attacked by a purse-wielding woman, who is incensed over his treatment of Krystle on "Dynasty."

Election night, 1986. On television, a shot of Governor George Deukmejian's victory celebration at a cavernous Los Angeles ballroom. As the camera pans the crush of dignitaries gathered on-stage, the governor introduces the state's junior senator, a small, bland Yalie by the name of Pete Wilson, who gives a tentative wave from the second row. One's eye is arrested, however, by the sight of a tall, familiar, white-haired figure standing front and center. Cesar Romero.

Hollywood can supply more glitter than a Society which has grown a trifle weary of its past magnificence and also a little timorous of its future. Hollywood's strings of pearls are longer, its Cattleyas rarer, its Hispano-Suizas newer, and its divorces bigger and better. And to some extent it has stolen the show.

The passage above, from Dixon Wecter's *Saga of American Society,* was quoted in chapter 1 (as the reader may recall) to point up the manner in which Hollywood Celebrity during the 1930s was displacing Eastern Society as a symbolic royalty. The passage will serve as well to point up the manner in which Hollywood Celebrity during the 1980s was displacing politicians, too. The first stage of the usurpation occurred in 1980 itself, when Ronald Reagan routed George Bush in the Republican primaries, thereby producing the final victory of Western Celebrity over Eastern Aristocracy. Later on, against Reagan's buttery Hollywood persona, mere politicians such as Jimmy Carter and Walter Mondale didn't stand a chance.

There were other California explanations for Ronald Reagan's ascendancy. In 1978, the voters of the state passed the now famous Proposition 13, which dramatically reduced their property taxes. (Frederick Jackson Turner was apparently right: in the West, "the tax gatherer is viewed as a representative of oppression.") Soon, state after state was infected with "referendum fever," as voters far and wide sought to cash in on the newfound bonanza. Theodore White was less jubilant: "The filter of representative government has slowly been eliminated between emotion and its electoral results. . . . California's popular initiatives have been one of the truest indexes of what people think or want, and thus, disturbing."[62] Never mind. The country was caught up in a wave of anti-government populism—which, as it happened, was exactly what Reagan had been preaching. ("Government is not the solution; government is the problem.")

There was a broader backdrop for the Reagan revolt. During the 1920s, following its defeat in the First World War, the nation of Germany, under the Weimar republic, went through a period characterized by weak national leadership, rampant inflation, a loss of faith in national institutions and a contempt on the part of the urban elite for ordinary Germans and German patriotism. This was soon followed, under the National Socialists, by "strong" (to put it mildly) national leadership; an emphasis on family, work and Fatherland; a display of the trappings of Christianity; racial polarization (to put it mildly); a movement to the right among the young; and a veneration of German mythology. Periods such as the latter have been described by Arnold Toynbee as ones of nationalistic archaism—that is, of a nation's attempt to restore a mythical past.

During the 1970s, following its defeat in Vietnam, the United States underwent a similar transition. There was the "weak" national leadership of Jimmy Carter, followed by the "strong" national leadership of Ronald Reagan. During the latter period, there was also the growth of religious fundamentalism, the appearance of neo-Nazi citizens groups in several Western states, and the spread of racial polarization. In addition, several academicians published books suggesting the United States had entered a period of national decline.

But what about the matter of national mythology—specifically, the attempt to restore a mythical past? The United States, we like to believe, is a country unencumbered by myth. Dreams, of course, we have, but not myths. Americans, after all, are a rational people; and myths are things that perturb the primitives (or at the outside, the crazies like the Germans).

The truth, however, is that we have a very potent national myth, one which is so obvious and so pervasive it's rarely recognized as such: the myth of the cowboy.

"The brief historic period of the opening of the west," writes James K. Folsom in a book of critical essays called *The Western*, "has become *the* great vehicle for American cultural myth."[63]

"Fleeting figures of these brief, broken moments," write Frank Bergon and Zeese Papanikolas in *Looking Far West*, "could not have hardened into legend and endured as myth if there had not been such a need and a longing for mythic sustenance in America."[64]

Adds Jenni Calder in another book on the Western: "The Western myth continues to live after a hundred years and more repetition than any other basic myth in the world's history."[65]

Nor is this myth merely an idle fantasy. "It contains a conceptual analysis of society that provides a model of social action," writes Will

103

Wright. "The receivers of the myth learn how to act by recognizing their own situation in it and observing how it is resolved."[66]

Certain American political figures understand this fact. As Henry Kissinger reportedly replied to Oriana Fallaci's question as to why he was so popular: "The main point . . . Well, why not? I'll tell you. What do I care after all? The main point stems from the fact that I've always acted alone. Americans admire that enormously. Americans admire the cowboy leading the caravan alone astride his horse. Without even a pistol, maybe, because he doesn't go in for shooting. He acts, that's all: aiming at the right spot at the right time. A Wild West tale, if you like."[67]

But Henry Kissinger, of course, was hardly the ideal actor to play the cowboy. Reagan was.

Perhaps the most systematic study of the Western movie is found in the book by Will Wright. Wright points out that in the classic Western, the hero is at first unknown to the community; but he is soon revealed to have an exceptional ability, which earns him a special status. Nonetheless, the hero initially avoids involvement in the conflict; eventually, of course, he fights the villains and defeats them.

This basic plot, spare as it is, could well describe the career of Ronald Reagan. More important, it is probably the way both he and the public subconsciously *perceive* his career.

For years, Reagan labored away as a run-of-the-mill movie actor, then as the host of "Death Valley Days." But in 1964, in a televised speech for Barry Goldwater, he was suddenly revealed to have an exceptional ability. ("His was a splendid performance," wrote Teddy White. "A few days later, I visited the Goldwater headquarters on Los Angeles's Wilshire Boulevard . . . where women sat . . . opening envelopes. Out of them came one-dollar bills, five-dollar bills, even an occasional Social Security check endorsed to Goldwater or Reagan. The Reagan personality had tapped a hidden mother lode of money—poor people's money, the contributions of those who must be called the underclass of conservative populism.")[68]

Not long afterward, several of Reagan's friends suggested he run for governor, but Reagan at first resisted. Eventually he won by a million votes. In 1968, his friends suggested he run for president, but Reagan at first demurred. Twelve years later, he won in a walk (with a vote that was much more Sunbelt than that for Ford in 1976). In 1984 he carried forty-nine states, something only Nixon had done before.

Throughout these years of ascendancy, Reagan's handlers took pains to identify him, of course, with the cowboy. All those shots of Reagan riding about on his California "ranch." The campaign posters of Reagan in broad-brimmed hat, which he frequently wore when making appearances. Best of all, the campaign button showing Reagan in the foreground, and in the background, the face of John Wayne. The billing said: "Win One for The Duke."

All well and good, you say, but how could Reagan have become a figure of Western myth? Weren't such characters usually to be found reclining somewhere on Boot Hill? As a matter of fact they usually weren't. "The obvious distortion of this mythic West," write Bergon and Papanikolas, "is not so interesting as its nearness to the surface of history. Legendary Westerners were not drawn from figures already eternalized by Arthurian mists of a dim past; they were real men who confronted their own myths and often helped shape them. Kit Carson faced himself as a melodramatic hero in 1849 when he found a sensationalized paperback novel about himself. . . . Twenty-four years later, Wild Bill Hickok was appearing on stage playing the popular role of Wild Bill Hickok. . . . With Buffalo Bill . . . myth completely overtakes reality."[69] So it did too with John Wayne, when Congress awarded him the Medal of Honor.

A similar apotheosis occurred with Reagan, following his plucky response to the attempted assassination. "A new legend has been born," declared David Broder. "From primitive days, heroic tales have been fashioned from incidents in which brave men escape danger. That tradition has been carried intact into the presidency."[70]

"Everybody knows that people seldom act at the margin between life and death with such light-hearted valor as they do in the movies," observed James Reston. "Yet Ronald Reagan did. No script writer could have improved on the carefree one-liners he tossed off on his way to the knife."[71]

William Safire wrote simply: "The President came through like John Wayne."[72]

Soon thereafter, Reagan's ratings soared in the polls.

*　　*　　*

One of the more interesting aspects of Reagan, however, is that he was not merely an *object* of mythmaking; he was also an active participant. This was true not only of his behavior on the way to surgery; it characterized his entire career. And it applied not only to himself, but to the country and the world at large. In this, Reagan was undoubtedly a perfect reflection of his adoring fans, which is one reason he was so popular. But in Reagan's case, the devotion to myth was so consistent and unshakable that one often wonders to what degree the man was in touch with reality. As Lou Cannon observes, in Reagan's mind, "the heroic world of make-believe and the real world coalesced. The man who lived in both of them could not always distinguish one from the other, and he came to believe in many things that weren't true."[73] A few examples:

· In his speeches, Reagan liked to tell the story of the B–17 pilot who was about to bail out of his stricken plane when he discovered a wounded gunner, trapped in his turret and unable to move. The pilot cradled the gunner in his arms and said, "Never mind, son, we'll ride it down together." Later, reported Reagan, the pilot was posthumously awarded the Congressional Medal of Honor. (A nice story, except that no such medal was ever given. Anyway, how would Reagan have learned what the pilot said, since the only two people left on the plane were presumably killed in the crash?)

· Another favorite story concerned the admiral standing on the bridge of his carrier and watching the planes take off. "Where do we get such men?" the admiral asked admiringly. (That's right, he did—in a movie called *The Bridges at Toko-Ri*.)

· In 1975, Reagan claimed that segregation in the armed forces had ended with World War II, citing as evidence an old war movie that showed a black seaman firing a machine gun at Japanese planes. When it was pointed out to him that segregation did not end until Truman's executive order of 1948, Reagan would not be budged. "I remember the scene," he said. "It was very powerful."

· Regarding his own war service, Reagan recalled: "By the time I got out of the Army Air Corps, all I wanted to do—in common with several million other veterans—was to rest up for a while, make love to my wife, and come up refreshed to a better job in a better world." (Uh-huh. Reagan spent the war years entirely in Hollywood, where his military duties consisted of working on air corps training films. He slept at home with his wife every night.)

· Another wartime recollection. A succession of Jewish visitors to the White House, including Israeli Prime Minister Shamir, listened attentively as Reagan described his service with an army Signal Corps unit that was filming the liberated Nazi concentration camps. The visitors were fascinated by Reagan's account of how he set aside a particularly revealing piece of film, just in case anyone he ever met should question the reality of the Holocaust. Sure enough, many years later, someone did just that, and luckily he still had this piece of film . . . Shamir and the others were quite moved by the story, until they discovered it was all a fantasy.

• Football. A subject as dear to Reagan's heart as World War II. While playing the game at Dixon High School, Reagan recalled, he committed a foul that went undetected by the various officials but was protested by members of the opposing team. Reagan fessed up, thereby costing his team the winning touchdown. (According to writer Garry Wills, no such game was ever played at Dixon High.)[74]

Then, of course, there's the case of George Gipp, the Notre Dame player whom Reagan portrayed in a movie, and who—in the movie—was the source of the now-famous line, "Win one for the Gipper." In truth, writes Richard Schickel, "Gipp was a thoroughly undesirable character, a pool hustler who smoked, drank, played pro football on the side, and regularly bet on Notre Dame games in which he played. In life he was never referred to as 'the Gipper'; and his death, before graduation, appears to have been hastened by his dissipations, which he never recanted."[75] Oh well. None of this mattered to Reagan. And in 1986, when Notre Dame unveiled a newly printed postage stamp in honor of Knute Rockne (the coach in the movie), Reagan joyfully attended the ceremony. "He's going home," said Patrick Buchanan, who had served as Reagan's communications director. "In his heart, that's where he thinks he went to school. . . . For Ronald Reagan, the world of legend and myth is a real world. He visits it regularly, and he's a happy man there."[76]

In the world of facts and figures, the one that most of Washington still regards, perhaps erroneously, as the real world, Reagan seemed rather less comfortable:

• In a nationally televised news conference just before the Geneva summit, Reagan insisted that "the United States is still well behind the Soviet Union in literally every kind of offensive weapon, both conventional and in the strategic weapons." Not true; although the U.S. trails the Soviet Union in conventional forces, it is Russia's equal (at least) in strategic, the ones that count.

• Reagan asserted that children were getting free school lunches in a community with an average income of $75,000. When White House assistant David Gergen was asked about the source of the president's information, Gergen replied, "He heard it at a dinner party."

• For nearly three years after becoming president, Reagan did not glom on to the elementary fact that most of the Soviet Union's nuclear arsenal consists of land-based missiles. This oversight, in turn, helps explain why his START proposal, with its tight restrictions on land-based missiles, was so one-sided.

• At a school in Illinois, the president told pupils about a British law requiring that anyone carrying a gun while committing a crime be tried for murder. When someone pointed out that Britain has no such law, a presidential spokesman replied, "Well, it's a good story, though." Four years later, in a newspaper interview, the president told the story again.

• Reagan said that OSHA has 144 regulations on climbing ladders. The actual figure is 2.

• Displaying his knowledge of American history, the president quoted Justice Oliver Wendell Holmes: "Keep the government poor and remain free." Holmes never said that. What Holmes did say was that "taxes are what we pay for a civilized society," a sentiment that the president would probably not have shared.

• Asked a simple question about arms control, the president was struck dumb for several long seconds. Nancy, standing beside him, murmured, "Doing everything we can." Reagan suddenly recovered his powers of speech: "We're doing everything we can."*

---

* Connoisseurs of Reaganisms are doubtless wondering why I have not included his famous assertion that missiles fired from submarines "can be recalled." The reason is that I'm not sure he made it. What Reagan said was: "Those [missiles] that are carried in bombers, those that are carried in ships of one kind or another, or submersibles, you are dealing there with a conventional type of weapon or instrument, and those instruments can be intercepted. They can be recalled if there has been a miscalculation." The White House later claimed that in saying, "those instruments can be intercepted. They can be recalled," Reagan was referring to the submarines rather than the missiles. While his statement is at best ambiguous, it seems to me that in this case, we'll have to give Reagan the benefit of the doubt.

• Reagan reported, in one of his radio talks, the case of a school district where "the venereal disease rate among young people in that district went up 800 percent in the first few years after sex education became a part of the curriculum." The VD division of the Atlanta Centers for Disease Control says it's never heard of any such case.

• At a press briefing, the president was asked how his brand-new MX missile system would actually be deployed (a topic of considerable speculation and debate). He answered: "I don't know but what maybe you haven't gotten into the area that I'm gonna turn over to the the, heh, heh, Secretary of Defense." Caspar Weinberger, standing beside him, said, "The silos will be hardened." The president said, "Yes, I could say this. The plan also includes the hardening of silos."

• Reagan pointed out that General Motors employs 23,000 people just to do federal paperwork. The actual number is more like 5,000, most of whom work on tax returns.

• Addressing the 1984 Republican National Convention in Dallas, the President said he wanted to share with his audience the vision of "a young boy who wrote to me shortly after I took office." His voice growing hoarse with emotion, Reagan then read from the youngster's letter: "I love America because you can join Cub Scouts if you want to. You have a right to worship as you please. If you have the ability, you can try to be anything you want to be. I also like America because we have about 200 flavors of ice cream." As it turned out, the "letter" was not written to Reagan at all. Its author, Mark Hawley, had composed it nineteen years earlier as an essay required for a Cub Scout merit badge. It was printed in *Scouting* magazine in the fall of 1969.

• During a trip to South America, the president proposed a toast "to the people of Bolivia." When someone pointed out that he was standing in Brazil, the president excused his error by saying that Bolivia was next in line on his tour. In fact, his next stop was Colombia." Bolivia was not on the tour at all.

• After doggedly pursuing his plan to lay a wreath at the Bitburg cemetary, where members of SS units were buried, Reagan attempted to quiet the criticism by citing a letter he had received from a thirteen-year-old girl named Beth Flom: "One of the many who wrote me about this visit was a young woman who had recently been bar mitzvahed. She urged me to lay the wreath at Bitburg cemetary in honor of the future of Germany, and that is what we have done." In fact, Ms. Flom had urged him *not* to visit Bitburg.

• More trouble in Brazil. During a televised address calling for funding of the contras, the president pointed to a map of Brazil, tinted red to dramatize his claim that the Sandinistas were training Brazilian revolutionaries. Both the State Department and the government of Brazil denied the claim.

• In the same address, Reagan decried "the desecrating and firebombing" of Managua's only synagogue. Actually, the building was abandoned during street fighting in 1978, a year before the Sandinistas came to power.

• President Reagan on South Africa: "They have eliminated the segregation that we had in our own country, the type of thing where hotels and restaurants and places of entertainment and so forth were segregated—that has all been eliminated."

To be sure, the president's mental landscape—little mounds of trivia amid mojaves of neglect—did not go unnoticed in Washington. Clark Clifford early on began referring to Reagan as "an amiable dunce." Other assessments were scarcely more charitable:

• Lou Cannon, *Washington Post:* "Few presidents have been as lacking in intellectual curiosity—or as unconcerned about what they do not know. . . . Reagan's basic problem is not credibility but a frequently superficial understanding of complex issues. . . . He is so far distanced from arms-control decisions within his administration that he must be viewing them from another planet."[77]

• Martin Tolchin, *New York Times,* describing a White House meeting between Reagan and Congressional leaders:

> At one point, Representative Robert H. Michel, the House Republican leader, urged the President to indicate his support for a Federal insurance plan to cover catastrophic illnesses. Mr. Reagan responded by talking about a New York City welfare family living in a plush hotel at extravagant cost. Other leaders explained that catastrophic health insurance was not a welfare program, but Mr. Reagan reiterated his story about the welfare family.
>
> Some of those attending were dismayed at what they viewed as the President's inability to grasp this issue and some of the others that were raised.[78]

· Tip O'Neill: "He has a great tendency of going into space and stargazing. . . . The truth of the matter is, he knows less than any President I've ever met."[79]

· Richard Cohen, *Washington Post:* "This President is treated by both the press and foreign leaders as if he were a child. . . . He earns praise for the ordinary. . . . His occasional ability to retain facts is cited as a triumph."[80]

· Leslie Gelb, *New York Times,* in an article titled, perhaps optimistically, "The Mind of the President":

Previous Presidents have spent their days reading lengthy position papers, meeting with outside experts, keeping up to the minute on international developments. But President Reagan, according to legislators and others who see him privately, generally shows little knowledge about most subjects under discussion. They say that his participation in discussions is often exhausted after he has read aloud the information his staff has written for him on three-by-five index cards.

According to a member of the President's Commission on Strategic Forces, "He never participated in meetings beyond what he'd been told to say by Bud McFarlane. He didn't understand what it was we were trying to do with strategic programs and arms control."[81]

· *Time* magazine: "In a meeting with a foreign leader . . . he pulled out and read from the wrong cue cards."[82]

· Joseph Kraft: "Behind the confusion is a President clearly unequal in his own person to serious business. . . . a leader addicted to romantic fantasy."[83]

· William Fulbright: "Mr. Reagan offended me. . . . This was an unserious man in a serious job, a job that he treated like Hollywood for eight years."[84]

· David Broder, *Washington Post:* Those who work with Reagan quickly come to understand how little his policy views rest on information or facts—how much they rely on his own instincts and long-cherished beliefs. . . . No Democrat or no 'liberal reporter' has drawn as unflattering a picture of this President as his chosen associates in government—David Stockman, Alexander Haig, Michael Deaver, Larry Speakes and now Regan—in their books. The portrait they paint is appalling: a President almost devoid of curiosity, reflectiveness, energy or purpose, a man full of his own preconceptions, yet easily manipulated and fooled by others."[85] Elsewhere, Broder referred to "the arid dessert between Reagan's ears," and employed the famous phrase that inevitably springs to mind: "the emperor had no clothes."

Thus, the democratization of politics was finally arriving at its logical conclusion: a president who was the perfect embodiment of the ordinary American. But there was more to come in this political symbiosis.

Clearly, the people around the president had a problem. Never mind that the leader of the free world knew next to nothing about the substance of his job—foreign affairs, arms control, the deficit and so on. Of more immediate concern was the likelihood that on any given day, the Great Communicator might communicate something—some little-known "fact" from his odd scraps of clippings, some misinterpretation of this or that—which would make him an object of ridicule. What was needed, obviously, was some sort of system that would give the appearance of a president smoothly performing his duties, while preventing anyone from inquiring too closely about what it was he was actually doing. What was needed was the politics of illusion.*

> At 8:15 every morning, White House Deputy Chief of Staff Michael K. Deaver sits down with other presidential aides to shape what will be broadcast from the White House on the television news that night. Recognizing that the evening news shows will most likely offer no more than a 30- or 40-second report on President Reagan's daily activities, Deaver and his communications staff are determined to control the content of that spot.
>
> In a recent interview, Deaver said his staff tries to "plot out a decent story or a theme for every day"
>
> —Robert Scheer
> *Los Angeles Times.*[86]

In effect, what Deaver and company were creating was a daily series of thirty-second (unpaid) political ads; and it was not by

---

* The phrase is borrowed from Richard Schickel's book, *Intimate Strangers: The Culture of Celebrity.*

accident that Deaver referred to the president as "the talent" (TV lingo for the actor appearing in a commercial).

The essence of these spots was the famous "photo opportunity"—the president visiting a school, the president visiting a national park, the president visiting an aircraft carrier and so on. As the *Los Angeles Times* described it, "The Deaver strategy focuses on TV coverage, on serving up for the cameras only the images approved by the White House and on safe-guarding the President from chance encounters with reporters who might ask questions that the White House does not want to deal with."

Simple as it sounds, the strategy worked. In the words of the *Los Angeles Times:* "NBC White House correspondent Chris Wallace notes that although he and other reporters continuously [sic] pointed out that Reagan had, if fact, cut funds for education, the 'visual' of Reagan appearing frequently with school children and teachers conveyed the image that the White House wanted—that Reagan had made a strong commitment to bolstering education."

The main reason such "photo-ops" worked, of course, was that Reagan was very good at them. And like the consummate host that he played on television, he always knew just the right moment to drop in a touch of self-deprecatory humor. Scene: The Baltimore harbor redevelopment project. President Reagan, by way of providing a photo opportunity, is peering seaward through a telescope. After several moments, he turns to the cameras and announces, deadpan: "The Russians are coming." Johnny Carson could not have done it better.

By all accounts, the president was quite comfortable with this ceremonial role. In the words of a former senior administration official: "He once described to me how he got into politics by accident. He said he told someone, 'By God, what am I doing in politics?' The kinds of things I've done so far are far away from this. But then I thought that a substantial part of the political thing is acting and role playing and I know how to do that. So I used to worry, but I don't anymore.' "[87]

"Here's a man who by his disciplines has always been handled," says someone who served Reagan over many years. "In Hollywood you get up at an unusual hour and go to some place and the sun comes over the horizon and somebody is there to check the lighting. Somebody else goes over your lines with you. Then you have a few words with the director. You sit where you are supposed to. Somebody says 'Action!' and you go with what you've got. . . . A great deal of his presidency relates to this exercise."[88]

President Reagan was once asked whether he planned to visit the Vietnam Memorial. His answer was revealing: "I can't tell until somebody tells me. I never know where I'm going."[89]

"You had to treat him as if you were the director and he was the actor," says another former White House staff member. "You told him what to say and what not to say, and only then did he say the right thing."[90]

"This was a PR outfit that became President and took over the country," says Leslie Janka, a former Reagan deputy press secretary. "The Constitution forced them to do things like make a budget, run foreign policy and all that. . . . But their first, last and overreaching activity was public relations.[91]

The greatest opportunity for public relations was afforded by a summit meeting—the Super Bowl of photo-ops. At Geneva, however, the president's staff was somewhat worried. As one official put it, "We had a nightmare vision of world headlines saying: 'Summit Breaks Up Over Star Wars.' " Nonetheless, Reagan and Gorbachev appeared to get on quite well. Following a formal meeting, Reagan suggested on the spur of the moment that the two take a stroll; and they wound up having a long private talk before a roaring fire in a poolhouse. What the public didn't know at the time, though, was that the impromptu talk had been planned in advance by the White House—simply because a staff member realized that the fireside setting would afford a wonderful (yes) photo-op. What did the two leaders talk about? Who knows? Who cares? The important thing (from the White House point of view) was that the public's image of the Geneva summit was one of Reagan and Gorbachev beside a cozy fire.

Reykjavik was trickier. Reagan got snookered into talking about banning all nuclear weapons—an extremely dangerous step for the United States, since the Soviet Union is far superior in conventional forces. Fortunately, the talks collapsed, but the whole affair was rather a fiasco. Afterward, Reagan and his staff were downcast—until a White House poll revealed that the public had somehow formed the impression that Reagan had "stood up to the Russians." Suddenly, the summit was portrayed to the press as a triumph. Reagan's image glowed.

*　　*　　*

The 1984 election as seen on PBS. "The MacNeil–Lehrer Newshour," June 26, 1984. Judy Woodruff is interviewing a female
yuppie who had supported Gary Hart until he dropped out of the
race.

> *Woodruff:* "Who will you vote for in the general election?"
> *Yuppie:* "Reagan."
> *Woodruff:* "Why not Mondale?"
> *Yuppie:* "I don't think he has a good image."

I don't think he has a good image. There you have it.

The other ingredient in the politics of illusion was keeping Reagan
isolated from members of the press ("sons of bitches," Reagan
called them when he didn't realize a microphone was on). Franklin
Roosevelt averaged about seven press conferences per month;
Eisenhower, Kennedy and Johnson, about two; Ford and Carter,
better than one; Nixon and Reagan, one half. (Carter, at least, was
also available to the press in other ways. As ABC's Sam Donaldson
remarked during the Reagan administration, "Jimmy Carter was
terribly accessible to television reporters and to all reporters. . . .
When I compare that to today, why I was practically living with
Jimmy and Rosalynn Carter.")[92]
  When Reagan did deign to hold a press conference, recalled his
former press secretary Larry Speakes, getting him prepared
"would be like re-inventing the wheel."[93] Or as Lou Cannon observed: "Reagan's handlers understand far better than his critics
how uninformed he is on many of the day's major issues. It is not
accidental that they have made him the most isolated President of
modern times."[94]
  To be sure, reporters tried to penetrate the presidential cocoon.
As Reagan boarded his helicopter en route to Camp David, they
would bellow the major questions of the day (to which the White
House responded by having the pilot rev up the engines). For a
while, reporters took the trouble to write up the president's outrageous misstatements of fact, Lou Cannon going so far as to

introduce a feature called "Reaganism of the Week." But eventually they all more or less gave up. The public, it turned out, couldn't care less. In the words of James Reston: "Not since the days of H. L. Mencken have so many reporters written so much or so well about the shortcomings of the President and influenced so few voters."[95] Or as Lou Cannon put it: "We could double the number of Reaganisms a week and it wouldn't change a thing."[96]

The lesson of all this is chilling. It is, simply put, that facts don't matter; the truth doesn't matter. All that matters is myth, illusion.

In a sense, though, the press was guilty of a certain amount of complicity. The conventions of American journalism require that it report and discuss the doings of the president as if there really is a president, as if there is actually somebody there. This is particularly true of television, which, as Michael Arlen noted in his book *The Camera Age*, "has communicated political news increasingly on a mythic basis . . . as part of an ongoing dramatic pageant."[97] The grand marshall of that pageant was Ronald Reagan.

Reality occasionally intruded. During an ill-defined mission in Lebanon, 241 marines were killed in a terrorist bombing. But few people blamed the commander in chief the way they blamed Carter, for example, for the hostages in Iran. (One reason may have been that shortly after the bombing, the commander was commanding the *opera bouffe* invasion of Grenada.) At any rate, people soon began referring to Reagan as the Teflon president—an amusing metaphor which of course explains nothing.

Think of Ronald Reagan as—quite literally—an actor playing the role of president of the United States. He has the lead in a (he hopes) long-running television series, "The Reagan Years." As it turns out, he plays the role extremely well. In Russell Baker's memorable phrase, he is "a magnificent boarder of helicopters." Pretty soon, the audience—in exactly the same way it has come to think of Trapper John as an actual doctor (all those Ecotrin commercials, remember)—begins to think of Ronald Reagan as an actual president.

At the same time, however, it still regards him as the leading man in a television series (just as it does Trapper John). After all, how does the audience actually observe Mr. Reagan? It sees him on television—in a series of little nightly, forty-second dramas that are largely produced by the White House. Ostensibly these dramas are "news," but as Don Hewitt reminds us, the audience often confuses various types of programs—dramas, news reports, political ads, what-have-you. Studies have shown, for example, that people will remember a particular event they saw in a television drama—a shootout in a cop show, say—and think that they saw it on the evening news (and vice versa). In addition, the public has long perceived Reagan as an actor, and has identified him with the legendary cowboy. Ergo: Reagan as the star of a television series (just like Trapper John).

What this really means is that the public subconsciously regards him as the hero of a myth (which is what the typical American television series actually is). This hero—the Leading Man—may not know a lot in an "academic" sense; that is certainly not required. But his judgment is infallible. He does not make mistakes. Whatever happens, he can handle it. He is the one who always wins the shootout (whether in Tombstone or the streets of L.A.), and who always gets the girl.*

We come now to another interesting aspect of Reagan's personality, one which drew him even closer to his audience (and vice versa): Just as the public regarded the Reagan presidency in mythical terms, so did Reagan himself. That is to say, the myth-making tendencies he displayed in his personal life (fantasizing, for instance, that he had photographed the liberation of concentration camps, or that a fictional pilot had been awarded the Congressional Medal of Honor), he carried with him to the White House.

Take the case of SDI—Star Wars, as it came to be called. In March of 1983, Reagan suddenly sprang a plan to protect the entire population of the United States by means of an impervious missile shield—a proposal that caught most of his technical advisors by surprise. No one else believed that this was feasible, but Reagan was adamant in his belief that it was. How did he arrive at this conclu-

* When someone once suggested that Reagan had seldom played leading roles, he vigorously denied it: "I always got the girl."

sion? It's a safe bet that he did not do so by mastering the mechanics of SDI, which are numbingly complex. A more likely answer: In 1940, Reagan starred in a movie called *Murder in the Air,* playing the role of secret agent Brass Bancroft. It was Bancroft's mission to prevent a band of Communist spies from stealing a new American secret weapon, which used a sort of death ray to blast enemy planes out of the sky. Another character in the movie, in the sort of peroration that was typical of movies of the time, declared that the weapon "not only makes the United States invincible in war, but . . . promises to become the greatest force for world peace ever discovered." This, of course, was exactly the claim that Reagan made for Star Wars.

Or take the case of Reagan's economic plan: slash taxes, boost defense spending, and balance the budget, all at once. "Voodoo economics," said the man who is now the country's president. "A riverboat gamble," said the Senate majority leader (later the White House chief of staff). The gamble failed. In just four years, Reagan managed to *double* the national debt. (If a Democrat had done this, Reagan would have had him tarred and feathered.) Moreover, as George Will points out, the previous debt was mainly incurred in wartime. Reagan managed to do it in peacetime. But when asked about the matter, he blamed it on his predecessors and Congress. Polls revealed that the public believed him.

Other facets of the Reagan administration display a similar capacity for self-delusion:

• Government ethics: Although Reagan made a big to-do about restoring old-time moral values, his government did not reflect that stance. In early 1988, the *New York Times* declared that "President Reagan presides over one of the most corrupt administrations ever. . . . the amount of sleaze is awesome."[98]

• The public welfare. Because Reagan is personally a rather decent man, it was necessary for him to reconcile, in his own mind, the knowledge of his decency and the existence of suffering. Unemployment? Reagan said there were "hundreds of ads" in every Sunday's issue of the *Washington Post.* Homelessness? Reagan said there were shelters available, but some people preferred to live on the streets.

• Morning in America. Although several writers have recently argued that the United States is entering a period of national decline, Reagan has presumably not read their books. Interestingly enough, Leo Rosten found that one of the most noticeable characteristics of Hollywood in the early forties was a sort of relentless optimism—"a form of magical thinking, an effort to make reality conform to wish."[99]

In the spring of 1987, it looked as if Reagan had finally overplayed his hand. The Iran-*contra* scandal came crashing down around him. Apparently, the country was in for a rerun of 1973: a "conservative" Republican president from Southern California, re-elected by a landslide that carried forty-nine states, done in by a counterattack led by the Eastern Establishment.

Certainly the scandal was serious enough, at least potentially. Never mind Iran. The real offense was the second half of this hyphenated affair.

Invoking one of its fundamental powers—the power of the purse—Congress had passed a law that said, in effect, don't send guns to the *contras*. But instead of vetoing the measure, or challenging it in the courts, the White House promised to uphold the law in letter and spirit. Meanwhile, it went about doing exactly what the law prohibited. And make no mistake; Reagan was deeply involved. (Even lazy presidents get involved in things they care about; and Reagan was obsessed with the *contras*.) Although earlier he had claimed that he "had no detailed information" about the matter, he was soon contradicted by Robert McFarlane, his former national security advisor, in testimony before the Iran-*contra* Committee of the Congress. Whereupon Reagan did a breathtaking about-face. Sure, he said, the whole thing "was my idea to begin with"; the hearings were producing nothing "I didn't know about." (One suspects that George Bush could have said the same thing.)

This was serious stuff indeed. As Elizabeth Drew observed: "If a White House can decide that a law passed by Congress is inconvenient, and simply set out to circumvent it, then our constitutional system is finished."[100]

But the counterattack failed. What went wrong?

Part of the answer is tactical. The White House set loose a mechanical rabbit called Reagan-didn't-know-about-the-diversion-of-funds. Like a frenzied pack of greyhounds, members of the committee raced off in mad pursuit. Somehow they never quite caught it. Meanwhile, the larger issue got lost in the dust.

But a more basic reason was that times had changed. The script had received a rewrite. The good guys were now the bad guys. In 1973, it was the forces of reason and rectitude against the California mafia, with their flattops and five-o'clock shadows. Now it was the People against the Eastern Elite.*

It all became clear at the hearings. There was John Nields, Yale and Penn, counsel for the House, looking like a yuppie Ichabod Crane. There was Arthur Liman, Harvard and Yale, counsel for the Senate, speaking in the sort of outer-borough brogue that the rest of the country always calls a "New York accent" (which as far as the rest of the country is concerned is not a particularly good thing to have). And there was Oliver North, the All-American Boy.**

David Denby, film critic for *New York* magazine, described his impressions of North in an article for *The New Republic:*

> The movie antecedents are not just Gary Cooper and Henry Fonda, but, more centrally, James Stewart. Especially Stewart the small-town idealist in *Mr. Smith Goes to Washington,* the hick who almost falls victim to the capital's cynicism but triumphs in the end, his victory urged on and celebrated by a storm of telegrams. More than once, North was on the verge of dissolving into tears, as Stewart had, but valiantly he held back. John Wayne is there as well in the swaggering touches, the almost masochistic readiness to suffer, endure, die.
>
> But most of all, North is a chip off the old block. The model is not so much Ronald Reagan the star of *Kings Row* as it is Reagan the President. The superbly timed catch in the voice, the mixture of truculence and maudlin self-pity; the anecdotal view of world politics ... it is Ronnie all over.[101]

And in the end, Reagan reigned—the most popular president since polls began. He personified the triumph of many things, of

* In the 1984 Republican primary in Massachusetts, Elliot Richardson, one of the heroes of Watergate, had been soundly defeated by a man named Raymond Shamie. As the *Times* assessed the vote: "The Massachusetts party had long been dominated by moderate to liberal Republicans, often from aristocratic backgrounds, like Henry Cabot Lodge. Mr. Shamie, who founded his own high-technology company, the Metal Bellows Corporation, represents the Sun Belt brand of Republicanism come to Massachusetts, with its calls for no new taxes, its religious overtones and its frequent assertions of patriotism." Said a Richardson supporter: "Elliot was the last of an era."[102]

** Incidentally, North's former secretary, the famous Fawn Hall, now works for a Hollywood talent agency.

course: California, Hollywood, the politics of illusion. But most of all he was Exhibit A in the case for the apotheosis of the average man.

All of this was supposed to change with the 1988 campaign. For the Republicans, George Herbert Walker Bush: vice-president of the United States; son of the late senator Prescott Bush, who was Skull and Bones at Yale; himself a product of Greenwich Country Day School, Andover, and Skull and Bones at Yale.* For the Democrats, Michael S. Dukakis: governor of Massachusetts; son of a graduate of Harvard Med School; himself a graduate of Swarthmore and Harvard Law.

Although Bush was the more patrician of the candidates, Dukakis was clearly the smarter. Either way, the country was in for a rather high-minded election: two intelligent, moderate, well-educated men, both of them serious about the function of government, discussing the major issues of the day.

But of course things didn't work out that way. They didn't work out that way at all.

George Herbert Walker Bush was not really a New England politician, to be sure. Early on, like Teddy Roosevelt, he had opted for a spell out west. But unlike Roosevelt, Bush remained essentially the Eastern dude. (After being elected president, comparing himself to Roosevelt, Bush remarked: "I'm an Oyster Bay kind of guy.") In the 1980 primaries, wrote Theodore White, "His steering committees in the key states came of the best people; 'they looked,' said someone, 'as if they'd been picked from the Harvard and Yale crew rosters of the past 20 years'. . . . And Bush disdained, as a gentleman, any cultivation of the hard-rock primitives, so large a part of the Republican revival. As a civilized person, he could not, or would not, court the Moral Majority, the right-to-life movement, the National Rifle Association."[103]

But Bush ran up against Ronald Reagan, who did not disdain any

* The counterpart to Harvard's Porcellian Club, Skull and Bones lists among its members and former members: President William Howard Taft, Senator Robert Taft, Henry Stimson, Averell Harriman, Potter Stewart and William and McGeorge Bundy.

of those things. Nor did he disdain the quick one-liner. "I'm paying for this microphone," he said in New Hampshire. (A spontaneous remark? No, it came from a movie, *State of the Union.*) "Not until 48 hours later, watching television," wrote Teddy White, "did I realize that Ronald Reagan had won the Republican nomination, hands down, right there in the Nashua High School."[104]

Bush suffered other indignities in New Hampshire. According to Kevin Phillips, he was "savaged (in an effort at the time encouraged by Reagan lieutenants) for his connections with David Rockefeller's Trilateral Commission."[105]

In 1980, Bush ran a reasonable, gentlemanly, Eastern campaign. He would not make the same mistake again.

For the 1988 effort, he hired the services of a media consultant named Roger Ailes, who had first gained notoriety in *The Selling of the President,* Joe McGinniss's classic account of the 1968 Nixon campaign. (In the book, Ailes is the source of the famous description of Nixon: "Now you put him on television, you've got a problem right away. He's a funny-looking guy. He looks like somebody hung him in a closet overnight and he jumps out in the morning with his suit all bunched up and starts running around saying, 'I want to be President.' "[106] Needless to say, Ailes is more circumspect today.)

Later on, Ailes had coached Reagan for his second debate with Mondale, and had handled the advertising for Dan Quayle's 1986 Senate re-election campaign. (Later still, he would persuade George Bush to add Dan Quayle to the ticket.)

As Paul Taylor observed in a *Washington Post* article called "Pigsty Politics": "What Ailes and his colleagues do for a living is help candidates get elected by calibrating what sells and what doesn't in the political marketplace. They have discovered—through decades of polling, ad testing, focus group interviewing, and trial and error in creating television commercials—that the traffic will bear a good deal more than they had once believed: more attacks, more distortions, more contrivances, more trivia, more half-truths."[107]

One thing that Ailes and others advised Bush to do was to try to take advantage of the campaign's surprisingly populist tone. As political writer William Schneider explained the phenomenon: "anti-establishment feeling in the American electorate is very nearly inexhaustible."[108] Thus, aristocratic Albert Gore—satirized in "Doonesbury" as "Albert, Prince of the Tennessee Valley"—was reduced to crying: "My family's *never* been accused of being aristocratic. I shoveled *pig manure* on a regular basis."[109]

Bush followed much the same course. He recalled that "I am a man who 40 years ago threw everything he had into the back of a Studebaker and tooled out to West Texas"—as though he had been some destitute Okie striking out for California. He let it be known that he was extremely fond of pork rinds and country music. He drove eighteen-wheelers and fork-lifts. Punched people in the shoulder. Talked tough ("read my lips"). He disowned the word *patrician* ("I don't even know what it means; I'll have to look it up.") When photographers appeared at Kennebunkport, Bush's aides insisted they aim their cameras away from the rocky shoreline. Rocks, said the aides, looked "elitist."

In other words, it was the Log Cabin Campaign all over again. Or in the words of Kevin Phillips: "It was the ultimate triumph of the populist revolution in Republican politics. Here we have the nation's leading preppy—an ornament and offspring of the Establishment—winning as a barefoot populist."[110]

Nearly as surprising was what Bush did to Dukakis. Bush managed to portray this son of Greek immigrants as the leader of the "liberal elite." His policy ideas, said Bush, had been "born in Harvard Yard's boutique" (whatever *that* might be). In a stump speech in California's Central Valley, Bush again invoked the *H* word: "You shouldn't have people from Harvard telling you that you can't own guns."

Bush's greatest advantage, however, was his role as heir to Ronald Reagan; and in many ways, the Bush campaign resembled very closely the Reagan White House. The message was doled out in daily "themes," by means of photo opportunities (the most famous of course being Bush's visit to a flag factory). And in order to ensure that the candidate did not actually *say* anything—thereby "stepping on the message"—he was carefully shielded from the press.

Finally, there were Roger Ailes's ads—on such weighty national matters as furloughs and flags. Campaign manager Lee Atwater, a good ol' boy from South Carolina, offered no apologies. The message, he said, was "an emotional, populist appeal to traditional values."[111] At the same time, the terms in which the message was couched did much to produce, in the words of Paul Taylor of the

Washington Post, "an election year that featured more negative television advertising than ever before in the 36 years that televised commercials have been part of the political landscape."[112] For this, Roger Ailes was unrepentant. "There are three things that get covered," he said. "Visuals, attacks and mistakes. You try to avoid mistakes and give them as many attacks and visuals as you can."[113]

There was another reason for such measures. The great mass of voters swallowed them hook, line and sinker. In a statement that sounds like an eerie echo of Clem Whitaker's dictum of sixty years ago, Republican consultant Charles Black remarks: "We have adapted ourselves to the voters. They have a short attention span. They don't follow government and politics every day—they don't want to. They won't sit around the kitchen table and read the two parties' platforms. They want things put simply."[114]

This political laziness was encouraged by the way the campaign—like all campaigns—was covered by the media, especially television. In interviewing potential voters—the cracker-barrel scene in a small midwestern town, a favorite television device—reporters simply asked them their opinions on this and that. There was never a suggestion that opinions should be based on information. An individual's feelings were all that mattered, and these were deemed to be mighty important.

"A lot of people are wondering why the candidates never talked about the issues," wrote William Schneider in the *Los Angeles Times.* "Here's why: the voters didn't want to hear it."[115]

"My work suggests that most people can only conceptualize politics in simple, personal terms," says Ann Crigler, a professor of political science at USC and a specialist on mass media in political campaigns. "They can't manage abstract ideas. In-depth interviews suggest that no matter how much people may complain about negative commercials, they remember them and believe them, especially if the other side fails, as the Democrats have this time, to counter with slogan-like thoughts of their own."[116]

Ah yes, the other side; the Dukakis campaign. Sequestered in Boston, writing position papers, its members didn't understand until far too late the visceral, populist appeal of "issues" such as the Pledge of Allegiance and prison furloughs. In many ways, they were running a campaign like that of Bush in 1980, only less effective. (None of them came up with an epithet half as funny as "voodoo economics.") As Boston's Ellen Goodman observed prophetically in early April: "the governor's weakness might be . . . his deep, even irrational, belief in reason."[117]

It was, in the end, a dreadful election—"The Dirty Campaign," read the headline of an editorial in the *Los Angeles Times;*[118] "An Embarrassing Campaign," read that of an editorial in the *Washington Post;*[119] "a terrible election year," John Chancellor called it;[120] "This low, dishonest campaign," wrote George F. Will.

In his *Washington Post* article called "Pigsty Politics", Paul Taylor wrote:

> Many consultants expect the boundaries [of taste] to be driven still lower in 1990 and 1992, as they and their colleagues scramble to come up with the best spinoffs of the hardball campaign that Bush's team of consultants threw at Michael S. Dukakis. Campaigns in this regard are much like TV series—a hit one season spawns imitators the next.
>
> "In a way, Roger Ailes has done the whole industry a favor," said [Democratic pollster Paul] Maslin. "Because from now on, candidates are going to be more convinced than ever that they need to hire a consultant who can really . . . nail the other guy."
>
> Similarly, Maslin says, the more that political campaigns are waged as a rat-a-tat-tat of distorted, 30-second charges and countercharges, the more cynical and disbelieving the viewing public becomes. And that raises the threshold for grabbing their attention. "Unless you jolt them, you won't get results," Maslin says.
>
> "Jolting" apolitical voters hasn't meant engaging them in a discussion of the deficit, national defense, the savings and loan and nuclear waste crises or any of the other issues that politicians confront once in office. Increasingly, it has meant finding "hot button" issues that are more accessible to the voters' daily lives, more personality-oriented, more entertaining.[122]

Other recent developments on the political scene are having much the same effect—to wit, the democratization of politics. Take the proliferation of presidential primaries, for example.

In 1980, Teddy White described presidential primaries as "the madness of a good idea run wild."[123] Since then the madness has only increased. Here's how Paul Taylor of the *Washington Post* assessed the scene in 1987:

> It's now been 18 years and four elections since Democratic Party reformers set about to transfer power in the nomination process

from the bosses to the masses. What they wanted was more democracy, small "d".

They got it. The jerry-built system of direct election primaries and caucuses they concocted is unlike anything practiced anywhere else in the world. It was born of fine intentions, and it still has much to recommend it. It gives play to an egalitarianism (everybody gets a chance to be President) and an anti-elitism (in theory, nobody but the people now choose their leaders) that are at the core of our political culture. It forces the candidates to learn the country (though they invariably wind up better versed in the folkways of Des Moines than Detroit).

But it also contains a set of tail-wags-dog distortions that grow more baroque with each passing election. It has created a new class of politicians who demonstrate their good sense by not running for President.[124]

The obstacles, as Taylor and others point out, are many. For one thing, the primary and caucus season now extends across dozens of states and several years. Financing this effort requires a great deal of fund-raising from people who by law are allowed to contribute only $1,000 apiece. That takes more time—lots of time. "In 1968," writes Taylor, "the last election for which the old rules were still in force, the winning Democratic nominee declared for the presidency 121 days before his party's convention. In 1984, the winning Democratic nominee announced his candidacy 511 days before."[125]

But the actual time required is much longer. "For four years," recalls Walter Mondale, "that's all I did. I mean, all I did. That's all you think about. That's all you talk about. That's who you're around. That's your schedule."[126]

The result is that we now draw our Presidents exclusively from the ranks of the ambitious unemployed. That's where we got Nixon, Carter, Reagan, and Bush. (Of course Bush was vice-president, but that doesn't count.)

The pool of potential presidents is reduced still further by the nature of the primary campaigns themselves. After all, what serious-minded, literate, statesmanlike person wants to spend several years sleeping in Holiday Inns, eating rubber chicken, wooing local activists and swilling cups of coffee with Iowa farmers, knowing all the while that every detail of his personal life is being pawed through by a press that is now prepared to gratify the public's

126

ravenous appetite for sexual titillation, while thereby imposing a standard of "morality" more appropriate to the election of a deacon in Peoria?

"The process puts a premium on sitting in someone's living room and being a pleasant fellow," says Austin Ranney, a political science professor at Berkeley. "But that isn't what a President is supposed to do."[127] Most of all, of course, it puts a premium on televised performance. "Primary and caucus voters," writes William Schneider, "have never shown much inclination to vote for professionalism."[128] Adds Flora Lewis: "The qualifications for success as a candidate and success in office have diverged dramatically."[129]

In theory, this gap was going to be narrowed somewhat by televised debates; but as often happens, the reform had unintended consequences. "The debate schedule quickly got out of control," wrote Andrew Rosenthal in the *New York Times,* "with invitations from obscure groups in much of the nation. 'It was a little like the Sixties, when people said, "Gee, primaries are great; why don't we have more of them," ' said David Keene, a senior advisor to Senator Bob Dole of Kansas. 'Before you knew it, we were up to our necks in primaries.' "[130] As a result, few people watched very many of the debates, which soon degenerated into efforts to produce "sound bites" for the network newscasts. (In one "debate," George Bush stole the show, in a sound-bite sense, by saying: "To hear the Democrats wringing their hands about all that's wrong—I'm sorry; I'm depressed. I want to switch over and watch 'Jake and the Fatman.' " Actually, Bush had never seen "Jake and the Fatman." The line was supplied by his media man, Roger Ailes. Ailes was very good at sound bites.)

The verdict on primaries, then, is not encouraging. Historian James MacGregor Burns writes that the United States has "the worst system of top leadership selection in the Western world."[131] Looking back on the period from the death of Kennedy through the election of Reagan, Teddy White beheld "a parade of Presidents almost as discouraging as the clowns' pageant that ran from Grant to McKinley."[132]

Several observers, therefore, argue that the primary system is in need of considerable reform. Both Walter Mondale and the *New York Times* favor a system that would begin with small-state contests, as now, but with different states chosen for each election. These early contests would then be followed by a series of regional primaries from late March to the middle of June.

Such a system, while more "rational," no doubt, would still be demanding and costly. Which is why several other observers—including John Chancellor, James Reston, Newton Minow, Stewart Udall and James MacGregor Burns—argue for a return to the old method of choosing nominees by open party convention. In the words of Chancellor: "Abolish the primaries. The United States is the only democracy that holds primary elections to choose candidates for the highest national office. No other country allows its leaders to be chosen in a series of roll-the-dice contests that depend more on mass marketing than on rational discourse."[133]

And the public? By three to one, the public favors the primary—a *national* primary. It has favored one, in fact, since the question was first asked by the Gallup Poll in 1952. Needless to say, a national primary would embody virtually all the problems of the present system, writ very, very large.

At the moment, though, the *real* example of "the madness of a good idea run wild" is not the American primary system. It is the California system of "direct democracy," in the form of the initiative and referendum. What's more, the system shows renewed signs of spreading to the rest of the country.

It all began with Proposition 13, the tax-cutting initiative passed in 1978. (The following year, California voters also passed Proposition 4, which placed tight restrictions on government spending. In the wake of Proposition 13, at least fourteen other states adopted tax-limiting measures, the best-known of these being Massachusetts's Proposition 2½.)* But eventually, of course, the flurry subsided, and most people probably assume that despite the dire warnings of government officials, everything has worked out fine. Most people are wrong.

In 1983, five years after the tax revolt began, the *Los Angeles Times* published a lengthy series of articles describing its effects. At the conclusion of the series, the editors of the *Times* (as editors like to

---

* Initiatives are allowed in twenty-six states, mainly in the West. Massachusetts is thus an exception.

do) wrote an editorial summarizing its findings. Referring to deterioration in everything from schools and libraries to parks and
roads to police and fire departments, the editorial warned of "the
slow rot of California's present" and "the wreckage of its future."
"The worst," it said, "is yet to come."[134] Ten days after the editorial
appeared, the school district of San Jose, capital of Silicon Valley,
declared itself bankrupt. (The final irony: only about a third of the
tax savings from Proposition 13 went to the average homeowner,
the foot soldier in the crusade to pass the measure. Nearly all the
rest went to business, including such mammoth corporations as
Chevron. But of course this is what happens when voters pass
judgment on Byzantine measures the implications of which they
cannot begin to comprehend.)

In 1986, journalist Peter Schrag (who is also associate editor of
the *Sacramento Bee*) wrote an article on California for *The New
Republic*. "In the early sixties," said Schrag, "when California surpassed New York as the largest state in the nation, thousands of
journalists came out to wonder at it, and to lavish the place with
sunbaked hyperbole about the future." And now? "California,
which was once regarded as a leader among states in progressive
government, public education, and social service, is now not much
better than average. . . . something important is . . . being lost, and
that loss is deeply regrettable, not only for California but for the
country whose future California once was. Things better work
here, Joan Didion said, 'because here, beneath that immense
bleached sky, is where we run out of continent'. . . . in settling for
average or just better than average, the state denies both itself and
the country the sense of greater possibilities it so long
represented."[135]

In 1988, ten years after the passage of Proposition 13, the *Los
Angeles Times* published another editorial assessment. The effects,
it said, had been "disastrous."

> The structure of government has been undermined. California's
> sense of community and social fabric are being torn apart. The
> economy is riddled with hidden costs. . . . Ten years ago the first
> reductions hit such local programs as libraries and parks. Now they
> have cut into the muscle of public services statewide: education,
> highways, mass transit. . . . A united California used to plan and

build for the future and for excellence. Today a fractured California fails to cope even with the growth that it has.[136]

In Shasta County, north of Sacramento, officials closed the county hospital and all nine branches of the public library.

And did all this prompt any popular misgivings, any second thoughts about the wisdom of "direct democracy"? Nope. In the 1988 general election, California voters were faced with twenty-nine state propositions, several of staggering complexity.* Peter Schrag wrote a *New Republic* article called "Initiative Madness," describing "an eruption of initiatives that is rapidly crippling representative government."[137]

In San Francisco, the situation was even worse: the number of state *and local* measures came to fifty-four. Officials worried that glassy-eyed citizens might violate a state law prohibiting anyone from spending more than ten minutes in the voting booth. Of course, a voter could bone up beforehand by studying the official San Francisco Voter Information Pamphlet, *plus* the official California Ballot Pamphlet—a total of 350 pages of solid type.

The notion that the average voter would master all this was obviously absurd. California had finally fulfilled the description suggested several years earlier by the chief of the *Los Angeles Times's* Sacramento bureau: it had become "a participatory nightmare."[138]

Not according to the participants, however. A poll conducted in March of 1989 found that 73 percent of California residents like the initiative system just fine. When respondents were asked what they disliked about the process, the largest group—44 percent—couldn't think of anything at all.

Meanwhile, across the country, the number of initiative and referendum measures is again on the rise. In 1988, there were a total of 176, the most since 1982.

Use of the initiative and referendum, however, is merely the most salient example of a far more pervasive phenomenon: the rise of

---

* The most notable measure to pass was Proposition 103, which provided for an eye-popping 20 percent rollback in insurance rates for autos, houses and many types of businesses. Since then, however, the measure has been partially nullified by the California Supreme Court, which held that insurance companies must still be allowed a reasonable rate of return.

"plebiscitary democracy."[139] As Jeffrey Abramson, Christopher Arterton and Gary Orren point out in a recent book called *The Electronic Commonwealth,* it is this phenomenon that has characterized American politics in the twentieth century.

Kevin Phillips makes much the same point:

> One of the more intriguing—and so far least understood phenomena in Republicanism and New Right populist conservatism is the extent to which advanced communications technology is being used by both to pursue an increasingly plebiscitary politics. By this I mean five particular new practices and biases: First, we can see growing emphasis on the presidency as a vehicle to get the attention of the public and mobilize the electorate . . . second, we can see unprecedented mobilization of grass-roots communications and voter support to pressure senators, congressmen . . . third, we can note mushrooming and massive use of direct mail for issue agitation and fund raising; fourth, we can see a growing philosophic embrace of plebiscitary mechanisms. . . . Jack Kemp and his "tax revolt" allies have called for adoption of a national initiative-and-referendum mechanism; and fifth, we can see GOP strategists making specific use of initiative and referendum as an ideological and institutional tool. . . . in states like California. . . . I think that this trend is enormously important. Moreover, there is nothing conservative about it in the traditional sense, and New Right populist conservatives are among the strongest proponents of the plebiscitary approach.[140]

This approach, though, does not depend solely, or even primarily, upon the specific mechanisms to which Phillips refers. For in a sense, we live in a plebiscitary democracy all the time. As *The New Republic* pointed out in an editorial called "The Electronic Plebiscite":

> The most striking feature of the system of electronic plebiscitary democracy is direct, continuous, highly intense communication between Presidents (and would-be Presidents) at one end, and scores of millions of people at the other. The politicians reach the people via television; the people reach the politicians via polls.[141]

This relationship is growing in many ways. On the politicians' side, for example, candidates in the 1988 presidential primaries often used satellite hook-ups to take their message directly to local

131

television stations across the country—thereby evading the "elite" network monitors in New York and Washington. Richard Gephardt, sitting in Austin, Texas, was able to grant "exclusive" five-minute interviews, in turn, to local stations in El Paso and Lubbock; Presque Isle, Maine; Lake Charles, Louisiana; Augusta, Georgia; and Tulsa, Oklahoma. The cost to Gephardt: $2,000.

On the citizens' side of the relationship—that is, the polling side—things have also been getting more interesting.

• Paul Taylor of the *Washington Post* describes a technique used in the White House during Reagan's second term:

> Every time the president gave a televised speech or news conference during the past four years, his pollster, Richard Wirthlin, would assemble a focus group somewhere in the country and hook them up with "people meters"—little dials they could turn to register a running commentary of approval or disapproval.
>
> The next day, Wirthlin would give the White House a chart that looked like an electrocardiogram—marking down to the word, the gesture and split second, exactly what had and hadn't worked the night before. Phrases that drew positive responses were repeated by Reagan in speech after speech; the turnoffs were discarded.[142]

• George Bush's television commercials—the famous flag-and-furlough campaign—were also produced with the aid of focus groups. Thus, the eventual audience for those spots saw not so much the candidate's positions as its own emotions reflected back at itself. Which is what plebiscitary democracy really is.

• For major politicians, polling is becoming a virtually nonstop affair, especially during a campaign. And the polling itself is becoming highly sophisticated. For example, telephone poll-takers use something called CATI—computer-assisted telephone interviewing. The questions to be asked are flashed on a computer screen; the respondent's answers are fed into the same computer. Additional questions are then determined by what the respondent initially says. Inappropriate questions are skipped over, and a much greater depth of information is obtained.

• In the future, plebiscites may well be conducted by means of "interactive" television systems. Cable subscribers punch a button on a hand-held console, which instantly transmits their opinion on a given issue—Star Wars, a tax raise—to a central computer. Moments later, results of the plebiscite are flashed onto television screens in houses across the country, including, presumably, the White House. When that happens, representative government will more or less cease to exist.

A taste of what may lie in store was recently provided by the issue of a congressional pay raise. The issue involved considerably more than the pay raise itself. One of the scandals of Congress is the fact that members regularly accept "honoraria" for speaking before various interest groups—munitions makers, savings-and-loan executives, what-have-you. Amounting to $10 million a year, these payments are not made in the form of campaign contributions; they go directly into the members' pockets.

Thus the recent understanding, agreed to by the leaders of both parties in both houses. The members would get their pay raise. In return, they would give up the honoraria.

It all made a lot of sense—until the issue was suddenly seized by the nation's radio talk-show hosts (the new arbiters of plebiscitary democracy), who banded together to launch an attack. Immediately the issue became a simple matter of Congress planning to gorge itself at the public trough. Capitol Hill was inundated with letters of protest, many containing tea bags, which the radio jocks had suggested their listeners send along to remind their representatives of the Boston Tea Party.

It was an exercise in mass stupidity. Or as David Broder put it—"cockeyed populism. . . . know-nothing demagoguery."[143]

Congress, nonetheless, capitulated.

"The French, under the old monarchy," wrote Tocqueville in *Democracy in America,* "held it for a maxim that the king could do no wrong. . . . The Americans entertain the same opinion with respect to the majority."

5

California Dreamin':
Democratization
and the
American Mind

> The public has long since cast off its cares. The people that
> once bestowed commands, consulships, legions and all else, now
> meddles no more and longs eagerly for just two things—Bread
> and Circuses.
>
> —Juvenal, *Tenth Satire*[1]

THE FINAL QUESTION to be raised in Part I is whether democratization has adversely affected American culture. In an effort
to shed some light on the question, we'll take a look at three of the
country's socio-cultural institutions—the theater, publishing (both
books and magazines) and television news. In addition, we'll examine some recent developments in movies and television entertainment (those two great engines of democratization) to see what
may lie in the future.

To be sure, the sort of question we're raising is not new. During
certain periods in Western history, it has seemed almost a preoccupation. In Periclean Athens, for example, opinion was somewhat
divided as to the likely effects of democratization, but democracy
did not fare any too well. Socrates was none too keen on the notion,
and Plato argued that "the many" are generally irrational. Both
believed that democracy was merely a way station (and a rather low
one at that) on the inevitable decline from aristocracy to tyranny.

In a modern sense, the idea that democratization means cultural
decline arose mainly in response to the mass production and mass
consumption of nineteenth-century industrialism. Often the response came from artists, adumbrating the reaction of twentieth-

century artists to even newer technologies (such as television). Wordsworth, for example, expressed horror at the appearance of *The Illustrated London News*—"Avaunt this vile abuse of pictured page! Must eyes be all in all, the tongue and ear nothing? Heaven keep us from a lower stage"[2]—while Flaubert vociferated: "Let us cry against imitation silk, desk chairs, economy kitchens, fake materials, fake luxury, fake pride. Industrialism has developed the ugly to gigantic proportions"[3]

The really lasting condemnations, however, came from critics who made a virtual career of Cassandraism. Nietzsche bewailed the death of tragedy, the "herd instinct" and "socialist dolts and flat-heads," and decided that Wagner (whom most Americans regard, of course, as very high culture indeed) was the worst sort of mass-cult charlatan. Oswald Spengler in 1918 foresaw *The Decline of the West* in "Caesarism" growing out of "Megapolitanism": great world-cities weakened from within by a rootless, valueless, urban under-class, "cohering unstably in fluid masses," its members "utterly matter-of-fact," "parasitical," "ready for anything."[4] Jose Ortega y Gasset, writing during the rise of Franco, Hitler, Mussolini and Stalin, observed: "The characteristic of the hour is that the commonplace mind, knowing itself to be commonplace, has the assurance to proclaim the rights of the commonplace and to impose them wherever it will."[5]

Like Ortega, T. S. Eliot believed that culture could be transmitted only by an educated elite, and as far as Eliot was concerned, the eliter the better. Also like Ortega, Eliot was skeptical of the value of mass education: "Whether education can foster and improve culture or not, it can surely adulterate and degrade it. For there is no doubt that in our headlong rush to educate everybody, we are lowering our standards, and more and more abandoning the study of those subjects by which the essentials of our culture—of that part of it which is transmissible by education—are transmitted; destroying our ancient edifices to make ready the ground upon which the barbarian nomads of the future will encamp in their mechanized caravans."[6]

In referring to barbarians, Eliot was echoing a refrain that was sung by all such critics: that the present precipitous decline (whenever the present might be) was to greater or lesser degree a reca-pitulation of the decline and fall of the Roman Empire. There were other geographical references as well. Often such critics seemed to feel that decline emanated from the west. "Mechanization," Baude-laire complained, has "thoroughly Americanized us,"[7] a complaint that his countrymen have been making in various forms ever since. (Oddly enough, as we shall see in the section on television, the complaints are subsiding as Americanization is making its final assault.) A more modern critic, Pitirim Sorokin, suggested in the 1940s that America might play Rome to Europe's Greece.

Cultural warning flags have gone up on this side of the water as well. In a 1944 essay entitled "A Theory of Popular Culture," Dwight Macdonald described the spread of a counterfeit culture among the masses. Unlike Ortega and Eliot, however, Macdonald regarded the masses mainly as victims: "Mass Culture is imposed from above. . . . The Lords of kitsch, in short, exploit the cultural needs of the masses in order to make a profit and/or to maintain their class rule."[8]

A different note is sounded in the recent broadside from Allan Bloom. In *The Closing of the American Mind* (a disingenuous title to which we'll return in Part II), Bloom takes the measure of the current crop of college students and finds them wanting—unacquainted with books and narcotized by rock music, which Professor Bloom likens to "a non-stop . . . masturbational fantasy."[9] (My goodness.) Such failings Bloom blames mainly (as did critic Hilton Kramer, several years earlier) on the sixties, and on the universities for caving in to their values.

There are, to be sure, some critics on the other side of this dirty little question—John Dewey, Herbert Gans, Irving Howe. In an essay entitled "Toward an Open Culture," Howe states his case as follows:

> Democratic cultures move ahead, or perhaps only move along, through internal struggle: the struggle of classes, ethnic groups, literary schools, and popular audiences. We should be honest enough to admit that this can lead to a momentary decline or even, in some respects, a permanent decline in cultural standards. There is no inevitable upward progression in cultural any more than in political life, and there may even be—a thought which surely haunts all democrats—an inverse relationship between cultural and political progress. Still, as one looks back upon the cultural struggles in America these past two centuries—the Emersonians against the Brahmins, the realists in fiction against the genteel writers, the crude immigrants against the nativists, the avant-garde modernists against

academic traditionalists—it seems that the price of change was usually worth paying. Or that it simply *had* to be paid. Through cultural
conflicts both revealing and masking social conflicts, the deprived
and neglected would assert their claims upon a culture that, in
principle, announced its readiness to embrace all humanity.[10]

It is impossible, of course, to resolve this sort of complex cultural
debate (at least in a book as broadly focused as this one). What *is*
possible, however, is to examine some socio-cultural precincts—
theater, publishing, television news—in which democratization has
clearly led to cultural decline, or at least shows promise of doing so.
But first, some general observations.

Whatever the precise condition of American culture, several of
its vital signs are tracing erratic patterns on the societal oscilloscope.
In 1984, a Louis Harris survey found that more Americans were
attending arts events than ever before. "The basic news," Mr.
Harris observed at a press conference in New York, "is that live
attendance at arts presentations continues to grow, despite the fact
that many have proclaimed that ours has become a culture dominated by the electronic media, especially television. The arts are a
real, positive thing in a time when all you have is bad news and
stress."[11]

In truth, however, the art news was somewhat less positive than
that. Although attendance at arts events was indeed on the rise, it
was growing at a slower rate than it had before. Theater attendance, for example, had grown by 12 percent between 1975 and
1980, but by only 3 percent between 1980 and 1984.

By 1988, the positive news had virtually vanished. Attendance at
dance events was down 14 percent; at the theater, down 25 percent;
at classical and pop concerts, down 26 percent; and at opera and
musical theater, down 38 percent. (The only artistic exception was
museum attendance, which rose by 24 percent, probably because of
the number of new museums that had recently opened their doors.)

How to explain these dramatic declines? One reason given by the
Harris organization was the decrease in per capita leisure time,
from about eighteen hours a week in 1984 to seventeen hours in
1987. But this explanation becomes less convincing when one
discovers that leisure time dropped by the same amount between
1980 and 1984, during a period when attendance at the arts was still
growing.

A much more persuasive explanation, as Mr. Harris concedes, is the rapid rise in the ownership of video cassette recorders. Such ownership grew from about 3 percent of the population in 1980, to 17 percent in 1984, to 55 percent in 1988. Paradoxically, this growth did not produce a decline in movie attendance, as many had predicted. Between 1984 and 1988, attendance at movies rose by 9 percent. The only losses, apparently, were felt by the performing arts.

Some of those losses have been severe indeed. Nowhere were they more apparent than in the life (and death) of the symphony orchestra, traditionally the center of musical culture in American cities (as opposed, say, to German cities, where musical life revolves around the opera company). Although the American Symphony Orchestra League reports that attendance increased during the first half of the decade (from 22.8 million concertgoers in 1980 to 25.4 million in 1985), by 1988, attendance had declined to 23.6 million. Two-thirds of the League's eighty largest symphonies ended the season in debt, with an aggregate net deficit of $10 million (compared to only $500,000 six years earlier).

Orchestras actually called it quits in New Orleans, Oakland, Nashville and Vancouver, B.C. (as did ballet companies, by the way, in Chicago and Dallas). Although those in New Orleans and Oakland have since been revived (at least for now), there is still a long list of cities with orchestras in trouble: Detroit, Columbus, Rochester, Denver, Houston, Honolulu, San Diego, San Antonio and so on.

Part of the trouble lies in the period of orchestral expansion that began soon after World War II and continued right through the sixties and seventies. In 1960, there were 42 orchestras classified by the league as professional; by 1984, there were 166, with the major growth occurring in the Sunbelt. The only problem was that many of these cities, anxious for the trappings of "culture," had failed to face up to what is required to support a symphony orchestra. "There just isn't a history out here of giving in general, and to the symphony in particular," says Richard Contee, managing director of the Phoenix Symphony, which is also in debt.[12]

Meanwhile, in cities across the country, symphonies were losing their social cachet, and with it their traditional subscription audiences. They responded, quite naturally, by going in search of replacements. Marketing research became very big, and promotions took on a jazzy, insistent tone. "It is hard not to hear in such promotions," wrote Will Crutchfield in the *New York Times,* "a suggestion that symphonic music is enjoyable in something of the same way that prime-time television, popular movies and sports are enjoyable."[13]

In Denver, the suggestion was not nearly so subtle. Members of the orchestra (who recently took a 20 percent cut in pay to save the symphony from bankruptcy) donned blazing orange Bronco T-shirts to perform at a pep rally just before a Super Bowl. The following season, symphony ushers began hawking copies of a "players book" (similar to a football program), which informed the concertgoer that a particular clarinetist, say, was a rabid fisherman, or that the tympanist's favorite movie was *Apocalypse Now.* Invitations to a cocktail party, promoting a benefit foot race, were printed on pairs of boxer shorts. Despite such efforts, the symphony was forced to make still more cutbacks. The director, Phillipe Entremont, resigned.

Other promotions have been equally bizarre. Dallas running back Herschel Walker performed as a dancer with the Ft. Worth Ballet. In New Orleans, when a supermarket came to the aid of the orchestra, music director Maxim Shostakovich (son of the composer) agreed to appear in a grocery commercial.

In a similar vein, many orchestras have had to water down their programs in order to appeal to popular tastes. Thus, the orchestra has become even more of a musical museum than formerly. And despite such concessions, several major orchestras are still having trouble filling the house.

Partly as a result of all these problems (as well as many others), American orchestras have fallen far behind their European counterparts in producing orchestral recordings. And this in turn has contributed to a sort of musical malaise. Donal Henahan of the *New York Times* has pondered "the end of an orchestral tradition that survived nicely for centuries until we came along."[14] Ernest Fleischmann, executive director of the Los Angeles Philharmonic, recently pronounced the American symphony orchestra a dead institution. André Previn, the Philharmonic's music director, has since resigned.

Meanwhile, as the statement by Donal Henahan suggests, all is not well these days in cultural New York, never mind the hinterlands. Although New York will remain for the foreseeable future the cultural capital of the country, if not the Western world, in some fields, at least, its culture may well be losing ground.

One such field is music. In the words of critic Samuel Lipman, publisher of the *New Criterion:* "The performance level of major New York musical institutions seems to me low, both absolutely and relative to what goes on outside the city."[15]

High on every critic's list of troubled, major musical institutions is the New York Philharmonic, directed by Zubin Mehta. According to the *New York Times,* "many major music critics simply ignore the Philharmonic except on special occasions."[16] Several years ago, the orchestra lost its long-term recording contract with CBS. (As a sort of consolation prize, CBS suggested that the orchestra cut a record with Stevie Wonder. Mehta, miffed, declined.) "The New York Philharmonic," concludes Samuel Lipman, "is now the sick man of the American orchestral world."[17]

Recently, Mehta has submitted his resignation (effective at the end of the 1990–91 season), which poses the problem of finding a replacement. Reportedly, several major conductors have already declined the post. A further complication: Herbert von Karajan has retired as director of the Berlin Philharmonic;* and the Berlin position is more prestigious than the one in New York.

Second on the critics' list of troubled New York institutions is the Metropolitan Opera, where, writes Donal Henahan, "the strenuous business of selling familiar art to a consumer society has reached the point of creative sterility."[18] Suggestive, perhaps, of the tone of the Met these days is the fact that the institution's major benefactor is one Sybil Harrington, of Amarillo, to whom the Met recently dedicated its main auditorium. Widow of a Texas oilman, Mrs. Harrington is given to gold lamé gowns and elaborate hairdos, while her money is given to equally elaborate productions of everybody's favorites. The results of all this, argues Bernard Holland of the *Times,* "turn the Metropolitan from house of art into tourist attraction, a nice conclusion, perhaps, to a bus tour including lunch at Mama Leone's."[19]

Even some of the Met's staunchest friends concede that the institution has suffered a loss of prestige. In the words of Sherrill Milnes, perhaps the world's leading baritone: "The Met is not as important as it once was to a singer, especially a European singer,

* Karajan, of course, has since died.

looking at what is going to make a career. The big power-broker conductors—the Karajans, Mutis, Kleibers—are not here. A lot of recording used to be planned in New York; I don't think any decisions are made here now. The Met is no longer the only opera that goes on television. The glamor opera movies do not come from New York . . ."[20]

All of which is not to assert that New York is about to lose its position as music center of the Western world. It is still the place where recitalists and orchestras come to perform and be heard (and reviewed), its only real rival in this sense being London.

Nonetheless, there are those who maintain that New York's vaunted status is more apparent than real. Among these observers is Gerard Schwarz, one of the country's most talented young conductors, who at the moment serves as music director of the Seattle Symphony, the Mostly Mozart Festival at Lincoln Center and the Y Chamber Symphony of New York. Schwarz points out that New York's influence as a musical leader is exercised primarily in the United States. "Artistic leadership," he explains, "deals with the creation of new works, and it deals with significant performances, whether by individuals, orchestras, or opera companies." But today, notes Schwarz, "composers are no longer primarily living in New York."[21] And while New York's chamber groups have done very well in performing new music, "New York's major institutions have not produced the major new works in their field. If it were not for the visiting orchestras from outside New York, the major works for orchestra would not have a forum here. In opera, significant contemporary works are rarely programmed in New York by our major institutions." Schwarz also mentions that "most conductors of the new generation are not, at this time, in New York. In the field of conducting, we still look to Europe as our cultural superior . . ."[21]

General speaking, Schwarz is concerned that the weakness at the core of New York's musical culture could eventually affect the city as a whole:

The cultural vitality of New York has changed a great deal over the last two decades. I think it is very difficult for New York to be a cultural leader when some of its resident ensembles are so severely criticized. The major ensembles affect the entire cultural life of this city. If the performance of music is perceived as mediocre, unexciting, not of the highest level, then the repercussions will be negative for all of New York's performing ensembles. . . . New York has the real potential of becoming, at least in the performing areas, less significant.[22]

Other observers point out that New York's decline in the field of music has been so far concealed, ironically enough, by the presence of the media. Here again, Samuel Lipman: "Because both the electronic and print media are so powerfully concentrated here, what New York wants to sell is perforce bought, more or less irrespective of its content. This operation of a cultural Gresham's law may be seen at its most potent in the prominence of Lincoln Center institutions and personalities in the musical presentations of public television." Lipman then alludes to "the overexposure on PBS of the now sadly secondrate Philharmonic" and to "the carte blanche given the Metropolitan Opera's James Levine to be America's television *primo maestro assoluto.*"[23]

"The result of this stranglehold," he continues,

> is that we have little if any chance to see on television such great orchestras as the Cleveland and the Chicago, or such important opera companies as San Francisco or, in the summer, Santa Fe. . . .
>
> I don't think that much can be done to take from New York the national cultural primacy it has had since the decline of Boston well back in the nineteenth century; it has that primacy not because of specific achievements but because of its size and economic power. The power of New York, contrary to its critics, comes from the brute economic strength they despise. But because of that strength, there is talent here, and the money to back it, to burn. The pity of it all is that the real resources of the city, so much greater than anything in the imagining of its present detractors, could be used to lead with excellence rather than level with mediocrity. But mediocrity, I suppose, sells in a way excellence does not.[24]

There are, to be sure, some fields in which the culture of New York is still in flower. "New York leads the world in dance," writes dance critic Arlene Croce,

> and not only in the modern dance, where the strength of a native tradition has been unquestioned for 40 years; we also have the best ballet—the soundest in schooling, the most artistically distinguished—of any that currently exist. True, the creativity that pro-

duced this supremacy is past or passing. But so is the struggle for recognition which marked the careers of the older generation of American dancers. On the gifts of this generation American dance rose from penury and insignificance to the pre-eminence it now enjoys. . . . This is all new power, and in the dimming lustre of the Golden Age the future looks bright enough. At any rate, no other world capital has what New York has in dance, or the potential to acquire it.[25]

Another constellation where New York still shines is painting. "New York remains the center of attention and of attention-giving," writes arts critic Clement Greenberg. "It's where new art gets validated, for better or worse."[26] Even so, there remains the question of where the art gets produced. "In the visual arts," writes editor and critic Hilton Kramer, "the heralded new talents are today as likely to come from Germany, England, and Italy as from New York."[27]

One of the reasons, oddly enough, might be what New York painter Chuck Close describes as the city's atmosphere of "hot-house production":

New York devours art and artists. What is good for the New York art world, with its voracious need for successive crops of new talent as grist for the critical mills, is not necessarily good for individual artists. . . . The need to "make it" in such a short period of time has fostered a new and rather frantic careerism. That thinking, no matter how understandable given today's climate, doesn't allow much time for the development of a personal vision. . . . The ideal-ism of other times seems quite often to have been replaced by the necessity for a strategy. . . . the importance of having a good eye or a good hand has been replaced by the importance of having a good nose. . . . I worry about a generation of artists who feel washed up by the age of 30 or 35 if something miraculous (and spectacularly remunerative) hasn't happened to them.[28]

The importance attached to remuneration is hardly surprising, considering the astronomical costs of renting quarters these days in New York. Nor is the problem peculiar to painters. All over Man-hattan, everyone from dance instructors to theater directors is engaged in a frantic search for affordable space. For some, the search ends in places such as Brooklyn and Queens (raising the question of how far out such artists can go and still be considered "in the city"); for others, it simply ends. A few years ago, the New York School of Ballet, one of the leading institutions in the city, had to close up shop when its lease expired on its studios on the Upper West Side. Since moving into the space in 1969, the school trained students such as Cynthia Gregory and Twyla Tharp (whose own company was recently forced to merge with American Ballet Theater, partly because it was without a home). Before that, the space housed the Balanchine–Kirstein School of American Ballet, where Balanchine and Stravinsky created *Agon,* one of the great works of American dance. "I don't feel the city is a cultural center anymore," said Richard Thomas, head of the New York School of Ballet, when it closed its doors. "A cultural center is a place that nurtures and develops the artist. New York is a showcase. But it is more difficult every day for young people to come to the city as I did 40 years ago and be able to live in a dignified manner and to study and pursue a career in the arts."[29]

In many ways, New York's devotion to mammon (in the form of high rents, in this case) is understandable. A country's cultural capital is also invariably its financial capital. Thus, in Italy, the cultural capital is Milan rather than Rome; in the United States, it's New York rather than Washington (or Boston or Chicago). Nonetheless, some people feel that in New York, at least, the devotion may have been carried too far. One such person is Leon Wieseltier, a native of Brooklyn, a graduate of Columbia, Oxford and Harvard, and at present the literary editor of *The New Republic* (which is published in Washington). "The problem is not only that New York is expensive," he writes. "Many places are expensive. The problem, rather, is that New York has granted money a most undeserved cultural prestige. There used to be glamor in being brilliant but broke. No more. If you're broke, you lack local ontology. The streets of Manhattan now remind me, almost every time I traverse them, of what the streets of London said to one of Jean Rhys's crushed heroines: 'Get money, get money, get money, or forever be damned.'"[30]

That may be putting it a bit strongly, but there are those who suggest that such an atmosphere may have contributed to the decline (some say extinction) of another local institution: the New York Intellectual.

The species flourished from the thirties through the fifties, primarily in the pages of *Partisan Review*. In politics, it was Marxist (though anti-Stalinist). In culture, it was Modernist, seeking to effect what Philip Rahv called "the Europeanization of American literature."

At the same time, the group was violently opposed to American middlebrow culture, which had the effect, wrote Clement Greenberg in *Partisan Review*, of

> devaluating the precious, infecting the healthy, corrupting the honest, and stultifying the wise. . . . This culture presents a more serious threat to the genuine article than the old-time pulp dime novel, Tin Pan Alley, *Schund* variety ever has or will. Unlike the latter, which has its social limits clearly marked out for it, middlebrow culture attacks distinctions as such and insinuates itself everywhere. . . . Insidiousness is of its essence, and in recent years its avenues of penetration have become infinitely more difficult to detect and block.[31]

"The danger," added Dwight Macdonald in a classic essay called 'Masscult and Midcult,' "is that the values of Midcult, instead of being transitional—'the price of progress'—may now themselves become a debased, premanent standard."[32]

For the New York Intellectual, things fell apart in the sixties— over the war, the student revolt and the counterculture (the last two of which, you may recall, originated in San Francisco). Philip Rahv moved sharply to the left (and was eventually ousted from *Partisan Review*). Lionel Trilling, Sidney Hook, Norman Podhortez et al. moved sharply to the right.

Since then: disarray and dispersal. The conservatives—or neoconservatives, as they came to be called—swung their telescope 180 degrees: rather than looking east, toward Europe, they now peered west, across their own formerly ridiculed country. As Irving Kristol explained their mission, "It is the self-imposed assignment of neoconservatives to explain to the American people why they are right, and to the intellectuals why they are wrong."[33] Eventually, this particular group of New York Intellectuals found their champion in Ronald Reagan, who, to paraphrase Voltaire's description of the

Holy Roman Empire, is neither from New York, nor is he an intellectual.

Equally important, the intellectuals themselves are abandoning New York, mainly in favor of the university. For one thing, the gentrification of Greenwich Village has made it difficult for intellectuals to live there, while the decline of literate culture has made it difficult for them to support themselves, in the Village, the West Side or elsewhere. "The intellectual," writes James Atlas in the *New York Times Magazine,* "has gone the way of the cobbler and the smithy."[34] At the same time, the anti-Semitism that formerly barred so many of them from university teaching has largely disappeared.

The effect on New York is another matter. "The emphasis in the city's cultural life has shifted away from the production of art and ideas to their consumption as fashion," writes Thomas Bender, chairman of the history department at New York University. "Such an elevation of cultural consumption has profound implications for the meaning of the city as a center of intellectual and artistic life. It threatens to turn the metropolis into a museum of its own culture."[35]

"New York is not what it was," writes Irving Kristol.

Mind you, New York is still the national center for the arts. . . . Moreover, it will probably remain such a national center for a long while yet, because that is where the money is, and all these arts need generous subsidies as well as affluent consumers. . . . But one thing New York will *not* be: the nation's intellectual center, where "literary intellectuals" live and write and excoriate one another. It ceased being that about 20 years ago. The writers who contribute to the *New York Review of Books, Commentary,* even the *New York Times*'s Sunday magazine and book review sections live elsewhere for the most part. Established novelists are published in New York but also live elsewhere, as do our best-known poets and literary critics. Columbia and New York University are still respectable schools, but they have very few famous "intellectuals" on their faculties. That generation is without heirs. There are some survivors. But they do not constitute a community; in fact, they frequently are not on speaking terms with one another. . . . As the city with the most consumers and the most purveyors, New York retains a semblance of an intellectual center. But the reality is not there.[36]

About the time he wrote those words, Mr. Kristol decamped for Washington, where he ensconced himself at the American Enterprise Institute, one of the potent think tanks in which the city now abounds. Along with him, he took his magazine, *The Public Interest,* perhaps the leading journal of neoconservatism.

As it happens, Washington is also home to the leading magazines of neoliberalism, *The Washington Monthly* and *The New Republic* (though the latter, whose editorial office used to be in New York, has lately been veering to the right). Taken together, these isolated facts point up a trend—to wit, the degree to which Washington has usurped New York's traditional role in setting public policy.

In noting this trend, one should also note that Washington and New York are very different towns. For one thing, the former is considerably more egalitarian, a characteristic that is reflected in its publications. At *The New Republic,* editor Michael Kingsley, in the guise of columnist TRB, seldom passes up a chance to look askance at "elitism," while over at the *Monthly,* publisher Charles Peters is positively rabid on the subject of class. Recently, for example, Peters went so far as to write a cover story on "How I Was Saved from Snobbery," a condition into which, it might be added, he was never in danger of falling.

Meanwhile, democratization has also reared its head at the other new home of the New York Intellectual: the university. So far, most of the attention has centered around the so-called Great Books debate at Stanford, where a coalition of black, female and other minority students recently persuaded the faculty to drop its required course in Western Culture in favor of a set of courses which, in addition to a shorter list of works by traditional Great Thinkers, will also include books on non-European cultures, books by "women, minorities and persons of color," and at least one work each quarter explicitly addressing the issues of "race, gender and class."

The questions raised at Stanford, however, go far beyond the matter of a single course. Joseph Berger reports in the *New York Times:*

Many college professors around the country are rethinking the very notion of what is literature. . . . The radical reexamination . . . has now begun to question the very idea of literary quality and has made for the teaching of writers principally for historical and sociological importance, for what they have to say rather than how well they say it. Once honored standards like grace of style, vigor of prose and originality of expression have been downgraded or questioned while the importance of historical and social impact and rhetorical strength has grown. Courses are proliferating on popular romance, detective stories, Gothic fiction and westerns.[37]

Proponents of the new way of thinking, writes Berger, "argue that those who have usually been included in American literature . . . were largely chosen by an informal establishment strongly concentrated in Northeastern colleges, publishing companies and periodicals."[38]

Changes in the field of history have been even more sweeping. Whereas historians formerly devoted their attentions to the careers of kings and parliaments, they now examine the lives of the little people, the forgotten ones: workers, women, blacks and homosexuals. At the most recent convention of the American Historical Association, for example, panel discussions covered topics such as: "Jazz in Society and Politics," "Women's Definitions of Love throughout Western History," "Sex, Gender and the Constitution," "Black Women in the Work Force," and "Sodomy and Pederasty Among Nineteenth-Century Seafarers." In the words of Gertrude Himmelfarb, a professor of history at the Graduate Center of the City University of New York and an outspoken critic of the current trend, the new history is "history with the politics left out." (As one who spent a couple of years in a college history honors program, I can well understand a certain disenchantment with the history of kings and parliaments. But the appropriate antidote, it seems to me, is a history that encompasses the whole broad sweep of Western culture (or Eastern culture): Stravinsky and Sartre, as well as Edward VII and David Lloyd George. The current trend goes in the opposite direction, toward the mundane if not the trivial.)

On the other hand, considering the level of knowledge of today's young students, maybe it's better to keep things simple. A recent survey of 8,000 high school juniors found (in answer to a series of multiple-choice questions) that 36 percent did not know that Watergate occurred after 1950, 39 percent could not place the Constitution within the correct half-century, 43 percent did not know the approximate dates of World War I and 68 percent did not know the dates of the Civil War. (But perhaps such findings are unfair to students. In its billing for a 1985 cover story on E. L. Doctorow, the *New York Times Magazine* felt it necessary to identify the subject as a novelist. A current *Times* circulation ad offers the comforting assurance that, "You can read as much or as little as you want.")

Surveys of general literacy are equally disquieting. Although estimates differ as to the size of the problem (which is understandable, since there are varying degrees of "illiteracy"), everyone concedes that the numbers are very large. Anywhere from 20 million to 80 million adult Americans can be regarded as unable to read and write.

Yet despite all this, American culture is not entirely moribund. The problems of the symphony orchestra notwithstanding, there is still a noticeable migration of cultural activity from east to west. In Atlanta, there's the splendid new High Museum of Art, designed by Richard Meier. In Houston (one of the country's brightest showcases of modern commercial architecture), the new Wortham Theater Center houses highly rated companies of opera and ballet. In San Francisco, the opera company has long been recognized as second only to the Met, while the local ballet troupe has also ascended to the ranks of the best. Dance is making a debut as well in Los Angeles, which the Joffrey Ballet now considers its second home. In addition, Los Angeles has launched an opera company, with Placido Domingo as principal consultant (and, presumably, frequent participant, either as tenor or conductor).

But Los Angeles is making its biggest splash in the visual arts (traditional playing field of the *nouveaux riches,* in New York and Florence as well as California). At the end of 1986, the city dedicated not one but two new art museums—the Robert O. Anderson wing of the Los Angeles County Museum of Art, and the Museum of Contemporary Art, the latter designed by all-the-rage architect Arata Isozaki of Japan. (It remains to be seen, though, how well the museums will get along, since both are devoted to more or less modern art. At the time of their opening, many critics noted that MOCA may have bitten off more than it can chew.)

Meanwhile, the J. Paul Getty Trust, which already operates a museum in Malibu, is planning a new museum and fine-arts center for a 110–acre hilltop site above Brentwood. With an endowment of $2.9 billion—more than *eight* times that of New York's Metropolitan Museum of Art—the Getty Museum will be by far the richest museum in the country, if not the world.

At the same time, Los Angeles is developing a sizable number of private collectors of modern art—more than a thousand, according to the *New York Times*. As a result, many local artists (whose tribe includes such "grand old masters"—Grace Glueck's term—as Sam Francis and Richard Diebenkorn) are deciding to stay put rather than pull up stakes for the East.

But even after considering such continental cultural movement westward, one is still left with some major questions concerning the future of the arts in America. Many of them have to do with money. "For a variety of unrelated reasons," writes William H. Honan in the *New York Times,* "the three traditional financial supports of the arts—the Federal and state governments, corporations and individuals—have cut back at the same time." As a result, says Honan, "arts institutions are now financially squeezed as never before since the Federal Government first got into the business of supporting them in 1964."[39]

Although the arts community managed to defeat President Reagan's attempt to abolish the National Endowment for the Arts in 1981, federal funding since then has not kept pace with inflation. In effect, that funding has declined by 24 percent over the past eight years.

At the state level, the story has been much the same. In Massachusetts, for example, the head of a group called Citizens for Limited Taxation lambasted the state arts council as "trendy, tony, pretentious, presumptuous and elitist." Faced with a mounting government deficit, the state legislature cut the council's $19 million budget in half.

In 1987 (the most recent year for which figures are available), corporate contributions declined by 10 percent. In the words of

William S. Woodside, former chairman of Primerica Corporation and the president of the Whitney Museum: "It's becoming practically un-American for a businessman to spend time on anything but his quarterly income statement." Individual contributions, meanwhile, have been discouraged by a variety of changes in the tax laws.

The consequences of all this, writes Honan, have in many cases been "devastating." In addition to the symphonic casualties already noted, the death toll includes the Oklahoma Symphony; the Boston Shakespeare Company; the Hartman Theater Company of Stamford, Connecticut; the Mosaic Theater Company of the 92nd Street Y; and the Alaska Repertory Theater. The Arizona Theater Company will probably be next. Meanwhile, between 1986 and 1987, twenty-seven opera companies were forced to cut back their operating budgets.

To be sure, times are tough all over. Nonetheless, the United States still suffers badly in comparison with Europe. For example, in France, West Germany, Austria and the Scandinavian countries, the major opera companies receive 70 to 85 percent of their income from the government. Even in Margaret Thatcher's England, the figure for the Royal Opera House is 46 percent. In New York, the figure for the Met is 3 percent. In West Germany, the government contributes $1 billion a year to theater alone. The comparable figure for the United States is $11 million out of a total yearly budget for the National Endowment for the Arts of $170 million.

In the end, however, government funding (or the absence thereof) is merely a reflection of the larger culture—as we'll see in examining three institutions in more detail: namely, the theater, publishing (books and magazines), and television news. In addition, we'll take a brief look at movies and television entertainment.

THEATER

When the revolution that has changed the social and political state of an aristocratic people begins to penetrate into literature, it generally first manifests itself in the drama, and it always remains conspicuous there. . . . If you would judge beforehand of the literature

151

of a people that is lapsing into democracy, study its dramatic productions. . . .

At the theater, men of cultivation and of literary attainments have always had more difficulty than elsewhere in making their taste prevail over that of the people and in preventing themselves from being carried away by the latter. The pit has frequently made laws for the boxes.

—Alexis de Tocqueville,
Democracy in America[40]

The influence of the games gradually pervaded the whole texture of Roman life. One of the victims . . . was the theater. Tragedy and comedy had to compete with gladiatorial combats and chariot races for spectators, and the arena won a slow victory over the stage. Terence had audiences walk out of his plays to watch rope dancers. . . . The theaters themselves came to be used for combats and displays of wild beasts. Cruder types of dramatic entertainment, pantomime and farce, evolved partly to meet the competition of the games, and these relied heavily on stage effects . . . and other forms of sensationalism.

—Patrick Brantlinger,
Bread & Circuses[41]

When I go to Broadway, I don't recognize the audience anymore. They seem to have wandered in from an appreciation of some other art form—like Las Vegas club acts. . . . They're too easy to please. How can people be so impressed with tits and feathers?

—Hal Prince,
Harper's, August 1983

As the Broadway mega-spectacle *Starlight Express* moves toward its finale, the extravagant melange of flashing lights and moving trusses, bridges, ramps, platforms and turntables that is the show's set begins to shift and turn and rise and fall. The set's gyrations are at first puzzling, and then it becomes clear: a moment or two before the cast will take its final bows, the set is having *its* curtain call. And what could be more appropriate? This $2.5 million set, after all, is the real star of the show.

—Paul Goldberger,
The New York Times, April 12, 1987

Time was, forty or fifty years ago, when Broadway served as one of the principal focal points of the intellectual life of the country. The latest play by Eugene O'Neill, Tennessee Williams or Arthur Miller was eagerly awaited and attended, and just as avidly dissected and discussed. In addition, the Great White Way (as it was known to outsiders; it was the Stem to insiders) supported a rich agglomeration of less lofty fare—from the pens of Cole Porter, George S. Kaufman, the Gershwins, Rodgers and Hart, Jerome Kern and Oscar Hammerstein. The peak year occurred quite early—1927—when a total of 257 productions made their way through the city's 71 theaters.

Today, of course, much of that scene has disappeared. Serious drama has a tough time making a run on Broadway—where nearly half the audience is composed of tourists—while the popular fare is apt to consist of glitzy spectacles (many of them imported from London). A quick review of the past seven seasons will set the stage:

1982–83: Attendance fell by 17 percent. By the end of May, 14 of Broadway's 39 theaters were dark. Frank Rich of the *Times* called the season "a gloomy burial ground, now and then brightened by unexpected shafts of light."[42]

1983–84: Attendance slipped a bit farther, and the number of new productions declined from 49 to 36, 20 of which were commercial failures. Critical reaction was decidedly mixed. "When this season was good, it was very, very good," wrote Frank Rich. "But when it was bad, it was almost non-existent. . . . It would be gratuitous to label such admirable creations as *The Real Thing, Glengarry Glen Ross* and *Noises Off* the best new plays of the season—they were virtually the *only* new plays of the season. . . . Subtract the English imports from the 1983–84 line-up, and *Glengarry Glen Ross* [which originated in Chicago] is left as the single worthwhile new American play of the entire Broadway season."[43] Noting the dearth of "fresh American work," Benedict Nightingale complained in the *Times* of the theatergoer's "thin and watery diet" and of Broadway's "intellectual emptiness."[44]

1984–85: Attendance dropped to the lowest point in nearly a decade, and the number of new productions declined to 33—the fewest of any season this century. Because of the paucity of musicals, three Tony Award categories in that field were summarily scrapped. "Underlying the statistics," wrote Frank Rich, "is the widespread fear that the whole notion of a Broadway theater community may be a nostalgic fantasy." There were other revealing facts underneath the statistics. "It's paradoxical, not to mention alarming," Rich continued, "that Broadway's decline in attendance ... comes when the quality of serious plays is up.... Such is Broadway's state that three of the Tony-nominated best plays are currently struggling to survive."[45] Summations of the season were despairing. Frank Rich: "The New York theater is in sad shape."[46] Robert Brustein in *The New Republic:* "Broadway, once the major force in our theater culture, has gone into a coma."[47] John J. O'Connor in the *Times:* "Is Broadway dying, or even dead?"[48]

1985–86: "The Broadway theater's attrition continued unchecked," wrote Frank Rich. Describing the Tony awards as "a last-ditch attempt to rewrite the history of an arid Broadway season,"[49] he went on to note "the sorry truth that this Broadway season failed to produce the four presentable new plays required to fill the best play category." His assessment of the situation: a "hemorrhaging crisis."[50]

1986–87: Broadway began to experience a turnaround of sorts, with a rise in both attendance and the number of new productions. But the reasons did not lie in any sudden outpouring or discovery of new American plays and musicals. Rather, they lay primarily in the importation of musicals from London—shows such as *Me and My Girl, Les Miserables, Starlight Express,* and the long-running *Cats.* While this trend was no doubt beneficial to big-time landlords such as the Schuberts, it represented, in a sense, Broadway's final indignity. The American musical, in Frank Rich's words, had been "Broadway's one undisputed contribution to world theater. . . . For the New York theater, the rise of London as a musical-theater capital is as sobering a specter as the awakening of the Japanese automobile industry was for Detroit."[51]

1987–88: Broadway's rebound continued, with attendance up 16 percent and box office receipts up 21 percent, making the season the richest in Broadway's history. More important, the season contained several new American plays of genuine merit—*Speed-the-Plow,* by David Mamet; *M. Butterfly,* by David Henry Hwang, which won the Tony; and *Joe Turner's Come and Gone,* by August Wilson, whom Frank Rich described as "the theater's most astonishing writing discovery in this decade."[52] (Wilson's *Fences* had won the Tony and the Pulitzer the previous year.)

At second glance, however, the season seemed somewhat less

glowing. The number of new productions dropped to 32, setting a fresh record for the fewest of any season this century. But that figure also failed to tell the story. The number of musicals actually increased—especially splashy British imports such as *The Phantom of the Opera* (which Frank Rich called "a perfect symbol of our times, the Trump Tower of the musical-theater landscape"). It was the popularity of these productions which accounted for Broadway's overflowing coffers.

The number of new productions of *plays,* on the other hand, declined. In 1986–87, there were 15 new plays and 8 revivals, for a total of 23 new productions. In 1987–88, the respective figures were 8 and 3, for a total of 11. And their popularity was hardly encouraging. "Theater is driven by the big musicals," explains John Breglio, an entertainment lawyer with the firm of Paul, Weiss, Rifkind, Wharton & Garrison, "and they drive ticket buyers away from the straight plays."[53] Apparently so. *Joe Turner's Come and Gone* almost came and went faster than anyone expected. Although the play was nominated for a Tony, it nearly closed after less than a month on Broadway when only about 400 people began showing up for performances at the 1,100–seat Barrymore Theater.* Meanwhile, over at the Majestic, other people were lining up around the block in hopes of getting tickets to *Phantom.*

1988–89: "Since every New York theater season is the worst in history," wrote Frank Rich, "why should the one just concluded have been any different?"[54] As Rich made clear, it wasn't. True, he did try to look for a silver lining (maybe we're going through a period of transition, etc.). But he was soon forced to return to what he called "the woes of our latest year of perpetual sorrows." To wit: "There were few good new plays and no good new musicals." Overall, the number of new productions declined to a record low of 30, down from the previous season's record low of 32.

Even those figures were somewhat misleading. As Rich pointed out in an article that appeared at the time of the 1988 Tony Awards, "Broadway cannot to any substantial degree take credit for the achievements it will be celebrating tonight. As usual in recent seasons, American drama on Broadway continues to be largely the fruit of nonprofit theatrical institutions off Broadway . . . or beyond New York."[55]

---

* The play was finally saved when it won the Drama Critics Circle Award.

Off-Broadway (and Off-Off) have been undergoing a revival of sorts in recent years—with such plays as Alfred Uhry's *Driving Miss Daisy* (which won a Pulitzer Prize), Terrence McNally's *Frankie and Johnny in the Claire de Lune,* A. R. Gurney's *The Dining Room,* Stephen Sondheim's *Sunday in the Park with George* and Wendy Wasserstein's *The Heidi Chronicles* (which won a Pulitzer and a Tony). In addition, there is the work of Sam Shepard, perhaps the country's leading contemporary playwright, who has never been produced on Broadway at all.

Two other institutions offer further evidence that there is still plenty of life in New York theater. At the New York Shakespeare Festival, Joseph Papp is in the process of staging all the works of the festival's namesake, in addition to a variety of recent plays. At Lincoln Center, director Gregory Mosher is rescuing the Beaumont and Newhouse theaters from four years of inactivity. For example, Mosher presented the first performances of David Mamet's *Speed-the-Plow,* which eventually went on to great success on Broadway.

Yet despite such success (or in some cases because of it), there are still plenty of drawbacks to the world of non-Broadway theater. For one thing, many of the institutions are under the same financial pressures that beset other arts organizations in New York, and companies such as the Phoenix Theater and the Chelsea Theater have been forced to close after decades of operation. By the same token, few of the smaller theaters can offer the sort of production values—not to mention remuneration—that playwrights have traditionally enjoyed on Broadway.

Another disadvantage to Off-Broadway is that its productions are not eligible for the annual televised extravaganza known as the Tony Awards (a ceremony administered by the Broadway powers-that-be and designed primarily to encourage attendance at Broadway theaters). Thus, plays produced Off-Broadway do not, as a rule, receive the sort of national attention (which in this day and age means televised attention) that attracts the trade of out-of-towners and guarantees a sold-out run in regional theaters. As a result of all this, much of the effort expended Off-Broadway is designed to move productions to Broadway.

Admittedly, there are arguments in favor of such a policy. Joseph Papp's Shakespeare Festival has amassed the largest endowment of any theater in the country ($24 million before the stock market crash, $21 million after), mainly from the proceeds of its production of *A Chorus Line,* which went on to become the longest running show in Broadway history. Not surprisingly, Papp himself is a strong defender of theaters whose productions are Broadway bound. "Are they selling out?" he asks. "Absolutely not. What has happened historically is that Broadway has shown it cannot initiate dramatic works because they're too costly and the potential revenue is small compared to a musical. Broadway has abdicated that role. Only Neil Simon writes drama regularly for Broadway. The others write for Off Broadway and the regional theater. And if there's a market for those plays on Broadway, then great. That's what we're after."[56]

The danger, of course, is that Off-Broadway will be controlled by the demands of Broadway. Take the case of *Ain't Misbehavin',* which was first produced by the Manhattan Theater Club in the late seventies and then moved on to Broadway. "In the five years since we did *Ain't Misbehavin','*" remarked Lynne Meadow, the club's artistic director, in 1983, "there's no question I've gotten more calls from Broadway about the plays we're doing. Some people on our board of directors have asked if we could do an *Ain't Misbehavin'* every year. But it's not that simple. The thing is: Do you make getting a play to Broadway your main product, or do you keep it a by-product?"[57]

Three years later, some critics felt that the verdict was in. Writing in *The New Criterion* in 1986, Mimi Kramer complained of "the commercialization of New York's institutional theater":

> The fact is . . . that Broadway's growing reliance on the "non-profit sector" has radically changed the nature of what is being produced there. More and more, the "little" theaters of Manhattan are ceasing to serve as cultural resources, centers for the fostering of developing art, and becoming showcases for commercial productions on their way to Broadway. . . . At the Manhattan Theater Club, long one of New York's most impressive outlets for interesting new work, Lynne Meadow seems suddenly to be devoted to yuppie comedy and contemporary revivals—which, two years ago, would have been Roundabout Theater fare. Meanwhile, at the Roundabout, Gene Feist has

developed an unaccountable taste for Broadway-type "star" vehicles and will have Jason Robards on his stage any minute if he's not careful."[58]

Similar observations have been made about the relationship between Broadway and the Beaumont Theater at Lincoln Center. For example, director/critic Robert Brustein points out that "in a perplexing demonstration of confused purpose, Lincoln Center Theater has actually begun *originating* shows on Broadway"—to wit, David Mamet's *Speed-the-Plow.*[59] At the Beaumont itself, the Center has been presenting revivals of decidedly "commercial" Broadway fare such as *The Front Page* and *Anything Goes.* A musical called *Sarafina,* which began at the Center's Newhouse Theater, subsequently moved on to Broadway.

At the end of the 1987–88 season, the Center had planned to move *Anything Goes* to Broadway as well—until it discovered that the move would cost about $1.75 million. So instead, the Center decided to leave *Anything Goes* at the Beaumont and move the Beaumont's next season to Broadway (specifically, to the Lyceum Theater on West Forty-fifth Street).

Now there is nothing really *wrong* with any of this. Nor does it appear to be a simple case of the Beaumont climbing the theatrical ladder. (For one thing, productions at the Beaumont are already eligible for Tony Awards.) Rather, the Beaumont's behavior seems to arise from the background of the theater's new director, Gregory Mosher. At his previous address, the Goodman Theater in Chicago, Mosher was successful in sending productions to Broadway; at the Beaumont, he is merely doing the same.

Even so, there is reason to wonder whether the Beaumont should be functioning as an extension of Broadway. After all, the Beaumont is supposed to serve as the theatrical counterpart to the Metropolitan Opera and the New York Philharmonic, and while this should not necessarily entail a steady stream of Sophocles and Shakespeare, neither should it mean that anything goes.

As Mimi Kramer remarked in 1986:

> The purpose of subsidized theater is to free theater from the constraints imposed by the commercial market. To free it from having to worry about the Tony Awards and rave reviews from Frank Rich. If Lincoln Center continues to try to market theater as a

commodity as Messrs, Mosher and Gersten [the executive producer] are doing now—subscribing to commercial standards and practices—what Lincoln Center will wind up with is a Broadway audience. And I don't think that's what Lincoln Center really wants.[60]

But considering the fact that the Center has since moved the Beaumont to Broadway (temporarily, of course), perhaps it does.

At the country's "regional" theaters (as they are known in New York, much to the annoyance of those who run them, who prefer a geographically neutral term such as resident theaters), the chief source of controversy is much the same—the long arm of Broadway. Zelda Fichandler, longtime artistic director of Washington's Arena Stage, states flatly that "the transfer of a play to New York does damage to the resident theater. It is esthetically disruptive and psychologically disruptive."[61]

Up in Cambridge, a few years back, the American Repertory Theater staged the first performances of Marsha Norman's *Night, Mother,* which much to the theater's surprise, moved on to Broadway. The following season, Ms. Norman was back with a new play, *Traveler in the Dark,* complete with a cast that included Sam Waterston and Hume Cronyn. The ART's artistic director, Robert Brustein, swallowed hard, then gave the production the go-ahead; he now believes he made a mistake. "I look back on this experience," he says, "with a sense of defeat and not a little shame."[62]

The problems, says Brustein, are several. When a play that is cast from a resident company moves intact to Broadway, the company is robbed of its resident cast. When a play brings in its own cast (often including a star or two), the resident theater is reduced to the status of real estate. It becomes a commercial tryout house, "with Broadway producers hovering in the wings, often contributing 'enhancement' money . . . and exercising control over artistic decisions."[63]

There are other concerns as well. A play intended for Broadway is usually tried out not just in one resident theater but several. In Brustein's words:

the growing practice of circulating these works to a network of nonprofit franchises, their final destination being New York, has resulted in a subsidized version of the old Broadway farm system, with every resident theater sharing the same play, the same production, the same style, the same kind of audience and much the same cast—a network one observer has called "McTheater."

The result is not only the abandonment of company work by people once committed to advancing theater art, it is the gradual transformation of theaters once devoted to risk and experiment into arenas of packaging and showcasing. . . . The paradox is that by cannibalizing these theaters, Broadway is effectively reducing their capacity to generate innovative work.[64]

In another, and perhaps broader sense, however, the growth of theater beyond New York represents not so much an extension of Broadway, but rather Broadway's relative decline. As theater writer Don Shewey observed in the *New York Times,* "Theater in America used to mean Broadway. The great playwrights wrote for Broadway and Broadway was their showcase, the place where things began. All that has changed."[65]

Indeed it has. Over the past thirty years or so, there has arisen across the country a network of nearly two hundred nonprofit companies that constitutes, as many have argued, a sort of national theater. For example the 1988 Tony Award for excellence in regional theater went to the South Coast Repertory of Costa Mesa, California, a theater especially notable (and commendable) for its policy of commissioning new plays from four or five writers a year.

"What New York's theatrical producers are having difficulty understanding is how much less important Broadway has become to America's playwrights," says Peter Stone, a Tony, Oscar and Emmy-winning author and president of the Dramatists Guild. "Increasingly, the reputations and fortunes of playwrights are being made on more modest stages across the country and around the world."[66]*

Nonetheless, there is no question that Broadway is still the theater's penultimate showcase. Nor is there much doubt that the showcase is becoming increasingly opaque.

Although the rest of the country is not much aware of it, a major wave of commercial development is rolling through the Broadway

---

* In San Francisco, however, several theaters are in what is known as a period of retrenchment.

neighborhood. At the center of the wave is the city's Times Square redevelopment project (consisting mainly of a series of trendy, postmodern office buildings, designed by Philip Johnson, of which New York is going to be awfully tired about a dozen years from now). Partly in response to this project, other private developers are planning to add as many as 10 million square feet of office space to the Broadway district over the next ten years. As a result, hundreds of small businesses catering to the theater industry—prop makers, lighting suppliers, rehearsal studios, casting concerns—have already been forced to leave. Many more will surely follow, and there is serious question whether they will ever return.

Meanwhile, in an effort to save the theaters themselves, the city has been designating the buildings as landmarks. In response, the theaterowners have filed a lawsuit, charging a taking of property without just compensation. Thus, the forty-six Broadway theaters (some of which have already been turned over to other uses, many of which are often dark) are in as much danger of disappearance as ever. Several years ago, the Helen Hayes and Morosco theaters were demolished to make way for the glitzy new Marriott Marquis Hotel. At this writing, the historic Biltmore Theater—a showcase for director George Abbott during the thirties and forties, home of *Barefoot in the Park* and *Hair*—has been abandoned and is being carried off piece by piece by vandals.

One reason such theaters are often dark is the cost of mounting productions. For example, a one-man show called *Edmund Kean* cost five times as much to produce on Broadway a few years ago as it did in London a few months earlier. Because of such costs, ticket prices have soared to a high of $55 for the splashiest musical; and Broadway has adopted the sort of blockbuster mentality that many allege is characteristic of Hollywood. Millions are wagered on mammoth productions that often fail to return their investments (while more modest works go begging). During a single week in the spring of 1988, $11 million worth of Broadway musicals—including the $7 million *Carrie*, based on the Hollywood horror film—sank without a trace.

Over the years, a number of proposals have been put forth to alter the economics of Broadway. In 1984, for example, the Mayor's Theater Advisory Council proposed the creation of a multi-million-dollar Theater Trust that would subsidize new productions, especially those of serious plays, in underused theaters.

But so far, nothing much has come of the proposal, and producer Joseph Papp has quit the council in disgust. "Who thinks, 'Wither Broadway?' " Papp asked rhetorically a few years back. "Nobody. It's one of the great institutions, and it's going down the drain."

That conclusion may be a bit premature, but certainly Broadway has cause for concern in yet another problem that lurks in the wings: the vanishing American playwright. True, there are companies such as the South Coast Rep in Costa Mesa that are actually paying people (albeit modestly) to write new plays. In New York, a similar program, called the American Playwrights Project, was announced in the summer of 1988 by Jujamcyn Theaters and three independent producers, James B. Freydberg, Max Weitzenhoffer and Stephen Graham. "The idea came to me," says Freydberg, "when I realized that there were fewer new American plays on Broadway this season than ever before—six by my count. Writers are no longer writing for the theater. . . . For the first time in years, I didn't have projects that interested me. I looked around and I was petrified."[67] So far, the project has commissioned plays from David Henry Hwang, Christopher Durang, Marsha Norman, David Rabe, Wendy Wasserstein and Terrence McNally, all of them established playwrights. Each will be paid about $20,000, which is intended to cover the cost of readings and workshops for the completed play, in addition to the writer's living expenses.

Enlightened though such projects may be, there is reason to wonder whether they can succeed in reversing what many perceive as a general decline in playwriting. "It is sometimes hard not to feel like I'm presiding over the American theater's going-out-of-business sale," writes Jack Viertel, dramaturge at the Mark Taper Forum in Los Angeles. "The new Michael Wellers, Marsha Normans, Christopher Durangs, Lanford Wilsons, David Mamets and Sam Shepards—the ones we're being paid to search out—do not seem to be anywhere in sight. As a longtime Taper employee said recently, 'I've seen lulls before. This isn't a lull.' "[68]

Even some of the writers who've more or less made it do not come in for universal acclaim. In an article entitled "Is the Best of What We Have this Season Really Good Enough?" John Gross of the *New York Times* described David Mamet's *Speed-the-Plow* as "an over-blown anecdote. The characters are too limited and the writing too coarse for it to be anything else."[69]

The chief problem in getting better plays, of course, is money. A writer can spend years creating a play, years more getting it produced—say at a resident theater or Off-Broadway—and then, despite good reviews, earn maybe $1,000. Even if the writer makes it to Broadway, his troubles may have only begun. Under the existing arrangement, the writer earns 10 percent of the weekly receipts. If a play is grossing $200,000 a week, this can amount to quite a bit of money. Which is exactly why the League of New York Theaters and Producers has brought an antitrust suit against the Dramatists Guild, seeking to overturn the arrangement. Never mind that according to the odds, this play is likely to be the writer's only big success of his life. The producers argue that they need to pay back theater investors in order to keep the system chugging along.

Pending the outcome of the suit, producers have been pressuring playwrights to waive or defer a portion of their royalties; and most playwrights have gone along with the new arrangement. "We are humiliated by it; we hate it and loathe it," says Peter Stone, president of the Dramatists Guild. "But you can either have no money with a play open or have no money with a play closed. Which is more advantageous?"[70]

The classic case of royalty waiver occurred with a play called *Bent,* which ran on Broadway in 1979. Two days before the play was to open, the producers asked the playwright, Martin Sherman, to give up much of his royalty money, which the producers said they needed to pay for advertising. Ultimately, *Bent* ran on Broadway for seven months, but Sherman says he received full royalties for only one week. "The most frustrating thing," he adds, "is how many people think I got rich on *Bent.*"[71]

At this point in a playwright's career (if not long before), he is apt to turn his attentions toward Broadway's bugaboo—Hollywood. "Film and television studios," writes Samuel G. Freedman in the *New York Times,* "are dangling six-figure sums in front of writers who are in debt or are barely breaking even—if only the writer will desert the theater for Hollywood. To talk to a selection of writers with one or two critical hits behind them is to realize how quickly writing talent can be diverted from the theater to television or film."[72]

163

*   *   *

In the end, it is Hollywood that is the basic cause of Broadway's decline. "This is an industry that doesn't have the common cold; it has cholera," says longtime Broadway producer Emanuel Azenberg. "The short-term problems are economic—royalties, unions, irresponsible management. The long-term problems are artistic, and they started 40 years ago with the advent of television and the upgrading of films. Our writers are writing books or films because they're more remunerative than plays. So, will the theater disappear? No. Is it healthy? Also no."[73]

Like Azenberg, Broadway in general is well aware of the cause of its distress. Which accounts in part for the periodic salvos fired in the direction of the opposite coast—beginning with Kaufman and Hart's lighthearted *Once in a Lifetime* in 1930 and continuing with David Mamet's poison-tipped *Speed-the-Plow* in 1988. The latter play, however, contained an unintended irony. Much of the production's drawing power stemmed from the presence in the three-person cast of Madonna, who is nothing if not a creature of Hollywood.

Drawing power (along with technology) is the basis for Hollywood's gradual ascendancy over Broadway. It explains why so many of Broadway's two-score theaters are so often dark and why Hollywood commands an audience that Broadway cannot even begin to match. In this country, that is the measure of success, the mechanism by which the pie is sliced. It accounts for what Stanley Kauffmann refers to as "a shift in cultural energy." Describing a first-time screenwriter, Kauffmann notes that "A few decades ago, his gift for sharp scene construction and for glittering chat might have impelled him toward a Broadway career. Today those gifts in people of his age move toward film."[74]

"In the late 1960's," writes Aljean Harmetz, the *New York Times*'s Hollywood correspondent, "when George Lucas was going to film school at the University of Southern California and winning first prize in the National Student Film Festival for 'THX–1138,' there were six film schools. And the road from them into the movie industry was circuitous and full of potholes. Today, there are 20 film schools; 1,000 more colleges and universities offer courses in everything from screenwriting to situation comedy. And if you can write or direct a film that seems slick and assured, the road is paved with Porsches."[75]

Thus, a lot of might-have-been playwrights (the ones you never hear about) are lost to Hollywood right at the outset. For others, the move comes later. "You can write a significant play, have it done on Broadway and still be in economic trouble," says Lloyd Richards, who has worked with hundreds of playwrights as artistic director of both the Yale Repertory Theater and the O'Neill Theater Center. "And then there are these people offering you money to write for the movies. That's when the decision is made. That's when you define yourself."[76]

To be sure, this sort of role change has been going on for quite some time. Sixty years ago, there were Ben Hecht and his partner Charles MacArthur. Later came Robert Sherwood, Thorton Wilder, Lillian Hellman and Clifford Odets. "The movies have taken over the field of entertainment in this country," Odets declared in 1937. "The theater, which once had a potent and powerful voice, has dwindled to a little squeak that sometimes, but not often, sounds like something cultural."[77]

Despite such sentiments, many of these playwrights eventually returned to New York; and the same is true for several of those who work in Hollywood today, among them, Michael Weller, David Mamet, Christopher Durang and David Rabe. It's a safe bet, though, that most will soon be back in Hollywood. "I don't know any playwright today," says Wendy Wasserstein, "who makes a living only in the theater,"[78] In Hollywood, it's much, much easier. A playwright can earn anywhere from $50,00 to $100,000 for a television assignment. Which is why a lot of them end up hanging around. Jason Miller, who won a Pulitzer Prize for *That Championship Season* and who was once regarded as another Arthur Miller, has more or less disappeared into acting for films and television. Paul Zindel, who won a Pulitzer for *The Effect of Gamma Rays on Man-in-the-Moon Marigolds,* has been mainly writing television scripts, as has Mart Crowley (*The Boys in the Band*), who recently batted out the script for "Bluegrass," a glitzy mini-series. In the case of Hollywood, wrote theater critic Walter Kerr in the *New York Times* a few years back, "writers are lost by the carload, permanently."[79]

More recently, another Hollywood attraction has begun to appear (or rather, reappear). As the movie audience grows older and presumably less frivolous, Hollywood is turning to the theater for "product." Thus, the transformation of plays—such as *The Miss Firecracker Contest, Steel Magnolias* and *Driving Miss Daisy*—into films. Which is fine for the playwright, of course. But in an age when the theater offers so little chance for remuneration, there is a danger that plays will be written less as plays than as embryonic Hollywood movies.

The Hollywood attraction for actors, of course, is equally strong, if not stronger.

"Ten years ago," writes playwright Albert Innaurato in the *Times*, "there was just enough theater and television in New York, just enough work on tour, to keep a large contingent of actors alive (tenuously, sometimes) in this city. When an actor or actress left town to do a movie or television show, he or she came right back. There was an attitude about the sanctity and value of stage work that made actors unwilling to settle permanently away from the source of new plays. That attitude is disappearing. It isn't only greed. It's the impossibility for many in the theater of making even a modest income in New York."[80]

To be sure, there have recently been cases of actors who've made it big in Hollywood returning to do a play in New York—Dustin Hoffman in *Death of a Salesman,* Glenn Close in *The Real Thing* and *Benefactors,* William Hurt in *Hurlyburly.* Such cases may even increase as more moviemaking is done in New York. But for the time being, they remain the exception; and they also have some drawbacks. Theater producers sometimes complain that movie actors seek limited runs or contracts allowing them to leave the show should a movie role pop up. When a movie actor (or rather an actor best known for movies) appears in a play, it's often the actor the audience comes to see rather than the play. Thus, a play called *Cuba and His Teddy Bear,* which received mixed reviews, did boffo business, simply because it starred Robert De Niro and Ralph Macchio. Meanwhile, much better plays with New York casts played to half-filled houses Off-Broadway. The message to young actors is clear: get thee to Hollywood.

All of which serves to point up the striking difference between New York and London in this regard. In the latter city, where movies, theater and television are concentrated, actors circulate among the three media with ease, sometimes even filming a movie during the day and appearing on stage in the evening. The same holds true for playwrights. "In America," writes theater critic Benedict Nightingale, "television sucks playwrights from the stage; in Britain it feeds them to it."[81] There are other differences as well. In London, theater is still first. It has not been relegated to the third-class status that theater occupies in America.

Such differences have countless manifestations. "British television comes from a theater tradition," observes Jonathan Powell, a high-level executive with the BBC. "It is rooted in literature and drama. American television comes from the cinema tradition—Hollywood film making. That difference in origin tells a great deal about our approach and yours to television dramatization."[82] It also tells, increasingly, a great deal about the effect of television on American playwriting.

"Speaking as someone who enjoys watching television—and not just British imports on Channel 13," writes Frank Rich, "I nonetheless find myself worrying increasingly about the medium's impact on the theater. That impact is spreading on all fronts." He goes on to give a number of examples: "the substitution of gimmicks for true comic writing that springs from character;" reliance on "facile sitcom situations;" creation of characters who aren't real characters, "but types summed up by a single, instantly recognizable personality trait;" "open-and-shut intellectual simplicity;" and closing a play "with an unearned, sentimental message." "The result," he concludes, "is not just a coarsening of the theater, but an assault on the very definition of theater."[82a]

This lack of definition leads, in turn, to an even more basic dilemma. Once again, Mr. Rich:

> Of all the ills that plague the American theater right now, none is more disturbing that the widespread perception that American plays simply do not matter anymore. There was a time when writers like O'Neill and Williams and Miller were at the center of this country's intellectual life—when a major play on Broadway was as fit a subject for universal comment and debate, pro or con, as the latest major novel or museum show or ballet. These days, theater is a special interest, occupying a ghetto on the cultural landscape. While the fluffiest Broadway entertainments are consumed by the masses (or at least the wealthiest masses), serious American theater is followed by a far smaller coterie—and is often either ignored or viewed with contempt by the general public and the arts-minded elite alike.[82b]

167

To be sure, the stage is not entirely dark: witness the growth of regional theater. But generally speaking, the most dramatic scene onstage today is that of the decline of a major East Coast institution, namely, theater itself. And theater is not alone.

PUBLISHING

Magazines

Back in the sixties and early seventies, there came to pass in the United States a sort of Golden Age of magazine journalism. Part of the reason, of course, was the temper of the times. Part of it was the advent of the so-called New Journalism, although not all the best pieces, by any means, were written in the *nouveau* fashion (which, in its assumption of omniscience, could often be annoying). At any rate, each month in the pages of *Esquire* and *Harper's* in particular, writers such as Norman Mailer, Tom Wolfe, David Halberstam, Gay Talese, Joan Didion and Garry Wills turned the magazine article into a kind of art form. In addition, *Esquire* carried it all off with a certain deadpan "style," and its covers, especially, became minor monthly events.

Beyond all this, there was the wealth of other magazines: the *Atlantic* (notable for its pieces on Vietnam), *The Reporter, Saturday Review, Look, Life,* the *Saturday Evening Post, Colliers,* and so on.

Today, of course, all this has changed considerably. Many of the more popular, general-interest magazines no longer exist (or are published much less frequently). One would be hard-pressed these days to find many examples of the article-as-art-form, partly because the magazines that published such pieces no longer exist in the form they did before:

Esquire, after slipping through the fingers of new owner Clay Felker, was acquired by a pair of parvenus from Nashville, who turned it into *Playboy* without the centerfold. (Sample bit of advice to Man at His Best: "A proper before-dinner cocktail is an engine revver, a delightful tease, and, like foreplay, should be eventually abandoned in favor of the entree."[83] To which *The New Yorker* would doubtless respond: "Noted.") Naturally, circulation and advertising rose rapidly. In early 1988, after the Nashville pair split up, the magazine was bought by the Hearst Corporation, which has more or less continued the Tennessee style.

168

Harper's, faced with annual losses of more than $1.5 million, announced in 1980 that it was folding. The magazine was subsequently rescued by the MacArthur and Atlantic Richfield foundations, a step that entailed its reorganization as a nonprofit entity. Since then, *Harper's* has been reduced to a shadow of its former self, its contents composed mainly of excerpts from often obscure publications; panel discussions; brief pieces of criticism; and collections of the recherché ("Amount Nancy Reagan's hairdresser charges for a haircut: $100. Amount he charges for a speech: $1,000"). In other words, a magazine on a very tight budget.

The *Atlantic* has likewise undergone some changes. In the same year that *Harper's* announced it was folding, its New England counterpart was sold to real estate tycoon Mortimer Zuckerman, whom the *Times* describes as "Boston's all-purpose bête noire."[84]* Soon, the new and former owners were entangled in a series of lawsuits, with Zuckerman claiming he had not been told that the magazine was losing about a million dollars a year. The suits have since been settled, with both sides claiming victory, but under replacement editor William Whitworth, formerly of *The New Yorker*, the *Atlantic* remains rather retiring. It still publishes lengthy, substantive pieces—it's one of the few magazines in the country that does—but except for the famous David Stockman article (which was actually set in motion by Zuckerman), many of these are either excerpts from forthcoming books (notably, Paul Kennedy's *Rise and Fall of the Great Powers*) or are singularly unarresting (cover stories on the diamond industry—which sounds a lot like one of those interminable *New Yorker* pieces—and on "Translating the Bible: An Endless Task." Indeed.) No doubt such pieces are a reflection of Whitworth's personality, but "perhaps the real issue," the *Times* concluded in an article on the *Atlantic*, "is whether any editor—however Promethean—can overcome the crises of identity and finances fettering the magazine industry today."[85]

A few years ago, such troubles advanced, like a lapping sea, to the sacrosanct chambers of *The New Yorker*. The magazine was sold to Samuel Newhouse, Jr., head of a publishing empire that includes twenty-six newspapers and the Conde Nast magazines (among them *Vogue, Vanity Fair, GQ, Glamour* and *House & Garden*), as well as Random House. A year or so later, Newhouse replaced longtime

* Zuckerman has also purchased *U.S. News and World Report.*

editor William Shawn, setting off an extraordinary protest by more than one hundred fifty *New Yorker* contributors and staff members. Since then, the more dire predictions of some of the protesters have failed to come to pass under Shawn's successor, Robert A. Gottlieb, former president and editor-in-chief of Alfred A. Knopf (a subsidiary of Random House). But this is not to say that *The New Yorker's* traditions have remained inviolate. For example, the magazine has begun billing articles on a tear-off cover card, a remarkable step for a publication that not too long ago did not even deign to provide its readers a table of contents. (Ironically, the innovation has served primarily to point out how few real articles the magazines runs: In order to fill the cover card, the editors have had to resort to trumpeting pieces by regular columnists—"Andy Logan on City Hall"; "Roger Angell on Baseball.") More significantly, the magazine has begun to publish "advertorials"—lengthy advertising sections that are designed to look like editorial matter.

Of late, *The New Yorker* has tried to broaden its appeal a bit. It ran a profile of Paul Shaffer, the bandleader/sidekick on "Late Night with David Letterman." It also ran an ad in *Adweek* and *Advertising Age* which featured Teri Garr (a regular, as it happens, on the Letterman show), along with the caption: "Teri Garr reads *The New Yorker* in Malibu, CA." Such efforts strike one mainly as odd, but in any case, they've apparently failed to do the trick. Ad pages for 1988 were down by 15 percent. A recent article in the *Columbia Journalism Review* alluded to the magazine's "anemic financial condition" and ended by observing that Samuel Newhouse "doesn't seem any closer . . . to finding a way to ensure *The New Yorker's* survival."[86]

The most consistently interesting magazine in the country—in fact, the only such magazine—is *The New Republic*, with its lively writing, entertaining columns and first-rate art direction. (The magazine's Ed Meese cover in the style of a Vargas Girl painting was at least as good as anything ever seen at *Esquire*, which is to say it was among the very best magazine covers ever produced.) One should mention, however, that *The New Republic* does not run lengthy articles— what I think of as real magazine pieces—and it is published in Washington, which may suggest the difficulty of publishing a substantive, public-policy magazine anywhere else.

Other substantive magazines have had a rough time of it. *The Reporter* folded long ago. *Saturday Review* never recovered from the departure of editor Norman Cousins in 1971. The last item I saw regarding the magazine, in 1987, had to do with its supposedly imminent purchase by Bob Guccione, the publisher of *Penthouse*.

For the unreconstructed magazine junkie, such as myself, the chief difficulty in buying substantive magazines is finding them. I have been living in San Francisco for better than ten years now, and I have yet to come across a first-rate magazine stand, either in the city itself or in the university towns of Berkeley and Palo Alto. Accordingly, I get my weekly magazine fix at a neighborhood shop called the Gramophone, near the corner of California and Polk. But the Gramophone—like many similar shops—has undergone a lot of changes over the years. The number of substantive magazines has steadily diminished. The store no longer carries *The New Criterion, Columbia Journalism Review, Daedalus, Foreign Affairs, Foreign Policy* or *The Public Interest.* What it does carry, in increasing profusion, are video cassettes. Now don't get me wrong. I rent a lot of video cassettes, and I'm glad the Gramophone carries them. But if I inquire of one of the hip young clerks whether he's seen anything of *The New Republic,* I'm apt to encounter a quizzical stare. The *what?*

There is an explanation for all this. Over the past ten years or so, the total number of magazines has dramatically grown—from 368 in 1977 to 504 in 1987. Subscription sales (often boosted by discounts) have likewise grown—from 170 million to 260 million. Newsstand sales, on the other hand, have noticeably declined—from a high of 93 million in 1978 to 80 million in 1987. Thus, the individual shopowner, faced with a bewildering variety of publications and a diminishing number of sales, is apt to weed out those magazines (such as the *Washington Monthly,* say) which sell only a few copies a week. If sales decline further, he is apt to devote his magazine space to something that moves a lot faster.

For the magazine reader—especially the younger reader—the trend is clearly negative. A magazine stand is where one goes to check out what is being written this week on any given issue, maybe to come across an issue that one was not even aware existed. It is, in a sense, a sort of intellectual marketplace. For the younger or potential reader, a magazine stand is where he or she discovers a new publication, picks it up, thumbs through it, maybe even buys it, maybe even reads it. One thing is certain, though. As the newsstand sales figures clearly demonstrate, young people these days are not buying magazines. What they're taking home are video cassettes.

The video invasion is significant in a broader sense as well. It symbolizes the myriad ways in which the magazine business is increasingly colored by show biz. To begin with the most salient example, the largest selling magazine in the country today is *TV Guide* (yes, it does publish articles—of a sort), circulation: 17.2 million. (Recently, *TV Guide* was bought by media mogul Rupert Murdoch—a Westerner, incidentally, in the sense that he comes from Australia. Murdoch also owns the fledgling Fox network— along with *New York* magazine and many other things—and it will be interesting to see whether he uses *TV Guide* to promote Fox programs at the expense of those of his television competitors.)

Another prominent example of the influence of show biz is the growing number of magazines devoted, in whole or in part, to celebrity (which these days nearly always means the show biz variety). *People* magazine (circulation about 3 million) makes more money for Time Inc. than any other magazine except *Time* itself, in its national and international manifestations. *Ms.* magazine has been sold (again); all the old editorial staff is gone; and *Ms.* is running cover stories on Cindi Lauper. Meanwhile, lowbrow tabloids such as the *National Enquirer* and *Star* are "repositioning" themselves to appeal to middle-class women at the supermarket checkout stand. (Translation: less sex, more celebrities.) Toward the other end of the monetary spectrum, the nouveaux "lifestyle" magazines—*GQ, M, Connoisseur, Fame, Vanity Fair, Esquire,* etc.— often feature celebrities on their covers (research having revealed that celebs sell better than models). And while it's true that such magazines don't compete directly with the *Atlantic* for readers (although this too is beginning to change), what they do compete for is advertising dollars and shelf space, which are often far more important. Needless to say, the lifestyle magazines are winning.

People magazine is not the only connection between Time Inc. and show biz. The company also owns American Television and Communications Company, the nation's second-largest cable operator, and Home Box Office, the largest pay television service.

Ten years ago, these businesses barely existed; today, they provide about 45 percent of the company's operating profit, a percentage that will almost certainly increase. Recognizing this new balance of power, Time Inc. recently named as its new president one Nicholas J. Nicholas, who had made his mark as head of the company's television subsidiaries.*

Meanwhile, the company's magazines have begun to branch out into video. *Sports Illustrated,* in the space of eight months, sold more than 180,000 copies of an action video called "Get the Feeling—Speed," at which point it launched the sequel ("Get the Feeling—Power"); two more are on the way. *Money* magazine has produced a video called "Making Your Money Count." Other magazines, such as *American Health* and *American Baby,* have also been getting into the act, with shows for public television and cable, respectively. In effect, such publications are forging an alliance between television and one of the fastest growing magazine species of the past ten years, namely, special-interest consumer magazines, sales of which grew by 31 percent between 1977 and 1987.

Another way to chart the course of magazines is to compare those of the East Coast with those of the West. The former location, while producing more than its quota of junk, nonetheless still supports (precariously) the *Atlantic,* the *Washington Monthly* and others. In California, one can look far and wide without finding more than a grain of substance. The leading magazine by far—and perhaps the fattest in the country—is *Los Angeles,* which features on every cover a Hollywood celebrity and a billing that reads: "Great New Getaways." (Actually, the billing varies from month to month, but not by much.) Inside the cover are four hundred pages of absolute fluff.

Books

Democracy not only infuses a taste for letters among the trading classes, but introduces a trading spirit into literature.

---

* There is also, of course, the recent merger between Time Inc. and Warner Communications Inc. (technically, an acquisition of the latter by the former). About the same time as that was taking place, Time Inc. launched another new magazine—*Entertainment Week.*

In aristocracies, readers are fastidious and few in number; in democracies, they are far more numerous and far less difficult to please. The consequence is that among aristocratic nations no one can hope to succeed without great exertion, and this exertion may earn great fame, but can never procure much money; while among democratic nations a writer may flatter himself that he will obtain at a cheap rate a moderate reputation and a large fortune. For this purpose he need not be admired; it is enough that he is liked.

The ever increasing crowd of readers and their continual craving for something new ensure the sale of books that nobody much esteems.

—Alexis de Tocqueville,
Democracy in America[87]

Until relatively recently—say thirty years ago—American publishing was a rather gentlemanly affair, more reminiscent of nineteenth-century Boston than twentieth-century New York. The houses, for the most part, were small and privately held; and though they were operated as businesses (after a fashion), their proprietors nonetheless regarded themselves, to varying degrees, as custodians of a culture.

The first signs of change appeared, rather innocently, around 1940, with the introduction of paperback books. The initial impulse behind most of these books was the same as that animating the early stages of televised drama several years later. That is to say, it stemmed from a basically aristocratic inclination (or to employ the present-day pejorative, an elitist inclination) to bring culture to the people. The attempt, in a way, succeeded wildly. For the first time, the book became a medium for the masses; and by 1960, paperback sales had risen to 360 million a year. But just as in the case of televised drama, success transformed the medium. Rather than remaining an elitist instrument for bringing culture to the people, the paperback book—and the book in general—became a democratic instrument for giving the people what they want.

One of the chief mechanisms of this transformation was a change in the manner in which books were sold. Before the sixties, the great majority of books (other than mass-market paperbacks) were sold through independent bookstores, many of which bore a passing resemblance to the staid Scribner's store on Fifth Avenue. To the average person, such stores were as intimidating as a restaurant with a wine list. "When I was growing up," recalls Richard Snyder, chairman of Simon & Schuster, one of today's more "commercial" houses, "you could walk into Scribner's and unless you were out of Harvard the clerks looked down their noses at you."[88] (Snyder can relax now. In yet another sign of the times, the Scribner's store on Fifth Avenue has been closed.)

In 1966, the Minneapolis department store firm of Dayton Hudson opened its first B. Dalton Bookseller; two years later, Dayton took over Pickwick, a chain of bookstores in Southern California. In 1969, a Los Angeles conglomerate called Carter-Hawley-Hale absorbed Waldenbooks; soon, Waldenbooks were sprouting like crocuses on the landscape at the rate of about forty stores a year. By 1979, the tally stood at 380 B. Daltons and 560 Waldenbooks—nearly all of both in suburban shopping malls, where the new breed of buyers hung out. (On television sit-coms, characters no longer spoke of "going downtown"; they spoke of "going to the mall." This was true even on "The Cosby show," featuring an all-black family that lived in an urban townhouse.)

By 1982, there was at least one Waldenbooks in every state in the union. Two years later, the chain was taken over by the mammoth 2,100-store K Mart Corp., to which it also began supplying books. (For those of you unfamiliar with K Mart: Whenever Johnny Carson finds his monologue sagging—owing, as a rule, to his mistakenly having assumed that his audience had recently perused a newspaper—he grabs the overhead mike and intones, "Attention, K mart shoppers . . ." The line is not meant as a put-down, and invariably it gets a big laugh.)

By 1986, when B. Dalton was acquired by the discount book chain of Barnes & Noble, the tally stood at 778 Daltons and 1,000 Waldenbooks. Together, the two chains accounted for 40 percent of all bookstore sales and a much higher percentage of "trade book" sales (trade books are the sort of books that are carried in the usual, general-interest bookstore).

Meanwhile, a parallel sequence of events was radically altering the other end of the book business—publishing. Beginning in the sixties, and continuing right up to the present day, house after house was devoured by a huge conglomerate. And just to add insult to injury, many of these conglomerates were heavily involved in the entertainment industry—Gulf & Western, which bought Simon &

Schuster, also owns Paramount Pictures;* MGA, which bought
G. P. Putnam's Sons, owns Universal Films, Universal Television,
MCA Records, etc.; Rupert Murdoch, who recently bought 170-
year-old Harper & Row, owns Twentieth Century–Fox, the Fox
television network, *TV Guide,* etc., etc. Other acquisitive conglomerates arrived from abroad: Bertelsmann Verlag of Germany
bought Bantam Books and Doubleday-Dell; Penguin Publishing of
Britain bought New American Library, Viking and E. P. Dutton.

Today, nearly all the most prominent American publishers are
owned by conglomerates; and the editor-in-chief of *Publishers
Weekly,* John F. Baker, estimates that the leading publishing conglomerates now control about 45 percent of book sales in the
United States. Many industry analysts predict that over the next ten
years or so, half-a-dozen international corporations will come to
dominate the entire American book trade.

Perhaps the most salient effect of this concentration of ownership
in both publishing and sales has been the increasing focus on The
Big Book—what Thomas Whiteside termed, in a pathfinding series
of *New Yorker* articles, "The Blockbuster Complex." Whiteside's
articles appeared in 1980, and since then the complex has grown
complexer and complexer. Here is how Edwin McDowell began a
couple of his book reports in the *New York Times:* "The publishing
industry's appetite for the 'big book' has always been hearty, but
recently it has become voracious."[89] "Book publishers have always
looked for titles that would keep the check-out registers whirring,
but their preoccupation with big books now borders on the
obsessive."[90]

One of the more notable manifestations of this obsession has
been the sums that publishers have been laying out in the form of
advances for unwritten books. Vanna White was paid $250,000 by
Harper & Row for her autobiography. (Incidentally, Vanna did not
go in search of this pot of gold, since she is paid quite handsomely
as hostess of television's blockbuster "Wheel of Fortune." Rather,
Harper & Row approached *her.* "My first reaction," she says in
admirable candor, "was: What will I write? I turn letters for a
living."[91] No problem. *Vanna Speaks* easily ascended to the *New York*

* The company today, in fact, is known as Paramount.

Times bestseller list.) Barbara Taylor Bradford has reportedly signed a contract with Random House for $9 million for her next three novels. Warner Books paid nearly $5 million for the sequel to *Gone With the Wind,* to be written by a woman named Alexandra Ripley. But for the absolute record, we must go to a book that actually existed at the time of sale. James Clavell (*Shogun, Noble House*) was paid an even $5 million by William Morrow & Company and Avon Books for his latest novel, *Whirlwind.* Bidding began at a stipulated "floor" of $3 million.

Sales figures for blockbuster books have been equally impressive. As Edwin McDowell reported in 1987, "A dozen or more have sold more than one million copies in the last two years, and *Iacocca* and Bill Cosby's *Fatherhood* have sold more than two million—totals that not long ago were considered unattainable."[92]

So much for the winners. The chief losers in this unequal struggle (aside from those readers who are not especially interested in the early years of Vanna White) have been those writers whose names are less than household words. "As trade publishers raised their expectations about the number of copies that a book must sell to be considered successful," writes Walter W. Powell, co-author of *Books: The Culture and Commerce of Publishing,* "they became less willing to take on eminently worthwhile books that had modest sales potential."[93] "Particularly hard hit was the 'mid-list book', one written by a little-known author or one that deals with a subject for which there is no well-defined market," writes Ray Walters, a longtime observer of the publishing scene. "As a result, authors who had once been able to count on incomes of $40,000 to $100,000 a year are being advised by their agents to take full-time jobs and do their writing at night or on weekends."[94]

Another effect of the new patterns of ownership in the publishing industry has been the increasing connection with show biz in general and Hollywood in particular. This connection, of course, is not new. As Bennett Cerf, then president of Random House, remarked in 1941, "Until a sweeping readjustment takes place . . . in the motion picture world, writers will not be interested enough in either books or book publishers to regard them as very much more than little way-stations on the royal road to Beverly Hills. . . . The thing that an author wants most from his publisher these days is a letter of introduction to Darryl Zanuck."[95] As demand for mid-list writers on Publishers Row continues to drop, such feelings will likely increase.

For bestselling authors, however, the royal road to Beverly Hills has usually seemed clear and wide. Twenty-five years ago, nearly every big novel was bought by the movies; and by the end of the seventies, million-dollar book deals were not uncommon. In a sense, the royal road proved to be a two-way street. The Blockbuster Complex—which was actually conjured up in Hollywood—made its way east.

Pretty soon, books and movies came to be regarded by many people on both coasts as more or less interchangeable versions of the same "product." Publishers, agents and producers became bound up in the "deal fabric;" and the subject of the deal might result from the "spontaneous generation of a literary property."

Under the system of "spontaneous generation," the "literary property" might originate in the office of an agent or producer, then be made into a movie, then be "novelized" as a book. Conversely it might be published as a hardback, then sent to Hollywood, then published as a paperback timed to coincide with release of the movie.

By the early- to mid-eighties, however, this particular Hollywood cycle appeared to have more or less run its course. For one thing, the "novelization" technique had produced a number of awkward offspring. Then too, several books that were turned into movies were box-office failures (for example, *The Island,* by Peter Benchley, author of *Jaws*); and several others (Gay Talese's *Thy Neighbor's Wife*, acquired for $2.5 million) were never made into movies at all. Meanwhile, Hollywood had decided that the movie audience was now composed entirely of teenagers, and that books at any stage of the process were more or less superfluous.

In a way, though, the connection between Hollywood and Publishers Row had merely shifted from movies to television; and here the connection proved particularly potent. Books that several years earlier might have been turned into films were now produced as television mini-series; and the effect on sales of the book was often dramatic. During and immediately after the airing of "James Clavell's *Shogun,*" the book sold an additional three million copies.

One of the reasons for this was that "James Clavell's *Shogun*" is exactly the way the series was presented on television, night after night. "The trick is to become a brand name," says Clavell. "That's what sells the books. People see your name on television and remember it the next time they're in a bookstore. Something I've written is always being aired somewhere . . ."[96] So it was that television also presented "James Clavell's *Noble House,*" a mini-series starring Pierce Brosnan and Deborah Raffin, with Clavell as executive producer. (Incidentally, although Clavell now resides in Switzerland, he lived off and on for twenty-five years in Los Angeles, where many of his fellow blockbuster writers—Judith Krantz, Sidney Sheldon, Jackie Collins—also reside. Together, they comprise a sort of Hollywood Bloomsbury. Meanwhile, the community's favorite literary couple—Joan Didion and John Gregory Dunne—have moved back to New York.)

But by the mid-eighties or so, the mini-series had begun to lose a bit of its luster. Audiences began to balk at setting aside several hours for each new "major event." Fortunately, Hollywood soon decided that the movie audience (like the country at large) was growing older, so books-for-the-movies began returning to favor. *Presumed Innocent* became the object of a frenzied bidding war, with author Scott Turow eventually choosing among competing million-dollar offers. Two of the most popular yuppie movies—*Fatal Attraction* and *Wall Street*—were "novelized," with first printings of 250,000 and 500,000, respectively. And off in the distance, somewhere among the Spanish moss and magnolia blossoms, lurks the biggest movie book of all: *Gone With the Wind II* (the publisher of which, Warner Books, is a subsidiary of Warner Communications, Inc., parent company of Warner Brothers).

Publishing is affected by movies and television in much less dramatic ways as well. There is, for example, the apparently insatiable demand for books written by or about celebrities: Shirley MacLain, Carol Burnett, Elvis Presley, Marilyn Monroe, Charles Kuralt, Bill Cosby, Vanna White, Lee Iacocca and Chuck Yeager (the last two of whom have become household names through their television commercials).

There is the importance of television exposure to the career of any new writer. As Ray Walters put it: "Writing well was no longer enough. To be a successful author, one had to be a public personality."[97] Several publishers began screening prospective authors for suitability for television; and McGraw-Hill drew up a "Memo on Media Exposure," advising its authors that, "By agreeing to appear before a TV camera or behind a radio mike, you have temporarily assumed the obligations of a show-biz personality. You must radiate self-confidence, charm, charisma."[98]

Crown Publishers spent $15,000 to produce what it ballyhooed as "the first literary video," starring Tama Janowitz, author of *Slaves of New York*. As Michiko Kakutani, book critic of the *New York Times*, described the final product: "The video opens with the sort of pulsing, syncopated music usually associated with fashion shows. . . . Later, there are shots of Ms. Janowitz sitting at an electric typewriter, dressed in a black T-shirt, black leggings and a pink, polka-dot tutu. . . . we see her dressed in an evening gown, walking down a garbage-laden street; talking with Andy Warhol and some other trendy-looking folks at a restaurant. . . . Publicity for the book gives a whole new meaning to the phrase, 'a writer's style.' "[99]

Show biz is also evident on the retail side of the book trade. Not long ago, for example, Waldenbooks ran a newspaper ad announcing an appearance by Martina Navratilova, who would be autographing copies of—no, not her book, her "workout video," as the ad described it. The list of such non-book items stocked by the chain stores is growing. In addition to videotapes, there are audiotapes (usually highly abridged versions of popular classics), calendars, maps, computer software, lap desks, tarot cards and Sendak dolls. At Waldenbooks, items such as these will eventually account for 30 percent of sales—if they don't already.

As this sort of figure suggests, the owners of the book chains keep a very sharp eye on what moves and what doesn't. In the main, this practice is prompted by a simple desire to make a buck. But it is also prompted by the fact that the number of new books appearing each year has been rapidly growing, from 12,000 in 1960, to 55,000 in 1980, to 90,000 in 1988.

To cope with this rising sea of print—and more important, to ride the biggest waves—the chain stores operate computer systems that monitor the sales of every title in every store. Books that move quickly are quickly reordered; those that don't are quickly returned to the publisher. At Waldenbooks, for example, a new hardcover can disappear in a hundred days; a paperback can vanish in a matter of weeks. "The key to the chain stores' success," writes Walter Powell, "is selling large quantities of a limited stock of titles; diversity is emphatically not their concern."[100]

Such a policy has some obvious drawbacks. Books that appear without the fanfare of a major ad campaign depend for their sales on word of mouth, which travels relatively slowly. Then too, the policy inevitably entails an emphasis on the here-and-now, hot-off-the-press, at the expense of books that might have been published a year or so (or, God forbid, a century or so) before. "A few years ago," says Harry Hoffman, head of Waldenbooks, "backlist was 65 percent of our business, and frontlist—titles out less than a year—was 35. Now it's the reverse. People are interested in what's happening—whether it's diet or sports."[101] They're also interested, says Hoffman, in brevity: "People want something short that they can read in a night."[102]

But backlist, of course, is more than just old books. Writ large, it is a society's literary culture, its repository of knowledge, its memory. Oh well. Times change. "The chains serve a different community of book readers from any that the book business has ever had before—book readers with different tastes," says Richard Snyder of Simon & Schuster. "The elitism of the book market doesn't exist anymore."[103]

The book market is likely to become even more democratic in the future. Waldenbooks, for example, has begun to enter the publishing business, putting out a series of genre fiction (mystery, romance, western, science fiction, etc.). "There is a demand," says Harry Hoffman, "for series fiction that you read in a couple of hours."[104]

There are, to be sure, some countertrends. During the past few years, several books of substance have risen rather high on the bestseller lists—Allan Bloom's *Closing of the American Mind,* James Gleick's *Chaos,* Paul Kennedy's *Rise and Fall of the Great Powers.* One should also note, however, that both Bloom's and Kennedy's books were introduced to the public through independent bookstores, which have been declining in number.

Another countertrend is reflected in the saga of the National Book Awards. Begun in 1950, the awards were traditionally handed out on the basis of literary merit, as determined by a panel of writers and critics. But in 1980, the publishing community decided that the awards were too stuffy, too "elitist." Accordingly, the National Book Awards became the American Book Awards, to be conferred by a panel that now included booksellers and librarians. The number of categories was greatly expanded, to include such things as westerns, mysteries, and books dealing with "lifestyle, sports and self-improvement." In response, more than fifty well-known authors and critics boycotted the 1980 awards ceremony; and by 1984, the number of categories had been cut back to three. In 1987, the American Book Awards became once again the National Book Awards, with a panel composed of writers and critics.

Finally, one should mention the growth of small publishing houses across the country. (In 1948, there were 357 American publishers; today there are more than 21,000.) Although most of these houses publish works of limited interest (and value), an increasing number—David R. Godine of Boston; North Point Press of Berkeley—publish books of genuine merit. In so doing, they provide a refuge for some of the mid-list writers abandoned by the publishing conglomerates. There is, however, a catch. As Walter Powell points out, "what is advantageous for readers may not augur as well for authors, particularly for those whose writing constitutes their primary source of income. Books produced by smaller houses generally get less exposure and sell fewer copies than they would had they been published by large trade houses."[105] In other words, writers, get thee to a university (or hie thee to Hollywood).

Even allowing for such countertrends, one cannot be exactly sanguine about the future of American publishing. The trends themselves are simply too overwhelming. As Ted Solotaroff, a senior editor at Harper & Row, remarked toward the end of a lengthy article in *The New Republic*, "I have been painting a bleak picture of the book business, because this bleakness is dominant and spreading." Said business, he concluded, is beset by a "heedless momentum in the direction of mediocrity."[106]

American publishing, writes Jonathan Yardley, book critic of the *Washington Post*, is "an industry that's doing well commercially but seems to care less and less about its larger cultural responsibilities, about perpetuating and strengthening the literary tradition that once was its principal raison d'etre . . ." It is, he concludes, "a publishing industry that now cares almost entirely for glitz and glitter . . ."[106a]

Or in the words of Felix Rohatyn, whose firm arranged several of the publishing takeovers: "Everything in this world has turned into show business."

MOVIES AND TELEVISION

Although this chapter is concerned primarily with certain institutions centered in the East, we must also take note of some recent developments in movies and television. One such development is the runaway growth of videocassettes, which like some insidious army of Hollywood gremlins now occupy more than half of American households and produce more revenue for the movie industry than the showing of movies in theaters themselves.

For a while, it looked as if the effects of the invasion would be largely benign, and indeed even salutary. Theater ticket receipts did not hit the skids, as many had predicted. Instead, following a temporary decline in 1985, they rose to a record $4.3 billion in 1987; and a record $4.4 billion in 1988. Theaters did not close; instead, they increased in number to a record 23,000. At the same time, the availability of videocassettes meant that many people could enjoy just about any movie they chose, whenever they chose. A variety of video shops sprang up, some of which functioned like neighborhood bookstores—stocking classic and even esoteric selections, offering advice on various movies, phoning customers when particular tapes arrived.

Perhaps best of all, the newfound market for videocassettes seemed to encourage the production of interesting, offbeat films from independent studios, as opposed to the blockbuster movies churned out by the majors. True, there were some casualties along the way. Revival houses—such as the Regency, the New Yorker, the Carnegie Hall, the Thalia, the Metro and the Hollywood Twin, all in New York—were either closed or transformed into first-run theaters; but these seemed to be necessary losses.

By the latter part of the eighties, however, things had started to turn sour. Along with the interesting, offbeat films, Hollywood had begun to regurgitate hundreds of films of every description. Many of these were intended primarily for the videocassette market, but in order to attract attention and to be certified as "movies," they first had to be shown in movie theaters.

The new movie theaters were ideally suited to this purpose.

Rather than being cavernous, rococo, urban palaces—or smaller, unpretentious, neighborhood bijoux—most of them were "multiplexes" owned by giant theater chains and situated mainly in suburban shopping centers (the ultimate example being the eighteen-screen Universal Cineplex in Los Angeles). Thus, a movie could be opened before a large number of relatively small, middlebrow audiences in a variety of locations. If it became an instant hit, it could quickly be expanded to additional screens. If not, it could just as quickly be dispatched, as most of the movies were (and are). The only problem was that the interesting, offbeat films—lacking major advertising budgets and time to build an audience through word of mouth—were quickly dispatched.

Meanwhile, major changes were taking place in the video stores. Increasingly, the neighborhood video "bookstores" found themselves squeezed from two directions: from below, by such places as convenience stores and grocery stores (some of which charged as little as forty-nine cents per rental); and from above, by newly formed video chain stores (one of the largest of which is called, so help me, the Blockbuster Entertainment Corporation. In 1988, Blockbuster claimed to be opening a new store every forty hours).

At the same time, all the video stores were faced with a flood of "product"—some six hundred tapes a month—along with a flood of television ads for the latest must-see movie. The results were more or less predictable. Video stores (like chain bookstores) began stocking up on the latest hits and giving short shrift to the rest. And since the demand for each new blockbuster lasted for only about ninety days, the stores were then forced to unload those tapes to clear space for the next incoming wave. Another result was also predictable. Production funds for independent films began drying up.

Back on the theater front, another new development was moving things in the same general direction. The new theater chains were being taken over by the major Hollywood studios. Forty years before, the federal government had barred the studios from just this practice—on grounds that it violated the antitrust laws—but in the present era of deregulation, the feds had apparently changed their minds.

The new era of moviegoing—and the popularity of video-cassettes—will likely have some other effects as well. When people choose to see a movie in a theater, they usually do so with some deliberation, reading reviews and so on. (Or at least they used to. Increasingly, writes Charles Champlin of the *Los Angeles Times,* studios are releasing films without benefit of press screenings, in order to try to avoid the critics. In newspaper ads, the studios usually quote television critics—who can be depended upon to say things such as "I cheered and stomped" (an actual quote that ran in an ad)—rather than print reviewers, who are perceived as elitist.)

When people choose to rent a movie on cassette, however, they usually do so much more casually, often on the basis of "who's in it." Once they're home, the same attitude holds sway. Watching a cassette, for many people (especially younger people), is an occasion to call a couple of friends, send out for pizza and crack one open for Spuds MacKenzie. Movies will become more ordinary, like a part of the furniture, like—well, teevee. They will be designed to hold the attention of people who are talking among themselves and passing the pizza, and who can just as easily change the channel.

Thus, the net effect of the video craze will be increased democratization—of movies, and by extension, of the culture as a whole.

On television, the choice of programs is of course much greater than ever before—or is it? Cable television, which was supposed to usher in the millennium, is now to be found in more than half of American households; but with certain exceptions, the fare is hardly different from what is broadcast over the commercial networks.

To be sure, there are many more programs and services. There is round-the-clock news, round-the-clock weather, round-the-clock shopping, lots of sports, lots (and lots) of movies, stand-up comedy with four letter words, three-hour game shows in Spanish, talk shows on fashion and pop psychology, and rock videos without end.

Some of the programs are even worthwhile. C-SPAN, the Cable Satellite Public Affairs Network (a nonprofit service funded by the cable industry), provides gavel-to-gavel coverage of proceedings on the floor of the House, as well as footage of Senate and House committee hearings and various public policy forums.* HBO, in

---

* Unfortunately, the service is carried by perhaps one cable system out of three.

addition to running an endless stream of Hollywood movies (and a few of its own), recently offered "Tanner '88," a presidential campaign satire written by Garry Trudeau and directed by Robert Altman. For the most part, however, cable has largely failed to fulfill the widespread expectations that it would tender an alternative to the medium's lowest-common-denominator fare.

For a time, it appeared that things would turn out differently. In 1980, various cable companies joined forces to offer a service called Bravo, which was designed exclusively for the performing arts. In the spring of 1981, ABC and the Hearst Corporation launched a service called ARTS, which likewise was intended to present plays, dance and opera. In the fall of 1981, CBS begat CBS Cable, a cultural service that would produce about 60 percent of its own programming. In the summer of 1982, RCA (then the parent company of NBC) and Rockefeller Center begat the Entertainment Channel, which was originally intended (at least by the board of Rockefeller Center) to be much like CBS Cable, but which later announced that it would acquire about half of its programs from the BBC. In other words, New York—yet again—was making an effort to bring culture to the people.

CBS Cable, after losing $30 million, folded within a year. The Entertainment Channel, after losing $34 million, folded in nine months. ARTS, which had reportedly been losing money at the rate of $8 million a year, picked up the remnants of the Entertainment Channel to form the Arts & Entertainment Network, or A&E.

Since then, A&E has been surviving at a rather modest (if rising) level, partly on the basis of programs from the BBC. Recently, the channel has begun to commission more of its own fare (for example, the production of a series of four one-act American plays for the 1989–90 season). But a good bit of its programming still consists of stand-up comedy. And in order to attract the male viewer sought by advertisers, A&E offers a lot of historical documentaries (a history of aviation, for example) and programs about war (the Normandy invasion). The Bravo arts channel, meanwhile, has survived at an even more modest level, mainly by running movies of the sort that used to play at the neighborhood art houses that videocassettes (and now cable television) have largely replaced.

Of course, there is still the promise of new technology looming in the distance like an obelisk. Pay-per-view, for example, allows cable subscribers to select individual programs for which they are later billed. So far, though, the system has been used mostly for movies. (In effect, the viewer avoids a trip to the video store, in return for which convenience he arranges to watch the movie at one of its scheduled air times.) There are other emerging technologies—direct-broadcast satellites, satellite master-antenna systems, fiber-optic telephone lines—all of them promising, all of them ultimately disappointing.

At the moment, in fact, one might almost say that the chief effect of cable television and its assorted variations, both commercial and technical, has been to blur the case for the *real* alternative to network television—yes, good old-fashioned *public* television. After all, goes the argument of the born-again laissez fairists, if people can get culture on cable, why should the government get into the act? Come to think of it, why should the government get into the act in any case? In the words of Mark Fowler, chairman of the FCC, "If there's a marketplace need for public television, it'll survive; and if not, it shouldn't." (How he would apply this reasoning to, say, the Metropolitan Opera or the National Philharmonic is not quite clear.)

At any rate, such was the attitude of the Nixon and Reagan administrations, both of which attempted to do away with public television entirely. (Nixon, of course, was convinced as well that PBS was infested with liberals.) Fortunately, Congress refused to go along, but even so, funds for public television during much of the Reagan reign were sharply reduced. In addition, PBS suffered from funding cuts for agencies such as the National Endowment for the Arts and Humanities, the National Science Foundation and the Department of Education, all of which had provided money for PBS programs.

As a result, the United States continued to lag far behind other western countries in support for public television. In 1985, for example, per capita expenditures for public television in Canada were $25; in Britain, $18; in New Zealand, $38; and in the United States, 57¢. Thus, the U.S. has nothing to compare to the public television production systems of countries such as Britain and West Germany; and according to Lawrence K. Grossman, former president of PBS, there is no way that a private television service—cable, satellite, what-have-you—could ever fill the void.

Faced with the shortage of funds, the member stations of PBS have resorted to various measures to try to close the gap. WNET in New York—one of the country's flagship stations, along with WGBH in Boston—announced that it is cutting back on national programming, thereby further expanding the American void. Meanwhile, the stations continue their annoying (though necessary) "pledge weeks," but since the audience has begun to tire of these seemingly endless exhortations, the stations have had to sweeten the pot. During the three-week pledge period on WNET, "Masterpiece Theater" and "American Playhouse" have been replaced by specials on everybody from Bing Crosby to Grace Kelly and Marilyn Monroe. Most of one Saturday was devoted to the Beatles, Elvis Presley and a prime-time program entitled "Shake, Rattle and Roll."

Another strategy being employed by many stations (following a suggestion by the Reagan administration) is what is euphemistically known as "enhanced underwriting"—in other words, commercials. Thus, viewers of public station KERA in Dallas have been treated to the sight of a local automobile dealer standing next to a brand-new Cadillac topped by a giant bow.

But automobile dealers, of course, are not interested solely in enhancing their image. They're interested in ratings, cost-per-thousand, sales. And perhaps because of this fact, a growing number of public stations have deliberately set out to expand their audience. Close to a hundred are now running syndicated commercial programs, such as "Star Trek," "Lassie" and "Leave It to Beaver."

Yet another dilemma facing public television is the fact that cable companies, though created mainly by people from the entertainment industry, are being increasingly treated by Congress and the courts as though they were journalistic enterprises (like newspapers, say) that are entitled to the protections of the First Amendment. Thus, cable companies are now allowed to drop any services they do not wish to carry—even if the replacement service (a movie channel, let's say) is one in which the cable company is a financial investor, and even if the service being dropped is a public television station. In fact, public television officials claim that such actions—either dropping a public station completely, or switching it to a higher, less desirable position on the cable dial—have so far affected more than two hundred stations, resulting in the loss of some three million viewers.

Moreover, such actions will likely continue as the cable companies follow the Hollywood studios' lead toward vertical integration. In the case of the studios, this means buying movie theaters. In the case of the cable companies, it means buying or investing in cable services (such as movie channels) and software (such as movies). Between April 1987 and April 1988, cable companies became equity partners in every major new service introduced.

The result of all this is that cable television and public television are becoming more and more a part of the system of middlebrow commercial television—to which, it was originally hoped, they might provide an attractive alternative.

An analogous process of democratization—or in this case, one might simply say Americanization—has begun to take over television in Europe. Historically, European television has been publicly owned, and its mission has been simple: culture to the people. In France, for example, one of the most influential programs is called "Apostrophes." Broadcast in prime time every Friday evening, it attracts as much as 15 percent of the viewing audience and consists entirely of a discussion of books. (Books! One explanation: 44 percent of the adult French population reads ten or more books a year, and 18 percent reads at least twenty-five. And not fluff, either. Serious fiction, politics, history . . .)[107]

But all that is beginning to change. France now has six television channels, only two of them government owned, and viewers are crowding around their sets to watch "Miami Vice," "Mannix," "Cagney and Lacey," "Columbo," "Hill Street Blues" and "Starsky and Hutch," along with the earlier available "Dallas." "La Roue de la Fortune" ("Wheel of Fortune") has reportedly caused near-riots among people seeking to appear on the show.

"The French film industry is being wrecked," writes James M. Markham in the *New York Times*.[108] Recently, reports Steven Greenhouse, also in the *Times,* French moviegoers, for the first time, have been going to see more American films than French films. Overall attendance, however, is down; local production is declining; and many of the French films that *do* get made are designed with an eye toward television. "Television wants proven films, without problems, with stars and very facile story lines," says Anne Andreu, filmwriter for *L'Evenement du Jeudi,* a French news weekly. "It's all very worrisome."[109]

"What we're seeing is the banalization of French cinema," says Serge Toubiana, editor-in-chief of *Cahiers du Cinema.*[110] In the land of Truffaut, Rohmer, Resnais, Godard and Malle, people are worried about the future of filmmaking.

For Hollywood, of course, the whole affair is a bonanza, especially since the French experience is being repeated, in varying degrees, all over Europe. (The matter of European residuals, in fact, was one of the chief reasons for the recent Hollywood writers' strike.) Other outposts of American culture have been equally blessed. Big Macs are sprouting like toadstools, even on the sacred Champs-Elysées. Europe's first Disneyland is now under construction on the outskirts of Paris. In the hills of Provence, where Jean de Florette farmed, the cynosure now is a roadside theme park known as the O. K. Corral.

American network television, to be sure, is undergoing its own transmogrification. In 1977, the three commercial networks could command about 90 percent of the viewing audience. By the spring of 1989, their percentage had declined to 61. Robert C. Wright, president of NBC, said the networks' share could drop to 55 percent within the next few years.

For the networks, the nightmare is not merely the zillions of spiffy new videocassettes just begging to be rented, nor the fifty new national networks on cable. There are also now more than three hundred independent television stations (up from just eighty-three in 1976); five superstations (including Ted Turner's hydra in Atlanta); plus the fledgling Fox "fourth network," owned by Rupert Murdoch.

Just what rough beast will emerge from all this turmoil, only time will tell, as they say on teevee. But for the time being, it might be useful to think of the process as a transfer of power from East Coast to West Coast, and from the few to the many.

East Coast to West Coast. Even as the networks are waning, the Hollywood studios are waxing. This is simply because there is now such a great and growing demand for "product," which the movie studios and television producers are all too eager to satisfy. "What is going on right now is a grab for power," writes Aljean Harmetz, the *New York Times*'s correspondent in Hollywood, "with the small getting big and the big getting huge, immense, gargantuan. . . . The buzzword in Hollywood is vertical integration. The major studios—and even some of the minor ones—intend to make and distribute movies, show them in their own theaters, manufacture and sell the videocassettes six months later, then syndicate their films to their own television stations, bypassing the networks, and, in the case of Disney, play them on a studio-owned pay-cable channel."[111]

To be sure, not all the flow of power is toward Hollywood. A great many movies these days are being filmed elsewhere, often New York. Television, too, is rediscovering Gotham. The number of television movies, specials and series made in New York rose from 45 in 1982 to 152 in 1988.

Part of the reason for New York's rebirth is the development and redevelopment of studios, notably the old Astoria Studios in Queens. Where the Marx Brothers, Gloria Swanson, W. C. Fields, Louise Brooks, Lillian Gish and Claudette Colbert made movies in the twenties and early thirties, now movies are made by Dustin Hoffman, Albert Finney, Paul Newman, Woody Allen, Francis Coppola and Sidney Lumet. Astoria is also being used for television—"The Cosby Show" is taped there—as is a new studio on a pier at West 23rd Street. Other shows taped in New York include the afternoon soaps, "Kate and Allie," "The Equalizer," "Saturday Night Live," and "Late Night with David Letterman."

For the most part, however, production remains in Hollywood. In 1987, California earned more than $6 billion from movie and television filming, compared to $2.3 billion for second place New York. (Florida was a distant third with $144 million.) It is significant that Rupert Murdoch has chosen to build his "fourth network" around a major Hollywood studio rather than around an entertainment company—or an evening newscast—centered in New York.

While many people question whether four "real" networks can actually survive, neither is it likely that all the networks will wither away. Two or three will presumably continue commissioning prime time programs for the foreseeable future. Meanwhile, the networks are also starting to get into cable. ABC, in addition to part-ownership of A&E, also has 80 percent of ESPN, the highly successful sports channel. NBC, which also owns a part of A&E,

recently acquired a cable network called Tempo, which it plans to merge with Cablevision, the country's twelfth-largest cable operator.

At the same time, the independent stations are also changing. Increasingly, they are broadcasting programs in what is known as first-run syndication. In other words, the programs are not network reruns (or even rejects, as a rule), but were produced specifically for the "network" of independent stations. In 1980, there were 25 such programs; in 1987, there were 96. Just to make matters more confusing, however, the most popular of these programs—such as "Wheel of Fortune," "Jeopardy," and "Entertainment Tonight"—are as apt to air on network affiliates as they are on independents. And if the program is popular and prime-time—as is the case with "Star Trek: The Next Generation"—it is apt to air on a network affiliate at the expense of a network program. Because of all this, first-run syndication is attracting the Hollywood biggies: Paramount, MCA, Disney, Lorimar.

Over at the PBS affiliates, meanwhile, things are equally confusing, as stations air not only reruns of "Leave It to Beaver," but Hollywood movies as well. In addition, PBS engages on occasion in production co-ventures with cable and the networks.

The result of all this bed-hopping is increasingly to blur the lines between the various types of television channels, and, in general, to reduce everything to a fairly low common denominator—which is more or less where we began. At the same time, though, there is still a growing demand for "product"; and now as before, product is made in Hollywood.

In the not too distant future, there will be more of that product. True, the cyclical financing of the movie business may cause a decline in the number of new films over the next year or so. But beyond that, there appears to be only perpetual gravy.

The reason is mainly that foreign demand for Hollywood entertainment—the only true mass global culture—is growing by leaps and bounds, not only in Europe but in Asia as well. American film companies earned $1.13 billion from foreign distribution in 1988—compared to $800 million in 1985. Foreign television sales in 1988 rose 30 percent, to $1.3 billion—a figure that is expected to jump to $2.3 billion by 1990. In the words of *The Economist:* "the ancillary markets are exploding. Satellite television, deregulation and privatisation promise almost unlimited opportunities world-wide for Hollywood."[112]

The transfer of power from the few to the many. By *the few* in this case is meant once again the three commercial networks; and by *the many* is meant not the new commercial networks but rather the individual viewers, all 245 million of them. *The transfer of power* is simply the fact that viewers today have so many more choices, and so much more control in making those choices, than they ever had before.

The process is similar to the transition from movies to television. Or from network radio to station-by-station radio. Or from national, general-interest magazines such as *Look* and *Life* to the multiplicity of special-interest, "lifestyle" magazines. In each case, the transition produced a greatly expanded number of choices (although not a flowering of American culture). It also produced a heightened sense of individual power and control, of individual self-importance. It engendered a feeling that each individual's tastes and values—no matter how mundane—are all that matter.

Such feelings are likely to increase in the very near future. Computer owners, for example, are using their PCs to practice what is known as desktop publishing, thereby producing professional-looking copies of their very own work—poetry, short stories, what-have-you. After all, who needs some publisher back in New York to tell him what's good?

On the television front, cable companies have been experimenting with various forms of "two-way TV," which allow the viewer to interact with his television set. In one system, a person watching a sporting event can actually select the shots he wants to see—a zoom-in on the quarterback, a wide-angle shot of the nickel defense . . . If that isn't good enough, he can start up his own little television station. (Just the thing for televising the high school football game.) Hundreds, in fact, have already done it, and thousands more have applied to the FCC for licenses. Too much trouble? How about home video? Roll off some footage of Flo and the kids and send it off to Johnny Carson. Next thing you know, you're on national TV.

Or in the words of Tom Wolfe: "Me . . . Me . . . Me . . . Me . . ."

NETWORK TELEVISION NEWS

There will, of course, be a certain number of casualties on the road to renewed democratization. In addition to cultural programming and possibly public television, one of the casualties may well turn out to be network television news.

Part of the difficulty in understanding network news stems from a common misconception: namely, that the content of the news is determined by an all-out race for ratings. It isn't, exactly. Rather, it is determined by a continuing tug-of-war. On one side are the networks' old-guard journalists—along with the New York television critics—who still believe that news should be substantive and serious. On the other are the newer video people, who think that news should be entertaining and profitable. And for much of the recent past, the younger side has been winning.

It is hard to know exactly what date to choose for the start of the decline of network journalism. One could go all the way back to January 31, 1961, when Edward R. Murrow announced his resignation from CBS after the network had taken away his program, "See It Now." (In the eyes of the network, Murrow had become too "controversial"; but a few years later, after Murrow had died, CBS would take great pride in being known as Murrow's bailiwick.)

Or one could go back to the middle of February 1966, when Fred Friendly (Murrow's former producer) resigned as president of CBS News following the network's decision to broadcast a rerun of "I Love Lucy" rather than the Senate Foreign Relations Committee hearings on Vietnam. (Sodden afterthought: nobody resigns from the networks anymore; they just get fired.)

But these events were early warning signs. After all, the half-hour evening newscast, network journalism's principal weapon, was not wheeled out of the hangar until 1963. During much of the sixties, the networks' devotion to documentaries noticeably increased. True, the networks' motives were not entirely pure. In part, the broadcasters were trying to atone for the quiz-show scandals of 1959. In part, they were trying to placate Newton Minow, the Kennedy-appointed chairman of the FCC, who in a now-famous speech in 1961, described American television as "a vast wasteland." Even so, at the time of Ed Murrow's resignation, the networks' crucial coverage of the civil rights movement, the Vietnam War and the Watergate crisis was yet to come.

As it happened, the seeds of the eventual decline of network news were not sown primarily at the networks themselves. Instead, they took root at the networks' local affiliates.

By the start of the seventies, many of those affiliates had discovered that local newscasts could be a big source of revenue. Accordingly, they set about fattening the goose. First they hired teams of consultants, who in turn came up with recommendations for a newscast that would appeal to a "broader audience." Such a newscast would include: a friendly anchor team (usually consisting of male and female anchors, the man often a few years older; a zany weatherman; and a clean-cut, fast-talking sports guy); lots of jokes and chatter (thereby enabling the team to fulfill its function as a surrogate family); reporter participation in stories; news you can use (how to cure back pain, etc.); fewer stories from city hall, the county courthouse and the state capitol (people are not really interested in government); more sex; more crime; more "human interest" stories (kids saved from certain death are always good); faster pacing; more action—fires, car wrecks, disasters. As Frank Magid, one of the best-known consultants, explained his philosophy of broadcast journalism: "ratings are improved not when listeners are told what they should know, but what they want to hear."[113]

The CBS affiliate in San Diego expanded on this notion in a memo posted in the newsroom:

> Remember, the vast majority of our viewers hold blue-collar jobs. The vast majority of our viewers never went to college. . . . The vast majority of our viewers have never seen a copy of the *New York Times*. The vast majority of our viewers do not read the same books and magazines that you read . . . in fact, many of them never read anything. The vast majority of the viewers in this television market currently ignore TV news.[114]

"To encourage more of these people to watch," writes Barbara Matusow in *The Evening Stars: The Making of the Network News Anchor,* "local newscasts took on a homier, more casual, purposely anti-intellectual atmosphere, in recognition of the fear with which the average American is thought to view anything even faintly smacking of intellectualism."[115]

Newspaper ads for those newscasts adopted much the same approach. In San Francisco, one station ran a full-page ad that featured its reporters wearing dog masks. (News hounds, get it?) A rival station responded with a full-page ad featuring *its* reporters dressed as cowboys. (Just why, I've forgotten.)

At the networks themselves, things did not reach quite this level, but they came pretty close. During the mid-seventies, NBC was run by a man named Herbert Schlosser, a former West Coast programming executive with a background in the motion picture end of television. When Schlosser became president of NBC in 1974, he brought with him a coterie of Los Angeles executives that quickly became known around network headquarters as the California mafia.

Schlosser was impressed by the show biz techniques that had elevated the network's station in Los Angeles, KNBC, from third place to first place in the ratings for the evening news. In particular, he was impressed by the station's anchor, a spellbinding figure named Tom Snyder. Soon after taking over as network president, Schlosser resolved to make Tom Snyder the anchor for the "NBC Nightly News." (John Chancellor, who then held the post, was regarded by the California mafia as much too stuffy, too serious, too "Eastern.") Toward this end, Schlosser brought Snyder to New York, installing him as anchor of WNBC, as well as host of the network's late-night "Tomorrow" show. There, Snyder was to bide his time until Chancellor could be eased out of his network chair.

In the end, of course, cooler heads prevailed. Schlosser was replaced as network president in early 1978 by Fred Silverman, who had recently engineered ABC's ascent from number three to number one in the ratings. With one eye cocked toward the New York critics—who by now were alert for any signs of "creeping localism"—Silverman decided to keep John Chancellor around for a while. When Chanceller was eventually made network commentator, his replacement as anchor was not Tom Snyder but Tom Brokaw.

The appointment of Brokaw, however, did not entirely assuage the critics. For one thing, Brokaw had also served as anchor of KNBC in Los Angeles. From there, he had been promoted to the prestigious post of NBC White House correspondent—a move that raised a great many Washington eyebrows. (Today, of course, Brokaw presents himself as a serious fellow, as perhaps he is, but I recall an appearance of his on the Johnny Carson show when he remarked, in passing, that his grades in college had been decided "on a case-by-case basis—a case of Miller, a case of Bud . . .") Finally, in choosing Brokaw as its sole evening anchor, NBC at the same time rejected the much more knowledgeable—but less photogenic—Roger Mudd.

Meanwhile, "localism" was also seeping into the evening news at ABC. During the mid-seventies, for example, ABC News vice-president Bill Sheehan wrote a memo to the staff of the "Evening News," suggesting that, "After the major stories of the day, we must go after the stories that grab people where they're involved. . . . I want more stories about the 'pop people.' The fashionable people. The new fads. Bright ideas. Changing mores and moralities. . . . The back of our show must be different from the competition's. Provocative. Funny. Interesting, because we're getting to the subjects that many people are interested in, and people are interested in many things that are not intrinsically important."[116]

Sheehan's memo prompted a hostile reaction from television critics when it was leaked to the press, and for a while, ABC appeared to back away from putting it into effect. In the meantime, though, the network came up with another idea to boost the ratings of its third-place newscast. In the spring of 1976, ABC hired Barbara Walters to co-anchor the evening news, with Harry Reasoner.

Apparently the network was trying to create that surrogate family so beloved of local news directors; but in any case, it badly miscalculated. Response to the Walters hiring was almost uniformly negative. Within the television community, this feeling was increased by talk about Walters's contract. Negotiated by a pair of show business agents, it called for a salary of slightly more than a million dollars a year (at the time, an unheard of amount for a "journalist"). In addition, it required that she be provided a makeup consultant, a "wardrobe person," and, when traveling, "first-class hotel accommodations (suite if available)," as well as a hairdresser.[117] Naturally, the boys on the bus all hated her for it. Walter Cronkite allowed as how he had "the sickening sensation that we were all going under, that all of our efforts to hold network news aloof from show business had failed."[118]

As it turned out, of course, the marriage between Barbara Walters and Harry Reasoner was a disaster. And largely because of this fact, Bill Sheehan was replaced as head of the news division, in June of 1977, by a man named Roone Arledge. In his role as president of ABC Sports, Arledge had already become something of a legend for televised glitter and flash, a reputation that was not diminished by his fondness for safari jackets, foot-long cigars, and a silvery, chauffeur-driven Jaguar.

Not long after taking over at ABC News, Arledge expressed his admiration for a young man named Geraldo Rivera, who was then employed in ABC's entertainment division. Not long after that came the capture of "Son of Sam," a serial killer who had been terrorizing metropolitan New York. In response to the arrest, Arledge himself showed up at Manhattan police headquarters at 3 A.M., dressed, according to a news account, "as if for a touch football game, a glass of scotch in one hand, a portable two-way radio in the other, directing his network's 'feeds to the Coast.' "[119] On that evening's ABC newscast, the Son of Sam story filled an entire 19½–minute segment (out of a total news program of only 22 minutes). Prominently featured, dressed in jeans and a T-shirt, was Geraldo Rivera. Overlooking the fact that the suspect had yet to be convicted, Rivera referred to him as a "fiend" and a "murderer." Not surprisingly, the whole performance drew some sharp rebukes from television critics, as well as from the network's Washington correspondents.

Following this episode, Arledge and his newscast sobered up considerably. Even so, ABC continued to confer with consultant Frank Magid (the same Frank Magid who had done such wonders for local stations) over how to broaden its newscast's appeal.

CBS, during all this time, had more or less disdained such gimmickry, partly because of the legacy of Murrow et al., partly because of the presence of Cronkite et al. But in March of 1981, Cronkite retired; and under his replacement, Dan Rather, the ratings for the "Evening News" began a steady decline. By November CBS was dead last for the first time ever; and thirty-second commercial spots, which had previously gone for $40,000, were now down to $30,000. This was getting serious.

Before the month was out, CBS had brought in someone to fix things. The new president of CBS News was Van Gordon Sauter, a burly, bearded man who (like Roone Arledge at ABC) was head of the network's sports division. Before that, he had become a specialist at reviving the ratings of local newscasts, most recently at KNXT (now KCBS), the network-owned-and-operated station in Los Angeles. While there, he married the sister of Jerry Brown, the governor of California.

Traditionally at CBS, the production of the "Evening News" had consisted, in a sense, of taking the front page of the *New York Times* and putting it on the air. Under Van Gordon Sauter, this system was to undergo a radical change. The old way, he said, was elitist. It was news put together by people who bought their clothes at Saks and Bloomingdale's, rather than at shopping centers, "where the real people in this country spend their time."[120] The "Evening News" should appeal, he said, to the interests and emotions of the average American. When a producer would insist that such-and-such a story was important—a story, say, on Parliamentary elections in England—Sauter would ask why. If the producer persisted, Sauter would again ask why.

Thus, on an evening when NBC and ABC led their newscasts with a report on House passage of the tax reform bill, CBS led with a story on a prison rebellion in Oklahoma, where the inmates had taken several guards hostage. Then it was on to Louisiana, where the trial of flamboyant governor Edwin Edwards had ended in a hung jury. Next came some footage of a high-rise building collapsing in Los Angeles (three dead, six injured), followed by an update from Madison Township, Ohio, on the condition of nine-year-old Jeremy Ghiloni. The evening before, CBS had filled its newscast with film of Jeremy being rescued from the icy waters of a local pond. Tonight it showed his schoolmates writing get-well cards. And so it went.

Even when CBS did cover national stories, it covered them from the viewpoint of the average man. Thus, a report on the balance of trade would consist mainly of interviews with laid-off automobile workers in Detroit. Some critics have praised this "populist" approach, but it seems to me that its dangers generally outweigh its advantages. What it says to the average viewer is that if this story affects you personally, right now, then it's important. If not—if it deals with arms control, say, or the federal debt or the EEC—why bother?

On the "Evening News" under Van Gordon Sauter, the bother quotient was very low. As Michael Massing remarked in the *Columbia Journalism Review,* "CBS often seemed like a network version of local television."[121] There were endless stories on the weather, for example (a snowstorm in Denver, fog in Dallas). There were stories on Herschel the sea lion, on a flying Santa who carries gifts to lighthouses, on a California town overrun by peacocks. There were moments of excruciating cuteness, all delivered in an upbeat manner that at times approached that of Mary Hart (the Queen of Cute) on "Entertainment Tonight." (Rather's opening line at the Geneva summit: "Ready, set, Gorbachev!") Finally, there were moments of . . . "Moments"—Sauter's term for those poignant little scenes that supposedly capture the essence of a story. (Sauter's example: Nancy Reagan attending a military memorial service and dabbing a tear from her eye.)

There was one thing to be said for all this treacle, of course. It worked. CBS regained the lead in the ratings.

Not everyone, however, was pleased. Walter Cronkite complained of the network's repeated attempts to "lighten up the news."[122] Richard Salant, who served as president of CBS News for sixteen years, alluded to a famous speech in which Edward Murrow had warned of the dangers of show business and advertising. Salant then remarked that, "the seeds of trouble Murrow talked about have turned into forests."[123] Bill Boyers, who worked at CBS off and on during the first half of the eighties, was even more expansive. Referring to "the encroachment of entertainment values," he went on to say:

> Not only were those values invited in, they were exalted. The line between entertainment and news was steadily blurred. Our center of gravity shifted from the standards and practices of the news business to show business. In meeting after meeting, "Entertainment Tonight" was touted as the model—breezy, entertaining, undemanding. . . . Pretty soon, tax policy had to compete with stories about three-legged sheep, and the three-legged sheep won.[124]

But CBS was not the only culprit. By the mid-eighties, the three network evening newscasts were actually quite similar: shorter, faster-paced stories, with "interviews" that went by in the blink of an eye; news you could use, especially on health; Hollywood-style theme music (NBC's was composed by John Williams, who also did the music for *Star Wars, E.T.* and *Superman*); fewer weighty reports out of Washington, and more human-interest stories from the hinterlands; pages from the *People* magazine school of journalism (ABC's Person of the Week); a dearth of commentary (except for John Chancellor on NBC); a growing number of sports stories, which ABC used in a shameless effort to promote its "Monday Night Football"; and so on.

Traditional news had said to the viewer: what is important is what is happening in Washington, New York, London and Paris; and we're going to tell you what it is. Now came the *new* news, saying to the viewer: what is important is what is going on in Peoria and Van Nuys; in a word, you. And we're going to let you tell us about it. The hero of the new news was the average man.

A similar strain of democratization had infected the other facets of television news. Documentaries, which the average viewer found much too dull, had largely disappeared (an outcome that was hastened by the FCC's evaporating interest in what had formerly been referred to as public service programming). In 1966, the three commercial networks aired 69 such programs (39 on CBS, 16 on ABC, 14 on NBC). In 1986, the total was 14.

What few documentaries remained were almost never referred to as such (since the average viewer supposedly found the term too serious). Camouflaged as "white papers," they were hidden away at Siberian locations on the programming schedule (Saturday night at ten, say), where they usually dealt with "lifestyle" subjects, rather than the weighty issues of the past. In place of "Harvest of Shame" and "The Selling of the Pentagon," we got "Scared Sexless," an NBC report on the social effects of the AIDS panic, broadcast on December 30, 1987. Narrated by Connie Chung, who often appeared standing between a pair of beds, the program featured such well-known sex experts as Goldie Hawn, Alan Alda and Marcus Allen, running back for the L.A. Raiders, who was described by

Chung as being "as close to a single stud as one gets." Just to make doubly sure the viewer stayed awake (and away from the dial), the program also featured a female comic, who popped in from time to time with some sexual innuendo. As it turned out, "Scared Sexless" was the highest-rated NBC "documentary" since "UFOs: Do You Believe?" in 1974.

CBS also weighed in—very lightly, as it happened—with a replacement for the allegedly dying documentary. Following the more or less unanticipated success of a sort of fast-food documentary called "48 Hours on Crack Street," the network, in the best show biz fashion, came up with the idea of doing a sequel. Which of course begat another sequel . . . And so it came to pass that the nation was blessed with "48 Hours in Las Vegas," "48 Hours in Hollywood," 48 Hours in a big-city hospital, 48 Hours at a big-city airport, and 48 Hours at the Westminster Dog Show. As if that weren't enough, we were also presented with 48 Hours in college basketball, a program that was aired just a few days prior to the college basketball championship game—which, in one of those odd little coincidences of network programming, was also aired on CBS.

Since "48 Hours" is produced by CBS News, some of the programs concern substantive issues, on a few of which the programs even manage to shed some light (for example, a report in September 1988 on the Yonkers racial housing dispute). As a rule, though, the program's quick-and-dirty production approach succeeds in generating mostly heat. Thus, a program on the West Bank and Gaza (February 9, 1988) managed to consume the entire hour without really explaining what the shouting was all about. In the main, the program consisted of the sort of footage one sees every night on the evening news.

In addition to pseudo-documentaries, the networks have been much taken of late by a television mongrel called the docudrama—an animal with numerous deficiencies. For one thing, docudramas are invariably produced by a network's entertainment division rather than its news division, which means the programs' creators are often given license to play fast and loose with the facts. Thus, in a five-hour CBS docudrama called "The Atlanta Child Murders" (seen by an estimated 50 million people), Hollywood screenwriter Abby Mann conducted a "crusade," as he put it, to convince the viewer that the defendant in the case was wrongfully convicted. In so doing, however, he omitted crucial testimony that did not conform to his crusade. In the words of *Newsweek*'s Atlanta bureau chief, Vern E. Smith, who covered the case from its beginning, the program "distorts much of the official record. . . . Events are taken out of context, characters created, scenes invented and trial testimony altered. Real people are either savaged or omitted."[125]

Another problem with docudramas, claim many critics, is that they weaken the viewer's already tenuous distinction between fiction and reality. But Don Hewitt, executive producer of CBS's "60 Minutes," demurs. Alluding to a *New York Times* editorial that was sharply critical of "The Atlanta Child Murders," Hewitt observed: "The fact is, the *New York Times* thinks the public is dumb, and has to be constantly educated about what it's watching. The public isn't dumb. They know very well what they're watching, and they know a drama when they see one."[126]

That's what Hewitt observed in Los Angeles, at a luncheon hosted by the Hollywood Radio and Television Society. In New York, however, on an earlier occasion, Hewitt offered a rather different assessment (quoted in the previous chapter). What he said was this: "The TV set is a stage, and on that stage, the audience watches 'Dallas' and 'Dynasty' and newscasts and paid political ads, and after a while they can't tell which is which."

One suspects that the latter statement is closer to Hewitt's actual beliefs—and certainly closer to the truth. Referring to people who watch several different programs during an evening of television, Michael Morgan, assistant professor in the department of communications studies at the University of Massachusetts, reports that, "People can't remember whether they heard something on the news or elsewhere; all of television looks very realistic."[127]

Shortly before leaving CBS, Bill Moyers made one last pitch for the moribund documentary. Over dinner at the Polo Lounge, Moyers was asked by Gene Jankowski, then president of the CBS Broadcast Group, just what would keep him at the network. As Moyers recalls it:

I said, "You own the title to the best known name in broadcasting history: 'See It Now.' Resurrect it. Give me a 52–week commitment, your worst time slot—a slot you haven't won for years. Give me call on some of CBS News's best producers and reporters, and a little patience. In return, this is what you'll get: ratings as good as or better than you've had in that slot, and—because of the lower costs—profits better than you can get in the same slot, the prestige of a first-class broadcast and the next generation of '60 Minutes' correspondents—the only way to prepare those people is to give them hard journalistic assignments. At the end of one year, you decide the success or failure. If it fails, send me $1 in the mail. If it succeeds, give me any payment you want—no agents."

He looked at me and said, "Bill, I'm going to stick with 'West 57th' "[128]

"West 57th," of course, is one of the network's pair of magazine shows, the other being "60 Minutes." Of the two, "60 Minutes" is far and away the more profitable, earning the network upwards of $70 million a year. As everyone knows, it is also far older, having recently celebrated its twenty-first season (an eternity in television).

"60 Minutes," however, "has changed radically over the years," according to Ernest Leiser, who worked as a CBS News correspondent, producer and executive for twenty-nine years and is now a senior fellow at the Gannett Center for Media Studies at Columbia University. Writing in the *Washington Journalism Review,* Leiser reports:

I looked a while back at the "60 Minutes" story logs going back to autumn of 1968, when it first went on the air. Granted, that was an election year, but it was striking how heavily and topically Hewitt and his correspondents, Mike Wallace and Harry Reasoner, covered politics. And for years thereafter, there was at least one top-of-the-news report on the broadcast. That was what Salant, as president of CBS News, thought he had agreed to. "I thought of it as coming right out of the hard news in pieces that couldn't be handled in two or three minutes and weren't worth the hour of a documentary," he says. When it began, Salant recalls, "60 Minutes" could only have been a product of the CBS News operation. Now, it is self-contained and it could just as easily come out of an independent syndicate, like Grant Tinker's TV version of *USA Today.*[129]

To be sure, "60 Minutes" still does some hard-news segments, but these seem to have been lifted from local news stories and local lawsuits (for example, the recent report on the problems of the shipboard Phalanx gun). And while all the stories on "60 Minutes" are still done with a certain "style," one suspects that from a journalistic standpoint, few of them really "matter." (My own theory is that "60 Minutes" *seems* more important that it is—mainly as a result of a device that is usually overlooked: the ticking stopwatch. As employed at the start of each program, the stopwatch seems to be counting down to something—such as a bomb explosion. Of course, the bomb almost never goes off anymore, but after fifteen minutes of Harry Reasoner or Morley Safer, the viewer has usually forgotten all about it.)

"West 57th" matters even less. Produced by a man who made his reputation through commercials for mouthwash and diapers, the program caused a mild sensation when it hit the screen in 1985, what with its whiz-bang style and its crew of young reporters who bopped around town like some sort of yuppie Mod Squad. William Leonard, former president of CBS News, allowed as how "it came closer to show biz than our biz. I thought it was well photographed and attractive to watch, but I don't think it was journalism by any stretch of the imagination. But I don't think that counts any-more."[130] Fred Friendly called the show "a piece of glitz."[131]

To be sure, the MTV-look of "West 57th" is somewhat under-standable in an age when sit-coms and cop shows (not to mention MTV) have conditioned viewers to expect something to happen every few minutes (if not every few seconds). If it doesn't, those viewers change the channel. In fact, a recent study by *Channels* magazine found that more than half the viewers aged 18 to 34 use remote-control devices to watch more than one program at a time, while 20 percent watch *three* or more shows. "Grazing," it's called.

One should also note that the premiere edition of "West 57th" had its admirers. "Entertainment Tonight" conducted a poll. Eleven hundred people didn't like the program; eighty-three hundred did.

At any rate, the show has improved a bit since then. The number of segments has been reduced from five to four, and some of these have been relatively respectable. (A segment on religious con men, for example, was just the sort of penny-ante exposé that enabled "60 Minutes" to make a name for itself.)

But "West 57th" still has a long way to go. For one thing, the program has been shifted to Saturday night at ten, an hour when not many yuppies are watching network television. Then, too, most of the segments are still pretty vapid: an embarrassingly obsequious interview with Bess Myerson; a superficial piece on Larry King; an interview with Tom Hanks while the subject was hitting baseballs at Dodger Stadium. (Why?)

One suspects that "West 57th" showed its true colors in October 1988. Toward the end of the month, CBS ran a two-part mini-series on Jack the Ripper. In between the two parts, "West 57th" also did a piece on Jack the Ripper. All week long, ads for the two programs—the mini-series and the "West 57th" segment—ran back-to-back on CBS.

ABC's "20/20" is beset by similar shortcomings. Many of its segments have tended toward the tabloid (Elvis Presley's "long and troubled abuse of drugs"); and the program has been shifted to Friday night at ten. The change in time slot, along with other complaints, prompted widespread dissatisfaction among the staff; and by mid-summer of 1988, half the program's twenty-five producers were reported to be looking for other employment. Meanwhile, NBC had failed for the umpteenth time to develop a "successful" weekly magazine (meaning one that would attract a sizable audience), its latest effort being "American Almanac" (later called "1986"). At the same time, CBS and ABC had also failed with two new magazines: "American Parade" (later called "Crossroads") and "Our World." As you can see, the names get lighter and sappier as we go along.*

In the end, perhaps the best way to regard such "news magazines" (including "60 Minutes") is not as news magazines at all, but rather as entertainment programs that happen to deal with factual material ("reality-based programming," as the genre is known at the networks). They do so because this is the type of programming that television audiences, conditioned by television news, have come to like best. Also because an hour of "West 57th" is a lot cheaper to produce than an hour of "Miami Vice." Otherwise, the fact that the magazine programs deal with "reality" is more or less incidental.

This fact has become even more apparent in the relatively new

---

* At this writing, NBC is about to introduce yet another magazine—"Yesterday, Today and Tomorrow"—which has already drawn fire for its use of "dramatic re-creations." ABC, meanwhile, is introducing a magazine called "Prime Time Live," which will apparently depend heavily on the "chemistry" between its hosts, Diane Sawyer and Sam Donaldson—the odd couple. CBS, for its part, has put a new face on "West 57th." It's now called "Saturday Night with Connie Chung."

types of programs known collectively as tabloid television, or simply, trash TV. Ranging from talk shows such as "Geraldo" to "magazine" programs such as "Inside Edition" and "A Current Affair,"** tabloid television represents an all-time low for the country's most powerful medium. Typical subjects: gang rape, grave robbing, teenage satanic killers, female mud-wrestlers, and re-creations of countless murders, including one in which a man disposed of his wife by shoving her body through a wood-chipping machine. (At this writing, ten more such shows are planned for the fall of 1989.)

Aside from debasing the television audience, such shows tend to drag down more respectable programs to their own low level. Thus, on a recent program devoted to transvestitism, host Phil Donahue appeared on camera wearing a red dress and hose. A few months later, during a panel discussion led by Fred Friendly, Donahue accused his critics of "elitism." Geraldo Rivera, during the same discussion, claimed that he was merely "democratizing" the news.

According to Walter Cronkite, that's exactly the problem. During a dinner in his honor at New York's Museum of Broadcasting, Cronkite told the assembled guests that he was "horrified at the proliferation of tabloid journalism."[132] Later, he explained to the *New York Times* that he was very much concerned that tabloid journalism could ultimately influence network news.[133]

His concern is well founded. A recent edition of "60 Minutes" opened with a lengthy report of a bizarre Australian murder case in which a mother accused of infanticide claimed that her child had actually been carried away by a "dingo"—a wild dog. And how did "60 Minutes" justify this descent into tabloid journalism? As correspondent Ed Bradley explained, the story had just been made into a movie starring Meryl Streep. About the same time the movie was released, the "CBS Evening News" broadcast a tabloid piece about mothers who kill their babies.

Thus, the larger danger of tabloid journalism is that it will blur the already indistinct line between news and entertainment. Even now, these two forms of television are converging on a small universe of quasi-fact epitomized on the news side by the political

** "A Current Affair" is hosted by Maury Povich, who is married to CBS newswoman Connie Chung. Not long ago, the couple was interviewed on "Entertainment Tonight," an occurrence which inevitably suggested that their two careers are more or less the same.

photo-opportunity and programs such as "West 57th," and on the entertainment side by the docudrama and shows such as "Entertainment Tonight." The common product of these converging efforts is best described by the awful but apt neologism *infotainment.*

Infotainment is certainly the word for another facet of television news—the morning shows. For a while, the descent into show biz was led by ABC, with its folksy, homey "Good Morning America" (produced by the network's entertainment division). Then CBS, in an effort to boost the ratings of its perennially third place "Morning News," hired Phyllis George, a former Miss America with no journalistic experience, to serve as the program's co-anchor. When this too failed, the program was taken away from news and given to the entertainment division, which devised its own version of "Good Morning America." (First choice for host was Alan Alda, who declined.) Failure again. Finally, the network threw up its hands and gave the program back to news, which is where it resides today.

Meanwhile, *mirabile dictu,* there has been a return to harder news on the "CBS Evening News" as well. Following a corporate shake-up (and a barrage of criticism of CBS News in the press), Van Gordon Sauter was ousted as president of CBS News in the fall of 1986; and with him went much of the penchant on the "Evening News" for cuteness and "human interest." Coincidentally or not, the other two networks also returned to a harder evening news (in addition to which, ABC should be given credit for "Nightline" and for "This Week with David Brinkley").

It soon became apparent, however, that the networks' newfound seriousness had its limits. The documentary remained as moribund as ever, and the weekly magazines as cloying. The newscasts themselves were not above some backsliding. CBS gave more coverage to the Mike Tyson divorce announcement than it received the same evening on "Entertainment Tonight." Another lengthy CBS feature followed the progress of a midwest sugar beet harvest. Sunday night promos for still other features: the joys and dangers of ferrets as pets, and South Carolina sightings of a swamp creature known as "the lizard man."

ABC (in addition to continuing its Person of the Week) offered a feature story on a Swiss army bicycle brigade "that gives new meaning to the term 'cycle-logical' warfare." ABC and NBC covered the national spelling bee, but both Peter Jennings and Tom Brokaw felt compelled to let the viewer know that the winning word—*elegiac*—was Greek to them. All three networks covered the story of the ice-trapped Alaskan whales with the fervor they had earlier devoted to Little Jessica Trapped in the Well.

Other recent stories: Jane Fonda's marital separation (NBC), a high school reunion (ABC), the winning numbers for the Pennsylvania Lottery, a tabloid piece about a "spoiled rich kid" who tried to kill his girlfriend and then spent his days playing tennis next door to her house, overweight pets, goats in Tennessee that faint when frightened and two reports on a pig named Jerome being evicted from the city of Houston (all on CBS). On the day that George Mitchell was chosen the new Senate majority leader, NBC led off its "Nightly News" with a lengthy filmed report about explosions in Kansas City, followed by another filmed report about a bus wreck in New Jersey. More recently, ABC has been roundly criticized for its use of simulated news footage.

Two other developments that did not bode well for the future of television news: In July 1988, CBS announced that its owned-and-operated station in New York, WCBS, would broadcast the "CBS Evening News" at 6:30 instead of its traditional time of 7:00, in order to make room for a game show called "Win, Lose or Draw" (one of the dumbest shows on television, by the way, which is saying a lot).* The move had been strongly resisted for at least two years by CBS News, largely because the earlier hour would provide the newscast with a smaller audience. But when the move was finally announced, no one in the news division uttered a word.

In October 1988, Linda Ellerbee appeared in a television commercial in which she endorsed a particular brand of personal computer. During the course of the commercial, she was identified as a "broadcast journalist." The following year, she appeared in a coffee commercial in which she impersonated the host of a television news-magazine. (Ellerbee was cashing in on the fact that she

---

* Two years earlier, WABC in New York had done the same thing in order to make room for the game show "Jeopardy."

had actually hosted three such shows during the course of her career.)

These are terrible precedents (for which Linda Ellerbee, who now does commentary three days a week on the Cable News Network, should be drummed out of the corps). For one thing, they suggest that journalists are no different from any other "celebrities"—movie stars, rock stars, what-have-you. For another, they suggest that journalists, who after all have something special to offer in return for their endorsement fee—namely, favorable press coverage, or what used to be referred to simply as the truth— are now up for sale to the highest bidder.

But developments such as these, disquieting though they be, can only begin to suggest the problems that are now confronting network news. First of all, the network news audience is steadily shrinking—down about a quarter since 1980. In addition, the audience is steadily aging, which is another way of saying that young people are otherwise occupied.

Meanwhile, the networks themselves have undergone fundamental changes. NBC and ABC have acquired new corporate parents (General Electric and Capital Cities, respectively), and CBS has acquired a new president and CEO in the person of Laurence Tisch, its largest stockholder. ABC finished 1988 in the red (although accounting procedures disguised the fact), and all three networks have made drastic cuts in personnel—some thirty-five hundred people in the past two years alone, including hundreds in the news divisions. At CBS, the cutbacks in news prompted anchorman Rather to write a stinging column for the Op-Ed page of the *New York Times,* in which he accused the new management of trying to bring about "a tragic transformation from Murrow to mediocrity."[134] Not since the days of Murrow himself had a CBS newsman delivered such a public rebuke to his corporate bosses. (As a result of this outburst, Rather's subsequent silence when his newscast was shoved aside to make room for a game show was all the more resounding.)

The corporate plan, apparently, is to turn the evening newscasts into money-making operations—business, after all, is business, and the public trust be damned. But whether the plan will succeed is open to serious question. For one thing, there is more and more competition in national newscasts. "Independent Network News," produced by the Tribune Company of Chicago, originates at WPIX in New York and is shown on 150 other independent stations. The program is anchored by Morton Dean, formerly of CBS. The *Christian Science Monitor*'s new "Monitor News" is anchored by John Hart, also formerly of CBS. The "MacNeil–Lehrer Newshour" on PBS embodies one of the networks' fondest hopes for their own newscasts—an hour-long nightly report, which the networks abandoned when their local affiliates refused to give up the extra time.

Finally, there is CNN, the Ted Turner operation headquartered in Atlanta, which offers the latest national and international news 24 hours a day, 365 days a year. (The program's principal Washington anchor is Bernard Shaw, who during the second presidential debate of 1988 asked Michael Dukakis the extremely dumb but attention-getting question about whether he would favor the death penalty if his wife Kitty were raped and murdered. Other journalists on the panel tried to persuade Shaw to ask the question in a different fashion, but Shaw refused.)

Operating with non-union labor and specializing in on-the-spot coverage of fast-breaking stories (the TWA hijacking, the bombing of Libya, Hurricane Gloria, the space shuttle disaster), CNN earned a profit of $60 million in 1987. As a result, CNN is expanding its list of foreign bureaus at a time when the Big Three networks are closing bureaus both here and abroad.

Those who look to CNN as a replacement for network news, however, might wish to recall the storm of controversy that erupted in 1985 when Ted Turner attempted to take over CBS. The takeover was opposed by a sizable number of black, Hispanic and women's groups, including the NAACP, the Urban League, the Hispanic National Bar Association and the National Organization for Women. In its petition, the Hispanic Bar Association stated that Turner's activities and comments "have demonstrated an insensitivity (and at times disdain) for blacks, Hispanics, women and Jews."

In a column that appeared in the *Los Angeles Times,* Daniel Schorr (formerly of CBS and CNN) added to the controversy when he accused Turner of "anti-Semitic slurs," of statements in favor of government censorship, and of "mixing editorial and programming decisions with his business interests."[136] Noting that he had worked for CBS for twenty-six years and Ted Turner for six,

Schorr wrote: "I pray that the latter does not succeed in winning control over the former."

Now the fear is that Turner may gain through the back door what he failed to gain through the front.

In addition to CNN, network news faces increased competition from a rather different source—namely, the entertainment shows that are crowding into the news hour. Among them: "Wheel of Fortune," "Jeopardy" and "Entertainment Tonight." In San Francisco (a relatively sophisticated television market), the combined audience for Dan Rather and Peter Jennings at 7:00 P.M. barely exceeds the audience for a single competitor—that's right, Vanna White. In New York, during a recent week in October, Tom Brokaw came in fourth at 7:00—behind "Jeopardy," a rerun of "The Cosby Show" and "Win, Lose or Draw."

"Entertainment Tonight"—already hugely successful as a dossier on the doings of the Hollywood crowd—has begun to include reports on such things as presidential politics. (And why not?) I'm just waiting for the day when the program opens (after a teaser about the latest hot stuff on Madonna) with a rundown of the latest national news. At that point, viewers can simply forget Dan Rather, and, in more or less good conscience, tune in each night to John Tesh and Mary Hart. (Come to think of it, John Tesh, like William Hurt in *Broadcast News*—clean-cut, blond and very cool—makes a better Dan Rather than Dan Rather.) Considering the direction that news and politics have taken of late, "Entertainment Tonight" won't even have to change its name.

At the moment, however, the *real* competition to network news comes from still another source: local news. The reason is not simply that local news broadcasts a lot of news (as much as two or even two-and-a-half hours a day on many stations); it's that within those hours, local news is broadcasting a lot of national news as well.

Much of this national news, ironically enough, is provided by the networks, through the daily news "feeds" that link them to their affiliates. But increasingly, local stations are generating their own national coverage as well. Scores of local stations now own elaborate mobile television vans, which are linked by satellite to the local newsroom. These provide coverage of regional disasters such as floods and hurricanes, of political campaigns (including those for president), and of political conventions such as the recent gatherings in New Orleans and Atlanta.

In addition, the mobile vans are connected to one another through consortia—or "networks"—such as Conus, which now has roughly eighty member stations. Thus, when a local station covers a forest fire (or better yet, a mass murder), the coverage is quickly relayed to stations all over the country—even though many of those stations are also members of other national networks: namely, ABC, NBC and CBS. What's more, Conus has joined forces with the Associated Press to form a second consortium called TV Direct, which provides a daily news feed out of Washington.

Finally, some of the better and larger local stations, such as KRON in San Francisco, maintain their own correspondents in Washington,* as well as sending reporters on trips abroad. KRON, for example, has sent reporters to the Far East; and a herd of local anchors showed up for Reagan's summit in Geneva.

The result of all this is that by the time local viewers tune in the network news at 7 o'clock (if they bother to do so at all), they are more or less "newsed out." And the big national stories that Dan and Tom so breathlessly divulge, many of the viewers have already heard several times over. Partly for those reasons, local news outdraws network news in about 80 percent of the country's television markets—often by sizable margins.

There is one more step in this progression. Local affiliates could come to regard their network connection as merely one source of news among many. They could then put together their own "complete" newscasts of local, national and international news, just as many independent stations do already. At the same time, they could drop their network newscasts, fill the slot with a game show—and pocket millions of dollars a year in additional revenue. According to Frank Magid, the television consultant, a few affiliates are privately talking of doing just that. "Television executives operate on a herd instinct about what will bring maximum profits," he says. "If one station abandons network news and is successful, it could trigger a stampede."[137]

To avert such an outcome, the networks are experimenting with

---

* KRON, however, has recently closed its bureau in Sacramento.

213

several different strategies. In an effort to beat Conus at its own game, for example, they are supplying their affiliates with more important stories on the daily news feed, and making it easier for affiliates to exchange their own stories via satellite. At the same time, the networks are trying to devise newscasts that could not be easily duplicated at the local level.

One such notion is rather revealing. As ABC's Roone Arledge described it to Barbara Matusow a few years back: "We could put on a program tomorrow, a pop news program . . . If we hired Alan Alda and Gregory Peck, did celebrity interviews and so on, we could wipe out the competition."[138] Of course, Arledge insisted that *he* had no desire to present such a program. But as the networks continue their downward slide, Mr. Arledge (or his successor) might not remain quite so scrupulous.

Meanwhile, the networks are considering less radical remedies. At ABC, one plan calls for a newscast consisting largely of lengthy feature stories, another for a program made up mainly of analysis. Under the heading of simply saving money, CBS has talked about moving its news operation from New York to Washington.

There is one other possibility: the networks could close down their news divisions. Of course they'd keep the money-makers such as "60 Minutes" and "20/20," but everything else—meaning mainly the evening newscasts—would go. NBC, in fact—which has no "60 Minutes" and which is under orders to put its news division in the black by 1990—has already considered this choice.

Such a step, however, could lead to pitfalls of its own. As Ed Joyce, former president of CBS News, remarked in his recent book, *Prime Times, Bad Times: A Personal Drama of Network Television,* the news division is "the cement that helps hold the whole affiliate system together." Without the news division, he added, the network "wouldn't have a network."[139]

"If we're not in the news business," says Thomas Murphy, chairman of Capital Cities/ABC, "we might as well be a Hollywood studio."[140]

Even so, several observers expect that the network news divisions will eventually disappear. In the words of Robert Wussler, a former president of CBS, "There is no longer a financial place in the networks for their news organizations. It's just a matter of time."[141]

Or in the words of Fred Friendly: "I see a great national resource just going down the drain."[142]

We would still have local national news; but before we resign ourselves to that eventuality, perhaps we should consider just what it might mean. First of all, the percentage of the population that reads newspapers continues to decline.* Instead, most people today get their news from television. Frank N. Magid Associates found that 54 percent of Americans depend on television as their primary source of news, while a recent Roper Poll found that 50 percent of Americans use television as their *only* source of news.

Disturbing as such figures may be, they also remind us that over the past quarter-century or so network news has played a major role in shaping the national agenda. The civil rights movement, the Vietnam War, the Watergate crisis—all of these traumatic events were profoundly affected by the way they were covered by Cronkite et al. (Indeed, Lyndon Johnson reportedly concluded that he had lost the country's support for the Vietnam War when he lost the support of Cronkite. And while the Watergate affair began as a story in the *Washington Post,* it became a national scandal only after becoming a major story on CBS.)

At the same time, we should recall that many local station-owners *hated* the coverage such stories were given by the networks—especially Watergate: all those smart-ass reporters tearing down the president ... No doubt Richard Nixon would have much preferred a reporting system in which local stations were calling the shots. Whether the country would have been better served is another question.(At the time, I happened to be working for an ABC affiliate whose anchorman was asked by a college newspaper whether he thought the president should be impeached. "No," he replied, "I think we should impeach the Congress"—whatever *that* meant.)

Most local stations are owned and run by people whose chief concern in life is not at all the reporting of news—except insofar as news is their chief source of revenue. And since the FCC has abandoned its rule that owners of stations hold them for at least three years, many stations are now owned by people who are in it strictly for the buck, and the faster the better. (Stations in Houston and Dallas had three owners in less than a year.)

The result of all this is that television news on the local level is

* As David Shaw points out in the *Los Angeles Times,* "newspaper readership among the young has declined significantly."[143] In 1967, 60 percent of Americans aged 18 to 29 were regular newspaper readers. In 1988, the figure was 29 percent.

often simply a numbers game—no different, in a sense, from the latest game show. The number one news station (meaning the one that leads in the ratings) is often if not usually the one that reports the least actual news—as opposed to car wrecks, robberies and fires—while the best news station (meaning the one that reports on government affairs, and so on) often if not usually comes in last. (Thus, in San Francisco and Los Angeles, the best news stations are KRON and KCBS, both of which are last in the ratings.)

The populist approach is apparent as well in the stations' presence on the national and international scene, where their coverage is often parochial at best. At the Democratic Convention in Atlanta, few of the many local stations in attendance were interested in the larger issues confronting the party, but rather, as one station put it, in "issues of interest to Okie folks."[144] Or in the words of a cameraman for a CBS affiliate: "Our viewer wants to tune in and see the guy they work with or the woman they see at the grocery store. Not many people will ever see Dukakis, but if you see your next-door neighbor at a convention, that's important to you." A few weeks after that convention, stations in Minneapolis sent crews to Sweden to provide live coverage of a exhibition game by the Minnesota Vikings.

It is at the local level, though, that the stations' what-the-hell philosophy is seen to best advantage. Many stations are not at all reluctant to fill the time in their expanding newscasts by running "video news releases," and other such PR material. Hollywood studios, for example, send out "interviews" with the stars of major new movies—interviews into which a local station can insert one of its own reporters to make it look as if the station itself conducted the session. Many stations do just that.

At least twenty-three stations, including KGTV in San Diego, ran a "news report" in which an eleven-year-old girl re-enacted an asthma attack she suffered after switching to a different medicine. The message of the report (a false one, by the way) was that generic drugs are less safe than brand-name products. Naturally, the report was paid for by a firm called Key Pharmaceuticals, maker of a brand-name drug that received favorable mention on the tape.

During "sweeps weeks," of course, when the newscasts are given their Nielsen ratings, all restraint is cast aside and the stations air whatever they think might lure the viewers. New York is by no means immune to this virus. WABC ran a series titled "Killer Salad

Bars" and another called "The Great Gameshow Comeback," which offered viewers a "look behind the scenes at how you can get on a game show, the secret to winning and why they've become the hottest shows on TV." WNBC simply strung together footage of natural disasters in order to pose the question: "Is God Punishing Us?"

By all accounts, however, it is the West Coast, and especially Los Angeles, which is the unchallenged master of the sweeps. (Or as a writer asked in a recent issue of the *Washington Journalism Review*, "Why is it that the nation's number two television market has such a scant appetite for real news?"[145]) During 1988, KNBC aired a series on people who satisfy other's sexual fantasies, another on sex after forty (a ripe old age, apparently, in L.A.) and a third on UFOs—featuring a computer-animated spaceship landing in the station's parking lot.

The Olympic gold, though, goes to KABC, along with its San Francisco counterpart, KGO. During the February sweeps of 1988, the latter aired a series on "Sexual Addiction." It also invited its viewers to call in with answers to "ethical" questions such as whether they would watch a live execution on television. (Opponents of the death penalty sometimes argue, of course, that one way to end the practice would be to televise executions live; but I wonder whether the effect might not be just the reverse. Live executions might well become bigger than "Monday Night Football.")

KABC, meanwhile, came up with a brainstorm: a series of reports on the Nielsen families—who they are, how they are chosen, how the system works—which was aired during one of the sweeps periods. After all, what better way to entice the Nielsen families to watch your news than to make the newscast all about *them*? (KNBC cried foul, of course, but it was probably just sorry it hadn't thought of the idea first.)

Just in case that might not suffice, KABC devised some other enticements too: a six-part series on Vanna White ("Sheer Vanna," which also ran on KGO); a series on "Satanists"; another called "Beyond and Back," on near-death experiences; and—not to be outdone by KNBC's report on sex after 40—a series on "Frisky at 50."

> Quite unexpectedly as Vasserot
> The armless ambidextrian was lighting

A match between his great and second toe
And Ralph the lion was engaged in biting
The neck of Madame Sossman while the drum
Pointed, and Teeny was about to cough
In waltz-time swinging Jocko by the thumb—
Quite unexpectedly the top blew off:

On Sunday, May 22, 1988, KABC, in order to promote still another sweeps report, hired a plane to tow a banner through the skies above crowded Dodger Stadium.

And there, there overhead, there, there, hung over
Those thousands of white faces, those dazed eyes,
There in the starless dark the poise, the hover
There with vast wings across the canceled skies,
There in the sudden blackness the black pall
Of nothing, nothing, nothing—nothing at all.*

The banner read: "Is Elvis Still Alive?"

While there will be no doubt continue to be ebb and flow in the process of American democratization, it seems unlikely the river will ever reverse its course. For one thing, the hallmark of American society is the satisfaction of the needs and desires of the average man, usually expressed in the form of consumption. And with each new possession—the private house, the private car, the car telephone, the television set, the cassette recorder, the dish antenna, the private pool (all of which, incidentally, are more characteristic of Southern California than they are of New York)— the owner develops a heightened sense of self-importance, of individual power and control. Coupled to traditional American egalitarianism, this sense erases deference to learned opinion, producing instead a feeling that one's own tastes, thoughts and opinions are just as good as anyone else's—a feeling reminiscent of the American frontier, as opposed to the urbane communities of the East. As Michael Arlen, in *The Camera Age,* observed of the transition from televised hard news to televised soft news:

* The poem, by Archibald MacLeish, is called "The End of the World."

I wonder if the gradual institutionalization of soft news . . . doesn't lead to a perspective that is regressive, even "pastoral." . . . In other words, to say that the new, casual type of news is unauthoritarian begs the question. It is only that the locus of the authority has changed: from the dream of bureaucratic power to the dream of individual power. Thus, old-fashioned hard news tried to tell us (through its world view) that the official acts of statesmen, bureaucrats, governments, and world bodies were the only permissibly effective acts. . . . But now soft news threatens to turn us backward, into some garden, some Arcadian fantasy where individuals now count for *everything*— individuals smiling, talking, expressing their opinions.[146]

In the political realm, moreover, this process displays a sort of "ratchet effect." In other words, once a particular "reform" has been granted—the presidential primary, the initiative and referendum—it becomes very difficult to retract. As legislators in California have discovered, any such effort is inundated by cries that politicians are trying to steal power from the people. Thus, the only pressure left is that being exerted in the opposite direction— toward still more primaries, toward a national referendum. As a result, the democratization of politics, especially, will likely continue; and any remaining hope for wise national leadership will probably rest largely with chance—a Bill Bradley, say, who happens to have been a star on the basketball court.

This, then, would appear to be the future of the first half of the legacy of the European Enlightenment—namely, political and social rationalism. And the second half of the legacy—scientific rationalism—is also under siege.

In the latter case, however, the challenge arises not so much because of the shift of power within the United States, but rather because of the shift of power from the Atlantic Basin to the Pacific, and especially to East Asia. Insofar as the challenge exists in California (as indeed it does), it exists—at least in its older and more substantive forms—in Northern California rather than Southern.

In essence, the Oriental challenge is epistemological. That is to say, it poses the Eastern, intuitive, "mystical" approach to reality, against the Western, rational, scientific approach. Of course, that sort of philosophical debate is difficult if not impossible to resolve; and for the past few hundred years, Western rationalism has had the upper hand in terms of practical effects (and worldwide influence). Recently, though, Eastern mysticism has begun to impinge on Western culture in a variety of ways, most strikingly, in the "hard" physical sciences that the West has always claimed as its exclusive preserve—physics, medicine, and so on. In addition (although we won't have time to delve too deeply into this aspect of the matter), Western artists and intellectuals have begun to find in Eastern mysticism a more rewarding avenue to what might be described as ultimate reality.

To be sure, it is possible to argue that Asia, like Europe, is being Americanized at such a rapid pace that any evidence of "mysticism" is merely vestigial. Japan is crazy about Hollywood movies, and was ahead of Europe in building a Disneyland. Japanese capitalists seem more American than Americans themselves. In China, the students who erected a replica of the Statue of Liberty in Tiananmen Square called for "science and democracy."

In the end, however, Asia is likely to prove much more resistant to Americanization than Europe. For one thing, it has radically different languages (different, that is, from those of the West) and a sophisticated culture that is thousands of years old—facts that we in the West are only beginning to appreciate. Equally important are the traditional Asian feelings of separateness and superiority.

This last is what is likely to prove decisive. Historically, it has been the superior region—in terms of sheer power—that has exported its culture to the rest of the world. That is the great advantage that the West has enjoyed for four hundred years and the United States for forty. And that is the advantage that is about to disappear.

PART II

The Challenge to Scientific Rationalism

House of the Rising Sun:
The Shift of Power
from the Atlantic
to the Pacific

Black became the predominant color of men's clothes on the Continent of Europe after the third decade of the nineteenth century. The funereal fashion (which survives in our contemporary evening, morning, and dinner clothes, and in the uniforms of hotel concierges and waiters) came from Britain. . . .

Something similar had happened in Italy in 1530. The Spaniards had become the dominant power in Europe. That year, Charles V came to Bologna to be crowned both king of Italy and Roman emperor by the Pope and to pose for a portrait by Titian. He and his retinue paraded on horseback through the city streets. The gay Italians, dressed in silks of all colors, brocades, velvets, and damasks, cheered their guests and tossed flowers from balconies hung with multicolored cloths and tapestries. All the unsmiling Spanish dignitaries, as pale as El Greco saints, wore black with white ruffled collars. A few months later the Italians, most of them, wore black too, as if to show their sorrow for the end of the Renaissance and the loss of their liberties and joy of life.

—Luigi Barzini
The Europeans[1]

Drums rolled and 16 models took giant steps down the runway of one of the four tents set up in the courtyard of the Louvre. The French ready-to-wear shows for spring and summer had begun. On Thursday, the first significant day of more than a week of showings, the dominant accent was Japanese.

Japanese designers began showing here a few years ago, to empty houses. Now everybody arrives a day earlier than usual to see their shows. . . .

The first 10 mannequins to appear . . . were all in black, enlivened only by a dash of white on the forehead or cheek of the model. Other makeup was minimal. Black dominates the collection. The next dresses were in black and gray patterns. Gray is the next most important color.

The fashion world has obviously responded to this message. Most of the audience and the people milling about outside were wearing black or gray, as if they were actors in a black-and-white movie.

—Bernadine Morris
The New York Times[2]

JAPANESE DESIGNERS have tempered their approach somewhat since their first frontal assaults on the citadels of fashion a few years back. But the Japanese invasion of the world of Western commerce continues unabated. Nor, to be sure, is Japan alone. Over the past decade, it has been joined by the so-called Four Tigers: South Korea, Taiwan, Hong Kong and Singapore. Eventually it may be joined by the Big Enchilada: China.

This is not the place, of course, for a full-scale review of the rise of Asia, but a few examples will serve to set the scene. Initially, the Asian ascendancy was based on manufacturing (since the countries in question, except for China, have little in the way of raw materials or arable land). All of us are familiar with what Toyota and Nissan have done to Detroit, but we tend to forget that the damage would have been much greater still had it not been for the "voluntary quotas" that Japan imposed on its automotive exports to the United States (just as it did in the case of steel a decade earlier).

Japan has coped with these quotas in part by building manufacturing plants on this side of the Pacific—plants that by 1990 will have the capacity to produce nearly 2 million cars and trucks a year. But these figures don't complete the story. There are also the "American" cars that are actually made in Japan, as well as the "American" cars that are made in the U.S. using a number of Japanese components. Back in 1985, the Chrysler Corporation predicted that when everything was taken into account—meaning true imports, along with the various hybrids—Japan, within a couple of years, would capture at least 50 percent of the entire American auto industry. In the words of Chrysler chairman Lee Iacocca, "We have managed to take the biggest single industry the world has ever seen and give away over half the total value added."[3]

The results have been even more dramatic in consumer electronics—radios, television sets, VCRs, what-have-you. The market for VCRs, for example, is virtually a monopoly of the

224

Japanese (along with the Koreans); and color television sets are still being produced by only one major American company (Zenith). Moreover, it appears the Japanese may well capture the next big television market—HDTV, or high-definition television, which produces a picture twice as sharp as the current system. If the Japanese do prevail, the U.S. trade deficit will likely rise by $10 billion a year.

In advanced electronics (semiconductors, computers and so forth), the Japanese position is not quite as strong—but it may soon become so. Japan already leads the U.S. 45 percent to 40 percent in the worldwide market for semiconductors (the tiny silicon chips that constitute the heart of computers). And in memory chips (which store and retrieve data), the Japanese lead is overwhelming—88 percent of the market for one-megabit DRAMS, the most advanced type of dynamic, random access memory chips, which in this case can accommodate a million pieces of data. Because of such imbalances, the CIA recently concluded that "the U.S. semiconductor industry is at a crucial turning point in its history. It fundamentally cannot compete in its present form."[4]

Its competitive position may soon worsen. At least three Japanese companies are now developing sixteen-megabit DRAMS; and Japan's Ministry of International Trade and Industry (MITI) is reportedly spending $700 million in 1988 to perfect a process called X-ray lithography, which could conceivably produce a chip that could accommodate as many as a billion circuits. (The U.S. government, for the same purpose, is currently spending about $25 million.)

In computers themselves, the U.S. still holds the lead, but here again, its position may be in peril. Many of its computers, for example, are assembled largely from components manufactured in Asia. This is the same practice that enabled Japan to take over production in consumer electronics, and many observers fear the process will be repeated in the case of computers. The U.S. has already felt it necessary to impose a 100 percent tariff on imported PCs.

Meanwhile, Japan is hard at work on projects to develop a supercomputer 100 to 1,000 times faster than existing models, and to devise a computer with the capacity to "reason" (the so-called fifth-generation computer). Although both projects have run into snags, their directors insist the projects are still on course; and in

225

any case, the Japanese are legendary for their perseverance. "It could become a Japanese era," warn Sidney Karin and Norris Parker Smith in a recent book called *The Supercomputer Era.* "Complacence or inattention in the United States could lead to quick erosion of the American lead."[5] In a book called *The Fifth Generation,* Stanford computer scientist Edward A. Feigenbaum points out that, "The Japanese ... have audaciously made it a national goal to become number one in this industry by the latter half of the 1990s"—just as they set out to do, he adds, with automobiles in the sixties, consumer electronics in the seventies, and silicon chips in the eighties. But this time, says Feigenbaum, the stakes are higher. The Japanese "aim not only to dominate the traditional forms of the computer industry but to establish a 'knowledge industry' in which knowledge itself will be a salable commodity like food and oil. Knowledge itself is to become the new wealth of nations. . . . The Japanese could thereby become the dominant industrial power in the world."[6]

Nor are these the only means by which Japan is seeking industrial dominance. According to the *New York Times,* a new technique for analyzing the quality of patents reveals that, "Starting more than a decade ago, Japan has been achieving a level of innovation greater than that of the United States."[7] Thus, Japan leads the world in such important new fields as magnetics and fiber optics, and is working feverishly to overcome the American lead in biotechnology. As Bruce Nussbaum reports in *The World After Oil: The Shifting Axis of Power and Wealth,* "the Japanese fully expect to dominate the market" in biotechnology by the end of the eighties.[8] In robotics, the Japanese lead is already commanding. In a recent book called *Inside the Robot Kingdom: Japan, Mechatronics, and the Coming Robotopia,* Frederik L. Schodt points out that the Japanese have deployed 116,000 industrial robots, the United States, 25,000.[9]

Another cryptic message as to where the future lies can be read on the ouija board of worldwide trade. In 1960, the United States engaged in more than twice as much trade with Europe as it did with Asia. By 1980, Asia trade had pulled ahead. Today, America's Pacific trade is more than 50 percent greater than its Atlantic trade; and by 1995, it will be roughly twice as great.

But those numbers—significant though they be—do not tell the whole story. The growth in America's Pacific trade has consisted mainly of exports from Asia to the United States, rather than the other way around. Thus, in 1977, America's trade deficit with Japan amounted to roughly $12 billion; by 1987 it was $60 billion, about a third of the total American trade deficit. That same year, America's combined deficit with Singapore, Hong Kong, Taiwan and Korea came to $38 billion—$8 billion more than America's deficit with all of Western Europe. (In 1988, with the devaluation of the dollar, America's deficit with Japan declined to roughly $52 billion, but there were still significant increases in American imports of Japanese semiconductors and automobiles. In 1989, the deficit with Japan began rising again.)

But those figures do not complete the picture. The United States's exports to Japan consist mainly of low-quality bulk goods such as corn, soybeans, coal and timber; while Japan's exports to the United States consist mainly of high-quality goods such as cars, VCRs and office equipment. Any student of history will immediately recognize this relationship. It is the one that has typically obtained between a colony and a mother country, with the United States in the role of colony. Thus, when Japanese businessmen joke among themselves about the coming world order, they say that Europe will serve as Japan's boutique, while America will function as the Japanese farm.

The joke is becoming less funny every day. Spurred by recent trade agreements that open Japan to foreign beef and citrus products, Japanese investors are rushing to buy up American farmland, mainly in the West. In addition, they're snapping up feedlots and meat-packing plants, thereby establishing entire production systems.

In other words, while devaluation of the dollar did not solve the problem of the U.S. trade deficit (partly because Japan managed to hold down the prices of its exports, and partly because Japanese consumers are not very interested in buying American manufactured goods at any price), it did have at least one dramatic effect: a rising tide of Japanese investment in the United States. By the end of 1988, Japan's direct investments in American companies amounted to $53 billion. This level was still well below that of the British ($102 billion), but ahead of those of the Dutch, the Canadians, the West Germans and the Swiss, all of whom the Japanese had trailed in 1980. More important, perhaps, is the fact that the tide of Japanese investment appears to be only beginning. The Japanese already own more than 640 American factories employing upwards of 160,000 workers. Among their recent acquisitions: Firestone Tire and CBS Records. (Sony, which bought the latter, is also reported to be shopping around for a Hollywood studio.)

The Japanese invasion is especially conspicuous in real estate. In 1985, they spent a mere $2 billion; in 1988, about $16 billion, for a total investment of more than $42 billion.* As a result, the Japanese may well own more American real estate than anyone other than the Americans themselves. Their holdings include the Exxon, Tiffany, Mobil, ABC and 666 Fifth Avenue buildings in New York (where I. M. Pei, with Japanese money, is designing a forty-six story hotel); Arco Plaza in Los Angeles (where the Japanese own about a third of the downtown office buildings and Mitsui is putting up a fifty-story tower); and seven or eight wineries in the Napa Valley. In Hawaii, they own virtually all the major Waikiki Beach hotels, most of the major resorts on other islands, dozens of office buildings and shopping centers, and well over a quarter of the houses in the posh Kahala section of Honolulu. (The raid on Pearl Harbor is beginning to appear superfluous.)**

Another big source of Asian capital is the 40-odd-million member Chinese Diaspora that is scattered all over Eastern Asia. In particular, Hong Kong these days is hemorrhaging money as the city prepares for reunification with China in 1997; and most of that money is winding up in places such as Los Angeles, San Francisco, Vancouver, New York and Toronto. Meanwhile, Taiwan has lifted its long-standing restrictions on the export of capital, and the island's enormous cash reserves have likewise begun to find their way to the United States. (Taiwanese investors already reportedly own nearly two-thirds of the independent motels in Los Angeles.)

*   *   *

* Theoretically, the real estate figures are included in those for direct investment. But the most commonly used source for real estate figures—Kenneth Leventhal & Co.—uses a different classification system than used by the Commerce Department, which supplies the figures for direct investment. Thus, the Leventhal figures for real estate are higher than the real estate figures of the Commerce Department.

** In Japan, Hawaii is referred to as "the 48th Prefecture" (Japan has 47) and Los Angeles as "the 24th Ward" (Tokyo has 23).

In the end, that is the weapon with which Asia will finally conquer the West: money. Indeed, many would argue that Japan—not the United States—is now the leading financial power in the world. The following examples of that newfound strength are taken mainly from a recently book by Daniel Burstein called *Yen!: Japan's New Financial Empire and Its Threat to America.*[10]

• Japan is now the world's leading creditor nation, and the United States is its leading debtor nation. And in the words of Benjamin M. Friedman, author of *Day of Reckoning: The Consequences of American Economic Policy Under Reagan and After:* "Whichever country is the world's leading lending country has always held a dominant position."[11]

• Japan has become the principal buyer of long-term U.S. Treasury bonds, which finance America's budget deficit. And as was demonstrated on May 7, 1987, even a rumor that Japan might be growing reluctant to buy can send tremors throughout the U.S. economy.

• The world's ten largest banks (ranked by deposits) are all Japanese. Of the world's twenty-five largest banks, seventeen are Japanese, none are American.* Thirty years ago, no Japanese bank even ranked among the world's top fifty. In 1980, only one Japanese bank ranked among the (American-led) top ten. San Francisco's Bank of America—the world's leading bank about a decade ago—was recently rescued from dire straits by a Japanese consortium.

• In California, five of the top ten banks are now Japanese. The British banks, once the dominant foreign institutions, have all pulled out.

• In 1987, the total value of all stocks listed on the New York Stock exchange was surpassed by the total value of all stock listed on the Tokyo Stock Exchange.

• Goldman Sachs is now owned in part by Sumitomo Bank; Shearson Lehman Hutton, in part by Nippon Life; Paine Webber, in part by Yasuda Mutual Life.

• Nomura Securities, the largest securities firm in the world, is more than twenty times the size (in market capitalization) of Merrill

---

* Citycorp is still found in the somewhat more broadly defined category of the world's top ten bank holding companies.

Lynch, the largest American brokerage house. "In a takeover financed with stock," observes *Fortune*, "Nomura could swallow Merrill Lynch like a bit of predinner *sashimi*."[12]

Not long ago, Masaaki Kurokawa then chairman of Nomura Securities International, the company's New York–based subsidiary—gave a dinner for a group of American guests at a restaurant fifty floors above Tokyo. Over the predinner sashimi, Kurokawa remarked that he had devised a plan for solving the United States's huge trade deficit. The Japanese yen (which was then trading at about 140 to the dollar) would be further strengthened until it reached around 100 to the dollar. That way, Japanese exports would become too expensive for sale in the U.S. Eventually, Japan and the U.S. would create a single joint currency.

And what would Japan expect in return, asked one of the guests. "California," said the host.

Kurokawa went on to explain that California would be turned into a Japanese-American economic community. No visas would be needed for Japanese nationals to come and go. Soon, Japan would send over several million workers and build new factories to take advantage of "cheap" California real estate.[13]

Whatever the merits of Kurokawa's arresting proposal, it illustrates an undeniable fact. The economies of the U.S. and Japan are gradually becoming a single economy. But of course Kurokawa was only joking about California. Ha-ha.

Japan, to be sure, is not the only Asian country on the rise. For the past twenty years or so, East Asia has led the world in economic growth. This is particularly true of course of the Four Tigers of South Korea, Taiwan, Hong Kong and Singapore. And now another aspiring tiger is anxious to join the feast, namely, Thailand (much of whose ascendancy has actually been engineered by the country's resident ethnic Chinese).

Even so, Japan is still by far the leading player. It serves as the model for economic growth. It is the chief source of trade and investment (*lots* of investment), and the chief provider of foreign aid. Indeed, Japan has now surpassed the United States as the fountain of foreign aid; and two-thirds of that aid goes to Asia. In 1987, this amounted to nearly $3.5 billion. Thus, while all of these countries still harbor deep suspicions of Japan from the days of

World War II, Japan is well on its way to establishing the Greater East Asia Co-Prosperity Sphere that it came close to gaining in the forties.

Within that sphere, Japan's most far-reaching relationship is the one with China. Already, Japan has emerged as China's principal trading partner; and as Nicholas D. Kristof observed in the *New York Times:* "Japanese companies have taken such a lead in doing business with China that other countries have only a meager chance of catching up."[14] By the year 2000, the combined GNP's of China, Japan and the Four Tigers will surpass that of the United States.

The implications of all this are of course considerable. As far as Japan is concerned, Lawrence Krause, a former senior fellow and Asia expert at the Brookings Institution, testified before Congress that "Japan is replacing the United States as the world's strongest economic power. It is in everyone's interest that the transition go smoothly."[15] "If things continue as they are now," adds Richard Rosecrance, professor of International Affairs at Cornell, "it won't be much beyond 2010 before Japan becomes the leading power in world politics."[16]

If China—not to mention Korea, etc.—were added to the eastern end of the scales, the balance would tip decisively (if it hasn't already). As Roy Hofheinz, Jr. and Kent E. Calder observe in *The Eastasia Edge,* "If China's natural and human resources could be merged with Japan's skills and economic power, the combination would be insurmountable."[17] And according to geohistorian Immanuel Wallerstein, that is exactly what is happening.

Meanwhile, in Western Europe, things have not been going nearly so well. During the eighties, economic growth has lagged behind that of the United States and well behind that of Japan. Unemployment has been stuck at the astonishing level of 11 percent (compared to 6 or 7 percent in the U.S. and about 3 percent in Japan). Since 1980, Europe has created no net new jobs.

More serious still, Europe (and especially Germany, its leading economic power) has fallen behind in the high-tech race that is transforming the economies of Japan and America—and that will form the basis of international wealth in the twenty-first century. In 1986, for example, Japan produced nearly four times as many semiconductors as all the European countries combined.

For all these reasons, words such as Eurosclerosis and Euro-pessimism entered the language. Or as Flora Lewis reported in the *New York Times* a few years back, Europe is gripped by "a profound feeling of weakness and weariness as the world moves on."[18]

As an antidote to anemia, Europe has resolved to take yet another step on the protracted journey towards unification that began with the signing of the Treaty of Rome in 1957. By 1992, the European countries will supposedly remove the remaining barriers that stand in the way of a fully integrated common market.

That's the plan. The degree to which it will be implemented remains to be seen. Certainly the benefits would be considerable: an unobstructed market of 320 million well-off consumers (as compared to 245 million in the U.S. and about 125 million in Japan). But various obstacles remain. Three years ago, the European community began hacking away at a list of 300 barriers to unimpeded trade. At last report, they had cleared away only about 100—and those were the easy ones. Many observers fear that when 1992 rolls around, the community will still be trying to assuage Italian worries about a plunging lira, and so on. Another fear is that various countries will attempt to perpetuate state support for declining industries such as textiles and shipbuilding, whose employees, after all, still cast votes in national elections. Finally, there still remain fundamental differences over just how much togetherness is desirable, with the Germans exuding *gemütlichkeit*, and the British maintaining a proper British reserve.

Should all these obstacles be somehow overcome, it is not at all certain that the resulting Europe would be to America's liking. Instead, as the European countries remove the barriers among themselves, they may well decide to re-erect them at the ocean's edge, thereby creating what is coming to be known as Fortress Europe. The principal invaders whom the fortress would be designed to repel would be the Americans and the Japanese.

There are other forces encouraging the Continent to turn its back to the Atlantic. As Western Europe lurches towards unification, countries on the outside are wondering whether it might be better to be in. One of the likeliest candidates for membership is Austria, which has long served the function of a bridge between the eastern and western blocs. Another potential candidate is Finland, which of course has close ties to the Soviet Union. In addition, relations are growing between the European community and

Comecon, the Eastern European trading association. In July 1988, for example, the former signed a trade pact with Hungary, which probably presages similar pacts with other Communist countries.

Finally, there is Russia itself, which of course has historic connections to Western Europe (especially France) and which is making every effort to strengthen those ties today. Apparently, the feeling is mutual. Various countries in Western Europe recently extended the Soviet Union a total of roughly $10 billion in credit.*

As relations warm between Western Europe and the Soviet bloc, another tie between Europe and America will loosen—namely, NATO, which currently consumes about half the United States's defense budget. The immediate occasion will be American efforts to reduce the country's budgetary deficit, but there are deeper causes as well.

For reasons that might be difficult for the average American to appreciate, the close relationship between the United States and Western Europe (especially England) was to a large extent an affinity of class. Dating back to colonial times, the affinity reached its apogee in the chummy, clandestine alliance between Roosevelt and Churchill during the early stages of World War II. After the war, it continued among the upper levels of the State Department and the CIA and, in a more general sense, among the members of the Eastern Establishment.

Conservative Republicans, on the other hand, have long advocated that the United States turn its attention toward Asia. And for most of the past twenty years, conservative Republicans have controlled both the party and the White House.

A reduction of United States defense commitments would come not a moment too soon (and perhaps several moments too late). As Paul Kennedy points out in his influential book, *The Rise and Fall of the Great Powers: Economic Change and Military Conflict from 1500 to 2000,* nations at the height of their military dominance tend to incur commitments which their economies, in the long run, cannot support. As a result of this "imperial overstretch," as Kennedy calls it, the nations in question decline. That is what happened to Spain in the sixteenth century, to Britain in the early twentieth, and to the United States in the late twentieth.[19] (Ironically, as the U.S. pre-

---

* West Germany naturally has a strong incentive to ante up, since it is only through increased ties to the Soviet Union that it can ever hope for anything approaching reunification with East Germany.

pares for World War III—building $500–million Stealth bombers even as it ceases to make computer memory chips—it is losing World War II, or at least that part of it being waged in the Pacific.)

There is a great deal of additional evidence to support the thesis of American decline. Take the American labor force, for example. In Japan, where the mean IQ is 111 (compared to 100 in the U.S.), high school seniors rank second in the world in math ability. (A frightening thought: If Japan is second, who's first? Not the U.S., at any rate; its seniors rank twelfth.) Ninety-five percent of Japanese finish high school, compared to about seventy percent of Americans. "Much of the success of Japan," says Merry I. White, professor of comparative sociology at Boston University and author of *The Japanese Educational Challenge*, "stems from the fact that its blue-collar workers can interpret advanced mathematics, read complex engineering blueprints, and perform sophisticated tasks on the factory floor far better than blue collars in the U.S."[20]

Here, according to *Business Week*, "the nation is facing a monumental mismatch between jobs and the ability of Americans to do them."[21] The Educational Testing Service reports that the science achievement level of American seventeen-year-old students is significantly lower than it was in 1969. A quarter of high school graduates are only marginally literate. A National Assessment of Educational Progress report noted that only 60 percent of white young adults could locate information in a news article or an almanac. The figure for Hispanics was 40 percent, and for blacks, 25 percent. By the year 2000, nearly 40 percent of Americans age eighteen or younger will be black or Hispanic.

There is, however, an American ethnic group that performs far better than all the others, including the Caucasians. It is, of course, the Asians.

At the moment, Asian-Americans comprise only about 2 percent of the population (about 5 million people), largely because U.S. immigration law, for forty years, deliberately kept them out. (The Yellow Peril, remember?) But when the law was changed in 1965, Asians began arriving in growing numbers. Although we tend to think of large-scale immigration as something that occurred around the turn of the century, the fact is that the 1980s may well turn out to be the high-water mark for immigration in the country's history, exceeding the record of nearly nine million people who arrived between 1900 and 1910. Of the more recent record-setting group, the largest number (about 48 percent) are Asian. By the year 2000, the number of Asian-Americans will rise to 12 million.

Meanwhile, Asian-Americans are having an impact that far exceeds what one would expect from two percent of the population. They are, in effect, the new Jews.

In the Westinghouse Science Talent Search, the country's oldest and most prestigious high school science competition (which used to be dominated by Jews), Asians won twenty of the seventy scholarships awarded from 1981 to 1988. In 1986, they won all of the top five prizes.

At Harvard, Asians make up about 14 percent of the freshman class; at Stanford, about 16 percent; and at Cal Tech and MIT, about 22 percent. At MIT, a Vietnamese "boat person" named Tue Nguyen recently earned a record seven degrees (in seven years, mind you), including a doctorate in nuclear engineering. His brother Tien is also earning a doctorate in nuclear engineering at MIT, and his brother Tai is doing graduate work at Berkeley. And speaking of Berkeley, its freshman class is nearly 30 percent Asian; and its engineering departments are 40 percent Asian. Impressive as these numbers may be, Asians claim they would be even higher were it not for admissions systems that subtly discriminate against Orientals. Whatever the truth of that claim (which is now being investigated by several different organizations), it recalls the quotas that several Ivy League schools imposed on Jewish admissions during the twenties and thirties.

In median family income, Jews and Asians rank one and two.

The influence of Asia is manifest in other ways as well. On the academic front in 1987–88, students from Asia for the first time accounted for more than half the foreign students enrolled in U.S. colleges and universities. In fact, the top five countries of origin were all in Asia.

The interest is being reciprocated. Between 1977 and 1986, the number of American college students enrolled in Chinese language courses increased from 10,000 to 17,000; in Japanese, from 11,000 to 24,000. Many educators claim the growth is long overdue. In the words of Dartmouth president James O. Freedman: "We've lagged far behind in learning about Eastern civilization, and I am one of those who believes that we are on the threshold of the century of the Pacific."[22] (In this context, Allen Bloom's attacks on "openness" and "cultural relativism" appear rather silly.)

At the same time, there has been a dramatic rise in general Asian studies, especially on the West Coast. The University of California at San Diego has recently established a Graduate School of International Relations and Pacific Studies, which expects to enroll about four hundred students within a couple of years. UCLA has doubled the number of its faculty experts on Japan and China to about forty. Stanford has opened a Center for Technology and Innovation in Japan and will administer a general Japanese Studies Program for a consortium of universities, including Yale, Princeton and Brown. (Meanwhile, Stanford has closed its center in Austria.) Berkeley has set up an office in Tokyo—the first for an American university—to raise funds for the expansion of its East Asian Institute. Funds will be solicited from Berkeley alumni and—well, from Japan. (The office will also be used as a base for expansion to South Korea, Taiwan and Hong Kong.)

That an American university should be passing the hat in Japan is not at all surprising—not when one considers the recent expansion of Japanese philanthropy (and general PR) in America. "As Japan increases its investment in the U.S.," writes *Business Week*, "it is also becoming a full-fledged member of the American political, cultural, and intellectual debate in a way—and on a scale—that no other nation has achieved."[23] For 1988, Japan posted a membership fee of at least $310 million—which covered everything from corporate gifts to Washington lobbying to public television contributions to university research contracts.

Berkeley received $4 million from Japanese companies to build a computer lab. The University of California at Irvine (where the freshman class is one-third Asian) got $12 million from Hitachi Chemical; in exchange, Hitachi, for the next forty years, will use two-thirds of the space in a new biotech lab. At MIT, Japanese companies have endowed sixteen chairs at roughly $1.5 million each. Columbia and Johns Hopkins awarded honorary degrees to Prime Ministers Takeshita and Nakasone, respectively. Both schools then received what *Business Week* describes as "substantial endowments from Japanese sources."[24] According to Prof. Chalmers Johnson, a Japanese expert at the new graduate school at UC-San Diego, 80 percent of the money for research on Japan now comes from Japan itself.

Japanese funds flow to the Brookings Institution and the American Enterprise Institute. The Hitachi Foundation, which contributes money to public television (among many other things), is chaired by Boston poohbah Elliot Richardson. The Council on Foreign Relations (which has historically faced toward Europe) is now chaired by former Commerce Secretary Peter G. Peterson, whose Wall Street investment firm, the Blackstone Group, serves major Japanese clients. (In fact, 20 percent of Blackstone is owned by Nikko Securities, the third-largest securities firm in Japan.)

As significant as all these high-level goings-on, perhaps, is the growing Oriental presence in American daily life. More than a quarter of a million Americans now work for Japanese companies (10,000 in Tennessee alone), and MITI predicts that Japanese investment will create an additional 800,000 American jobs within the next ten years. Moreover, working for Japan, Inc. is not like working for the British or the Dutch. Japanese firms have a hands-on management style, and American workers are taught Japanese production methods by Japanese instructors. Japanese customs are also in evidence. The start of construction for a Mazda plant in Flat Rock, Michigan was preceded by a forty-minute Shinto service entitled "Sacred Groundbreaking Ceremony with the Principal Parent of the Universe."

In Edgewater, New Jersey, there is a new shopping plaza that consists entirely of Japanese stores. Owned by a company that already operates six stores in California, it is designed primarily to serve the 60,000 Japanese in the New York region; but signs in the stores are also written in Korean and Chinese. Others, naturally, are welcome. Across the river in New York, the number of Japanese restaurants has doubled to 600 in the past five years; and Japanese tourists have replaced the British as the city's most frequent foreign visitors.

But the Oriental presence is most visible in California—the new Ellis Island. Already, the state is home to about two-thirds of the country's Asians; and many of the Vietnamese refugees who settle elsewhere eventually migrate to California, where they encounter little of the prejudice they experience in other states. As of 1987, Asians made up roughly 7 percent of the state's population, a figure that will rise to 10 percent by the year 2000. California has attracted

237

more than 40 percent of the Japanese investment in the United States, including more than 750 Japanese companies.

In San Francisco, by 1990, Asians will comprise about 40 percent of the population, making them the city's dominant ethnic group. Their number will be four times that of the blacks, and roughly equal to the combined population of whites and Hispanics. The Chinese have already spread far beyond Chinatown, becoming the dominant group in North Beach, on Nob and Russian hills, and in the Richmond and Sunset districts. (Each month, I make out my rent check to a man named Ming Koo, who owns the building in which I live. I buy my groceries at a recently opened market just down the street, where the owners and clerks are all Chinese, the vegetable bins are filled with ginger and bean sprouts and the front wall is lined with bulky, fifty-pound bags of rice. For a while I also shopped at the market's next-door neighbor, a grocery store owned by a personable young Caucasian man with whom I used to enjoy making idle conversation. Then suddenly one morning the young Caucasian man was gone, and the store reverted to its previous owners, a family of Palestinians (who had earlier leased the place to a family of Italians). The Palestinians seemed very determined, and quickly rearranged the cans and jars on all the shelves. But a few months later, they posted signs for a going-out-of-business sale. Only the Chinese remain).

In the metropolitan Bay Area, Asians will comprise a quarter of the population of 6 million people by 1990. In Silicon Valley, there are 10,000 engineers with Chinese surnames, many of them immigrants from Taiwan. In the valley town of Mountain View, the Taiwanese government has set up a recruiting office in an effort to lure its emigrant engineers back home.

The Asian residents of metropolitan Los Angeles will increase by 1 million by 2010, rising from 6.2 percent to 9.3 percent of the total population. Over the past four years, Los Angeles mayor Tom Bradley has received more than $200,000 in campaign contributions from a dozen or so Japanese businesses. Another $100,000 in Japanese money was given for a monument the mayor wants to build to welcome immigrants. Another $4 million went to the Los Angeles County Museum of Art towards construction of its recently opened Japanese Pavilion. The city's new Museum of Contemporary Art was designed by Japanese architect Arata Isozaki (who has also just designed the addition to the Brooklyn Museum, and whom

Richard Meier calls "the best architect practicing today").[25] The plaza of the city's new Japanese American Cultural and Community Center (one of the largest such centers in the country) was designed by Isamu Noguchi.

As the examples just given suggest, Asia is likely to have a strong influence on America in the realm of art. In architecture, Isozaki's colleague Fumihiko Maki is designing a new cultural center in San Francisco, and was one of three finalists considered for the Getty Museum in Los Angeles. I. M. Pei, who left his native China in 1935, has since designed (among many other things) the East Building of the National Gallery in Washington and the new glass pyramid for the courtyard of the Louvre. Isamu Noguchi's sculpture and sculpture gardens may well have contributed to the current wave of interest in the art of Japanese gardening in general.

Other examples of the influence of Asian art are far too numerous to describe in any detail. A few samples will have to suffice:

• In music, Philip Glass's minimalist style was derived, in large part, from Indian *raga*. His opera Satyagraha is sung entirely in Sanskrit. John Cage was deeply influenced by Zen Buddhism. At the moment, roughly a quarter of the students at Juilliard are Asian. Yo Yo Ma will probably become the greatest cellist since Casals. The Boston Symphony is directed by Seiji Ozawa.

• Modern dance is an American creation, but Ted Shawn and Ruth St. Denis drew on their impressions of the movements and spirituality of Eastern temple performances. Their disciple Martha Graham went on to adopt many Asian elements in her work. Japanese disciples of John Cage have composed several pieces for Merce Cunningham.

• Asian influence in Western theater can be seen in examples as diverse as Samuel Beckett's theater of silences and Peter Brook's *Mahabharata,* a nine-hour realization of the Hindu epic. (Brook is also known for a film called *Meetings with Remarkable Men,* which dealt with the life of G. I. Gurdjieff, the Russian devotee of Eastern religions.) Beneath the red Chinese-lacquer ceiling in the study of his Tao House, about thirty miles east of San Francisco, Eugene O'Neill wrote *The Iceman Cometh, a Moon for the Misbegotten,* and *Long Day's Journey into Night.*

• Other writers strongly influenced by Asia: Kenneth Rexroth, Gary Snyder and Allen Ginsberg (a practicing Buddhist). Recently, young American novelists such as Brad Leithauser, Jay McInerney and John Burnham Schwartz have been spending time in Japan. In fact, writes Michiko Kakutani, book critic for the *New York Times,* Tokyo is becoming for the today's generation of young writers what Paris was for that of Hemingway.

• The Asian strain has been strongest, perhaps, in painting. Following the "opening" of Japan in the latter nineteenth century, a wave of *Japonisme* swept the French Impressionists, including Cezanne, van Gogh, Degas, Manet and Monet. More recently, Asian thought has informed the work of such West Coast painters as Mark Tobey and especially Morris Graves (whose 1983 retrospective at the Whitney and other museums was entitled "Vision of the Inner Eye").

For the most part, writes Michael Brenson in the *New York Times,* interest in Asia has tended to focus on one or two areas—Japanese prints, Chinese calligraphy, and so on. But "in the last ten years," he says, "Western art, particularly in America, has set both feet on the shores of the Orient for the first time. Numerous artists, coming from a great many directions, have been roaming through the artistic landscapes of Japan, India and China."[26] The list of such artists includes David Hockney, Robert Rauschenberg (who was introduced to Zen by John Cage), and (according to other critics) Robert Motherwell and Franz Klein.

"The interest in Oriental art," writes Brenson, "is not a trend. It is not a new suit of clothes that artists will wear this season and discard the next. . . . it touches deep needs. . . . What artists have found there is essential."[27]

Brenson's assertion, if I understand it correctly, is true. And it goes to the nub of the difference between Western art and Asian art. The former, in this secular age especially, is concerned primarily with art as a reflection of life, existential life, and little more. It has reached a kind of intellectual and artistic dead end. Asian art, on the other hand, is concerned with ultimate reality, which in the end is what art is all about.

Changing artistic sensibilities, in turn, are merely another indication, albeit an important one, that the world is undergoing one of those seismic shifts that periodically rearrange things. For the past four hundred years or so, the world has been dominated by European power and European culture. The standards of production, of perception, of art—in short, of what was important—have been those of Europe.

As heirs to that power and culture, we in the United States have inevitably assumed that such was the natural order. We are like the protagonist of Sartre's *Le Mur,* who has lived his life in the illusion of being eternal. But like the same protagonist, faced with imminent demise, we are beginning to see things differently. We are like the theatergoer who, dozing off, suddenly wakes to find the circular stage set slowly turning and a strange new world gliding into view.

The Meeting of East and West:
Mysticism, Rationalism
and the New Paradigm

There is an orientalism in the most restless pioneer, and the
farthest west is but the farthest east.
—Henry David Thoreau[1]

Go on to the limit of emptiness;
Hold fast to the stability of stillness.

—*from the Tao-Teh-King*[2]

THERE IS A PLACE along the California coast where the mountains roll down to the sea, row upon row, like a ghostly herd of lumbering bison. At the line where the mountains and water collide, the scene is strewn with debris. Jagged rocks jut up from the beach, and when met by the waves, send showers of sea spray soaring above the cliffs. And there above the cliffs: billows of wildflowers and waving grass.

Yet despite the allure of this magical place, it remains remarkably untouched. One can spend an entire afternoon here, lying on an eiderdown of oddly named ice plant at the edge of a cliff, pulsing to the pounding waves, swilling wine, making love to one's mate, without ever seeing (or being seen by) another living soul.

Yet people do come here. Robinson Jeffers, Jack Kerouac, Joan Baez, even a young Hunter Thompson . . . Henry Miller, who lived here for twenty years, wrote that "if the soul were to choose an arena in which to stage its agonies, this would be the place for it. One feels exposed—not only to the elements, but to the sight of God."[3] Robert Lindsey of the *New York Times* described it as "a place of almost mystical beauty."[4]

There is something mystical about the name as well. Echoing the

sound of the booming sea, it resonates in the mind like a mantra:
Big Sur.

On the southern edge of the hamlet of Big Sur itself—an assort-
ment of rustic tourist cabins tucked among the redwoods—is a
rough-hewn restaurant called Nepenthe, a Greek word denoting
an ancient potion that brought about oblivion. Built alongside an
adobe house that Orson Welles bought for Rita Hayworth, the
restaurant stands nearly eight hundred feel above the ocean.
Seated on Nepenthe's outdoor terrace, gazing southward at the
silent, sea-bound mountains, one thinks of a line from MacLeish:
"And the inertness of hills is a kind of waiting."[5] A rather Japanese
line; haiku minus four.

A few miles south of Nepenthe lies a colony of buildings perched
on the edge of a towering cliff. At first glance the colony is unpre-
possessing, but its name is probably as widely known as that of the
coastline itself. It's Esalen.

One hesitates at beginning a chapter on a weighty subject with a
reference to Esalen, which over the years (and in the hands of
reporters who didn't do their homework) has acquired a reputation
for frivolity. But the facts of the matter are somewhat different.

Esalen was founded in 1962 by Michael Murphy, a native of
nearby Salinas, California, where his father was a lawyer and his
grandfather the town's leading doctor.[6] (The latter delivered the
town's best-known citizen, John Steinbeck, who later, it is said,
modeled the brothers in *East of Eden* on the Murphy brothers,
Dennis and Michael.) After turning down a scholarship to Harvard,
Michael began pre-med studies at Stanford. But he soon fell under
the spell of noted Asian scholar Frederic Spiegelberg, and especially the writings of Indian philosopher Sri Aurobindo. (It was no
passing fancy. Today, the walls of Murphy's study are lined with the
works of Sri Aurobindo and Sri Ramakrishna; the Upanishads, in
various translations; books on Tibetan Buddhism and Vedanta; as
well as books on Christianity and Islam; and the works of Meister
Eckhart, St. John of the Cross, St. Theresa, Freud and Jung, Blake
and Coleridge, and Joseph Campbell, among others.)

After graduating from Stanford in 1952, Murphy eventually
made his way to Aurobindo's ashram at Pondicherry. Although
Aurobindo himself had died in 1950, Murphy remained at the

ashram for a year and a half, studying Indian philosophy and meditating for four or five hours a day.

Returning to Palo Alto, then San Francisco, Murphy ran into a Stanford classmate named Richard Price, who was interested in social anthropology. Together, the two decided to take a look at a house and property that Murphy's grandmother owned on the Big Sur coast, where the family had often gone for summer vacations. After doing so, the pair decided to turn the place into a sort of informal university, where people would come to study the meeting of East and West (a favorite topic of Aurobindo, who had gone to school at Cambridge). They named it Esalen, after the local Indian tribe, whose members had for centuries taken baths in the property's natural hot springs.

The next several years comprised what George Leonard, the former *Look* editor and later Esalen's vice-president, describes as the institute's "big-bang period." This was, after all, the sixties, and great expectations were in the air (especially the balmy air of California). And since none of the officers of Esalen had any particular dogma they were trying to propagate, the institute became fair game for those who wanted to remake it in their own considerable image. There was, for example, Fritz Perls, the bearded, beaded, jump-suited "therapist" whose favorite technique was to place a member of his group in the "hot seat" and then proceed to take the person's psyche apart. There was William Schutz and his encounter groups in which members were encouraged to wrestle each other or sometimes to take off their clothes.

At the time this all began, however, Michael Murphy had never heard of encounter groups, and he later developed serious doubts about their long-term value. In any case, such groups never comprised more than a small percentage of Esalen's activities; and Perls, at least, eventually decamped for greener pastures. Meanwhile, Esalen had begun to attract a growing list of more serious, less flamboyant visitors: Aldous Huxley, Alan Watts, Arnold Toynbee, Frederic Spiegelberg, Linus Pauling, Paul Tillich, Harvey Cox, Gary Snyder, Rollo May, Carl Rogers, B. F. Skinner, Abraham Maslow, Kenneth Rexroth, Susan Sontag, Herman Kahn, Buckminster Fuller, Ansel Adams. Anthropologist Gregory Bateson spent much of the end of his life at Esalen, as did fellow anthropologist Joseph Campbell.

Today, says Murphy, Esalen is in the best shape it's ever been in.

After years of precarious financing, the institute is operating comfortably in the black. It's booked year-round at 90 percent occupancy, which translates to about 10,000 visitors annually, a third of them from abroad.

What all these people encounter at Esalen is a smorgasbord of 500 seminars and workshops—The Body and Zen, Imagination as Healer, Tao and the Timewave, Alternative Realities, Morphic Resonance (taught by the theory's originator, Rupert Sheldrake), T'ai Chi Ch'uan, Peak Experiences (taught by the author of *The Outsider,* Colin Wilson), Vipassana Meditation, Psychic/Intuitive Abilities, Being Good Enough (taught by Bruno Bettelheim), Ashtanga Yoga, Shamanism, Aikido and on and on.

For professionals in various fields, there are conferences in which enrollment is by invitation only—Quantum Physics and the Nature of Reality, Biological Research and Evolutionary Theory, Mysticism Reconsidered, Psychic Research, Meditation Research, Applications of Intuition, Revisioning Philosophy. (A relatively recent addition to the conference list, Revisioning Philosophy was developed with the aid of a grant from Laurance Rockefeller. It's directed by Jay Ogilvy, who taught philosophy at Yale and wrote a book called *Many Dimensional Man,* which sought to combine Western rationalism and Eastern mysticism.)

Many of those who direct and participate in these conferences are (like Ogilvy) California writers who've done much to shape the current quest for the-nature-of-it-all. Among them: Fritjof Capra, author of *The Tao of Physics* and *The Turning Point;* Gary Zukav, author of *The Dancing Wu Li Masters* and the recently published *The Seat of the Soul;* Charles Tart, a well-known parapsychologist; Russell Targ, who conducted a remarkable series of "remote-viewing" experiments at the Stanford Research Institute; and Nick Herbert, author of a book called *Quantum Reality.* (We'll return to all these writers in the following chapter.)

Another writer who occasionally shows up at Esalen is Michael Murphy, who spends most of his time these days at his house in Mill Valley, north of San Francisco. There, he devotes himself to running, meditating and writing his latest book, which in this case is a lengthy work called *The Future of the Body.* Researched with the aid of a $50,000 grant from Laurance Rockefeller (and the assistance of Esalen president Steven Donovan), the book is a compilation of evidence from various fields—the martial arts, religion, parapsychology, sports, shamanism, medicine—concerning a person's ability to alter the body at will. Or as Murphy describes it, the book is "a neo-Aurobindonean marriage of science and metaphysics."

Clearly, an institution such as Esalen would not have come into being without the ideas of a Michael Murphy. But like all such phenomena, it owes much of its character to the peculiarities of time and place. Murphy, for example, compares his explorations of inner space to Lewis and Clark's opening up of the West; and indeed the California psychic voyage can be regarded as an extension of the country's great drama of westward expansion.

As Van Wyck Brooks observed, Americans were "permanently transitory."[7] Possessed of a "restless temper," as Tocqueville put it:

> In the United States a man builds a house in which to spend his old age, and he sells it before the roof is on; he plants a garden and lets it just as the trees are coming into bearing; he brings a field into tillage and leaves other men to gather the crops; he embraces a profession and gives it up; he settles in a place, which he soon afterwards leaves to carry his changeable longings elsewhere. . . . Death at length overtakes him, but it is before he is weary of his bootless chase of that complete felicity which forever escapes him.[8]

More than that of any other people, American life was one of becoming, of inventing identities and casting them aside, then inventing new ones somewhere else, usually to the west. In addition, the quest for identity had mythic overtones: the search for Elysium, for Eden, for El Dorado, for—*something*.

So long as there were still fresh lands to settle, this something could be located, psychologically, in the land itself. (As the Lime-lighters used to sing: "I wonder if it's greener on the far side of that hill.") But in California the land ran out; there were no more valleys farther west, and even if there had been, they could hardly be expected to surpass the splendor of the coastal declivities of the Golden State. Still, the question persisted (as it always does): Is this it? Is this all there is? And so the search continued. In sunny, Southern California, it found expression in Hollywood, with its promise of magical transformation, of El Doradan riches, Edenic surroundings, eternal life (at least on celluloid), and indeed of the wellspring of the fountain of youth. In the fog-bound, brooding north, the search turned serious. Instead of becoming preoccupied with the pleasures of Elysium, northern adventurers (in spirit, at least) continued the westward journey across the Pacific, toward a place that promised not merely ease but enlightenment.

In doing so, they were, in a sense, merely continuing a tradition long established in California—to wit, the abandonment of inherited cultural patterns in favor of experimentation. As we noted in an earlier chapter, historian Carey McWilliams pointed out that the novelty of California's physical environment had forced such abandonment in one field after another—mining, agriculture, and so on—and the success of the resulting improvisations had created the impression that in California, anything was possible. As McWilliams put it: "Californians have become so used to the idea of experimentation—they have had to experiment so often—that they are psychologically prepared to try anything. [This was written, mind you, in 1949.] Experience has taught them that almost 'anything' might work in California; you never know."[9]

SATURDAY. A quick trip out West—to Santa Barbara, county seat of the Reagan ranch. It's my first visit to this town of 70,000 on the cusp between Northern and Southern California. On Monday there will be a conference at the Center for the Study of Democratic Institutions, but for the moment there is nothing to do except—how do you say in Californian?—eat lotuses. I take a stroll along the curving beach, enjoying the exotica—palm trees, a miniature freeway for bicycles, macramé sellers. The ocean is tamer than my familiar Atlantic, and greener. . . . Back at the El Escorial Hotel, I page through the Saturday *L.A. Times,* which is as fat as a Sunday anything else. My attention wanders. To hell with the world situation! I head for the tiled outdoor Jacuzzi, near the swimming pool, and slip into the hot water. My Jacuzzi-mates are a couple from up the coast. He is a landscape architect; she is a masseuse. I ask her where she plies her trade. "Have you heard of a place called the Esalen Institute?" she asks. "I've heard of it," I say. I feel immensely smug. *I'm really in California.* And it's just the way I like it—more foreign than Europe, any day.

—Hendrik Hertzberg,
The New Republic[10]

As the foregoing quote suggests, there are other differences between California and the East Coast that account for the former's receptiveness to new ways of thinking—and I don't mean the matter of Esalen masseuses. Rather, I refer to the writer's final phrase: "more foreign than Europe, any day."

It's true, of course. A few of the reasons:

• Age. Being older, the East Coast shares Europe's sense of history, of human frailty and human folly—and especially the sense that there is nothing new under the sun. In addition, the East Coast is conscious of a responsibility (however unofficial) for preserving the European cultural tradition.

• Society. On the East Coast, a person's life is often largely predetermined—by social class, education, custom and so on. On the West Coast, there are few such constraints. How should a person spend his life? is a question that inevitably arises.

• Daily life. East Coast residents are preoccupied—in an Eastern Shuttle sort of way—with running the country and the world. This, in a sense, is their reality. West Coast residents bear few such weighty responsibilities, at least for now. They may (or may not) take the trouble to find out what is happening back at OMB or CBS, but even so, they will not necessarily regard it as any more real than a number of other things. In a sense, they are like a leisure class that, free from the business of earning a living, is inclined to wonder what it all means.

• Setting. The unspectacular, rather "quiet" natural environment of the East Coast, like that of Western Europe, inclines residents toward restraint, rationality and resignation. The spectacular setting of California, with its empty spaces and wild coastline, encourages a belief in infinite possibilities.

• Climate. Similar effects to those of setting. The East Coast elements (especially the winter ones) prompt residents to hunker down, hope for marginal improvement, but not expect too much of things; life, after all, is harsh. The West Coast elements (such as they are) nurture the feeling that since ordinary experience is so pleasurable, anything beyond that can only be more so. (To be sure, East Coast residents claim that Californians are made balmy by the very climate they profess to relish; and there may be a bit of truth to this observation. In a place where it virtually never rains between March and November, any deviation from the norm is apt to produce a peculiar reaction. A photo caption that appeared in the *San Francisco Chronicle* in 1983, for example, referred to "the first August storm since 1976." According to the same caption, this storm consisted of exactly four one-hundredths of an inch of rain.)

• The national consciousness. During recent years, medical scientists have discovered a basic difference between the left and right hemispheres of the human brain, the left being more logical and linear in its thinking, the right more intuitive. (The left, for example, deals in words and language; the right, in patterns and images.) Now imagine a map of the United States as a human face, or more precisely, forehead. You will note that the West Coast corresponds to the right hemisphere of the brain, and the East Coast to the left hemisphere. This division in fact reflects a basic difference in thinking between the two sides of the country. (I would not contend, of course, that the difference is actually a function of continental geography; the map and forehead are merely metaphors. Nonetheless, there are those who argue that with the spread of television, in particular, mankind is evolving a sort of global consciousness. As the *New York Times*—of all publications—observed in a recent editorial: "Televising shared events does not create merely a global village or universal bulletin board. It may well unify millions of minds around the world, like a brain unifying millions of nerve cells.")[11]* To expand the notion of a super-consciousness, imagine the left hemisphere as consisting of the East Coast plus Europe, and the right, of the West Coast plus Asia. Again, this division reflects a basic difference in perception of the world, and indeed, of reality itself.

At any rate, such differences in perception and so on not only help explain why the West Coast is open to new ideas, but why the East Coast is apt to dismiss such ideas as merely another "California thing." Which in turn perhaps explains why no national jour-

* For further discussion of this possibility, see Peter Russell, *The Global Brain: Speculations on the Evolutionary Leap to Planetary Consciousness*, J. P. Tarcher (Los Angeles: 1983).

nalist has taken a recent look at California to see what is really going on.

One of the best ways of approaching what is really going on is by reviewing a book that has had a noticeable impact on the sort of people who participate in seminars at Esalen—namely, *The Structure of Scientific Revolutions,* by Thomas S. Kuhn (who wrote the book while teaching at Berkeley). In his book, Kuhn points out that most people have been taught, at least implicitly, that science is a linear, cumulative enterprise that has led inevitably to our present body of "scientific facts." But that is not the way that science actually operates. Instead, he says, it proceeds by a series of revolutions.

First there develops, in any given science, what Kuhn calls a "paradigm"—that is, an intellectual model of reality. In Ptolemaic astronomy, for example, the principal paradigm held that the heavens revolved around the earth. (In practice, any science is apt to contain a number of complimentary paradigms, some of them broader than others.)

Once a paradigm has been adopted, it effectively determines the ground rules for further research. For quite some time, that particular science will be engaged in what Kuhn refers to as "mopping-up operations"—"an attempt to force nature into the preformed and relatively inflexible box that the paradigm supplies."[12]

But there's a problem: the paradigm can never explain all the facts with which it can be confronted. For a while, these inconvenient facts are simply ignored or brushed aside, but as they begin to pile up, the paradigm is modified to try to fit them in. In Ptolemaic astronomy, the orbits of the planets were altered to include a series of "loops." One thing, however, does not happen. "What scientists never do when confronted by even severe and prolonged anomalies," writes Kuhn: "they do not renounce the paradigm."[13] Instead, they construct new versions. Eventually, the paradigm becomes increasingly blurred. "Though there still is a paradigm, few practitioners prove to be entirely agreed about what it is."[14]

By this time, the paradigm has entered a state of crisis, even though the crisis may not be generally acknowledged. In Kuhn's words: "scientific revolutions are inaugurated by a growing sense, often restricted to a narrow subdivision of the scientific community, that an existing paradigm has ceased to function adequately in the exploration of an aspect of nature to which that paradigm itself had previously led the way."[15]

Gradually, though, the ground rules for research are relaxed somewhat, and a new paradigm begins to appear. "Often a new paradigm emerges, at least in embryo, before a crisis has developed far or been explicitly recognized. . . . In other cases, however— those of Copernicus, Einstein, and contemporary nuclear theory, for example—considerable time elapses between the first consciousness of breakdown and the emergence of a new paradigm."[16]

In any case, the new paradigm does not, as a rule, simply displace the old, the way the billings change on a theater marquee. Instead, the two engage in a prolonged and bitter war. Copernican astronomy—the heretical theory that the earth is not the center of the universe—made few converts for almost a century after Copernicus's death; and Copernicus himself was denounced as mad. As Max Planck observed in his *Scientific Autobiography*, "a new scientific truth does not triumph by convincing its opponents and making them see the light, but rather because its opponents eventually die, and a new generation grows up that is familiar with it."[17]

One of the reasons for this is that the new paradigm represents sweeping change (and, to its opponents, ridiculous change). It involves, as Kuhn puts it, "a reconstruction of the field from new fundamentals, a reconstruction that changes some of the field's most elementary theoretical generalizations."[18]

According to many observers in California, at least, Western science is now engaged in just this sort of transformation. In the words of Stanford neurologist Karl Pribram (best known for his investigation of the brain-as-hologram), "I believe we're in the middle of a paradigm shift that encompasses all of science."[19] Geoffrey Chew, professor of physics at Berkeley and theoretical group leader at the Lawrence Berkeley Laboratory, foresees the emergence of "a completely new form of human intellectual endeavor, one that will not only lie outside physics but will not even be described as 'scientific,' "[20] This endeavor, in the words of Willis Harman, former director of policy research at the Stanford Research Institute, constitutes "the new Copernican revolution."[21]

251

Part of the basis of this revolution lies in a series of anomalies—and theoretical disputes—that have begun to trouble Western science. These we'll examine in the following chapter.

But there is also a broader, more general basis. As Kuhn points out, the transition from one paradigm to another is never made solely on the basis of scientific analysis: "the choice is not and cannot be determined merely by the evaluative procedures characteristic of normal science, for these depend in part upon a particular paradigm, and that paradigm is at issue. When paradigms enter, as they must, into a debate about paradigm choice, their role is necessarily circular. Each group uses its own paradigm to argue in that paradigm's defense. . . . The status of the circular argument is only that of persuasion. It cannot be made logically or even probabilistically compelling for those who refuse to step into the circle."[22]

What prompts people to step into the circle, says Kuhn, is something analogous to "a change in visual gestalt: the marks on paper that were first seen as a bird are now seen as an antelope, or vice versa."[23] But of course the transition is more sweeping than that: "when paradigms change, the world itself changes with them."[24]

Prior to that point, "the proponents of competing paradigms practice their trades in different worlds."[25] In Kuhn's analysis, these different worlds are of course of the scientific variety, but he acknowledges that they can be geographic as well. In either case, the members of the different worlds presumably receive more or less the same stimuli, but as a result of being conditioned by different paradigms (either scientific or cultural), they perceive different things: birds on the one hand, antelopes on the other.

Kuhn also notes, in passing, that "the bulk of scientific knowledge is a product of Europe in the last four centuries."[26] That's about as far as he goes in the matter of cross-cultural differences, but there's no reason we shouldn't take the observation a step or two further.

First of all, we should recall that those last four centuries are also the period when Europe (partly because of its scientific knowledge) dominated the world, both politically and culturally. It was a time when the world succumbed to the Western paradigm of scientific rationalism.

But today, with the West in relative decline and the East in ascendancy, one might wonder whether we are about to witness the rise of a paradigm of a different sort. For paradigm shifts, remember, are not made solely on the basis of reason and logic. They do not occur in a vacuum, or even a laboratory, but rather within the changing tides of history.

This is not to suggest, of course, that we are about to observe the wholesale rejection of one cultural paradigm in favor of another. While such neat transitions may occur in the world of science (at least in an earlier era), in the messy world of international politics, things are seldom so clear cut, especially in the age of the global village. Instead, what we are more likely to see is what F.S.C. Northrop referred to in a now-classic book as *The Meeting of East and West*.

Northrop's analysis of Western thought is strikingly similar to Kuhn's analysis of Western science. (Actually, one should say that Kuhn's analysis is similar to that of Northrop, since the latter's came first. But perhaps any intellectual historian would come up with more or less the same observations.)

Western man, says Northrop, is devoted to spinning elaborate, logical theories (that is, paradigms), the more elaborate the better. Such theories, however, are never exactly congruent with the facts. "This theoretical conception [of man and nature], even when determined by empirically and experimentally controlled scientific methods, always affirms more . . . than bare facts by themselves provide. In short, scientific theory always asserts more than observation gives, and is not verified directly . . . instead, it is a hypothesis proposed *a priori*, verified in part at least indirectly through its experimentally checked deductive consequences. . . . This *a priori* is, however . . . a hypothetical *a priori*, subject to change in its formal as well as its empirical content."[27]

All this, in turn, leads to what Northrop describes as "the revolutionary character of Western civilization." Theories are continually found wanting and overthrown, to be replaced by new ones. Even so, the emphasis remains on theory, or as Northrop puts it, on "things in their theoretic component." (Westerners, he notes, tend to be positivistic only during periods of transition.) Indeed, much of what we in the West take to be hard, factual knowledge is actually supplied by our theoretical concepts, our paradigms.

In the Orient, the emphasis is quite different. Rather than approach natural objects as mere grist for experimentation—theory fodder, as it were—the Oriental approaches them in an intuitive, esthetic attempt to comprehend their true nature, and through it, the nature of what Northrop calls "the undifferentiated aesthetic continuum," the ground of all being—the Tao, of which all things are transitory manifestations.

"The Oriental . . . positivistic concern with things in their aesthetic immediacy," writes Northrop,

> has had two consequences which to a Westerner seem self-contradictory. First, there is a stark kind of realism, a this-worldly concern with the concrete. . . . Second . . . there is what seems to a Westerner an excessively speculative other-worldliness. However . . . what [the Easterner] immediately apprehends is not merely the atomic, transitory qualities, but also the otherwise undifferentiated aesthetic continuum in which these occur. . . .
>
> Thus it is to be emphasized that when the Oriental designates the Tao, Nirvana, Brahman . . . to be something which is not given through the specific senses, he does not mean that it is a speculatively postulated . . . entity such as the mathematical . . . space in Newton's physics, or the unseen God the Father in the traditional Christianity of the West. He means . . . something . . . which is immediately experienced, its "transcendency" of the senses being due to the fact that the senses deliver specific, limited, determinate data within it, whereas it is indeterminate and all-embracing.[28]

During this experience, distinctions between subject and object fall away. (As Lin Yutang remarked, the Western artist paints an object from the outside, the Eastern artist from within.) Indeed, distinctions disappear between subject and all else that is; and the universe is experienced as it really exists, as One. But the accompanying knowledge cannot very easily be reduced to words; it must be experienced to be understood (like the color red). The result is a good deal less than provided by Western theory—and a good deal more.

Northrop points out that the basic cultures of East and West, although fundamentally different, are nonetheless complementary (rather than incompatible, as Kipling insisted). And as the two cultures increasingly meet and merge (especially in places such as California) we may begin to witness the accuracy (or inaccuracy) of Northrop's observation. But for most of recent history, Western culture, and specifically Western science, has moved increasingly away from the "unitary universe" perceived by Eastern mystics.

For much of the past four hundred years, Western civilization has been dominated by a view of reality—a paradigm—characterized by the primacy of matter, by a more or less strict separation between matter and mind, and by reason and logic (and especially mathematics) as the sole avenue to truth. The universe, in this scheme of things, is regarded as a well-oiled machine, and in order to understand it, one has merely to break it down into its elemental components of particles and laws.

This mechanistic, reductionist approach has been apparent not only in physics, but in sciences such as biology and medicine as well. (It is also apparent in such disciplines as philosophy, which for the most part no longer addresses the big questions concerning the meaning of life, but instead—in an effort to mimic the sciences—has become bogged down in highly technical analyses of language, logic and empirical data.)

During recent decades, however, this long-standing paradigm has begun to weaken. As we shall see in the following chapter, the change first became apparent in the field of physics, where it has continued unchecked. (Today, for example, physicists describe reality in terms of as many as a dozen dimensions, instead of the usual three.) From there it expanded to involve such fields as medicine and sports, as well as what has usually been referred to as "parapsychology"—instances of "mind over matter" and "ESP" which have turned up repeatedly in laboratory experiments and personal accounts, but which cannot be explained by conventional Western models of reality. Although he was not referring specifically to parapsychology, Northrop stated the problem well: "The trouble which constitutes the contemporary demoralization of Western culture is not that there is a present scientifically grounded philosophical theory adequate to all contemporary knowledge which some future discovery might render inadequate; but that we do not know how to relate and thereby give meaning to even contemporary factual knowledge. The immediate need is not for some theory which will remain adequate for all future time but merely for a theory which is adequate to the present accumulation of Western scientific knowledge."[29]

To be sure, there are many people in California who are fond of referring to "the new paradigm," but as Northrop suggests, there is no new paradigm as such. (Which is one reason the old paradigm is still in force: as Kuhn points out, an old paradigm is never rejected until a new one is available to replace it.) Instead, what we have, in a variety of fields, is a mingling of Western "science" and Eastern "thought."

Even so, it is possible to discern some elements of an emerging paradigm. For one thing, the primacy of matter, and the distinction between matter and mind, are gradually dissolving. As astronomer James Jeans puts it, "The universe is more like a great thought than a great machine."[30] Or in the words of astronomer Arthur Eddington: "The stuff of the universe is mind stuff."[31]

There are a great many more things that one could toss into this countercultural stew. Some of them are serious and substantive (at least potentially): James Lovelock's Gaia hypothesis; Rupert Sheldrake's theory of "morphic resonance"; the reborn concern for the environment. Some of them are less so: the California State Task Force to Promote Self–Esteem and Personal and Social Responsibility; crystals; channelers; Zen Master Rama (a.k.a. Frederick Lenz) of Malibu . . .

Which brings up, in turn, the whole New Age thing, a movement that is apparently growing by leaps and bounds. The number of New Age bookstores, for example, has doubled in the past five years, to more than twenty-five hundred. Stanford's highly rated business school offers a seminar on Creativity in Business, which features meditation, chanting, "dream work," tarot cards and discussion of the "New Age Capitalist." Major corporations such as Ford and Westinghouse have sent employees to "human potential" workshops conducted by groups such as Transformational Technologies, Lifespring and Insight. (Transformational Technologies is a recent brainchild of Werner Erhard, founder of the famous and now defunct EST; the founder of Lifespring is a former Erhard associate.) In Los Angeles, a couple of enterprising publishers have produced the New Age Telephone Book, a 160–page directory of psychics, healers, acupressurists, numerologists, channelers, ghost hunters and gurus galore.

The only problem with all this is that the subject soon turns to mush—as *Time* demonstrated in a captious and rather silly New Age cover story in December of 1987. (The cover photograph, inevitably, featured New Age convert Shirley MacLaine proffering a handful of crystals and beads.)

Thus, in the following chapter, we'll try to steer clear of the subject's more ephemeral aspects, and instead get to the heart of the matter: the decline of the paradigm of scientific rationalism, a view of reality that has governed Western society, and much of the world, for the past four hundred years.

8

Westerly Winds:
Birds Into
Antelopes

THERE ARE A NUMBER of fields of human endeavor—especially scientific endeavor—in which the culture of the East is beginning to influence the culture of the West. As a result, Western perceptions of physical reality are undergoing a change: what were formerly seen as birds (in Thomas Kuhn's analogy) are now seen as antelopes. In the present chapter, we'll take a look at several of the fields in which change is most noticeable, beginning with the one which, in the West, at least, is perhaps the most fundamental of all.

PHYSICS

"One of the best-kept secrets of science is that physicists have lost their grip on reality," writes physicist Nick Herbert in his book *Quantum Reality*. "News of the reality crisis hardly exists outside the physics community."[1]

What Herbert means by the "reality crisis" is simply the fact that many physicists are no longer certain what reality is "like," what it "consists of." One prominent theory—the so-called "many worlds" interpretation—goes so far as to argue that reality consists of a huge and growing number of "parallel universes."

Clearly, this curious, not to say alarming, state of affairs is a far cry from the one that obtained for the bulk of the four-hundred-year history of modern physics (and indeed from the one that most people erroneously assume still characterizes physics today). For most of that period, physics was the physics of Newton, who formulated among other things the famous laws of motion. In Newton's clocklike universe, time and space were absolute; all physical events could be reduced to the motion of solid bodies caused by the force of gravity.

During the latter half of the nineteenth century, Newtonian physics were modified somewhat by Maxwell's theory of electromagnetism; but by the end of the century, the physicists' paradigm of the physical universe seemed complete. Lord Kelvin declared that all the important discoveries had been made, and that physicists would soon have little to do except refine their measurements (Thomas Kuhn's "mopping-up operations"). Max Planck's teacher, expressing a similar view, advised his student to become a concert pianist instead.

All of this changed, of course, during the early twentieth century with the publication of a series of papers by an obscure, twenty-six-year-old patents clerk named Albert Einstein. In one of them, Einstein set forth his Special Theory of Relativity. In another, he laid the groundwork for quantum mechanics, which was later developed by such scientists as Niels Bohr and Werner Heisenberg. The effects on physics were profound.

"It was as if the ground had been pulled out from under one," wrote Einstein in his autobiography, "with no firm foundation to be seen anywhere, upon which one could have built."[2]

"The great extension of our experience in recent years," wrote Bohr, "has brought to light the insufficiency of our simple mechanical conceptions and, as a consequence, has shaken the foundation on which the customary interpretation of observation was based."[3]

"I remember discussions with Bohr," wrote Heisenberg, "which went through many hours till very late at night and ended almost in despair; and when at the end of the discussion I went alone for a walk in the neighboring park I repeated to myself again and again the question: Can nature possibly be so absurd as it seemed to us in these atomic experiments?"[4]

It seems (as we shall see) even more so today, especially in the field of quantum physics. As a result, the field is manifesting several characteristics which suggest that a fundamental paradigm shift may well be underway.

For example, the more traditional physicists, in an effort to preserve the primacy of matter, are engaged in a relentless attempt to discover the most elemental particles, the so-called building blocks of nature. (Nontraditionalists speculate that there *are* no such particles in any meaningful sense, that their colleagues are off on a snipe hunt.) An attempt of this sort recalls Thomas Kuhn's observation that during periods of paradigm crisis, traditionalists are apt to respond by fine-tuning the paradigm:

> Faced with an admittedly fundamental anomaly in theory, the scientist's first effort will often be to isolate it more precisely and to give it structure. Though now aware that they cannot be quite right, he will push the rules of normal science harder than ever to see, in the area of difficulty, just where and how far they can be made to work. . . . Probably the best illustrations of all come from contemporary research . . . on fundamental particles. . . . Like much other research in physics during the past decade, these experiments were in part attempts to localize and define the source of a still diffuse set of anomalies.
>
> This sort of extraordinary research is often, though by no means generally, accompanied by another. It is, I think, particularly in periods of acknowledged crisis that scientists have turned to philosophical analysis as a device for unlocking the riddles of their field. . . . It is no accident that the emergence of Newtonian physics in the seventeenth century and of relativity and quantum mechanics in the twentieth should have been both preceded and accompanied by fundamental philosophical analyses.[5]

The second paragraph quoted above brings up another characteristic of contemporary quantum physics—namely, the emergence of fundamental philosophical analysis. While the great majority of physicists (like the moppers-up in any age) are content to practice their craft without worrying much about its deeper dimensions—quantum theory works, after all, so what the hell—a small but growing minority has begun to wonder *why* it works. What sort of reality, they ask, underlies the theory?

And this question, in turn, has brought about what physicist Nick Herbert calls the "reality crisis": nobody knows, any longer, what "reality"—deep, dark, quantum reality—is "really like."

There are, as I say, a number of theories (eight, according to Herbert). There is, for example, the ever popular Copenhagen interpretation (named after Niels Bohr's Copenhagen Institute), according to Part 1 of which (says Herbert) there *is* no deep reality; and according to Part 2 of which the phenomenal reality observed by quantum physicists is actually created by observation. (I know this doesn't make sense; we'll return to it later.) There is David Bohr's theory that reality is an undivided wholeness. There is David Finkelstein's theory that reality obeys a nonhuman logic, namely, quantum logic. And last but certainly not least, there is the many-worlds interpretation, which calls into being a zillion parallel universes.

All of which reminds one of another of Thomas Kuhn's observations—that in periods of crisis, a given paradigm becomes increasingly blurred: "Though there still is a paradigm, few practitioners prove to be entirely agreed about what it is."[6]

Yet despite such apparent confusion, several observers argue that the New Physics (meaning relativity theory and quantum theory) is actually moving toward a unified vision of reality—one which is strikingly similar, in many ways, to that embraced by Eastern philosophies. Perhaps the best known observers of this sort are Fritjof Capra, a European physicist who wrote *The Tao of Physics,* and Gary Zukav, a Harvard graduate and student of Eastern thought who wrote *The Dancing Wu Li Masters.* As it happens, both these people have lived for a number of years in the San Francisco area, where they've participated in physics conferences at Berkeley and Esalen. (This is not to suggest, however, that the two men are friends. Capra regards Zukav as having appropriated ideas from *The Tao of Physics,* which was first to appear.)

In exploring some of the parallels between the New Physics and Eastern philosophy, we'll begin with Einstein's theories of relativity. Although Newton's laws of motion are still the rule for normal objects traveling at normal speeds, these laws break down when one begins to deal with very great speeds (approaching that of the speed of light). At such velocities—says the Special Theory of Relativity—measurements of observed objects will vary according to the speed of the object relative to the position of the observer. An object such as a javelin (moving at a much greater speed than one could ever throw it) will measure shorter than "normal." A clock in motion will "slow down."

This latter peculiarity leads to the famous paradox of the twins. If a pair of twins is separated, one remaining on Earth and the other leaving on a long and speedy voyage in space, the latter, on his return, will be younger than his brother (or sister, as the case may be).

Clearly, space and time are not absolute (as assumed in Newtonian physics). Instead, they exist as a continuum—space-time—which seems peculiar (at least to us in the West) only because we perceive things in three dimensions rather than four. (Think of a circle trying to imagine a sphere.) As Gary Zukav explains the matter in *The Dancing Wu Li Masters:* "In . . . the space-time continuum, events do not develop, they just are. If we could view our reality in a four-dimensional way, we would see that everything that now seems to unfold before us with the passing of time, already exists *in toto,* painted, as it were, on the fabric of space-time."[7]

In Einstein's General Theory of Relativity, things become curiouser and curiouser. Space-time, it turns out, is "curved" by the force of gravity. Thus, around a "black hole"—a collapsing star so dense that not even light can escape—there forms something known as the "event horizon." At this horizon, time—to an outside observer—grinds to a halt; but beyond the horizon, time continues to flow "normally."

Physicists speculate that an object sucked across the "event horizon" might pass through a "wormhole" and re-emerge in another—and distant—time and place. Indeed, a trio of theoretical astrophysicists—two from Cal Tech and one from Wisconsin*—recently published a paper in the prestigious *Physical Review Letters* (an official publication of the American Physical Society) in which they suggested that such a "wormhole" might actually be constructed by some advanced civilization. As the authors observed in their summary: "If the laws of physics permit an advanced civilization to create and maintain a wormhole in space for interstellar travel, then that wormhole can be converted into a time machine with which causality might be violatable."[8] In other words, it might be possible to change the "past."

Another bizarre possibility is that objects drawn into the infinite density of a distant black hole—to a point that is known as "the singularity"—might re-emerge, as a matter of course, in another universe. By the same token, black holes in other universes might be spewing stuff out into our universe. In fact, some physicists speculate that we already observe this latter phenomenon in the form of "white holes," or quasi-stellar radio sources—quasars, for

* The two from the California Institute of Technology were Dr. Kip S. Thorne and Dr. Ulvi Yurtsever. The one from the University of Wisconsin was Dr. Michael S. Morris.

short. One reason for such speculation, reports Gary Zukav, is that while most quasars are only several times the diameter of our solar system, they emit more energy than a galaxy of 150 billion stars.[9]

Obviously, we are only beginning to understand the ins and outs of space-time; and yet the basic truths we've acquired so far are oddly similar to ones long held by another branch of learning, namely, Eastern philosophy.

First of all, ordinary ideas of absolute space and time have always been regarded by Eastern sages as constructs of the mind—just as relativity theory has (belatedly) shown them to be.

Second, relativity theory's (relatively) recent discovery that space and time are actually a continuum—space-time—was made long ago in the Orient. Architect Arata Isozaki, for example, points out that both dimensions are expressed in the Japanese concept of *ma,* or space-time. Equally important, space-time has always been a central concept of Eastern philosophy, particularly in the *Avatamsaka* school of Mahayana Buddhism. As D. T. Suzuki describes the state of enlightenment achieved by that school, "there is no space without time, no time without space; they are interpenetrating."[10]

Finally, there are the recent speculations by Western physicists that the "past" and "future" are somehow "accessible" (by means of "wormholes," perhaps); that they are somehow part of the present—"painted, as it were, on the fabric of space-time." Again, this concept—the "eternal now"—is central to Eastern philosophy. In the words of Hui-neng, the Sixth Zen Patriarch (as quoted in *The Tao of Physics*): "The absolute tranquillity is the present moment. Though it is at this moment, there is no limit to this moment, and herein is eternal delight."[11] Or in the words of D. T. Suzuki:

> In this spiritual world there are no time divisions such as the past, present and future; for they have contracted themselves into a single moment of the present where life quivers in its true sense. . . . The past and the future are both rolled up in this present moment of illumination, and this present moment is not something standing still with all its contents, for it ceaselessly moves in.[12]

To be sure, such notions have not been entirely unknown in the West, even before the advent of relativity theory. As William Blake wrote in his poem called "Auguries of Innocence":

To see a World in a Grain of Sand
And a Heaven in a Wild Flower,
Hold Infinity in the palm of your hand
And Eternity in an hour.[13]

Quantum theory—the branch of physics that deals with the very small—is, if anything, even stranger than relativity theory. Subatomic units of matter, for example, display a dual aspect, appearing sometimes as particles, sometimes as waves. Although the latter exhibit the physical characteristics of waves, they are not "real" three-dimensional waves, like sound or water waves. Rather, they are "probability waves"—abstract mathematical quantities related to the probabilities of finding the particles at particular places at particular times. Thus, at the subatomic level, matter shows only "tendencies to exist," and events, "tendencies to occur." Laws are expressed as probabilities. (Clearly, we've come a long way from Newton's clocklike universe.)

Yet despite such paradoxes, the world of quantum physics manifests some salient, consistent characteristics. One of these is the essential unity of all its ingredients. In the words of some noted physicists:

> Isolated material particles are abstractions, their properties being definable and observable only through their interaction with other systems. (Niels Bohr)[14]

> The world thus appears as a complicated tissue of events, in which connections of different kinds alternate or overlap or combine and thereby determine the texture of the whole. (Werner Heisenberg)[15]

> We have reversed the usual classical notion that the independent "elementary parts" of the world are the fundamental reality, and that the various systems are merely particular contingent forms and arrangements of these parts. Rather, we say that inseparable quantum interconnectedness of the whole universe is the fundamental reality. (David Bohm)[16]

A striking example of this "inseparable quantum interconnectedness" is provided by Bell's Theorem (which was demonstrated at the Lawrence Berkeley Laboratory in 1972). Suppose that we start with what physicists call a two-particle system of zero spin, meaning

264

one in which the particles are spinning in opposite directions. Suppose that we then separate the particles by some great distance—as great as you please—and change the spin of one of them. The other will change its spin instantaneously. How do the particles "communicate"? And at a speed faster than that of light—in fact instantly? No one really knows. What we do know is that the implications of Bell's Theorem are immense.

In the words of Henry Stapp, senior staff scientist of the theoretical physics group at the Lawrence Berkeley Laboratory:

> The important thing about Bell's Theorem is that it puts the dilemma posed by quantum phenomena clearly into the realm of macroscopic phenomena . . . [it] shows that our ordinary ideas about the world are somehow profoundly deficient even on the macroscopic level. . . . Bell's Theorem is the most profound discovery of science.[17]

Or as physicist Nick Herbert writes in *Quantum Reality:*

> Bell's Theorem shows that the holistic grammar of the quantum formalism reflects the inseparable nature of reality itself. Beneath phenomena, the world is a seamless whole.[18]

Of necessity, this seamless whole includes the human observer (a point to which we'll return later in this chapter). According to the famous Heisenberg Uncertainty Principle, it is impossible to determine simultaneously both the position and momentum of a subatomic particle. This is not because of any shortcomings in our measuring devices or our methodology. Rather, it results from a condition inherent in the nature of quantum reality, and especially in the interaction between that reality and ourselves. As Fritjof Capra explains in *The Tao of Physics:* "If we decide to measure the particle's position precisely, the particle simply *does not have* a well-defined momentum, and if we decide to measure the momentum, it does not have a well-defined position."[19] Which raises the question of whether, in choosing which attribute to measure, we somehow summon that attribute to existence.

In the words of John Wheeler, formerly of Princeton and now head of the Institute of Theoretical Physics at the University of Texas:

> May the universe in some strange sense be "brought into being" by
> the participation of those who participate? . . . The vital act is the act
> of participation. "Participator" is the incontrovertible new concept
> given by quantum mechanics. It strikes down the term "observer" of
> classical theory, the man who stands safely behind the thick glass wall
> and watches what goes on without taking part. It can't be done,
> quantum mechanics says.[20]

The extrapolations from this sort of thinking are various and
several. Physicists such as Wheeler subscribe to what Nick Herbert
refers to as Part 2 of the Copenhagen interpretation (see above):
namely, that the phenomenal reality observed by quantum physicists is created by observation. In Wheeler's words: "No elementary
phenomenon is a real phenomenon until it is an observed
phenomenon."[21]

Other physicists who subscribe to this general line of reasoning
go even further, arguing that reality is created not simply by
observation—by measurement—but rather by consciousness.

As to the question of what possible connection there could be
between consciousness, on the one hand, and the world of shoes
and ships and sealing wax, on the other, physicist David Bohm
offers an intriguing answer. Consciousness, he suggests, is actually
a subtle form of matter.

Here again, the findings and speculations of contemporary physics bear a striking resemblance to those of Eastern philosophy. The
concept of reality as a seamless whole—of universal "oneness"—for
example, is perhaps the central tenet of Oriental thought. Thus, in
a situation where a physicist such as Niels Bohr might state that
"isolated material particles are abstractions, their properties being
definable and observable only through their interaction with other
systems," a Buddhist such as Nagarjuna might remark that "things
derive their being and nature by mutual dependence and are
nothing in themselves."[22]

By the same token, Eastern philosophers regard the unitary
universe as including of necessity the human observer and human
consciousness. Indeed, in states of deep meditation, Eastern mystics arrive at a point where the distinction between observer and
object breaks down completely, and the experimenter sees himself
as part of an undivided whole.

Another salient characteristic of contemporary physics is its view of the universe as being essentially dynamic—that is, as continuously in motion and continuously changing. This concept involves considerably more than one might at first surmise.

All of us are familiar with Einstein's famous $E = mc^2$, but we usually associate it with an isolated event, such as a nuclear explosion. Physicists, however, increasingly view the universe as an undivided quantum field of energy that is continuously manifesting itself as particles and then "fading away" again into energy. In Einstein's words:

> We may therefore regard matter as being constituted by the regions of space in which the field is extremely intense. . . . There is no place in this new kind of physics for both the field and matter, for the field is the only reality.[23]

Or in the words of Hermann Weyl:

> A material particle such as an electron is merely a small domain of the . . . field within which the field strength assumes enormously high values. . . . Such an energy knot, which by no means is clearly delineated against the remaining field, propagates . . . like a water wave across the surface of a lake; there is no such thing as one and the same substance of which the electron consists at all times.[24]

Or in the words of physicist W. Thirring:

> The field exists always and everywhere. . . . It is the carrier of all material phenomena. . . . Being and fading of particles are merely forms of motion of the field.[25]

Once again, the parallels to Eastern philosophy are striking. In Hinduism, this "motion of the field" is regarded as the cosmic dance. In Chinese philosophy, it is expressed in the concept of *ch'i*, the vital energy animating the cosmos. In the words of Chang Tsai:

> When the ch'i condenses, its visibility becomes apparent so that there are then the shapes [of individual things]. When it disperses, its visibility is no longer apparent, and there are no shapes.[26]

And how do physicists on the East Coast of the United States in the latter part of the twentieth century regard all this? Dr. Heinz

R. Pagels, former executive director of the New York Academy of Sciences,* reviewed a physics book for the *New York Times* in April 1983, and pointed out that the author "shares the view of most professional physicists that modern quantum physics has nothing in common with the facile mysticism articulated in some recent popular books. He is not about to suggest that you 'trade in your calculator for a mantra.' "[27]

In October 1984, however, Dr. Pagels was asked by the *Times* to comment on any potential contributions of Oriental thought to Western science. He replied: "When I read some of those ancient texts, I sometimes think, my God, they're talking about modern physics. But they certainly didn't know anything about particles and waves, or quantum mechanics. You have to ask yourself what they had in mind. I don't know if there's a real connection between their insights and a modern understanding. Personally I'm rather skeptical, but I could be dissuaded. I'm all for these explorations of other points of view."[28]

Scientists on the West Coast, apparently, are rather more open to these other points of view. Take Geoffrey Chew, former chairman of the Berkeley physics department, now dean of the physical sciences at Berkeley and theoretical group leader at the Lawrence Berkeley Laboratory. Chew recalls that in 1969, on the eve of a family trip to India, his teenage son remarked that the physics his father pondered over at the lab sounded a lot like the Mahayana Buddhism he was studying in school. At first, says Chew, he was rather taken aback, but as he learned more about the subject of Buddhism, the comparison made a lot of sense. Today, Chew has developed a deep appreciation for the similarities between physics and Eastern thought ("I've become persuaded," he says, "that there's no sharp definition of physics"),[29] along with a certain bemusement concerning the dilemma faced by his fellow physicists when confronting those same similarities. As he remarked during a lecture delivered in Boston:

> Now, of course, other particle physicists, since they are working with quantum theory and relativity, are in the same position. However, most of them are reluctant to admit, even to themselves, what is happening to their discipline, which is, of course, beloved for its dedication to objectivity. But for me, the embarrassment that I felt

* Dr. Pagels was killed in a fall while hiking in Colorado in 1988.

in 1969 has gradually been replaced by a sense of awe, which is combined with a sense of gratitude that I am alive to see such a period of development.[30]

If the truth be known, Chew has a lot of distinguished company. David Bohm, who studied at Berkeley under J. Robert Oppenheimer and then taught at Berkeley and Princeton,* became a close friend of Krishnamurti, who served as his spiritual mentor. Others in the same company, in their own words:

The general notions about human understanding ... which are illustrated by discoveries in atomic physics are not in the nature of things wholly unfamiliar, wholly unheard of, or new. Even in our own culture they have a history, and in Buddhist and Hindu thought a more considerable and central place. What we shall find is an exemplification, an encouragement, and a refinement of old wisdom. (J. Robert Oppenheimer)[31]

The great scientific contribution in theoretical physics that has come from Japan since the last war may be an indication of a certain relationship between philosophical ideas in the tradition of the Far East and the philosophical substance of quantum theory. (Werner Heisenberg)[32]

For a parallel to the lesson of atomic theory ... we must turn to those kinds of epistemological problems with which thinkers like the Buddha and Lao Tzu have been confronted, when trying to harmonize our position as spectators and actors in the great drama of existence. (Niels Bohr)[33]

In 1947, Niels Bohr was knighted. As the motif for his coat of arms, he chose the ancient Chinese symbol of *t'ai-chi*—representing the complementary relationship between the archetypal opposites, *yin* and *yang*—along with the inscription *Contraria sunt complementa*.[34] In so doing, Bohr was no doubt making a sly reference to his belief that waves and particles are complementary aspects of the same reality; but in a larger sense he was clearly

* Bohm lost his position at Princeton when he refused Sen. Joseph McCarthy's demand that he testify against Oppenheimer. He left the United States, and today teaches at Birkbeck College, University of London.

suggesting a basic harmony between Western science and Eastern thought.

MEDICINE

Until recently, Western medicine operated (as it were) on many of the same assumptions that governed pre-twentieth-century physics. Mind and body—following the dualism of Descartes—were regarded as separate. And just as the universe was regarded as a large machine, so a person's body was regarded as a small one. In the words of Descartes: "I consider the human body as a machine. . . . My thought compares a sick man and an ill-made clock with my idea of a healthy man and a well-made clock."[35]

Like a clock, the body was looked upon as the sum of its parts. Through a process of reductionism, the causes of illness were sought in specific agents, as were the cures. As a result, the physician assumed the role of a sort of white-collar mechanic.

The rewards of this process have certainly been considerable—the development of surgery, the discovery of penicillin, the eradication of smallpox, tuberculosis and polio . . . At the same time, however, the system retains a number of flaws. According to Dr. Herbert Benson of Harvard Medical School, "only about 25 percent of the illnesses that bring a Western patient to a Western physician are successfully treated by specific agents and procedures. . . . Our Western medical approach is thus rather limited in its efficacy. . . . We in the West are now looking more carefully, and less condescendingly, at alternative practices of medicine."[36]

One such alternative practice is the traditional medicine of China, which operates on a very different set of assumptions. In part, the practice is based (like all other systems of Chinese thought) on the ancient concepts of *yin* and *yang*, the complementary opposites that supposedly inhere in every aspect of the universe. In a more specific sense, it is based on the concept of *ch'i*, the vital energy that flows through the body along a series of meridians. (This is the same ch'i, incidentally, that supposedly animates the cosmos.) Finally, the practice is based on the belief that health is affected by environment and diet as well as by thought and emotion. In other words, there is no separation of body and mind.

The principal method of treating illness is a complex system of herbal remedies. In addition, acupuncture and massage are used to direct the flow of *ch'i* along the system of bodily meridians.

Assessing the efficacy of such treatments can be somewhat difficult—as a Harvard medical student named David Eisenberg discovered in 1979 when he became the first American medical exchange student in the People's Republic of China. Following his stay in China, Eisenberg continued his study of Oriental medicine during his residency at UCLA, after which he wrote a fascinating book about his Chinese experiences called *Encounters with Qi.**

Dr. Eisenberg recounts, for example, his assisting in an operation for the removal of a brain tumor. Although the procedure involved sawing away a four-by-six-inch rectangle from the patient's skull, the only anesthetic used was acupuncture—six slender needles inserted in the patient and attached by wires to a twelve-volt battery that delivered its current at specific frequencies. Throughout the four-hour operation, the patient remained awake and alert; and when it was over, he stood up, shook hands with all around him, and walked from the room unassisted.

Eisenberg also describes the stroke victim who made a "remarkable recovery" in a matter of weeks with the aid of acupuncture (though the doctor feels compelled to note that the man might have recovered in any case). In general, Eisenberg feels that acupuncture is effective in controlling certain chronic pain syndromes, but that beyond that, things become a bit murky.

As for herbal remedies, Eisenberg recalls the "remarkable and impressive recovery" of a patient suffering "a severe flareup of ulcerative colitis;" and he reports that most patients "showed marked improvement over time." But he adds, not surprisingly, that "without looking at large numbers of patients and comparing one kind of therapy with another under controlled conditions, it is impossible to know the overall effectiveness of herbal remedies."[37]

Part of the problem, apparently, is that China, in effect, has two systems of medicine. There is traditional Chinese medicine, which in 1980 could claim about 370,000 doctors, but only about a fifth of the students in medical training. And then there is Western medicine, which could boast roughly 500,000 doctors and four-fifths of the students in training. Only about 2,000 doctors were trained in both systems, between which there was little communi-

* *Qi* is the modern spelling of *ch'i,* and thus refers to the body's "vital energy."

cation. As Eisenberg wryly notes: "Doctors running nuclear magnetic resonance scanning machines have little in common with doctors prescribing antelope-horn tea."[38] (In Japan, on the other hand, the situation is apparently rather different. As Fritjof Capra points out in his second book, *The Turning Point,* "there is an increasing number of Japanese doctors, known as *kanpo* doctors, who combine Eastern and Western techniques into an efficient system of medical care.")[39]

At any rate, Eisenberg informed this writer over the phone that since the time his book was published he has visited China several times, partly to recommend a series of tests of various claims of Chinese medicine—especially those pertaining to "vital energy." Discussions for such tests, he said, are continuing.

Meanwhile, Eastern medicine has already begun making noticeable inroads into the West. Acupuncture, for example, is now legally recognized by roughly thirty of the United States, and claims about fifty-five hundred qualified practitioners. Hiroshi Shiriashi, who serves as acupuncturist for the Japanese national track team, has also treated a number of American sports figures, including football players Jim McMahon, Willie Gault and Walter Payton, and tennis players John McEnroe, Jimmy Connors and Ivan Lendl. In Washington, D.C., a thirty-three-year-old registered nurse named Karen Greubel found that acupuncture relieved her rheumatoid arthritis when all other remedies had failed. The more sensational reaction to acupuncture has passed, says Dr. Joseph Helms, a Berkeley internist who is president of the American Academy of Medical Acupuncture. "Physicians are willing to look at it and seriously consider how they can incorporate it into their medical practices."[40] So far, an estimated fifteen hundred to two thousand physicians have elected to do just that.

The most significant confluence of Eastern and Western medicine, however, is found in the relationship between body and mind. Increasingly, Western doctors are discovering—partly through their own efforts, partly under the influence of the teachings of the East—that body and mind are not at all separate, that a person's thoughts and emotions can affect the course of a host of diseases and perhaps determine whether a person gets sick to begin with. Although a full account of this emerging field of study is beyond the scope of this book (one has to draw the line somewhere), a few examples will provide an indication of what the field consists of.

Some of the examples arise directly from Eastern medicine. At the University of California Medical School in San Francisco, asthma patients have employed a visualization therapy based on a technique practiced in Tibet. During the therapy, each patient imagined himself traveling through his body as a point of light, like a miner in a cave, touring the troubled cells. Patients who used the therapy needed less medication and had improved respiration as compared with patients in a control group. In the words of Dr. Kenneth Pelletier, a clinical psychologist who has written a number of books on Eastern consciousness and the healing mind: "The Tibetan system seems to be a testable inner science: it has specified techniques with predictable outcomes. It seems to me we have much to gain from studying it."[41]

In the Mind/Body Clinic at Boston's Deaoness Hospital (modeled on a similar clinic at that city's Beth Israel Hospital), Dr. Herbert Benson teaches patients how to employ "the relaxation response," a technique he popularized in a book of the same name. Based on Oriental meditation, the technique is used to treat disorders ranging from insomnia to ulcers to high blood pressure.

Other examples of mind-body interaction may not have originated in China, but the message is much the same. All of us are familiar with the so-called placebo effect (which Western doctors have usually regarded as something of a nuisance). During the sixties came biofeedback (the effects of which were eventually found to be similar to those achieved by Eastern yogis). More recently, Western physicians have begun to observe a rather more generalized mind-body effect, one which, in theory at least, could apply to more or less any illness.

Not everyone in the medical profession, however, has been pleased with the turn that things have taken. In a famous editorial that appeared in June 1985, the *New England Journal of Medicine* commented on a study concerning advanced stages of cancer, the results of which were published in that same issue. Concluded the *Journal:* "It is time to acknowledge that our belief in disease as a direct reflection of mental state is largely folklore."[42]

No sooner did the editorial appear, however, than it was challenged by other researchers in the field. Then came a still unkinder cut. The author of the cancer study published in the *Journal,* Dr. Barrie R. Cassileth of the University of Pennsylvania Cancer Center, wrote a column for the *Los Angeles Times* in which she, in effect, disowned the *Journal*'s editorial. And just to add insult to injury, Dr. Cassileth wrote the column in conjunction with Norman Cousins, former editor of *Saturday Review*, whose well-known book *Anatomy of an Illness* had done so much to popularize the mind-body connection.[43] (In his book, Cousins described how he managed to cure himself of a supposedly incurable illness with the aid of massive doses of Vitamin C and laughter. Today, he is alive and well and teaching at the UCLA Medical School.)

Recent studies have supported the Cousins prescription. For example, Dr. Sandra M. Levy of the Pittsburgh Cancer Institute found that, as expected, the best predictor of survival time for patients with recurrent breast cancer was the length of "disease-free intervals." But the second-best predictor was something of a surprise. It was the patient's sense of "joy."

Conversely, studies show higher rates of mortality among nursing-home patients who feel they have no control over their daily lives; among people who have recently lost a spouse; and among those who feel socially isolated.* (Unfortunately for nursing-home patients, they are apt to qualify in all three categories.)

Over the past year or so, research efforts have also indicated a possible link between mental attitudes and the progress of AIDS. During a meeting of the American Association for the Advancement of Science held in San Francisco in January 1989, papers suggesting such a link were presented by scientists from five major research institutions, including UCLA and the University of California Medical School in San Francisco.

Such a connection would hardly be surprising, since over the past few years there has developed a hybrid science devoted to exploring links between the brain and the immune system (and AIDS is a disease of the immune system). Known as psychoneuroimmunology—or PNI—the new discipline involves researchers from a variety of fields, including behavioral science, psychosomatic medicine, endocrinology and neurology.

One of the more intriguing findings to emerge from PNI is that

---

* Studies of this sort have spawned a slew of recent books on the mind-body connection. Among the better ones: *The Healing Brain*, by Robert Ornstein and David Sobel; *The Healer Within*, by Steven Locke and Douglas Colligan; and *Who Gets Sick*, by Blair Justice. In addition, there is Bernie Siegel's ever popular *Love, Medicine & Miracles*.

the brain and the immune system are far more intimately connected than scientists had heretofore imagined. For example, Dr.
Candace Pert of the National Institute of Mental Health has found
that monocytes—immune system cells that heal wounds and ingest
bacteria—are shaped in such a way that they invite chemical interaction with neuropeptides, which normally serve as messengers
between brain cells. Such findings have prompted Dr. Pert to
observe that "I can no longer make a strong distinction between the
brain and the body. . . . we need to start thinking about how consciousness can project into the body."[44]

We're starting a bit late. As David Eisenberg remarks toward the
end of *Encounters with Qi:* "Three thousand years before the birth
of the first psychoneuroimmunologist, Chinese doctors were struggling with the same mind-body relations."[45]

SPORTS AND OTHER STRANGE PRACTICES

Among the more interesting aspects of *Encounters with Qi* is the fact
that the author's research into Chinese medicine soon led him into
areas that most Westerners would regard as far afield (at least in
terms of medicine). Early on, for instance, he encountered the
ancient practice of *qi gong,* or "manipulation of vital energy." According to Eisenberg, it "combines the motions of Tai Ji Quan [also
known as *T'ai-Ch'i*] with meditation, relaxation, careful attention to
breathing, and a specialized series of exercises that enable the
practitioner to direct his or her internal energy throughout the
body."[46] Today, *qi gong* is enjoying a popular resurgence and is
practiced each morning by tens of millions of Chinese adherents.
For most of them, the ritual is "merely" a good form of exercise
(and a means of preventing disease), but for thousands of cancer
patients, it is practiced in the firm belief that it will aid in curing
their illness.

Qi gong, however, can also be a demanding discipline—it is, after
all, the oldest of the martial arts—especially as practiced by the
small and dwindling number of *qi gong* masters. When David
Eisenberg asked to meet such a master, he was told to wait one
afternoon in the alley alongside the medical institute. There, he was
introduced to a sixty-year-old man with shaven head, taut skin and
massive forearms. The man asked Eisenberg to find him a rock—
any rock—and after walking to the end of the alley, Eisenberg chose

a stone about four inches wide and eight inches long. The man studied the stone for a moment, then placed it on a concrete doorstep, inhaled three times, and with his left fist, broke the stone neatly in two. That evening, Eisenberg watched as the man swallowed a pair of iron balls—each about two and a half inches in diameter and a pound and a half in weight—and then brought them up again. Next he picked up a fish-sized stone (supplied by Eisenberg) and broke it open against his head.

China is not the only Oriental country where such feats have been recorded. The greatest number are found in the literature of India (where the "vital energy" is known as *prana*), and they are quite common as well in literature of Japan (where the vital energy is known as *ki*). In all these countries, however, the explanation for such feats (as well as for others even more startling) is more or less the same. Masters of the various mind-body disciplines are said to partake not only of their own vital energy but of that of the universe as well, since the former is simply an extension of the latter.

In the West, the thinking of those who engage in physical disciplines has not reached quite this stage. Even so, quite a few athletes have begun to take up mind-body practices that are clearly derived from those of the East.

Jack Nicklaus and Kirk Gibson, for example, practice "visualization," whereby they imagine the way they will swing at the ball just before they do so. Gibson, in fact, employed the technique as he stepped to the plate for his dramatic ninth-inning home run in the 1988 World Series. (For most Western athletes, of course, visualization is merely a mental rehearsal, but for devotees of Eastern martial arts, the technique has quite a different meaning. One such devotee is George Leonard, the former *Look* editor who is now a trustee of Esalen, an expert in aikido, and the author of several books on human potential. As Leonard suggests in a book called *The Ultimate Athlete*, the desired athletic motion, whatever it is, already exists, like a whirlpool. All the athlete has to do is move into the whirlpool, and everything else will take care of itself.)[47]

Meditation, likewise, has been taken up by Western athletes, among them Billie Jean King and Bill Walton. And while such techniques are gradually being adopted by athletes headed for the Olympics, U.S. teams, in this regard, still lag far behind those of the Soviet Union and Eastern Europe (which may help explain why the latter do so much better). According to Grigori Raiport, who has written widely on Soviet athletic training, the Russians check out their athletes by means of "Kirlian electrobioluminescence." In other words, they examine the athletes' auras. If an aura is out of whack, technicians adjust it by using laser beams to stimulate points on the athlete's earlobe which correspond to internal organs. (All of which sounds a lot like high-tech acupuncture.)

There is, however, a more general sense in which Western athletics and Eastern mysticism may well be headed for a meeting of the minds. As Michael Murphy and Rhea White observe in a book called *The Psychic Side of Sports*, "sport has enormous power to sweep us beyond the ordinary sense of self, to evoke capacities that have generally been regarded as mystical, occult, or religious. This is not to say that athletes are yogis or mystics. . . . It is simply to recognize the similarities that exist between the two fields of activity, both in their methods and in the states of mind they both evoke."[48]

Following an extraordinary training run, for example, Mike Spino was suddenly overcome by an acute sense of loss-of-self: "Conversation was impossible, because for a while I didn't know who I was. Was I the one who had been running or the ordinary Mike Spino? I sat down by the roadway and wept."[49]

More common are descriptions of an uncommon ecstasy. Russian weightlifter Yuri Vlasov told a reporter of "the white moment," when "all suddenly becomes quiet within you. . . . There is no more precious moment in life than this, the white moment, and you will work very hard for years just to taste it again."[50]

Equally common are tales of feats that seem to defy conventional laws. Former St. Louis Cardinal linebacker David Meggysey (who has since taken up yoga) once found himself playing football "in a kind of trance where I could sense the movements of the running backs a split second before they happened."[51]

Which brings us to what is undoubtedly the most unusual aspect of the meeting of East and West—the subject which in the Occident has traditionally been known as parapsychology but is now known simply as psi.

PSI

Once upon a time, a long time ago, I was sitting in class on a Friday afternoon at the Fletcher School of Law and Diplomacy, in Boston. The class was one in international law, and normally I would have been paying rather close attention. But for some reason I found that I was daydreaming; and what I was daydreaming was this: Suppose I had just learned that the president of the United States had been assassinated; would I interrupt the class to break the news?

A few moments later there was a gentle knock at the classroom door; then the door swung open and a fellow student announced that President Kennedy had just been shot.

Now, statistically speaking, this little incident in and of itself was not particularly significant. After all, there must have been dozens of people across the country who, when they heard the news, slapped themselves on the forehead and said, "My God, I was just talking about assassination last night with my uncle Ralph!" In all likelihood, pure coincidence.

My own case, however, was somewhat different. Later that afternoon, I had a little talk with the student who had made the announcement. Without explaining why I was curious, I asked him what he had been doing just before he opened the door. He replied that he had stood beside the door for several moments, wondering whether he should interrupt the class to break the news. I would guess that raises the odds against coincidence considerably.

No, this experience did not change my life, or even arouse an interest in ESP. Like many Americans, when confronted by evidence of the "paranormal," I simply dismissed the evidence. Now, having looked into the subject at considerable length, I'm not so sure. In fact, I'm a lot less sure than that.

Although most of us tend to think of "psychic powers" as something conjured up by the supermarket tabloids, they have actually been reported throughout the course of human history. Interestingly enough, such reports are rather rare in the case of classical Greece and Rome. Equally interesting, they have always been common in the case of China.

When David Eisenberg began hearing reports of *qi gong* masters, for example, he also heard that not only could such people direct the flow of *qi* within their bodies, they could likewise project *qi* *outside* their bodies. Thus, on the evening he watched the *qi gong* master break rocks against his forehead, Eisenberg asked the man whether he had ever moved an object without touching it. The man replied that he had never attempted this before, but after a few moments' reflection, he agreed to try. What would you like me to move, he asked. Eisenberg looked around the man's apartment and then pointed to a lantern hanging from the ceiling. About four feet tall, it was composed of six sections of handcut glass held together by strips of hardwood.

After completing a series of breathing exercises, the man stood a few feet away from the lantern and held out his right arm. Slowly the lantern began to swing back and forth. Eisenberg was speechless.

On another occasion—this one at the *qi gong* research laboratory of the Shanghai Institute of Traditional Chinese Medicine—Eisenberg suspended a small object by a string from the ceiling so that the object dangled about ten feet off the floor. Then he watched a *qi gong* master named Lin Ho-sheng slowly approach the object, like a cat stalking a bird. All the windows in the room were closed and Lin himself wore a surgical mask. Holding his hand about three feet under the object, Lin rotated his palm in a clockwise direction. The object rotated counterclockwise. Lin kept his hand still. The object stopped moving.

Lin repeated the twisting motion several times, and each time the object moved in synchrony with his hand. By using both hands, he increased the rotation; and by moving his hands in a horizontal plane, he set the object swinging back and forth.

Eisenberg's most memorable experience of this sort, however, occurred when he visited a pair of sisters named Bin and Qiang Wang, who (like many other children in China) were reported to be able to read words written on scraps of paper hidden from view. On his visit, he was accompanied by a dozen Chinese doctors who were trained in Western medicine and who were all extremely skeptical about the existence of "psychic powers."

After arriving at the Wang's tiny house in a run-down section of Beijing, Eisenberg presented thirteen-year-old Qiang with a black plastic film container. Inside was a slip of paper bearing a pair of Chinese characters that are pronounced "peng you," and mean "friend." One of the Chinese doctors handed eleven-year-old Bin a container constructed from thick, black protective jackets of the sort used to insulate X-ray film. Inside was a piece of paper that bore the word "ren," meaning man. Both Eisenberg and the doctor had prepared their packets several hours earlier, and neither had told anyone what words were inside.

The girls placed the packets, oddly enough, under their right armpits, and waited a few moments for the words to "appear" inside their heads. Suddenly, Qiang shouted: "Peng, peng, peng you!" A few seconds later, her younger sister stopped chewing gum long enough to shout: "Ren! My word is ren! And you wrote it in red ink!"

Thereafter, the visitors took turns walking hundreds of yards away from the house to scribble fresh words on scraps of paper and then returning. Out of seven words (actually, a mix of words and pictures), the sisters got six of them exactly right; and the one miss may not have been a miss at all. In that instance, Eisenberg at first wrote the words *Zhong Guo,* meaning China. But then he decided that that was too easy, so he tore up the first piece of paper and instead wrote the words *Mei Guo*—America. When Qiang attempted to read the words, however, she saw them as *Zhong Guo;* and Eisenberg concedes that his first choice may still have been strongest in his mind. In other words, the sisters may well have been employing telepathy rather than clairvoyance (seeing at a distance), or perhaps some mixture of the two.

At any rate, all of the dozen Chinese doctors became instant believers. A senior surgeon, in fact, was moved to quote that ancient Chinese text, the *I Ching,* or Book of Changes: "I am reminded that haughtiness invites ruin; humility receives benefits."

In discussing such feats with doctors of traditional Chinese medicine, Eisenberg discovered that they were not at all surprised. Telepathy, clairvoyance and psychokinesis (or "mind over matter") have always been part of the Chinese medical tradition, he was told, and are well documented in historical texts.

Another thing he discovered is that such abilities have recently been undergoing extensive testing in Chinese medical laboratories. The Wang sisters, for example, have been tested at the Beijing Institute of Traditional Chinese Medicine, where the faculty is thoroughly convinced that their feats are genuine. Lin Ho-sheng (the *qi gong* master who rotated the object suspended from the ceiling) has been the principal subject of research at the Shanghai Institute of Traditional Chinese Medicine, where the doctors are likewise convinced of his abilities. Among other things, he has reportedly provided "anesthesia" for fifteen major operations merely by directing "external *qi*" at acupuncture points. He did not use needles, and he never touched the patients.

At the Shanghai First Medical College, doctors trained in Western medicine tested the ability of a *qi gong* master to cure a group of children of severe myopia. Of 20 children treated by the master, using external *qi,* writes Eisenberg, "an astounding 16 showed marked improvement in vision."[52]

At the Beijing Institute of Traditional Chinese Medicine, a *qi gong* master was tested for his ability to affect the growth of bacteria in test tubes, both positively and negatively. After more than forty repetitions of the experiment, it was found that a "health-promoting" dose of *qi* caused a seven- to tenfold increase in the number of bacteria. A "lethal" dose of *qi* lowered the number of bacteria by at least a half.

There has been a great deal of psi research in other parts of the world as well—mainly in the Soviet Union and Eastern Europe, but also in Western Europe and the United States. The findings from this research are in fact voluminous. What follows, therefore, is a highly selective sampling.

Psychokinesis

In 1967, a series of bizarre events took place at a law office in the Bavarian town of Rosenheim. Light bulbs exploded; fuses blew; phones rang incessantly; phone conversations were abruptly cut off; calls were placed without anyone touching the phones; light fixtures swung violently about; a picture rotated on its hanger . . .

As the events continued, the German Association for the Advancement of Science appointed a committee to investigate. The committee soon learned that certain of the events had been recorded in photographs, and that the series as a whole could be attested to by forty first-hand witnesses.

Among the members of the committee were several distinguished physicists, one of whom, Dr. Friedbert Karker of the Max Planck Institute in Munich, issued the following statement:

> We have investigated with particular intensity a case of RSPK [recurrent spontaneous psychokinesis]. This was the Rosenheim case. In the course of this investigation we came to the conclusion that it cannot be explained by means of today's theoretical physics. . . . I cannot offer any model which seems to fit these phenomena. That

they really do exist could be established with the utmost certainty.[53]

Eventually, it was determined that the events were associated with a nineteen-year-old employee of the law firm named Anne-Marie, who was sent to another place to work. Thereafter, things at the law firm quieted down, but when Anne-Marie began visiting a local bowling alley, electrical disturbances repeatedly upset the equipment.

In 1984, some curious things occurred in a house in Columbus, Ohio. Appliances began turning themselves on and off—stereos, radios, television sets, electric lights, shower faucets . . . Objects flew through the air—telephones, candlesticks, coffee cups, glasses, an afghan rug, a baby's bottle . . . The hands of a clock moved faster than normal . . .

Eventually, the family concluded that the events were swirling around a fourteen-year-old daughter named Tina, who was often struck by flying objects and who was experiencing nausea and headaches. Meanwhile, the family had called in members of the local press, one of whom snapped a photograph of a telephone apparently flying across Tina's lap. The story was picked up by the wire services, and not surprisingly, it was given prominent play in a number of papers, including the *San Francisco Chronicle.*[54] Not surprisingly also, nothing about the story appeared in the *New York Times*. (This difference in press coverage, as one might expect, is characteristic of the media on the East and West coasts.) Shortly thereafter, in an unrelated article, the *Times* referred to psi as something that "many scientists believe to be preposterous."[55]

Preposterous or not, psi—including psychokinesis—has been turning up in a steadily growing body of laboratory evidence. Around 1970, for example, a former Boeing physicist named Helmut Schmidt designed a device known as a random-number generator, which (in this case) is powered by the process of radioactive decay. Left to itself, the device hums along in the expected manner, producing a chain of events that is completely—well, random. But when a test subject "wills" the device to produce a different result, it apparently "responds" to the subject's wishes. Thus far, at least nineteen scientists have replicated Schmidt's rather startling findings; and Schmidt himself has obtained results that are significant at odds as high as a billion to one.[56]

Dramatic evidence of psychokinesis has likewise been elicited by testing a number of particularly gifted subjects, the Western versions of *qi gong* masters. At New York's City College in 1972, a man named Ingo Swann was tested by Dr. Gertrude Schmeidler, who found that Swann was able to alter repeatedly the temperature registered by an electronic sensor known as a thermistor, even though the instrument was located several feet away and was sealed inside a thermos bottle.[57]

Later that same year, Swann reported for a series of experiments at the Stanford Research Institute (now known as SRI), in Menlo Park, California. Soon after arriving, he was asked by physicist Harold Puthoff to see whether he could alter the readings being produced by a superconducting magnetometer, which was housed in an elaborate vault beneath the floor of the building in which they were standing. Although Swann was somewhat taken aback, he nonetheless agreed to give it a try. A few seconds later, the frequency of the oscillation in the reading doubled for about half a minute. Swann was then asked to try to stop the oscillation altogether, and a few seconds later, the oscillation ceased. After about forty-five seconds, Swann announced that he couldn't "hold it any longer," and the oscillation immediately returned to normal.

Swann's explanation of how he did this was intriguing, to say the least. He explained that he could "see" the device inside the vault, which he then proceeded to describe in words and sketches. In his description, he went so far as to mention such details as a gold alloy plate, which he could not possibly have known about. During his description, the magnetometer registered further perturbations.

Physicist Puthoff then suggested they stop talking about the device for a while, and the magnetometer's reading returned to normal. But a few minutes later, when Swann again described the device, the reading jumped into a high-frequency pattern. As soon as Swann stopped, the reading reverted to its usual tracing. Swann and Puthoff then left the building, and the tracing continued its normal pattern, an undulating line of hills and valleys, over and over, undisturbed.[58]

One year later, Puthoff conducted a similar but more elaborate experiment with a gifted subject named Patrick Price. On this occasion, Price was able to affect the reading from a superconducting differential magnetometer that was housed in a separate room. (We shall return to Price and Swann in the following section.)

Like the *qi gong* masters, gifted Western subjects have also produced evidence of "psychic healing." During the 1960s, a man named Oscar Estebany was tested by Dr. Bernard Grad, a psychiatrist at McGill University, who found that Estebany was able to improve the healing rate of injured mice. In subsequent tests on plants, Grad found that containers of water that had been handled for thirty minutes by Estebany produced significantly larger plants than were produced by untreated water.[60] (Perhaps there's more to the term *green thumb* than we have thought.)

Finally, there is the famous case of Nina Kulagina, a Russian woman who has been tested extensively by Soviet scientists, as well as by several from other countries, including the United States. Among her reported accomplishments: moving various objects across a table top; rotating the needle of a compass; stopping and starting a pendulum; moving the pans of a scale; and producing images on photographic film.[61]

Extrasensory Perception

Several years ago, just for the fun of it, I had a freelance artist do a drawing of a jacket design I had in mind for the book you're now reading. Although the drawing she produced didn't quite seem to "work," I still thought the concept had merit. Accordingly, I made a mental note to discuss it with my publisher when the manuscript was finished.

As I was writing away one day, however, I received in the mail from Donald I. Fine, Inc. a medium-sized manila envelope. Inside was a printed copy of the jacket you acquired along with this book. The design struck me as handsome—and startling. It was the same design I had had the artist draw several years before.

That is to say, both designs consisted of a human face, cut off just below the eyes, and on its forehead, a map of the United States. Now of course it's hardly surprising that two jacket designs for a book called *East Coast, West Coast* would contain a map of the United States. But the human face, cut off just below the eyes . . . If that's a coincidence, it's a strange one indeed.

Whatever the verdict on this little tale, it illustrates (as does the account of the Wang sisters of Beijing) the difficulty of testing for mental telepathy, one of the three forms of extrasensory perception (the other two being precognition and clairvoyance). Although this is the form of ESP that many people have experienced in their personal lives, in the laboratory the experimenter often has a problem determining whether a given extraordinary result was achieved by telepathy rather than by clairvoyance or precognition. In the case of the jacket design, for example, if one assumes that some form of ESP was involved, it could well have consisted of the art director's "seeing" the drawing that's in my files (although she or he would have had no reason to try to do so).

The evidence for precognition presents no such ambiguity, simply because of the temporal element involved. In 1966, for instance, a crumbling mountain of coal waste buried the Welsh village of Aberfan, killing 116 children and 28 adults. In a subsequent study, Dr. J. C. Barker, a London psychiatrist, found that dozens of people had had premonitions of the tragedy, either in the form of dreams or visions. Many of these premonitions included specific details that were later observed in the actual event.[62] In a study of twenty-eight train wrecks that occurred in the United States between 1950 and 1955, William Cox discovered that the number of passengers on disaster-bound trains was always considerably fewer than the number on corresponding trains that ran one, two, three and four weeks prior to the accidents.[63]

Precognition has also been reported in hundreds of laboratory experiments. At Brooklyn's Maimonides Medical Center in the early seventies, an Englishman named Malcolm Bessent was asked to try to dream about a group of slides that he would be shown the following morning. The next day, a series of target slides would be chosen at random. On five nights out of eight, Bessent dreamed about the target slides.[64]

A few years ago, Robert Jahn, dean of the School of Engineering at Princeton, published *Precognitive Remote Perception,* a 178–page evaluation of 227 precognition trials. Jahn and his associates found the data in support of precognition to be significant at odds of 100 billion to one.[65]

The evidence for "simple" clairvoyance is also compelling. Perhaps the best known evidence is that compiled by J. B. Rhine in his famous "card guessing" experiments at Duke University in the 1930s. But while such experiments produced results that were statistically significant—even highly significant—they suffered from an annoying drawback, known among professionals as the "decline effect." That is to say, the number of correct responses declined as the experiments progressed. In other words, the subjects got bored.

This problem is particularly apparent in the case of gifted subjects. In the words of Dr. Charles Tart, a well known parapsychologist who teaches at the University of California at Davis, card-guessing experiments are "a technique for extinguishing psychic functioning in the laboratory."[66] Thus, as much as other scientists might bridle at the thought, psychic abilities cannot be tested in the same manner that one would test for more conventional responses. In other words, people aren't rats.

One possible antidote to laboratory boredom is to have subjects make what are known as "confidence calls"—that is, to respond only when they "feel" that they have the right answer. This was done in 1974 by experimenters Edward Kelly and H. Kanthamani, working with a gifted subject named Bill Delmore. In two test runs, Delmore shuffled a deck of ordinary playing cards (which were out of sight in a closed box) until he felt that their order matched that of a target deck. Then, as each card in each deck was about to be turned over, Delmore chose the pairs that he felt were in fact identical. During the two runs, he made a total of fifty confidence calls, and he was correct on every one. In each case, the cards matched in both suit and number.[67]

The most dramatic results in laboratory tests, however, are often achieved when gifted subjects are allowed to employ their abilities on a somewhat grander scale. This was the general procedure followed in a remarkable series of experiments in "remote viewing" that began at SRI in the early seventies and is still continuing today.

Before taking a look at the tests themselves, we should note in passing several facts. First, the people who conducted the experiments—Harold Puthoff and Russell Targ—are physicists, trained to look for verifiable evidence. Second, the experimenters happened upon psi research more or less by accident. Thus, they were not out to demonstrate a preconceived notion. In fact, they were initially quite skeptical that the experiments they were trying would actually work. Finally, their experiments have since been replicated at several other institutions, among them Princeton.

The first person to volunteer for the work at SRI was Ingo Swann. Following his encounter with the superconducting magnetometer, Swann was given a series of "simple" tests for clairvoyance (for example, determining whether a red laser or a green laser had been activated in an adjoining lab). These he easily completed and quickly grew bored. As a result, Swann suggested his experimenters try something different. Why not give him the map coordinates (that is, the longitude and latitude) for any place on the globe, and he would tell them what was there. Although Puthoff and Targ were extremely dubious, they agreed to go along. Coordinates were supplied; Swann gave a description—which turned out to be accurate. More coordinates were given, more descriptions rendered, nearly all of which were on the mark.

At this point, Puthoff and Targ began scratching their heads. Was Swann really doing what he seemed to be doing? Or was he "simply" reading their minds after they had chosen the sites from a map in the lab next door? Did Swann possess an eidetic memory that had enabled him, somehow, to memorize a map of the entire world, complete with coordinates for every single spot?

To try to answer such questions, they gave Swann a pair of coordinates that had been supplied by a skeptical colleague on the East Coast. The spot to which the coordinates applied (in degrees, minutes and seconds) was 3000 miles from California, and neither Targ nor Puthoff knew what was there. Swann proceeded to describe the spot—which he thought was some sort of military base—in graphic detail, drawing a map that included such features as roads, trees, buildings, walkways, fences and a flagpole. All the information was accurate, and the map was drawn exactly to scale. Apparently, Ingo Swann was on to something.[68]

About this time, Puthoff received a phone call from a man named Patrick Price (who was mentioned a few pages earlier). A former Burbank police commissioner, Price was then living in retirement at Lake Tahoe. Like Ingo Swann (an artist from New York), Price was convinced that he possessed what are usually referred to as "psychic abilities." After talking with Price for several minutes, Puthoff, on an impulse, read him the coordinates supplied by the

East Coast colleague. Although Price conceded he'd never tried anything quite like this before, he agreed to give it a go.

A couple of days later, Puthoff received Price's written response—a five-page commentary beginning with a description of the spot from an altitude of 1,500 feet and ending with a tour of building interiors. Included in the tour were descriptions of equipment, names from desks, and a dozen labels from folders locked in a file cabinet. Smiling indulgently, Puthoff sent the letter along to his colleague on the East Coast, knowing that such detailed information could not possibly be accurate.

Soon thereafter, the "skeptical East Coast colleague" wrote to say that Price's description was essentially correct. Furthermore, the colleague was certain that Price could not have obtained the information by normal means. Puthoff and Targ were stunned. Patrick Price—who wasn't—moved to the Bay Area to join the project.

As it turned out, Price had a number of unusual talents. On one occasion, he casually described to a visitor (presumably in this case a military man) the way in which he would build a particular type of airplane—*if*, you understand, he was going to build a plane. As it happened, his description was remarkably similar to what the visitor had been told in a closed-door briefing only two days before.

On another occasion, Price was asked to fly overhead in a glider and reproduce a drawing being produced by a visitor on the ground below. The visitor, for his part, poked through a garbage dump, randomly chose a label showing a moon and stars, and tucked it in the pocket of his shirt. On landing, Price gave the visitor his drawing, which showed a moon and stars, plus a curious addition—an ansate cross. The visitor chuckled, unbuttoned his shirt, and withdrew an ansate cross, which was hanging from a chain around his neck.

Impressed by the talents of Price and Swann, the experimenters set out to devise a series of careful tests of what they chose to call by the neutral name of "remote viewing." In the tests, a subject would sit in a laboratory at SRI while a "target team" departed for a site chosen at random. Thirty minutes later, the subject would begin, as best he could, to describe the site by means of words and drawings. After a series of several such attempts, a team of independent judges would visit the sites and compare them to the various descriptions.

The first subject so tested was Ingo Swann, who, in a series of eight attempts, supplied descriptions that were significantly accurate at odds of 2,500 to one. Although these odds are not as high as some of those obtained in more limited experiments (such as card-guessing), one should keep a couple of things in mind. First, in scientific experiments, any results at odds of greater than twenty to one are considered significant; and these results were quite a bit higher than that. Second, the scoring procedure used at SRI was quite conservative, since it ignored all details beyond those needed to match a given description to a given site. And many of those details were uncannily accurate. For example, in describing what turned out to be the plaza in front of the Palo Alto City Hall, Swann reported that the fountain at the site was not running (correct) and that the number of trees to the right of the plaza was four (also correct).

Pat Price was also obsessed with detail, even under difficult conditions. During a demonstration trial for a potential sponsor, Price began describing a large, curved building where the visitor, in fact, was standing. But at that moment, the visitor, wishing to "test the system," insisted that he and the target team get into their car and drive to a small, old building he had noticed along the way, one which housed a beer garden. No problem. Price switched in mid-description from a large, curved building to a small, old building with double-hung doors, a building he said had some sort of historical significance. (Later, the experimenters discovered a small bronze plaque which stated that the building had served as a stop for the pony express.)

In his "real" test series, Price correctly identified the first target site as Hoover Tower, on the Stanford campus. Another description began as follows: "What I'm looking at is a little boat dock along the bay . . . Yeah, I see the little boats, some motor launches, some little sailing ships, sails all furled, some with the masts stepped and others are up."[69] Price went on to describe the granite slabs leading down to the water, and gave the location as four miles northeast of SRI. All his details (of what turned out to be the Redwood City Marina) were correct. A subsequent description—of a shopping center built in the style of a Spanish mission—was even more detailed, and also accurate. In addition to describing the buildings themselves, Price noted the presence of fountains, trees and pathways, of specific species of flowers, and of arbors made of redwood. Overall, Price scored seven direct hits out of nine attempts, at odds of 35,000 to one.

To be sure, it is theoretically possible that Price and Swann were relying on "mere" telepathy (that is, by reading the minds of the target teams). But Puthoff and Targ point out that subjects would often "describe elements of a scene that would not be visible to an observer standing at ground level."[70] Price, for example, would say things such as, "I'm going to elevate again and go through a search quadrant," or, "Let's jack up a bit, maybe five hundred feet."[71] He would then go on to describe the scene—accurately—as if he were hovering directly above it. An accomplishment such as this comes very close to constituting what is known in the trade as an OBE—an out-of-body experience.

As research progressed, the experimenters discovered that Price and Swann were not the only people capable of "remote viewing." In fact, they found that more or less anyone could do it to some extent, especially if the experimenter let the subject know that remote viewing was "okay." Furthermore, they noted that scores tended to improve over time; in other words, there was no "decline effect." Overall, about two-thirds of the test runs have been successful.

But again, while the two-thirds figure is quite significant, it fails to convey the startling results of individual tests, including those by subjects who had never tried the practice before. Duane Elgin,* for example, an SRI research analyst, described a target site at which he saw "large metal plates," along with members of the research team. Three minutes later, at precisely 11:25 A.M., Elgin said: "Everything changes . . . I don't see them anymore." As it turned out, the research team had been standing in a BART rapid transit station. At 11:25, they boarded a train and were whisked away.

Susan Harris, a medical student who later went on to complete

---

* Although Elgin had never tried remote viewing, he had spent some time at SRI with an electronic random target generator, which tests a subject's ability to predict which of four pictures the machine will light up. Elgin's score was successful at odds of better than 3 million to one.

her residency in psychiatry at Harvard, was recruited for a series of tests to determine whether remote-viewing is affected by increased distance (it isn't). In completing the tests, she not only succeeded in describing target sites on the opposite coast, but displayed a remarkable facility for perceiving human activity. In the first test, she reported that members of the target team were tossing something back and forth. (Correct—a paper airplane.) During the second test, she reported that Russell Targ was holding some coins in the palm of his hand, then giving some to Nicky, another member of the target team. (Correct. He used them to buy a postcard of Grant's Tomb, the target site.) In the third test, she observed that Targ was opening a cellophane bag. (Correct. It was 95 degrees in Washington Square, and Targ had bought some ice cream.)[72]

Perhaps the most remarkable recruit of all was a professional photographer named Hella Hammid. In her first test, a "trial run," Hammid reported: "I see a little house covered with red, overlapping boards. It has white trim and a very tall, pointed roof. But the whole thing feels fake, like a movie set." (All accurate. The building was a "little red schoolhouse" on a miniature golf course.) Subsequently, in a series of nine formal tests, Hammid was successful at odds of better than 500,000 to one.

But she was still just warming up. She then went on to describe four more sites with what turned out to be, in each case, amazing accuracy. In one case, for example, she observed that the main focus of attention at the site was a "black iron triangle" that was "bigger than a man." She also reported that she heard a sound— "squeak, squeak, about once a second." The site was a small children's playground with a set of triangular, squeaking swings.

And now the punch line. All four descriptions were given *before* the sites were (randomly) selected. In other words, Hammid was employing not only clairvoyance, but precognition as well.

Her performance was interesting for other reasons too. Unlike Patrick Price, who prided himself on his wealth of verbal detail, Hammid gave her descriptions primarily in the form of drawings (and Hammid, you'll note, had the better score). According to Targ and Puthoff, the difference between these two approaches is revealing in that it suggests the manner in which psi may function within the brain. In general, they report, subjects are more nearly accurate when supplying information of a nonanalytical nature (shape, color, form) than they are when attempting analysis (for example, by reporting words, functions and names). From such information (as well as other experiments), Targ and Puthoff conclude that psi is primarily a function of the brain's right hemisphere.

Finally, a footnote. As suggested earlier, the SRI experiments attracted the interest of the U.S. military. In fact, part of the research was funded by the Pentagon and the CIA, and perhaps still is. (Harold Puthoff, incidentally, is a former employee of the National Security Agency.)* Although "much of this material is classified" (to use the standard phrase), some interesting tidbits have nonetheless appeared.

In April 1984, columnist Jack Anderson reported that the CIA had wanted to know the location of a Soviet Tu–95 Backfire bomber that had crashed somewhere on the continent of Africa. So the agency consulted a subject at SRI (probably Patrick Price), who was able to determine the location within a few miles of the actual wreckage.[73]

In another case, the CIA gave an SRI subject the longitude and latitude of a remote location and asked him to describe what was there. The subject proceeded to describe in considerable detail an airfield, which he said contained, among other things, a gantry crane. The CIA was impressed; the map coordinates it had given the subject were those of the Soviet Union's ultrasecret nuclear testing site at Semipalatinsk, Kazakhstan. But the agency pointed out that the site did not contain a gantry crane. The subject insisted it did. So the CIA commissioned a new set of photographs from American satellites, and sure enough, there was the gantry crane.[74]

What is one to make of all this? In the eyes of many scientists (not to mention journalists), it is all somehow a hoax. Although they

* For quite some time, both the United States and the Soviet Union—especially the latter—have funded research that might lead to military applications of psi. But like the man said, that's another story.

concede that the statistical evidence from psi experiments could not have resulted from chance, they nonetheless insist that because such results are impossible, they must have been produced by fraud. The skeptics then go on to concoct elaborate conspiracy theories for any given experiment, involving more or less everyone concerned.

The problem with such theories (at least for this observer) is that they quickly become much harder to believe than the evidence for psi itself, which is quite extensive. The theories remind one of nothing so much as the convoluted explanations that have often been produced by defenders of a paradigm in serious trouble. (By the thirteenth century, Ptolemaic astronomy had become so cumbersome that Alfonso X was moved to remark that if God had consulted Alfonso when creating the universe, He would have received good advice.)

Actually, much of the evidence for psi—contrary to popular and indeed to much scientific opinion—would not require a modification of existing theories at all. As Targ and Puthoff remark in a book called *Mind-Reach:* "There is still hope for a rational consideration of paranormal functioning, since many contemporary physicists are now of the opinion that these phenomena are not at all inconsistent with the framework of modern physics: the often-held view that observations of this type are incompatible with known laws is not only outdated but false, being based on the naive realism prevalent before the development of modern physics."[75]

Precognition, they point out, is probably the form of psi that the greatest number of physicists would find easiest to swallow: "The reason . . . lies in this fact: in physics, everything that is not forbidden occurs. And . . . physics does not forbid the transmission of information from the future to the present. The difficulty that one has in dealing with this problem is more linguistic than physical."[76] Or as Einstein remarked: "For us believing physicists, the distinction between past, present, and future is only an illusion, even if a stubborn one."[77]

Because of such realizations, argue Puthoff and Targ, "rejection of the possibility of paranormal functioning by the scientific community is fading rapidly. Physics seminars on the possible mechanisms involved in paranormal functioning are becoming part of the current scene. . . . The Loyal Opposition thus numbers fewer and fewer scientists among its ranks; the physicists by and large are leaving first, the psychologists last."*[78] In a subsequent book called *The Mind Race,* Targ predicted that "psi research findings and the discoveries of modern physics will soon come together."[79]

Meanwhile, there are still some gaps, perhaps more apparent than real. For one thing, "the discoveries of modern physics"—at least those of quantum mechanics—take place at the microscopic level, whereas psi research findings seem to occur in the macroscopic realm. It is not entirely certain how discoveries at the former level apply to the latter; and in any case, it is in the realm of ordinary objects that the great majority of scientists ply their trade. Thus, when confronted by reports of "psychic phenomena," many scientists are apt to brush them aside (much as astronomers used to brush aside reports of meteorites because everybody knew that rocks couldn't fall from the sky).

Another way of regarding psi phenomena, however, is simply as a well-established set of anomalies that cannot be explained by the current scientific paradigm. (A paradigm, remember, can never account for all the facts with which it can be presented.) Perhaps what is needed is a new paradigm.

Although such a paradigm is only beginning to emerge, one would do well to keep in mind some of the basic concepts of contemporary physics. One of these is the concept of the "unitary universe." Thus, physicist David Bohm, who argues that reality is "undivided wholeness," also points out that "there is no intrinsic reason why the paranormal should be impossible."[80]

The most dramatic demonstration of the unitary universe is Bell's Theorem (which showed that a pair of particles, widely separated, are nonetheless strangely "connected"). Apropos of which one might recall the observation of physicist Henry Stapp of the Lawrence Berkeley Laboratory: "The important thing about Bell's Theorem is that it puts the dilemma posed by quantum phenomena clearly into the realm of macroscopic phenomena . . . it shows that our ordinary ideas about the world are somehow profoundly deficient even on the macroscopic level."

Another basic concept of contemporary physics is that of the observer-as-participant. In the words of Werner Heisenberg, "Ob-

---

* In 1969, the Parapsychological Association was admitted to membership in the American Association for the Advancement of Science.

servation plays a decisive role in the event, and . . . the reality varies depending on whether we observe it or not."[81] Or in the words of Targ and Puthoff of SRI: "observation of a system perturbs that system. . . . to the degree that consciousness is involved in observation (and it always is), to that degree consciousness must also be seen to interact with the physical environment."

To be sure, there have been more specific explanations for psi phenomena, involving extremely low-frequency electromagnetic waves, and so on, but as Targ and Puthoff observe:

> An alternative viewpoint held by many physicists (including the authors) is that the reconciliation of observed [psi] data with modern theory may take place at a more fundamental level—namely, at the level of the foundations of quantum theory. There is a continuing dialogue, for example, on the proper interpretation of the effect of an observer (consciousness) on experimental measurement. There is also considerable current scientific interest in the implications . . . of "quantum interconnectedness," an apparent connection between distant events. This Quantum Connection is codified in a theorem of great elegance known as Bell's Theorem . . . which . . . reveals that parts of the universe apparently separated from each other can nonetheless act together as parts of a larger whole, a statement perhaps more expected to be found in mystical writing than in a theory of physics.[82]

Thus, quantum theory, psi and mysticism are occupying common ground. And one of the most salient features of this terrain is consciousness.

Historically, the East and West (that is, Orient and Occident) have been quite different in this regard. In the West, matter has been considered the primary reality, consciousness the stepchild of neurons. In the East, just the opposite. Consciousness is primary, the ground of being out of which all else arises.

Today, these two traditions are drawing closer, largely because Western science is gravitating toward positions that are rooted in the culture of the East. In physics, scientists are beginning to "conceptualize" a sort of ground of being in which matter becomes almost incidental, and to wrestle with the well-known "observer problem," whereby consciousness seems to play a role in the outcome of experiments. In medicine and sports, consciousness seems to influence the body in ways we had not thought possible. In parapsychology, consciousness behaves in strange ways indeed, insinuating itself into superconducting magnetometers, leaping continents and oceans.

Thus, Western scientists are beginning to refer to consciousness in heretical language. Physicist David Bohm proposes that matter be considered a form of thought. Or in the words of two astronomers quoted earlier: "The universe is more like a great thought than a great machine" (James Jeans); "The stuff of the universe is mind-stuff" (Arthur Eddington).

If scientists lead, can intellectuals be far behind? For Western writers and intellectuals, the past few hundred years have not been particularly happy ones. As science expanded, so spirit contracted, until eventually it more or less disappeared. In its place, most intellectuals adopted secular art as the new religion, but it turned out to represent a rather cramped creed. Serving merely as a mirror to man (and a diminished man, at that), it became a sort of circular exercise, promising little more than elegant or inelegant distillations of life's quotidian detail.

But art in the East, in theory, at least, is a horse of a different color, promising not merely esthetics but transcendence. It is an avenue not only to the nature of man and existential life, but to the nature of ultimate reality, to a sort of universal consciousness. "In short," writes F.S.C. Northrop in *The Meeting of East and West,* "the Oriental uses the purely esthetic to constitute the nature of the divine."[83]

Late afternoon at Big Sur. From the edge of the cliffs at Esalen, one can hear the sound of the incoming sea, booming softly against the massive rocks a hundred feet below. Out ahead, across the vast Pacific, a huge fireball hangs above the horizon, its pulsing shape glowing a molten red. Against one's face comes the rush of a warming, westerly wind, like the muffled wave of a distant, unknown detonation.

. . . It is colder now,
             there are many stars

296

                                        we are drifting
North by the Great Bear,
                        the leaves are falling,
The water is stone in the scooped rocks,
                                        to southward
Red sun grey air:
                the crows are
Slow on their crooked wings,
                                the jays have left us:
Long since we passed the flares of Orion.
Each man believes in his heart he will die.
Many have written last thoughts and last letters.
None know if our deaths are now or forever:
None know if this wandering earth will be found.

We lie down and the snow covers our garments.
I pray you,
                you (if any open this writing)
Make in your mouths the words that were our names.

I will tell you all we have learned,
                                I will tell you everything:
The earth is round,
                        there are springs under the orchards,
The loam cuts with a blunt knife,
                                beware of
Elms in thunder,
                the lights in the sky are stars—
We think they do not see,
                        we think also
The trees do not know nor the leaves of the grasses hear us:
The birds too are ignorant.
                        Do not listen.
Do not stand at dark in the open windows.
We before you have heard this:
                                they are voices:
They are not words at all but the wind rising.
Also none among us has seen God.
(. . . We have thought often
The flaws of sun in the late and driving weather
Pointed to one tree but it was not so.)
As for the nights I warn you the nights are dangerous:

The wind changes at night and the dreams come.

It is very cold,
>>>> there are strange stars near Arcturus,

Voices are crying an unknown name in the sky

>>>> —Archibald MacLeish,
>>>> "Epistle to Be Left in the Earth"[84]

NOTES

CHAPTER 1

Open the Door, Richard

1. Paul Fussell, *Class: A Guide Through the American Status System* (New York: Summit Books, 1983), p. 17.
2. Henry Fairlie, "Why I Love America," *The New Republic,* July 4, 1983.
3. Fussell, op. cit., p. 172.
4. Alexis de Tocqueville, *Democracy in America* (New York: Vintage Books, 1945), pp. 11–12.
5. Ibid., pp. 102–103.
6. Richard Hofstadter, *Anti-Intellectualism in American Life* (New York: Vintage Books, 1962), p. 145.
7. Quoted by E. Digby Baltzell, *Puritan Boston and Quaker Philadelphia: Two Protestant Ethics and the Spirit of Class Authority and Leadership* (Boston: Beacon Press, 1982), p. 4.
8. Cleveland Amory, *Who Killed Society?* (New York: Harper & Brothers, 1960), p. 254.
9. Baltzell, op. cit., p. 84.
10. Ibid., p. 83.
11. Ibid., p. 55.
12. Ibid., p. 38.
13. Quoted by Baltzell, op. cit., p. 53.
14. Quoted by Cleveland Amory, *The Proper Bostonians* (New York: E. P. Dutton, 1947), pp. 233–34.
15. Ibid., pp. 253–54.

16. Edith Wharton, *A Backward Glance*, (New York: Charles Scribner's Sons, 1985), pp. 61–62.
17. Quoted by Amory, *Who Killed Society?*, p. 270.
18. Richard Hofstadter, *The Age of Reform* (New York: Vintage Books, 1955), p. 14.
19. Baltzell, op. cit., p. 198.
20. Quoted by Amory, *Who Killed Society?*, p. 274.
21. Baltzell, op. cit., p. 282.
22. Ibid., p. 126.
23. Quoted by Baltzell, op. cit., p. 370.
24. Ibid., p. 199.
25. Ibid., p. 373.
26. Ibid., p. 399.
27. Quoted by Amory, *Who Killed Society?*, p. 274.
28. Ibid., p. 279.
29. Quoted by Amory, *The Proper Bostonians*, p. 246.
30. Ibid., p. 246.
31. Ibid., p. 247.
32. Allan Nevins and Henry Steele Commager, *History of the United States* (New York: Washington Square Press, 1986), p. 175.
33. Ibid., p. 312.
34. Quoted by Ray Allen Billington, ed., *The Frontier Thesis* (New York: Holt, Rinehart and Winston, 1967), p. 29.
35. Ibid., p. 17.
36. Ibid., p. 14.
37. Ibid., p. 16.
38. Ibid., p. 11.
39. Ibid., p. 26.
40. Ibid., p. 22.
41. Ibid., p. 28.
42. Ibid., p. 24.
43. Ibid., p. 10.
44. Hofstadter, *Anti-Intellectualism in American Life*, pp. 157–59.
45. Ibid., p. 159.
46. Nevins and Commager, op. cit., p. 166.
47. Hofstadter, *Anti-Intellectualism in American Life*, pp. 159–60.
48. Ibid., p. 164.
49. Ibid., p. 166.
50. Ibid., p. 166.
51. Billington, op. cit., p. 16.
52. Hofstadter, *Anti-Intellectualism in American Life*, pp. 161, 172.
53. Quoted by Amory, *Who Killed Society?*, p. 30.

54. Billington, op. cit., pp. 14–15.

55. Nevins and Commager, op. cit., p. 229.

56. Hofstadter, *Age of Reform*, p. 137.

57. Ibid., pp. 139–40.

58. Quoted by Amory, *Who Killed Society?*, p. 86.

59. Ibid., p. 508.

60. Wharton, op. cit., p. 226.

61. Ibid., p. 119.

62. Edith Wharton, *The House of Mirth* (New York: Bantam Books, 1984), p. 116.

63. Wharton, *A Backward Glance*, p. 58.

64. Henry James, *The American Scene* (Bloomington: Indiana University Press, 1968), p. 76.

65. Ibid., p. 97.

66. Ibid., p. xi.

67. Ibid., p. 115.

68. Ibid., p. 77.

69. Ibid., p. 102.

70. Ibid., p. 92.

71. Quoted by Matthew Josephson, *The Robber Barons* (New York: Harcourt, Brace and Company, 1934), p. 326.

72. Calvin Trillin, "A Reporter at Large," *The New Yorker*, Sept. 26, 1983.

73. Donal Henahan, "It's Nice to Know What is Happening in an Opera," *New York Times*, Oct. 2, 1983.

74. Editorial, "Hustling New York," *New York Times*, May 28, 1985.

75. Tom Wolfe, "Proper Places," *Esquire*, June 1985.

76. Charlotte Curtis, "Ted Turner, at Met Party, Is Awed by Walter Cronkite," *New York Times*, May 28, 1985.

77. Quoted by Sandra Salmans, "Author Explores Business Ethics," *New York Times*, Oct. 28, 1985.

78. Baltzell, op. cit., p. 26.

79. Michael M. Thomas, *Hard Money* (New York: Viking, 1985), p. 10.

80. Ibid., p. 49.

81. Quoted by Amory, *Who Killed Society?*, p. 9.

82. Ibid., p. 494.

83. Ibid., p. 494.

84. Ibid., p. 495.

85. Ibid., p. 492.

86. Ibid., p. 478.

87. Ibid., p. 518.

88. Ibid., p. 497.

89. Ibid., p. 85.

90. Ibid., p. 327.

91. E. Digby Baltzell, *The Protestant Establishment: Aristocracy and Caste in America* (New York: Random House, 1964), p. 149.

92. Ibid., p. 150.

93. Hofstadter, *Age of Reform*, pp. 258–59.

94. Amory, *Who Killed Society?*, p. 167.

95. Leo C. Rosten, *Hollywood: The Movie Colony, The Movie Makers* (New York: Harcourt, Brace and Company, 1941), p. 167.

96. Ibid., pp. 70–71.

97. Richard Schickel, *Intimate Strangers: The Culture of Celebrity* (New York: Doubleday & Company, 1985), p. 68.

98. Robert Sklar, *Movie-Made America: A Cultural History of American Movies* (New York: Vintage Books, 1975), p. 118.

99. Quoted by Rosten, op. cit., p. 170.

100. Amory, *Who Killed Society?*, p. 135.

101. Ibid., p. 135.

102. Ibid., p. 17.

103. Quoted by Rosten, op. cit., p. 165.

104. Ibid., p. 362.

105. Amory, *Who Killed Society?*, pp. 109–10.

106. Rosten, op. cit., p. 165.

107. Ibid., pp. 12–13, 16.

108. Sklar, op. cit., p. 230.

109. Hofstadter, *Anti-Intellectualism in American Life*, p. 50.

110. Hofstadter, *Age of Reform*, pp. 325–326.

111. Schickel, op. cit., pp. 74, 76, 79, 80.

112. Sklar, op. cit., p. 207.

113. Ibid., p. 210.

114. Ibid., p. 210.

115. Will Wright, *Six Guns and Society: A Structural Study of the Western* (Berkeley: University of California Press, 1975), p. 187.

116. Ibid., p. 57.

117. Quoted by Todd Gitlin, *Inside Prime Time* (New York: Pantheon Books, 1983), p. 150.

118. Ben Stein, *The View from Sunset Boulevard* (New York: Anchor Books, 1980), p. 105.

119. Ibid., p. 88.

120. Ibid., p. xi.

121. Ibid., p. 44.

122. Ibid., p. 109.

123. Quoted by Barbara Basler, " 'Bad Guys' Wear Pin Stripes," *New York Times*, Jan. 29, 1987.

CHAPTER 2

Westward the Course of Empire

1. Quoted by C. K. McFarland, ed., *Readings in Intellectual History: The American Tradition* (New York: Holt, Rinehart and Winston, 1970), p. 244.

2. Ibid., p. 229.

3. Quoted by George B. Leonard, *The Transformation: A Guide to the Inevitable Changes in Humankind* (New York: Dell Publishing, 1973), p. 136.

4. Quoted by Frank Bergon and Zeese Papanikolas, eds., *Looking Far West: The Search for the American West in History, Myth, and Literature* (New York: New American Library, 1978), p. 76.

5. Carey McWilliams, *California: The Great Exception* (Santa Barbara: Peregrine Smith, 1979), p. 35.

6. Ibid., p. 25.

7. Neal R. Pierce and Jerry Hagstrom, *The Book of America: Inside 50 States Today* (New York: W. W. Norton & Company, 1983), p. 27.

8. Ibid., p. 747.

9. Reported by Elizabeth Mehren, "California Ranked No. 1 in Innovation," *Los Angeles Times,* Dec. 4, 1985.

10. McWilliams, op. cit., p. 87.

11. Quoted by Thomas J. Lueck, "Pervasive Problems Threaten New York's Economic Base," *New York Times,* June 26, 1988.

12. Quoted by Jerry Hagstrom, *Beyond Reagan* (New York: W. W. Norton & Company, 1988), pp. 290–91.

13. Lester C. Thurow, "Up North, Rust is Showing Through Again," *Los Angeles Times,* Apr. 3, 1988.

14. Theodore H. White, *America in Search of Itself: The Making of the President, 1956–1980* (New York: Warner Books, 1983), p. 348.

15. Quoted by Hagstrom, op. cit., p. 44.

16. Ben J. Wattenberg, "The Census' Political Role," *New York Times,* Jan. 6, 1980.

17. Kevin P. Phillips, *Post-Conservative America* (New York: Vintage Books, 1983), p. 236.

CHAPTER 3

No Business Like Show Business

1. F. Scott Fitzgerald, *The Last Tycoon* (New York: Charles Scribner's Sons, 1941), p. 3.
2. Much of this account of the movies' early years was drawn from Sklar, *Movie-Made America.*
3. Rosten, *Hollywood,* p. 67.
4. Sklar, op. cit., p. 19.
5. Ibid., p. 18.
6. Ibid., p. 34.
7. Ibid., p. 33.
8. Ibid., p. 32.
9. Ibid., p. 34.
10. Bergon and Papanikolas, *Looking Far West,* p. 2.
11. David McClintick, *Indecent Exposure: A True Story of Hollywood and Wall Street* (New York: William Morrow and Company, 1982), p. 55.
12. John Gregory Dunne, *The Studio* (New York: Simon and Schuster, 1979), p. 11.
13. Quoted by Schickel, *Intimate Strangers,* p. 39.
14. Carey McWilliams, *Southern California: An Island on the Land* (Salt Lake City: Peregrine Smith Books, 1983), p. 343.
15. Ibid., p. 342.
16. Schickel, op. cit., p. 40.
17. Rosten, op. cit., pp. 67–69.
18. Wright, *Six Guns and Society,* p. 5.
19. Fitzgerald, op. cit., p. 118.
20. Stanley Kauffmann, *The New Republic,* Mar. 31, 1986.
21. Nathanael West, *The Day of the Locust* (New York: New American Library, 1983), pp. 192–93.
22. Schickel, op. cit., p. 85.
23. Ibid., p. 85.
24. *Newsweek,* Sept. 10, 1962.
25. *Life,* Oct. 19, 1962.
26. *Look,* June 28, 1966.
27. Alice McIntyre, "Depressed in California," *Esquire,* May 1963.
28. Richard Todd, "Turned-on and Super-sincere in California," *Harper's,* Jan. 1967.

29. Joan Didion, *Slouching Towards Bethlehem* (New York: Simon & Schuster, 1979), pp. 84–128.
30. "California Evil," *Esquire*, Mar. 1970.
31. "Whatever Happened to California?" *MORE*, Mar. 1975.
32. "Whatever Happened to California?" *Time*, Jul. 18, 1977.
33. Tom Wolfe, "The Me Decade and the Third Great Awakening," *Mauve Gloves & Madmen, Clutter & Vine* (New York: Farrar, Straus and Giroux, 1976), pp. 126–67.
34. Peter Marin, "The New Narcissism," *Harper's*, Oct. 1975.
35. Quoted by Charles Perry, "The Sour Apple," *New West*, June 2, 1980.

CHAPTER 4

Tippecanoe and Tyler Too

1. Tocqueville, *Democracy in America*, Vol. I, p. 207.
2. Quoted by McFarland, *Readings in Intellectual History*, p. 349.
3. Ibid., p. 390.
4. Samuel Eliot Morison, *The Oxford History of the American People* (New York: Oxford University Press, 1965), p. 359.
5. McFarland, op. cit., p. 167.
6. Morison, op. cit., p. 425.
7. Nevins and Commager, *History of the United States*, p. 165.
8. Morison, op. cit., p. 427.
9. Ibid., p. 424.
10. Hofstadter, *Anti-Intellectualism in American Life*, p. 51.
11. Ibid., p. 156.
12. Morison, op. cit., p. 424.
13. Ibid., p. 425.
14. Ibid., pp. 457–58. For more on the Log Cabin and Jackson campaigns, see chapter one, above.
15. Ibid., p. 457.
16. Ibid., p. 456.
17. Ibid., p. 423.
18. Hofstadter, *Age of Reform*, p. 60.
19. Nevins and Commager, op. cit., p. 251.

20. James Bryce, *The American Commonwealth* (New York: Macmillan, 1922), vol. 1, p. 79.

21. Hofstadter, *Anti-Intellectualism,* p. 4.

22. Hofstadter, *Age of Reform,* p. 261.

23. Richard Rovere, "The American Establishment," *Esquire,* May 1962.

24. White, *America in Search of Itself,* p. 36.

25. Rovere, op. cit.

26. Hofstadter, *Anti-Intellectualism,* p. 41.

27. Baltzell, *Protestant Establishment,* p. 287.

28. Ibid., pp. 284–85.

29. Richard Hofstadter, *The Paranoid Style in American Politics, and Other Essays* (Chicago: University of Chicago Press, 1979), p. 8.

30. Hofstadter, *Age of Reform,* p. 288.

31. Ibid., p. 289.

32. Ibid., p. 19.

33. Baltzell, *Protestant Establishment,* p. 261.

34. Hofstadter, *Age of Reform,* p. 21.

35. Hofstadter, *Anti-Intellectualism,* p. 12.

36. David Halberstam, *The Best and the Brightest* (New York: Fawcett Crest, 1972), p. 798.

37. Leonard Silk and Mark Silk, *The American Establishment* (New York: Basic Books, 1980), p. 203.

38. Ibid., p. 222.

39. Ibid., pp. 220–21.

40. White, op. cit., p. 55.

41. Ibid., p. 55.

42. Ibid., pp. 73, 81–82.

43. Ibid., p. 230.

44. Phillips, *Post-Conservative America,* p. 54.

45. White, op. cit., p. 285.

46. Hofstadter, *Paranoid Style,* p. 110.

47. Phillips, op. cit., p. 36.

48. Ibid., p. 38.

49. Ibid., p. 39.

50. Several of Reagan's factual errors noted in this chapter are drawn from Mark Green and Gail MacColl, *There He Goes Again: Ronald Reagan's Reign of Error* (New York: Pantheon Books, 1983).

51. Lou Cannon, "The Winning of the East," *California Magazine,* Aug. 1984.

52. White, op. cit., pp. 63–64, 66.

53. Ibid., p. 67.

54. Pierce and Hagstrom, *The Book of America,* p. 762.

55. Rosten, *Hollywood,* pp. 136–37.

56. Quoted by Joel Kotkin and Paul Grabowicz, *California, Inc.* (New York: Rawson, Wade, 1982), p. 86.

57. White, op. cit., p. 69.

58. Quoted by Ron Suskind, "The Power of Political Consultants," *New York Times Magazine*, Aug. 12, 1984.

59. Quoted by Kotkin and Grabowicz, op, cit., p. 110.

60. Interview from "Television and the Presidency," a Group W television documentary, 1984.

61. Tom Wicker, "A Star is Born for the Democrats," *New York Times*, Sept. 9, 1986.

62. White, op. cit., p. 66.

63. James K. Folsom, ed., *The Western* (Englewood Cliffs, N.J.: Prentice-Hall, 1979), p. 9.

64. Bergon and Papanikolas, *Looking Far West*, pp. 7–8.

65. Jenni Calder, *There Must Be a Lone Ranger: The American West in Film and in Reality* (New York: Taplinger, 1975), p. xiii.

66. Wright, *Six Guns and Society*, pp. 185–86.

67. Bergon and Papanikolas, op. cit., pp. 444–45.

68. White, op. cit., p. 178.

69. Bergon and Papanikolas, op. cit., pp. 9–10.

70. David Broder, "The Making of a Legend," *San Francisco Chronicle*, Apr. 3, 1981.

71. James Reston, "A City of Fantasy," *New York Times*, Apr. 5, 1981.

72. William Safire, "Haig Flunked the Test," *San Francisco Chronicle*, Apr. 6, 1981.

73. Quoted by Robert Sherrill, "How Reagan Got that Way," *The Atlantic*, Mar. 1984.

74. Quoted by Richard Schickel, "No Method to His Madness," *Film Comment*, June 1987.

75. Ibid.

76. Quoted by Steven V. Roberts, "Return to the Land of the Gipper," *New York Times*, Mar. 9, 1986.

77. Lou Cannon, "The Winning of the East," *California Magazine*, Aug. 1984; *Washington Post*, National Weekly Edition: "Credibility is Not Enough," Aug. 26, 1985; "Reagan's the Brother from Another Planet," Jan. 28, 1985.

78. Martin Tolchin, "An Inattention to Detail is Getting More Attention," *New York Times*, Jan. 14, 1987.

79. Ibid.

80. Quoted by Green and MacColl, op. cit., p. 17.

81. Leslie Gelb, "The Mind of the President," *New York Times Magazine*, Oct. 6, 1985.

82. Quoted by Anthony Lewis, "Dr. Pangloss Speaks," *New York Times*, Feb. 19, 1984.

83. Joseph Kraft, "White House Dirty Work," *San Francisco Chronicle:* Oct. 28, 1983; "A Windbag?," Aug. 3, 1983.

84. Quoted by R. W. Apple, Jr., "Fulbright Out of Politics But Not Out of Options," *New York Times*, Feb. 13, 1989.

85. David Broder, *Washington Post*, National Weekly Edition: "The Presidential Shield," Oct. 22, 1984; "Our President the Patsy," May 23, 1988; *San Francisco Chronicle*: "Ronald Reagan: Man of Conviction," Sept. 2, 1985.

86. Robert Scheer, *Los Angeles Times*, August 20, 1984.

87. Quoted by Leslie Gelb, "The Mind of the President," *New York Times Magazine*, Oct. 6, 1985.

88. Quoted by Carl Bernstein, "Reagan at Reel II," *The New Republic*, Feb. 4, 1985.

89. Quoted by Paul Slansky, "What He Didn't Know," *The New Republic*, Jan. 1, 1987.

90. Gelb, op. cit., p. 112.

91. Quoted by Mark Hertsgaard, "How Ronald Reagan Turned News Hounds into Lap Dogs," *Washington Post*, National Weekly Edition, Aug. 29, 1988.

92. Quoted by Robert Scheer, "White House Successfully Limits the News," *Los Angeles Times*, Aug. 20, 1984.

93. Quoted by Steven V. Roberts, "Ex-Reagan Spokesman Roils Capital with Book," *New York Times*, April 8, 1988.

94. Lou Cannon, *Washington Post*, National Weekly Edition, Sept. 24, 1984.

95. James Reston, "Reagan Beats the Press," *New York Times*, Nov. 4, 1984.

96. Quoted by Sidney Blumenthal, "Reagan the Unassailable," *The New Republic*, Sept. 12, 1983.

97. Michael J. Arlen, *The Camera Age: Essays on Television* (New York: Penguin Books, 1982), p. 271.

98. Editorial, "A Year of Shame," *New York Times*, Jan. 3, 1988.

99. Rosten, op. cit., p. 43.

100. not3Elizabeth Drew, *The New Yorker*, Mar. 30, 1987.

101. David Denby, "Ollie North, The Movie," *The New Republic*, Aug. 3, 1987.

102. Fox Butterfield, "Massachusetts Senate Race Offers a Sharp Choice," *New York Times*, Sept. 20, 1984.

103. White, op. cit., pp. 302–303.

104. Ibid., p. 32.

105. Phillips, op. cit., p. 39.

106. Quoted by Lloyd Grove, "The Selling of the Vice President, 1988," *Washington Post*, National Weekly Edition, June 27, 1988.

107. Paul Taylor, "Pigsty Politics," *Washington Post*, National Weekly Edition, Feb. 13, 1989.

108. William Schneider, "The Perils of Populism," *The New Republic*, July 15, 1985.

109. Maureen Dowd, "Gore Lashes Out at Rivals and Image," *New York Times*, Feb. 22, 1988.

110. Quoted in "Poppy the Populist," *Newsweek*, Nov. 7, 1988.

111. Ibid.

112. Taylor, op. cit.

113. Quoted by Marvin Kalb, "TV, Election Spoiler," *New York Times*, Nov. 28, 1988.

114. Quoted by Taylor, op. cit.

115. William Schneider, "New Rules for the Old Race," *Los Angeles Times*, Nov. 6, 1988.

116. Quoted by R. W. Apple, Jr., "Political Experts Offer Three Views of '88 Election," *New York Times*, Oct. 29, 1988.

117. Ellen Goodman, "Dukakis Woos the Democrats," *San Francisco Chronicle*, April 8, 1988.

118. *Los Angeles Times*, Oct. 25, 1988.

119. *Washington Post*, National Weekly Edition, Oct. 10, 1988.

120. John Chancellor, "Putting Zip, Juice—Interest—Into Campaigns," *New York Times*, Nov. 29, 1988.

121. George F. Will, "Our Servant Bush: Vaguely Admirable, Ominously Empty," *Los Angeles Times*, Nov. 6, 1988.

122. Taylor, op. cit.

123. White, op. cit., p. 284.

124. Paul Taylor, "Is This Any Way to Pick a President?" *Washington Post*, National Weekly Edition, April 13, 1987.

125. Taylor, "Is This Any Way . . .?"

126. Quoted by Taylor, "Is This Any Way . . .?"

127. Quoted by Taylor, "Is This Any Way . . .?"

128. William Schneider, "The Democrats in '88," *The Atlantic*, April 1987.

129. Flora Lewis, "The Wrong Reasons," *New York Times*, Jan. 10, 1987.

130. Andrew Rosenthal, "Candidates Have Become a Debating Society," *New York Times*, Jan. 31, 1988.

131. Quoted by Michael J. O'Neill, "Let Surrogate Candidates Smile for TV," *New York Times*, Apr. 9, 1988.

132. White, op. cit., p. 426.

133. Chancellor, op. cit.

134. *Los Angeles Times*, June 19, 1983.

135. Peter Schrag, "California Screamin'," *The New Republic*, June 23, 1986.

136. *Los Angeles Times*, June 26, 1988.

137. Peter Schrag, "Initiative Madness," *The New Republic*, Aug. 22, 1988.

138. William Endicott, "California's Initiative Process is in Drastic Need of Reform," *Los Angeles Times*, Sept. 4, 1983.

139. Jeffrey Abramson, Christopher Arterton and Gary Orren, *The Electronic Commonwealth: The Impact of New Media Technologies on Democratic Politics* (New York: Basic Books, 1988).

140. Phillips, op. cit., pp. 225–26.

141. *The New Republic*, Oct. 29, 1984.

142. Taylor, "Pigsty Politics."

143. David Broder, *Washington Post,* National Weekly Edition: "Having the Guts to Say Yes," Dec. 19, 1988; "Lonesome Dove in the House," Feb. 20, 1989.

CHAPTER 5

California Dreamin'

1. Quoted by Patrick Brantlinger, *Bread & Circuses: Theories of Mass Culture as Social Decay* (Ithaca: Cornell University Press, 1983), p. 22.
2. Ibid., p. 278.
3. Ibid., p. 126.
4. Ibid., p. 189.
5. Ibid., p. 186.
6. Ibid., p. 203.
7. Ibid., p. 128.
8. Ibid., p. 200.
9. Allan Bloom, *The Closing of the American Mind: How Higher Education Has Failed Democracy and Impoverished the Souls of Today's Students* (New York: Simon & Schuster, 1987), p. 75.
10. Irving Howe, *The New Republic,* Mar. 5, 1984.
11. Quoted by Douglas C. McGill, "More Americans Attend Performances of Arts," *New York Times,* Dec. 4, 1984.
12. Quoted by Tamara Jones, "A Crescendo of Crisis for Symphonies," *Los Angeles Times,* Aug. 11, 1987.
13. Will Crutchfield, "Why Today's Orchestras Are Adrift," *New York Times,* Dec. 22, 1985.
14. Donal Henahan, "Our Orchestras Are Splintering," *New York Times,* Sept. 13, 1987.
15. Samuel Lipman, "New York in the Eighties: A Symposium," *The New Criterion,* Special Issue, Summer 1986.
16. Crutchfield, op. cit.
17. Lipman, *New Criterion.*
18. Henahan, op. cit.
19. Bernard Holland, "Bottom-Line Economics and the Burial of Opera," *New York Times,* Nov. 12, 1987.
20. Quoted by Will Crutchfield, "New Era at the Met," *New York Times Magazine,* Sept. 22, 1985.
21. Gerard Schwarz, *New Criterion,* op. cit.

22. Ibid.

23. Lipman, *New Criterion,* op. cit.

24. Ibid.

25. Arlene Croce, *New Criterion,* op. cit.

26. Clement Greenberg, *New Criterion,* op. cit.

27. Hilton Kramer, *New Criterion,* op. cit.

28. Chuck Close, *New Criterion,* op. cit.

29. Quoted by Jennifer Dunning, "Small Dance Studios in New York Are Imperiled by Real-Estate Surge," *New York Times,* Aug. 22, 1985.

30. Leon Wieseltier, *New Criterion,* op. cit.

31. Quoted by Russell Lynes, "Highbrow, Lowbrow, Middlebrow," *Harper's,* February 1949.

32. Quoted by James Atlas, "The Changing World of New York Intellectuals," *New York Times Magazine,* Aug. 25, 1985.

33. Quoted by Joseph Epstein, "The Rise of the Verbal Class," *Harper's,* Mar. 1984.

34. Atlas, op. cit.

35. Quoted by Michael Oreskes, "Wilting City: Its Cultural Vigor Slips Away," *New York Times,* Sept. 3, 1987.

36. Irving Kristol, "Why I Left," *The New Republic,* April 11, 1988.

37. Joseph Berger, "U.S. Literature: Canon Under Siege," *New York Times,* Jan. 6, 1988.

38. Ibid.

39. William H. Honan, "Arts Dollars: Pinched As Never Before," *New York Times,* May 28, 1989.

40. Tocqueville, *Democracy in America,* Vol. II, pp. 84–85.

41. Brantlinger, op. cit., p. 75.

42. Frank Rich, "The Broadway Season Had Its Highs—And Too Many Lows," *New York Times,* June 5, 1983.

43. Frank Rich, "Directors Made a Difference This Season," *New York Times,* May 27, 1984.

44. Benedict Nightingale, "Kopit's 'End of the World' is Serious, Urgent Drama," *New York Times,* May 20, 1984.

45. Frank Rich, "At Season's End, the Theater Looks to a Brighter Tomorrow," *New York Times,* June 2, 1985.

46. Frank Rich, "The Best May be a Harbinger of Brighter Days," *New York Times,* Dec. 30, 1984.

47. Robert Brustein, *The New Republic,* July 29, 1985.

48. John J. O'Connor, "TV: Tony Ceremony on CBS," *New York Times,* June 4, 1985.

49. Frank Rich, "Of Yesteryear's Plays And This Year's Tonys," *New York Times,* May 8, 1986.

50. Frank Rich, "At Its Best, It Was a Season that Illuminated Our World," *New York Times,* June 1, 1986.

51. Frank Rich, "Broadway: The Empire Strikes Back," *New York Times*, Mar. 29, 1987.

52. Frank Rich, "Engaged Drama Treated Real Concerns," *New York Times*, Dec. 27, 1987.

53. Quoted by Mervyn Rothstein, "Record Regards for Broadway's 1987–88 Season," *New York Times*, June 2, 1988.

54. Frank Rich, "Signs of Intelligent Life in the Theater," *New York Times*, June 4, 1989.

55. "Broadway cannot ..." Frank Rich, "A Season for Eastern Sissy Playwrights," *New York Times*, June 5, 1988.

56. Quoted by Samuel G. Freedman, "As Off Broadway Thrives, Its Problems Mount," *New York Times*, Oct. 9, 1983.

57. Ibid.

58. Mimi Kramer, *New Criterion*, op. cit.

59. Robert Brustein, "The Siren Song of Broadway is a Warning," *New York Times*, May 22, 1988.

60. Kramer, op. cit.

61. Quoted by Samuel G. Freedman, "Will Success Spoil Nonprofit Theater?" *New York Times*, July 22, 1984.

62. Brustein, op. cit.

63. Ibid.

64. Ibid.

65. Don Shewey, "Has the Regional Theater Fulfilled Its Promise?" *New York Times*, Aug. 7, 1983.

66. Peter Stone, "Give My Regards to Off Broadway and Beyond," *New York Times*, June 21, 1988.

67. Quoted by Mervyn Rothstein, "Broadway to Cultivate Home-Grown Plays," *New York Times*, June 8, 1988.

68. Jack Viertel, "Theatrical Life Far From Broadway," *New York Times*, June 1, 1986.

69. John Gross, *New York Times*, Aug. 7, 1988.

70. Quoted by Samuel G. Freedman, "Playwrights Often Forego Royalties To Get and Keep Plays on the Stage," *New York Times*, Oct. 3, 1983.

71. Ibid.

72. Samuel G. Freedman, "Enter Success, Followed by Problems," *New York Times*, July 28, 1985.

73. Quoted by Samuel G. Freedman, "Last of the Red-Hot Producers," *New York Times Magazine*, June 2, 1985.

74. Stanley Kauffmann, *The New Republic*, June 3, 1985.

75. Aljean Harmetz, "At the Movies," *New York Times*, Sept. 6, 1985.

76. Quoted by Samuel G. Freedman, "Enter Success, Followed by Problems," *New York Times*, July 28, 1985.

77. Rosten, *Hollywood*, p. 316.

78. Quoted by Stephen Farber, "Playwrights See New Promise on the Small Screen," *New York Times*, Dec. 14, 1986.

79. Walter Kerr, "Fledgling Playwrights Are Being Lured From the Stage," *New York Times,* Sept. 6, 1981.

80. Albert Innaurato, "A Playwright Decries An Era of 'Hit Flops,' " *New York Times,* July 20, 1986.

81. Quoted by Julius Novick, rev. of Benedict Nightingale, *Fifth Row Center: A Critic's Year On and Off Broadway* (New York: Times Books, 1986), *New York Times Book Review,* March 23, 1986.

82. Quoted by Herbert Mitgang, "A British Producer Savors 'the Freedom to Get It Right,' " *New York Times,* Nov. 24, 1985.

82a. Frank Rich, "Broadway Can Live Without TV," New York *Times,* July 19, 1981.

82b. Frank Rich, "To Make Serious Theater, 'Serious' Issues Aren't Enough," New York *Times,* Feb. 19, 1984.

83. "The Drinking Man," *Esquire,* Sept. 1983.

84. Diane McWhorter, "The Atlantic: In Search of a Role," *New York Times Magazine,* Feb. 14, 1982.

85. Ibid.

86. Chris Wells, rev. of Gigi Mahon, *The Last Days of The New Yorker* (New York: McGraw-Hill, 1989), *Columbia Journalism Review,* March/April 1989.

87. Tocqueville, op. cit., Vol. II, p. 64.

88. Quoted by Thomas Whiteside, "The Blockbuster Complex," Part II, *The New Yorker,* Oct. 6, 1980.

89. Edwin McDowell, "Why O'Neill Is Getting $1 Million for His Thoughts," *New York Times,* June 23, 1985.

90. Edwin McDowell, "Publishing Obsession: The Biggest Sellers," *New York Times,* Mar. 26, 1987.

91. Quoted by William E. Geist, "A BioBoom: The Famous Write On," *New York Times,* May 23, 1987.

92. Edwin McDowell, "Publishing Obsession: The Biggest Sellers," *New York Times,* Mar. 26, 1987.

93. Walter W. Powell, "The Good Books Business," *The New Republic,* Sept. 15, 1986.

94. Ray Walters, "From Boom to Crunch," *New York Times Book Review,* July 17, 1983.

95. Rosten, op. cit., p. 366.

96. Roderick Mann, " 'Noble House' Miniseries Gets Clavell's Hard Sell," *San Francisco Chronicle,* Feb. 21, 1988.

97. Walters, op. cit.

98. Whiteside, op. cit., Part 1, *The New Yorker,* Sept. 29, 1980.

99. Michiko Kakutani, "What's in a Name? A Route to the Best-Seller List," *New York Times,* Oct. 13, 1986.

100. Powell, op. cit.

101. N. R. Kleinfield, "The Supermarketer of Books," *New York Times Magazine,* Nov. 9, 1986.

102. Ibid.

103. Whiteside, op. cit., Part II, Oct. 6, 1980.

104. Kleinfield, op. cit.

105. Powell, op. cit.

106. Ted Solotaroff, "The Literary-Industrial Complex," *The New Republic,* June 8, 1987.

106a. Jonathan Yardley, "Booksellers and Their Serious Shortcomings," *Washington Post,* June 5, 1989.

107. Whiteside, op. cit., Part III, Oct. 13, 1980.

108. James M. Markham, "Off-Screen TV: Scandal, Sex, Money," *New York Times,* Jan. 18, 1988.

109. Quoted by Steven Greenhouse, "Cinema in the Land of Truffaut and Godard Suffers Some Blows," *New York Times,* Dec. 6, 1987.

110. Ibid.

111. Aljean Harmetz, "Now Playing: The New Hollywood," *New York Times,* Jan. 10, 1988.

112. "The Return of Hollywood," *The Economist,* Oct. 29, 1988.

113. Quoted by Barbara Matusow, *The Evening Stars: The Making of the Network News Anchor* (Boston: Houghton Mifflin Company, 1983), p. 162. Much of the recent history of television news in Chapter 5 is drawn from her account.

114. Ibid., p. 163.

115. Ibid., p. 163.

116. Ibid., pp. 166–167.

117. Ibid., pp. 174–175.

118. Quoted by John Corry, "The Barbara Walters Prism," *New York Times,* Sept. 9, 1984.

119. Quoted by Matusow, op. cit., p. 225.

120. Ibid., p. 276.

121. Michael Massing, "CBS: Sauterizing the News," *Columbia Journalism Review,* March/April 1986.

122. Quoted by Peter Kerr, "Cronkite Now Critical of 'CBS Evening News,' " *New York Times,* Dec. 7, 1984.

123. Quoted by Jonathan Alter, "The Struggle for the Soul of CBS News," *Newsweek,* Sept. 15, 1986.

124. Ibid.

125. Vern E. Smith, "Atlanta's Nightmare Revisited," *Newsweek,* Feb. 18, 1985.

126. Quoted by Jay Sharbutt, " '60 Minutes' Executive Defends CBS Network," *Los Angeles Times,* Feb. 14, 1985.

127. Quoted by Sally Bedell Smith, "TV Docudrama: Questions of Ethics," *New York Times,* Feb. 14, 1985.

128. *Newsweek,* Sept. 15, 1986.

129. Ernest Leiser, "See It Now: The Decline of Network News," *Washington Journalism Review,* January/February 1988.

130. Quoted by Sally Bedell Smith, "Contention Over CBS's 'West 57th'," *New York Times,* Aug. 15, 1985.

131. Quoted by John Corry, "Magazine Shows: A Time for Decision," *New York Times*, Aug, 25, 1985.

132. "Cronkite 'Horrified' by Tabloid TV Trend," *San Francisco Chronicle*, Dec. 7, 1988.

133. Jeremy Gerard, "Walter Cronkite: Speaking His Mind Instead of Just News," *New York Times*, Jan. 8, 1989.

134. Dan Rather, "From Morrow to Mediocrity?" *New York Times*, Mar. 10, 1987.

135. *New York Times*, "Groups File Petitions Against Takeover of CBS," June 4, 1985.

136. Daniel Schorr, "Ted Turner at CBS Would Give Journalism a Black Eye," *Los Angeles Times*, June 2, 1985.

137. Quoted in "TV News: The Rapid Rise of Home Rule," *Newsweek*, Oct. 17, 1988.

138. Matusow, op. cit., p. 228.

139. Ed Joyce, "Playing Hardball at CBS," *Manhattan, Inc.*, Apr. 1988. Adapted from his *Prime Times, Bad Times* (New York: Doubleday, 1988).

140. Quoted in "TV News: The Rapid Rise of Home Rule," *Newsweek*, Oct. 17, 1988.

141. Ibid.

142. Quoted by Eleanor Randolph, "Is Network News Going Down the Tube?" *Washington Post*, National Weekly Edition, Feb. 23, 1987.

143. David Shaw, "For Papers, Generation Is Missing," *Los Angeles Times*, Mar. 15, 1989.

144. Quoted by Maureen Dowd, "Local TV Filling Hall and Airwaves," *New York Times*, July 19, 1988.

145. John Horn, "The Hard-News Bears: KCBS Fights Back in L.A.," *Washington Journalism Review*, July/Aug. 1988.

146. Arlen, *The Camera Age*, p. 268.

CHAPTER 6

House of the Rising Sun

1. Luigi Barzini, *The Europeans* (New York: Simon & Schuster, 1983), p. 35.

2. Bernardine Morris, *New York Times*, Oct. 15, 1983.

3. Quoted by John Holusha, "The Disappearing 'U.S. Car,'" *New York Times*, Aug. 10, 1985.

4. Quoted by Andrew Pollack, "U.S. Sees Peril in Japan's Dominance in Chips," *New York Times*, Jan. 5, 1987.

5. Quoted by Ken Fermoyle, rev. of Sidney Karin and Norris Parker Smith, *The Supercomputer Era* (San Diego: Harcourt, Brace Jovanovich, 1987), *Los Angeles Times Book Review*, July 26, 1987.

6. Edward A. Feigenbaum and Pamela McCorduck, *The Fifth Generation: Artificial Intelligence and Japan's Computer Challenge to the World* (Menlo Park, Calif.: Addison-Wesley, 1983), p. 2.

7. William J. Broad, "Novel Technique Shows Japanese Outpace Americans in Innovation," *New York Times*, Mar. 7, 1988.

8. Bruce Nussbaum, *The World After Oil: The Shifting Axis of Power and Wealth* (New York: Simon & Schuster, 1983), p. 45.

9. Frederik L. Schodt, *Inside the Robot Kingdom: Japan, Mechatronics, and the Coming Robotopia* (New York p.: Kodansha, 1988).

10. Daniel Burstein, *Yen!: Japan's New Financial Empire and Its Threat to America* (New York: Simon & Schuster, 1988).

11. Quoted by John Crudele, "The Ultimate Doomsday Book," *New York*, Nov. 7, 1988.

12. Quoted by Burstein, op. cit., p. 32.

13. Ibid., pp. 34–35.

14. Nicholas D. Kristof, "Japan Winning Race in China," *New York Times*, Apr. 29, 1987.

15. Quoted by Joel Kotkin and Yoriko Kishimoto, *The Third Century: America's Resurgence in the Asia Era* (New York: Crown Publishers, 1988), p. 7.

16. Quoted in "The Pacific Century," *Newsweek*, Feb. 22, 1988.

17. Roy Hofheinz, Jr. and Kent E. Calder, *The Eastasia Edge* (New York: Basic Books, 1982), p. 13.

18. Flora Lewis, "Europe on the Brink," *New York Times*, Mar. 18, 1984.

19. Paul Kennedy, *The Rise and Fall of the Great Powers: Economic Change and Military Conflict From 1500 to 2000* (New York: Random House, 1988).

20. Quoted in "Human Capital: The Decline of America's Work Force," *Business Week*, Sept. 19, 1988.

21. Ibid.

22. Quoted in "Ideas & Trends," *New York Times*, Aug. 23, 1987.

23. From "Japan's Influence in America," *Business Week*, July 11, 1988.

24. Ibid.

25. Quoted by Charles Fleming, "Isozaki," *California*, Mar. 1986.

26. Michael Brenson, "Why Asian Culture Answers the Needs of Western Artists," *New York Times*, Apr. 20, 1986.

27. Ibid.

CHAPTER 7

The Meeting of East and West

1. Quoted by Marilyn Ferguson, *The Aquarian Conspiracy: Personal and Social Transformation in the 1980s* (Los Angeles: J. T. Tarcher, 1980), p. 135.

2. Quoted by F. S. C. Northrop, *The Meeting of East and West: An Inquiry Concerning World Understanding* (New York: Collier Books, 1966), p. 336.

3. Quoted by Steven R. Weisman, "On Foot in Big Sur Country," *New York Times,* June 4, 1989.

4. Robert Lindsey, "Town Marks the Reopening of Scenic California Route," *New York Times,* Apr. 12, 1984.

5. Archibald MacLeish, "Lines for a Prologue," *The Collected Poems of Archibald MacLeish* (Boston: Houghton Mifflin, 1962), p. 24.

6. Historical information on Esalen is drawn largely from Calvin Tomkins, "New Paradigms," *The New Yorker,* Jan. 5, 1976.

7. Quoted in McFarland, *Readings in Intellectual History,* p. 413.

8. Ibid., p. 452.

9. McWilliams, *California: the Great Exception,* pp. 221–222.

10. Hendrik Hertzberg, *The New Republic,* Jun. 18, 1984.

11. *New York Times,* Jan. 30, 1986.

12. Thomas S. Kuhn, *The Structure of Scientific Revolutions* (Chicago: University of Chicago Press, 1970), p. 24.

13. Ibid., p. 77.

14. Ibid., p. 83.

15. Ibid., p. 92.

16. Ibid., p. 86.

17. Ibid., p. 151.

18. Ibid., p. 85.

19. Quoted by Ken Wilber, ed. *The Holographic Paradigm and Other Paradoxes: Exploring the Leading Edge of Science* (Boulder: Shambhala, 1982), p. 7.

20. Quoted by Gary Zukav, *The Dancing Wu Li Masters: An Overview of the New Physics* (New York: Bantam Books, 1980), p. 317.

21. Leonard, op, cit., p. 37.

22. Kuhn, op. cit., p. 94.

23. Ibid., p. 85.

24. Ibid., p. 111.

25. Ibid., p. 150.

26. Ibid., p. 168.

27. Northrop, op. cit., p. 294.
28. ibid., pp. 376–77.
29. Ibid., p. 298.
30. Quoted by Ferguson, op. cit. p. 182.
31. Ibid., p. 182.

CHAPTER 8

Westerly Winds

1. Nick Herbert, *Quantum Reality: Beyond the New Physics* (Garden City: Anchor Press, 1985), p. 15.
2. Quoted by Fritjof Capra, *The Tao of Physics: An Exploration of the Parallels Between Modern Physics and Eastern Mysticism* (New York: Bantam Books, 1977), p. 42.
3. Ibid., p. 42.
4. Ibid., p. 37.
5. Kuhn, *The Structure of Scientific Revolutions*, pp. 86–88.
6. Ibid., p. 83.
7. Zukav, *The Dancing Wu Li Masters*, p. 150.
8. Quoted by Malcolm W. Browne, "3 Scientists Say Travel in Time Isn't So Far Out," *New York Times*, Nov. 22, 1988.
9. Zukav, op. cit., p. 186.
10. Quoted by Capra, op. cit., p. 158.
11. Ibid., p. 166.
12. Ibid., p. 166.
13. Quoted in Zukav, op. cit., p. 149.
14. Capra, op. cit., p. 124.
15. Ibid., p. 125.
16. Ibid., p. 124.
17. Zukav, op. cit., pp. 290, 299.
18. Herbert, op. cit., p. 242.
19. Capra, op. cit., p. 127.
20. Zukav, op. cit., p. 29.
21. Herbert, op. cit., p. 18.
22. Capra, op. cit., p. 125.

23. Ibid., p. 197.

24. Ibid., p. 199.

25. Ibid., p. 208.

26. Ibid., p. 200.

27. Heinz R. Pagels, "Things of this World," *New York Times Book Review,* Apr. 24, 1983.

28. Quoted by Daniel Goleman, "Psychology of the Far East Gaining an Audience in the West," *New York Times,* Oct. 9, 1984.

29. Quoted by Don Lattin, "Physics, Mystics and the Essence of Things," *San Francisco Examiner,* Feb. 9, 1986.

30. Quoted by Fritjof Capra, *Uncommon Wisdom: Conversations with Remarkable People* (New York: Simon & Schuster, 1988), p. 54.

31. Capra, *Tao of Physics,* p. 4.

32. Ibid., p. 4.

33. Ibid., p. 4.

34. Ibid., pp. 145–46.

35. Quoted by Fritjof Capra, *The Turning Point: Science, Society, and the Rising Culture* (New York: Simon & Schuster, 1982), p. 62.

36. Herbert Benson, Foreword to *Encounters with Qi: Exploring Chinese Medicine,* by David Eisenberg, M.D., with Thomas Lee Wright (New York: Penguin Books, 1987), pp. 13–14.

37. Ibid., p. 133.

38. Ibid., p. 231.

39. Capra, *The Turning Point,* p. 319.

40. Quoted by Marcia Dunn, "Americans Get the Point: Some Try Acupuncture," *Los Angeles Times,* Nov. 27, 1988.

41. Quoted by Daniel Goleman, op. cit.

42. Quoted by Lynn Smith, "Mind Over Body: Doubt Rekindled," *Los Angeles Times,* Aug. 20, 1985.

43. Column by Barrie Cassileth and Norman Cousins. Reprinted in *Brain/Mind Bulletin,* Nov. 18, 1985.

44. Quoted by Daniel Goleman, "The Mind Over the Body," *New York Times Magazine,* Sept. 27, 1987.

45. Eisenberg, op. cit., p. 234.

46. Ibid., pp. 207–8.

47. George Leonard, *The Ultimate Athlete: Re-visioning Sports, Physical Education, and the Body* (New York: Avon Books, 1977).

48. Michael Murphy and Rhea A. White, *The Psychic Side of Sports* (Menlo Park, Calif.: Addison-Wesley, 1978), pp. 5–6.

49. Ibid., p. 114.

50. Ibid., p. 127.

51. Ibid., p. 137.

52. Eisenberg, op. cit., p. 203.

53. Quoted by Stuart Holroyd, *Psi and the Consciousness Explosion* (New York: Taplinger, 1977), p. 114.

54. "House Goes Crazy, Family Takes Off," *San Francisco Chronicle*, Mar. 7, 1984.

55. Richard D. Lyons, "New York Meeting is the Talk of Science," *New York Times*, May 22, 1984.

56. Holroyd, op. cit., pp. 97, 119–20. Also described in several other publications, e.g., Stanley Krippner, ed., *Advances in Parapsychological Research* (New York: Plenum Press, 1977), Vol. 1, pp. 56, 95.

57. Krippner, op. cit., Vol. 1, pp. 46, 100.

58. Russell Targ and Harold E. Puthoff, *Mind-Reach: Scientists Look at Psychic Ability* (New York: Delacorte Press, 1977), pp. 19–25.

59. Ibid., pp 58–60.

60. Krippner, op. cit., vol. 1, pp. 59–60, 101–104.

61. Krippner, op. cit., vol. 1, pp. 44, 116.

62. Holroyd, op. cit., pp. 89, 92–94.

63. Ibid., p. 94.

64. Krippner, op. cit., vol. 2, p. 79; Holroyd, op. cit., p. 98.

65. Cited by Russell Targ and Keith Harary, *The Mind Race: Understanding and Using Psychic Abilities* (New York: Villard Books, 1984), p. 68.

66. Quoted in Targ and Puthoff, op. cit., p. 11.

67. Krippner, op. cit., vol. 2, p. 177. See also Charles T. Tart, *Psi: Scientific Studies of the Psychic Realm* (New York: E. P. Dutton, 1977), pp. 63, 87.

68. Targ and Puthoff, op. cit., pp. 1–4, 33–34. The remaining experiments described in Chapter 8, unless otherwise noted, are from Targ and Puthoff.

69. Ibid., pp. 50–52.

70. Ibid., p. 102.

71. Ibid., pp. 66–67.

72. Targ and Harary, op. cit., pp. 33–38.

73. Jack Anderson, "The Race for 'Inner Space,' " *San Francisco Chronicle*, Apr. 23, 1984.

74. Ibid.

75. Targ and Puthoff, op. cit., p. 169.

76. Quoted by Holroyd, op. cit., p. 103.

77. Quoted by Targ and Harary, op. cit., p. 53.

78. Targ and Puthoff, op. cit., pp. 170–71.

79. Targ and Harary, op. cit., p. 6.

80. Wilber, op. cit., p. 196.

81. Holroyd, op. cit., p. 134.

82. Targ and Puthoff, op. cit., p. 170.

83. Northrop, op. cit., p. 404.

84. Archibald MacLeish, "Epistle to be Left in the Earth," *The Collected Poems of Archibald MacLeish* (Boston: Houghton Mifflin, 1962), p. 71.